G000150916

THE WHO
CONCERT FILE

by Joe McMichael and 'Irish' Jack Lyons

OMNIBUS PRESS

LONDON . NEW YORK . PARIS . SYDNEY . COPENHAGEN . BERLIN . MADRID . TOKYO

Contents

FOREWORD

By Pete Townshend

The co-authors of this book are both well known to me as rather more than fans of The Who. Through their respective qualities they have become celebrities in their own right. I have known Jack Lyons the longest, he was present in 1962 at one of the first occasions I played with Roger Daltrey in public in our home area of Shepherds Bush (I'd played in various school bands with John Entwistle since 1959). Jack has become rather distinguished in Who folklore as the character who inspired Jimmy in *Quadrophenia*. In fact Jimmy was a composite of several early Who fans, including one girl, but there is no doubt that Jack has become the most visible protagonist.

The authors undertake a staggering and daunting task here - to carefully document every single Who engagement they can, and if possible to gather opinion, critique and narrative evidence to bring the project properly to life.

The Who toured actively to support their recordings between 1964 and 1982. In 1982 the band broke up and came together again briefly in 1985 for Live Aid, a Brit Award, and finally a 25th anniversary tour in 1989. In '96/'97 The Who developed and toured a theatrical version of *Quadrophenia*. The most exciting part of our career was the beginning. Shows were crammed into every available space, even during recording sessions. I remember the college and university shows we played in the UK particularly fondly.

This book seems at first a strange idea, but it works very well. During its relentless account I am dragged through many black-holes in my memory (which friends call selective, but which is actually often just inactive). I find a rich mixture of emotions. I am amazed we worked so hard, especially when I realise that around all these shows I tried to fit in a normal family life, conducted interviews, and of course continued to write songs whenever I could.

I am pleased by the passion recounted here with which The Who's live performances were received over the years. We were very good most of the time, and in a life of so many variables it was wonderful to be able to rely not only on one another in the band, but also on our extraordinary managers and road managers. There are a few cancelled shows here, and a few that I remember with horror. There are incidents I'd prefer to forget, but I'm happy to see that my memories of such a helter-skelter of activity on the road are accurate.

Looking back it is also important for me to remember that most of our performing was great fun. There were difficult and genuinely tragic moments, but most of the time it was a good life. I have often said that I ended up hating touring, and it would be wrong for me now to correct myself, but today I am finding it enjoyable once again. It seems more natural, easier and in a very real sense spiritual than visceral, more joyous than vengeful. So I for one read this book with pleasure and I know it will serve as a vital document, especially to younger Who fans who are trying to piece together the real history of The Who and their part in the birth of real British rock in the early Sixties.

THE WHO

MANAGEMENT AND BOOKING ENQU
NEW ACTION LTD., 84, EATON PLACE, LONDON
BELGRAVIA 8989

PREFACE
"Who's Up 'ere Next Week"

At their peak The Who were the greatest live rock'n'roll band in the world, and since that time no one has quite been able to capture their sheer command of performance. The Who defined rock'n'roll energy and excitement on the stage but theirs was no meteoric rise, nor was it an easy road. It was a long struggle, proven over hundreds of nights, played out on hundreds of stages. They learned to play together the hard way, in front of demanding audiences, "by pounding stages like a clown", as Pete put it. They developed a sound and a style brimming with defiance, energy and emotion, all carried off with breathtaking fluency. The Who did not so much perform as assault their audience with sight and sound night after night. They wrote the book about live rock'n'roll; this book is about that book.

Pete Townshend's windmill guitar strum has never been equalled; more than a few have imitated his jumps and scissor kicks, but none have matched his athleticism on stage. Roger Daltrey swung his microphone on its cord in wide arcs, often over the first few rows of an audience, catching it seemingly out of nowhere. Keith Moon's manic attack on drums set him apart from all of his contemporaries, and he remains the greatest drummer that rock had ever produced. Only John Entwistle seemed detached from the musical maelstrom, but his outstanding bass lines were the group's foundation, the runway from which the others could fly. Together they established a new standard for live rock'n'roll, a standard that has never been matched.

The quartet that was The Who doesn't exist as a band any more, but several live tracks and film footage offer a taste of what they were about. Anyone who was there at the time, though, knows that nothing can ever quite rival the experience of seeing the original Who play together on a good night. There can never be another band like The Who.

Joe McMichael & Irish Jack Lyons.

ACKNOWLEDGEMENTS

This book would never have seen the light of day without the help, encouragement and personal endorsement of The Who – John Entwistle, Roger Daltrey and Pete Townshend.

The authors are also indebted to Bill Curbishley and Robert Rosenberg at Trinifold, Keith Altham, Bob Pridden, Cyrano Langston, John Wolfe, Mick Double, Rex King and Alan Rogan. Special thanks also to Nicola Joss and Paul Bonnick at Eel Pie, Richard Barnes, Nick Goderson, Carol Letham, Billy Nicholls, Mike Shaw, Chris Stamp, Jon Astley, Tim Young at Metropolis, Andy Catling, Jeff West, Ed Hanel, Doug Sandom, Mrs Queenie Johns, Mrs Kitty Moon, Mrs Betty Townshend and the late Mrs Irene Daltrey; also the Pete Townshend and Who websites (www.petetownshend.com)

Many thanks also to the following for their memories and personal contributions: Mark Aase, Peter Alecks, Nick Ames, Christer Ahlin & Per-Eric, BBC Libraries & Archives at Reading, Ken Benjamin, Annika Berg-Friholm, Lois Berman, Bernd Bexte, Pete Bishop, Wendy Blair, Reinhold Boedeker, John Booth, JC Bowden, Dan Brennan, the British Newspaper Library at Colindale, Kieran Burke at Cork City Library, Des Cassidy, Harry Clarke, June F. Clarke, Alan Clayson, Chris Chappel, Eric Collingridge, Helen Cook, Julia Courtney, Alan Crisp, Mike Crowder, Dewi P. Davies, Colin Dawson, Paul Derry, Mike Dickinson & the Doodlebugs, Clive Dickman, Pat Donegan, Bob Druce, Colin Durrant, Werner Dwenger, Robert & Jane Fearnley-Whittingstall, Tony Fletcher, Kevin Foley, Barry Foran, Carola Frauli, Fiona Fulger at NME Archives, Vincent Fumar, Janet Furlong, Sergio Gandiglio, Dave Gillings, Malcolm Gray, Richard Groothuizen, Ed Hanel, Norman Harris at BT Archives, Diane Hatz, Jared Hauser, Doug Hinman, Beat Hirt, Bob Hopkins, Margaret Howden, Lou Hunt, Steve Ingliss, Clemens Jaeger, Maria Jeffers & Ben Turner at Melody Maker Archives, Lennart Johansson, Jan Kacperek at ITC Archives, Bruce Kawakami, Greg Kelton, Matt Kent & Pete Norris at all at Naked Eye magazine, Paul de Kievil, David Kneale, John Knott, Gunther Kuhnke, Graham Larkeby, Earle Law, Diane Leeson, Ray le Heup, Mark Lloyd-Selby, Virginia Lohle, Rudolf Markle, Jim McMichael, Patrick Milligan, Pat Moorman, Helen Murphy and Mary Byrene at Statistical Solutions, Joe Murphy, Andy Neill, Torbet Neilson, Lou Newman, Manfred Nitschmann, Thierry Nydegger, Karen O'Connor, Jim Orlowski, Vivienna Pearce, John Quorm, Tim Renwick, Jan Reynaert, Diana Rico, Marc Roberty, Jess Roden, Brad Rodgers, Dorcas Sanders, Les Saunders, Brigitte Schokarth, John Schollar & Tony Brind of the Beachcombers, Roy Shelley and the (Goldhawk) Shepherd's Bush Club Committee & Archives, Linda Sonner, Kenny Spratling, Pat Stoddart, Romeo Strakl, John Sullivan, Christian Suchatzki, Dave Taylor, Jimmy Teare, Andrew Tong, Ole Vohnringer, Andrea Walsh, Dave Weedon, Brad Wheeler, Harry Wilson & family, Willie Wilson, Jeff Wolfe, Roy Woodcock and Tom Wright.

Special thanks also to Phil Hopkins and John Atkins of Generations magazine, Matt Kent and Pete Norris of Naked Eye and Olle Lundin of The Who In Sweden.

Thanks also to every local studies group and library in the British Isles, Europe and USA whose diligence we depended upon and whose photocopiers we wore out.

Much of the commentary was contributed or researched by John Atkins, editor and co-publisher of Generations magazine. John also wishes to acknowledge the help of Tim Joseph, Jan Reynaert, Elaine Atkins, Svante Borjesson, Chris Jones, Bruce Kawakami, Andy Catling, Andy Pierie, Brian Parrot, Nick Ryle, Mike Moore, Phil Hopkins, Scott Campbell, Gavin Hoare, Adrian 'Moony' Lee and Dominic Bacci.

The following publications offered valuable reference material: Who's News magazine, Maximum R&B by Richard Barnes, The Who Down Under, January 1968 by Andy Neill, The Complete Guide To the Music Of The Who by Chris Charlesworth and Before I Get Old by Dave Marsh. The use of material which was first published in the British Who magazine Generations and is here reproduced with permission.

Joe McMichael acknowledges the help of Chris Charlesworth, Richard Evans, Alan Grossman and Pam Lord.

'Irish' Jack offers his deep appreciation and thanks to his wife Maura and children Karen, Anthony, Keith and Glen who believed in him and stuck by their 'old man' during this seven year itch of writing and research. And to the finest 'old men' anyway, anyhow, anywhere… Pete, Roger, John and Keith, whose music inspired me and drove me beyond my imagination.

INTRODUCTION
The Detours

The group that became The Who began life in 1962 as The Detours, a band formed by Roger Daltrey with friends at the Sulgrave Boys' Club in Goldhawk Road, Shepherd's Bush, West London. Roger, recently expelled for unsociable behaviour from Acton County Grammar School, assembled the group with the help of Colin Dawson from North Acton. Meanwhile, in the year below Roger at Acton County Grammar, Pete Townshend and John Entwistle had left a school band called The Confederates and joined another called The Aristocrats, later The Scorpions. Neither lasted very long.

The original Detours featured Roger on lead guitar and trombone, Colin Dawson on vocals, Harry Wilson from Yew Tree Road, Shepherd's Bush, on drums, and Reg Bowen on rhythm guitar. One day Roger spotted John Entwistle, of Lexden Road, Acton, carrying his bass guitar down the street and enlisted him on the spot. They practised at Bowen's house and before long John proposed his classmate Pete Townshend join the group, assuring him (Pete) that The Detours not only had a reliable van to transport them to gigs but also a *real* Vox amp.

Colin Dawson introduced his girlfriend, Angela Dives, to the band and persuaded Roger to augment The Detours with Angela on vocals, maracas and tambourine on selected numbers. For a short time the band called themselves Dale Angelo & The Detours. No one is certain where the Dale came from but Angelo was a variation of the band's newest member.

This line-up was short lived, however, and the band reverted back to the original five-man line-up. With a set list largely comprising popular traditional jazz numbers and hits from the Top Ten, The Detours managed to pick up occasional engagements while filling in at weddings and bar mitzvahs. They also took on some company dances. One in particular was for a firm called Dublliers Condensers in North Acton where The Detours were in popular demand. Works outings also took the band to Bognor Regis, Dorking and even Doncaster in Yorkshire. Lacking a proper manager, The Detours were driven to gigs in a Bedford van by Harry Wilson Sr., father of the group's drummer.

Through a friend John met at Day Release college, The Detours secured a weekly engagement at a youth club at 3 Consort Road, Peckham, in Southeast London. The Paradise Club held dances each week for teenagers and, despite its geographical inconvenience from the band's west London base, The Detours were offered about five weeks work. They received the princely sum of six pounds a night for their efforts. On about the fourth week of the booking, Harry Wilson was told that another drummer would sit in for the second half of the show. The result was that Harry was ousted and Doug Sandom took over on drums.

The Detours line-up now comprised Colin Dawson on lead vocals, Roger on lead guitar and trombone, John on bass guitar and trumpet, Pete on rhythm guitar, and Doug Sandom on drums. Doug's first full engagement with The Detours was an unspecified date in July 1962 at The Paradise Club. An accomplished drummer with eight years more experience than the rest of them, Doug became the mainstay of the band. His ability gave his younger bandmates a new found confidence and the group gradually became busier. After about five weeks The Paradise Club was invaded by members of a rival club in Peckham who started a fight and broke up the premises. As a result The Detours lost the booking.

One regular engagement for the group around this time was The Jewish Club in Grange Road, Ealing. The Detours appeared here many times, the dates undocumented. Another source for engagements arrived through John Entwistle's

9

girlfriend, Alison Wise, who worked as a secretary at the CAV engineering plant in Acton. The company held frequent dances, or 'socials' as they were known, at their sports ground in Northolt and at the CAV Social Club in Turnham Green, Chiswick.

At some point in 1962, the five man Detours appeared at a large ballroom called Boseleys, on Faroe Road in Shepherd's Bush, and it was here that 'Irish' Jack Lyons saw them for the first time. Boseleys operated on Saturday nights and was run by Maurice Placquett, owner of a local music shop.

In November 1962, Pete Townshend's mother Betty contacted Bob Druce of Commercial Entertainments, the area's leading booking agency. Druce and partner Barry Foran successfully managed a string of clubs and pubs and booked their own stable of groups into these venues. An audition was arranged for the band at the Oldfield Hotel, Greenford, one of Druce's better venues. The group turned up for the audition, driven there by Pete's mother in her little Ford van. They were allowed a three song spot during the interval while the resident band The Bel-Airs, one of the most popular acts on the Druce-Foran circuit, took a break. The audience took to The Detours and as a result Druce signed them to his agency.

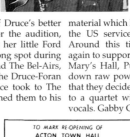

The Detours' first documented engagement for Druce was on November 23, 1962, when they appeared at the Grand Ballroom in Broadstairs, Kent. The Detours continued to play regularly at this venue all the way into May 1963, appearing at least once a month, usually on Friday nights. They also played support to Johnny Kidd & The Pirates at St. Mary's Hall, Putney, and Kidd's band had a profound effect on them. The Detours maintained the CAV contacts they had established during the year and played a number of Christmas dances as 1962 came to a close.

Another important series of engagements was

at the Douglas House, an American servicemen's club in Lancaster Gate, near Marble Arch. Again, Betty Townshend initiated the booking when she called up an old friend, Lesley Douglas. Betty and her husband Cliff (Pete's father) had been members of Douglas's dance band during the war. Lesley Douglas had a regular Sunday afternoon engagement at Douglas House (no relation), and within a couple of weeks, The Detours were given an audition and landed the gig. During their tenure at Douglas House (probably late January 1963) lead vocalist Colin Dawson left the band and was replaced by Gabby Connolly, who specialised in American country and western songs. Connolly had played bass with The Bel-Airs which enabled him to fill in on bass while John Entwistle was featured on trumpet.

When the Douglas House Sunday afternoon gigs dried up there was no further demand for the group's country and western material which had only really been popular with the US servicemen who frequented the club. Around this time, The Detours were booked again to support Johnny Kidd & The Pirates at St. Mary's Hall, Putney. This time Kidd's stripped down raw power impressed the group so much that they decided to scale down their own line-up to a quartet with guitar, bass, drums and lead vocals. Gabby Connolly was out and Roger abandoned his guitar altogether. Pete assumed the role of dual lead and rhythm guitarist while John developed a bass style that somehow filled in for the missing guitar. Doug Sandom was still on drums. With this line-up, The Detours let go of all pretensions to being "all round entertainers" and adopted the attitude of a serious minded "beat group".

Another Commercial Entertainments promotion which featured The Detours was a series of dances at the civic hall in Southborough, Tunbridge Wells. Bob Druce employed his stable of bands here every Saturday night, probably in the late spring of

1963. "Druce used to run this place every Saturday with a guy from Barnes," recalls Commercial Entertainments employee Ken Spratling. "I got lumbered with driving him and a mate who was a bouncer. It used to do very well until a punch-up started with the local gypsies. The other two were useless and I got a thumping trying to sort it out. The next week no one turned up."

The Detours also picked up a series of Friday night bookings at a venue known as Club Druane. Despite its French sounding name "Druane" was an amalgamation of the surnames of the promoters Bob Druce and Barry Foran. The club was in the basement of Notre Dame Church at 5 Leicester Place, an alley leading of Leicester Square in London's West End. Club Druane ran for a little over a year until nuns attending the church complained about the noise. According to Ken Spratling, the caretaker was perpetually drunk, although the venue served no alcohol, and constantly having his way with girls in the church while the band played!

The Detours also began to appear at the Oldfield Tavern, Greenford, which became one of their most popular venues. They eventually played there no less than three nights a week, and the venue has become an important shrine in Who folklore. It was at the Oldfield that they would be introduced to an audience as The Who for the very first time (on Thursday, February 20, 1964), and, equally crucial, it was here that Keith Moon first stepped up to the drum kit to play with them.

All that was in the future as the original Detours continued to play the West London circuit and support star attractions like The Searchers, The Big Three, Freddie & The Dreamers as well as the more powerful Johnny Kidd & The Pirates. One such booking was with Wayne Fontana & The Mindbenders on Saturday, December 7, 1963, at the California Ballroom, Dunstable. An even more important gig took place on Sunday, December 22, when the group played support to The Rolling Stones at St. Mary's Hall, Putney. It was here that Pete noticed Keith Richard's casual warm up swing of his arm just as the Stones hit the stage. Townshend would soon transform the gesture into one of rock-'n'roll's most inimitable trademarks: the Pete Townshend "windmill" strum!

NB: The dates that follow, for 1962 and 1963, represent only a tiny handful of the actual number of shows performed by The Detours during this period. They are, however, the only dates that the authors have been able to confirm authentically.

1962

July/August (exact dates unknown)
Paradise Club, Peckham, South London

The Detours played three shows at the Paradise Club during July and two in August. At the first of the August shows Harry Wilson recalls being informed that Pete's 'cousin' had been promised a sit-in on drums for the second half with the result that Wilson was out and new drummer Doug Sandom took over.

Saturday September 1
Acton Town Hall, West London

The Detours play support to The Ron Cavendish Orchestra, 7:45 to 11 pm.

Friday November 23
Grand Ballroom, Broadstairs, Kent

The Detours began a regular booking at the seaside town of Broadstairs that continued through to the early summer of 1963, their first regular engagement for agent Bob Druce. Druce ran Commercial Entertainments and booked the group for about eighteen months as they gradually attracted a large following on the pub and ballroom circuit.

On this début night they were billed as the "dynamic Detours", from 8 to 11 pm.

Friday November 30
Grand Ballroom, Broadstairs, Kent

1963

Friday January 4
Grand Ballroom, Broadstairs, Kent

Friday January 11
Fox & Goose Hotel, Ealing, West London

The Detours one and only appearance here, 7:30 to 11 pm.

Friday January 18
Grand Ballroom, Broadstairs, Kent

Saturday January 19
CAV Sports Ground, Northolt, West London, 7:30 to midnight

Friday February 22
Grand Ballroom, Broadstairs, Kent

Tuesday February 26
Oldfield Hotel, Greenford, West London

   The Oldfield became one of the group's regular venues during the next two years. This is the first verified date at The Oldfield.

Friday March 22
Grand Ballroom, Broadstairs, Kent

Friday March 29
Grand Ballroom, Broadstairs, Kent
   Advertised but The Detours played in Central London this night.

Friday May 17
Park Hotel, Carnival Ballroom, Hanwell, West London, 8 to 11:30 pm

Friday May 24
Grand Ballroom, Broadstairs, Kent

Saturday June 1
Oldfield Hotel, Greenford, West London, 7:30 to 11 pm

Friday June 28
Club Druane, Notre Dame Church Hall, Leicester Place, Central London

GREENFORD
Saturday Jiving with The Detours at the Oldfield Hotel, Greenford. 7.30-11

   The club took it's name from the combination of Bob DRUce and Barry ForAN(e), the two managers of Commercial Entertainments. The agency ran a total of 18 different venues in the west London area and The Detours probably played them all.

Friday July 26
Club Druane, Notre Dame Church Hall, Leicester Place, Central London, 8 pm to 12 midnight

Friday August 30
Club Druane, Notre Dame Church Hall, Leicester Place, Central London

Friday September 13
Club Druane, Notre Dame Church Hall, Leicester Place, Central London

   The September 7 issue of *Melody Maker* ran an ad for Marshall amplification with The Detours listed among the clientele. Pete in particular took great interest in, and contributed directly to, the development of Marshall's 100 watt amplifier, while he and John were the first to use the 4 x 12 speaker cabinets.

Friday September 20
Club Druane, Notre Dame Church Hall, Leicester Place, Central London

Friday November 15
Feathers Hotel, Ealing, West London, 8 pm to midnight

Friday November 22
Goldhawk Social Club, Shepherd's Bush, West London

Saturday November 30
Railway Hotel, Greenford, West London, 8 pm to midnight

Saturday December 7
California Ballroom, Dunstable
   The Detours played support to Wayne Fontana & The Mindbenders, 8 pm to midnight.

Sunday December 22
St. Mary's Hall, Putney, South London
   The Detours played support to The Rolling Stones. It was here, just before the Stones went on stage, that Pete saw Keith Richards swing his arm in a wide arcing motion, a gesture that inspired Townshend's trademark windmill strum. When approached about it, Richards said he didn't remember doing it and didn't care either!

C.A.V. APPRENTICE
presents
NEW YEARS R
to be held
THE SPORTS GROUND
SATURDAY, 19th JANU.
7.30 to 12 Midnight
FEATURING
THE DETOUR
Ticket 4/-

St. Mary's Hall, Putney

1964

Throughout 1964 The Detours continued to work steadily on the Bob Druce circuit, playing up to six nights a week. Occasional support slots to name acts offered the band wider exposure and experience, especially at shows that took them into proper theatres. However, it was still the hit record that brought any real recognition and there was no prospect of The Detours securing a recording contract. Despite their growing professionalism, they were no different from hundreds of other bands who in this era managed to sustain a living wage by regularly playing live.

Sometime in early February The Detours became The Who. The change was mooted when John saw a band called Johnny Devlin & The Detours on *Thank Your Lucky Stars,* and thought a change was in order to avoid confusion. It was Richard Barnes, Pete's room-mate, who suggested the name The Who. At the end of one of their usual Thursday night gigs at the Oldfield Hotel, Greenford, MC Lou Hunt taunted the crowd with the words "Who's up 'ere next week?" Uninformed of the name change the crowd chanted back "The Detours!" Lou taunted them further. "I said who's up 'ere next week?!" Again, the crowd responded, "The Detours, Lou! The bloody Detours!"

Whatever their name, the group desperately needed management who could secure the inter-

est of a record company. Through Doug Sandom's sister-in-law, they were introduced to Helmut Gorden, the owner of a local foundry. Gorden expressed interest and accompanied Sandom to watch them in action at the White Hart Hotel one Sunday night. Gorden mapped out a grand strategy of presenting them to some of the most influential agents in the music business, arranging for them to perform at the Stork Club at 66 Regent Street, showcasing for agents and impresarios such as Arthur Howes. Howes was one of Britain's top booking agents, and the audition led to the group taking part in a summer long series of Sunday concerts around the country, including a slot supporting The Beatles in Blackpool. A proposed autumn tour for Howes never materialised.

Helmut Gorden also arranged an audition with record producer Chris Parmeinter, and hired out a club called Zanzibar in Edgware Road for the occasion. Parmeinter made some favourable comments about the band but found fault with Doug Sandom's drumming. Doug, older than the rest, decided to quit, but not before honouring the next couple of weeks' work. His last known gig with The Who was in April at the 100 Club on Oxford Street.

In a move to make legal the contract he had drawn up, Helmut Gorden reimbursed the band for lost wages for time off from work and paid them £20 each a week. The contract was questionable since all four members were under 21 years of age. The only member of the band whose parents refused to countersign was Pete, and this invalidated the contract when the band subsequently decided to break away from Gorden.

In late April or early May, when The Who were relying on pick-up drummers, fate took a hand with the arrival of Keith Moon. They were playing one of their regular gigs at the Oldfield when Moon, then with The Beachcombers, another act on the Druce circuit, introduced himself. Challenging them to let him sit in, Moon blasted his way through Bo Diddley's 'Road Runner' and was accepted immediately. The line-up was now complete.

That spring the group was introduced to Pete Meaden, a committed Mod who was working as a pop publicist. The band took an immediate liking to Meaden, and it was largely through him that they adopted a Mod image and released a single on Fontana Records as The High Numbers. Each side was a rewrite of two existing R&B numbers, the A-side a reworking of Slim Harpo's 'Got Love If You Want It' and the B-side a new take on 'Country Fool' by The Showmen. 'I'm The Face' backed with 'Zoot Suit' was released as a single on July 3 but the record failed to make the chart.

Meaden also managed to get the group booked into the Scene Club in Soho for a residency that began on August 5 and ran until September 2, and it was thanks to him that the name he gave them – The High Numbers – first appeared in the editorial pages of the pop press.

At some point during the summer Pete smashed his first guitar – by accident – at the Railway Hotel in Harrow. In his frustration he deliberately reduced it to splinters, mesmerising the audience in the process. Two weeks later the same crowd brought along their friends and expected a similar display. Pete obliged and to demonstrate solidarity Keith smashed his drumkit. Pete would justify the destruction intellectually by citing pop art situationists, but the essence of the matter was that the display inspired a massive rush of adolescent adrenaline and was tremendously exciting to watch. The downside was the cost, but The Who's reputation as a great live band began here.

The band was playing a regular Tuesday at the Railway Hotel in July when an unlikely character approached the door. Well dressed, well spoken and suspiciously out of place, Kit Lambert conferred with Richard Barnes who had booked the group at the club. Lambert was looking for a band to appear in a film he was producing and Barnes introduced him to Pete Meaden. Lambert watched the show and began to think of the band on a grander scale than as mere subjects of a short pop music film. That night Lambert phoned his partner, Chris Stamp, about his discovery of The High Numbers while Stamp was in Dublin working as an assistant director on the film *Young Cassidy*.

Stamp flew back to London for the August Bank Holiday and joined Lambert in time to catch the last few minutes of The High Numbers at the Watford Trade Union Hall. Although the group had taken a liking to Meaden and he had a genuine understanding of the Mod scene, it was clear to them that any serious attempt at securing a recording contract was probably beyond his capabilities. A deal was therefore made to extricate the group from their obligations to Meaden, who graciously agreed to far less money than he might have asked for. Thus the maverick team of Kit Lambert and Chris Stamp became the managers of the band, whom they quickly rechristened The Who.

Unbeknownst to the band, despite their urbane appearance their new found mentors were completely ignorant about the music business. They had no experience in securing gigs, contacting agencies or approaching record labels. Managing the group from their apartment at 113 Ivor Court, Gloucester Place, Lambert and Stamp quickly applied themselves (and their finances) towards the band who were literally "on call" when the pair took on booking gigs, especially in the early days. They made a serious effort to secure a recording contract for the group in the autumn of 1964. A letter of tentative encouragement (but ultimate refusal) from EMI Records was dated October 22 after a test session at the Abbey Road Studios.

A run of Wednesday night shows was booked in Greenwich to expand the group's appeal to audiences outside their regular West London

stronghold. The dates were a failure and cancelled on October 28 after only the fourth week. Lambert and Stamp took out a display ad in the November 7 issue of *Melody Maker* with impressive white lettering on a black background announcing "The Who Maximum R&B" with a vertical arrow extending from the letter 'o'. Appearing in the same issue under the heading of Fan Clubs was "The Who Fan Club. Send SAE Jane Who, 74 Kensington Park Road, London, W11." This was the home address of Robert and Jane Fearnley-Whittingstall. Robert had been in the army with Kit Lambert as well as at Oxford

University. Jane, his wife, was The Who's first publicist and Fan Club secretary.

Now firmly re-established as The Who, the band appeared on November 18 at Wolsey Hall, Cheshunt, just as they were about to begin a notable Marquee residency. The Marquee series was booked for Tuesday nights, the slowest night of the week, which put the group in a make or break situation. If they could succeed in drawing big crowds on an off night, they would almost certainly make a name for themselves on the London club scene. Although the opening night was attended by no more than 30 Shepherd's Bush regulars, they gradually built up a larger and larger audience at the club. As fate would have it, their rising success at the Marquee coincided with the release of their second single and the chart success that would bring them national fame.

With a paucity of reviews, tapes or other documentary evidence, set lists for the Who/High Numbers shows through 1964 to early 1965 are difficult to establish. The wealth of material that the band drew upon included basic blues, rhythm and blues, and rock'n'roll that were fairly common to all up-and-coming bands of the era. Throughout 1964, however, an increasing number of soul and Tamla Motown songs were introduced into the act, which were fairly unique to the band and directly reflected the tastes of the Mods. Much of this latter material was obscure at the time and was drawn from discs imported from the States, as championed by Mod DJs such as Guy Stevens.

The following songs all featured in the act at some stage (some being retained, of course, for the remainder of their career). The artist in brackets after each title is the original performer, or the best known/most influential version at the time: 'Big Boss Man,' (Jimmy Reed), 'Green Onions,' 'Plum Nellie,' (both Booker T. & The M.G.s), 'I Don't Mind,' 'Shout And Shimmy,' 'Just You And Me, Darling,' 'Please Please Please,' (all James Brown), 'I'm A Man,' 'Here 'Tis,' 'Pretty Thing,' 'Road Runner,' (all Bo Diddley), 'Parchman Farm,' 'Back Country Suite: Blues' a.k.a. 'Young Man Blues,' (both Mose Allison), 'Baby Don't You Do It,' (Marvin Gaye), 'You Can't Sit Down,' (Phil Upchurch Combo), 'Ooh Poo Pah Doo,' (Jessie Hill), 'Heatwave,' 'Motoring,' 'Dancing In The Street,' (all Martha and The Vandellas), 'Leaving Here,' (Eddie Holland), 'Daddy Rolling Stone,' (Derek Martin), 'I Gotta Dance To Keep From Crying,' (The Miracles), 'A Shot Of Rhythm & Blues,' (Arthur Alexander), 'Jump Back,' (Rufus Thomas), 'Twist And Shout,' (The Isley Brothers), 'Fortune Teller,' (Benny Spellman), 'Anytime You Want Me,' (Garnet Mimms), 'Spoonful,' 'Smokestack Lightning,' (both Howlin' Wolf), 'Shakin' All Over,' 'Please Don't Touch,' (Johnny Kidd & The Pirates), 'Money' (Barrett Strong), 'I Just Want To Make Love To You,' (Muddy Waters), 'You Really Got Me,' (The Kinks), 'Bony Moronie,' (Larry Williams), 'Summertime Blues,' 'C'mon Everybody,' 'My Way,' (all Eddie Cochran), 'Good Lovin',' (The Olympics), 'Long Tall Shorty,' (Don Covay), and 'I Saw Her Standing There' (The Beatles). Other material was drawn from the repertoires of Chuck Berry, Elmore James, The Shadows, and (at Keith Moon's behest) The Beach Boys and other surf outfits.

NB: As before, the dates that follow, represent only a handful of the actual number of shows performed by The Detours/High Numbers/Who during this period. They are, however, the only dates that the authors have been able to confirm authentically.

Friday January 3
Glenlyn Ballroom, Forest Hill, South London
The group opened for The Rolling Stones for the second time in under two weeks. The Detours played support to at least three other acts at this venue, the Hollies (later in the month), Cliff Bennett & The Rebel Rousers and The Undertakers.

Friday January 24
Glenlyn Ballroom, Forest Hill, South London
The Detours played the Glenlyn again, this time supporting The Hollies.

Thursday January 30
Oldfield Hotel, Greenford, West London
The group had been gigging regularly at the Oldfield throughout 1963, eventually playing there as often as three times a week. Another already professional group, Johnny Devlin & The Detours, appeared on *Thank Your Lucky Stars* on ABC TV the following Saturday evening,

February 1. This necessitated an immediate name change. The band would now be called The Who.

Thursday February 6
Oldfield Hotel, Greenford, West London

Thursday February 13
Oldfield Hotel, Greenford, West London
This is the probable date of the group's last gig as The Detours. By their next regular Thursday appearance at The Oldfield, they had been renamed The Who.

Thursday February 20
Oldfield Hotel, Greenford, West London
This is the probable date of the first gig the band played as The Who.

Saturday March 7
Old Oak Common Institute, Shepherd's Bush, West London
The Who played at the wedding reception of Joan Wilson, whose brother Harry Jr. had played drums with The Detours for a brief period in 1962.

The March 14 issue of *Melody Maker* carried an article with the headline 'Massive Swing To R&B', about the emerging and increasingly popular R&B scene. The Who, in one of their first notices in the national press, were mentioned among the more notable groups of that scene. In the same issue, The Who were cited by name in an advert that listed groups using Marshall amps.

Sunday March 29
Florida Rooms, Brighton
This Easter weekend was the occasion of a famous battle between Mods and Rockers at the other seaside town of Clacton. Brighton would be the focus of riots during the Whitsuntide Bank Holiday in late May.

Saturday April 4
California Ballroom, Dunstable
The group, erroneously billed as The Detours, played as opening act for The Tony Meehan Combo.

Monday April 13
100 Club, Oxford Street, Central London
The Who played support to the Mike Cotton Sound, 7:30 to 11 pm. This was the last gig Doug Sandom ever played with The Who.

Saturday April 18
Florida Rooms, Brighton

Monday April 27
100 Club, Oxford Street, Central London
Supporting The Mike Cotton Sound, 7:30 to 11 pm.

Various session drummers sat in with the group for a short period, including Mitch Mitchell who would later drum for Jimi Hendrix, until Keith Moon turned up at one of their regular Thursday nights, most likely in May, at The Oldfield Hotel.

Thursday May 7
Oldfield Hotel, Greenford, West London
The group appeared at the Oldfield on Thursday nights for a lengthy but undetermined period in 1963 and 1964. The first four dates almost certainly include the night when Keith Moon, then aged 17 and working as a plaster salesman, sat in with the band for the first time. By all accounts he was dressed from head to toe in ginger, and his hair was dyed ginger too.

Keith's arrival, like everything else about him, was framed in hilarity. "I went down and they had a session drummer sitting in with them," he told *Rolling Stone* magazine in 1972. "I got up on stage and said 'I can do better than him'. They said go ahead and I got behind this other guy's drums and I did one song – 'Road Runner'. I'd had several drinks to get my courage up and when I got on stage I went arrrrggGGHHHH on the drums, broke the bass drum pedal and two skins and got off."

This display impressed Pete, Roger and John no end and he was asked along to the next gig. "Nobody ever said 'You're in'," recalled Keith. "They just said 'What you doing Monday?'"

Sunday May 10
Florida Rooms, Brighton

Thursday May 14
Oldfield Hotel, Greenford, West London

Thursday May 21
Oldfield Hotel, Greenford, West London

Thursday May 28
Oldfield Hotel, Greenford, West London

Sunday June 7
Florida Rooms, Brighton

Friday June 19
Granby Halls, Leicester
 The Who were on the bill for this concert, advertised as the 'Kinky Ball'.

Friday June 26
Golders Green Refectory, North London
 In a *Melody Maker* ad this week, the group was listed as 'The Who's'.

Sunday June 28
Florida Rooms, Brighton

Tuesday June 30
Railway Hotel, Harrow & Wealdstone
 Billed as The Who, 8 to 11 pm, the group began a 12-week, Tuesday night residency.

Tuesday July 7
Railway Hotel, Harrow & Wealdstone
 Billed as The Who, 8 pm to 1 am. Around this time the group changed their name to The High Numbers, but there were a number of gigs as late as the end of the month that still advertised them as The Who.
 They adopted the name The High Numbers for about four months, from July to late October of 1964.

Sunday July 12
Florida Rooms, Brighton

Tuesday July 14
Railway Hotel, Harrow & Wealdstone
 Billed as The High Numbers. It is almost certain that this was the show where Kit Lambert first encountered The Who, making it one of their most significant early gigs, although they didn't realise it until afterwards. Lambert was searching for a band, around which he hoped to produce a revolutionary pop film.
 As he recalled: "There was one very scruffy looking pub in Harrow where there was this great cluster of scooters outside, and I went in and there were The Who. They were playing there in this room with just one red bulb glowing and an extraordinary audience that they had collected. They were the loudest group I'd ever heard and they gave the whole thing a satanic quality. It just seemed to me that this had to be the face of the late Sixties. There was Keith Moon, the drummer, raised on a high stool dominating the group, battering away for all his life was worth. The rest of the group was playing on a stage made out of beer crates. And the ceiling came right down on top of them so that when Pete Townshend – the lead guitarist – was playing, he'd bang his guitar against the ceiling, and one night he physically poked a hole thorough the ceiling because it was getting in his way. It was only made of paper and cardboard, and he went straight through. This went down tremendously with the audience. And that's how the whole thing started." (From *Born Under A Bad Sign*, by Tony Palmer, 1969)

Saturday July 18
Trade Union Hall, Watford
 Billed as The Who with Chris Farlowe & The Thunderbirds as the supporting act. The Who played a series of Saturday night gigs here during July, and Farlowe had initially been billed as the headliner but was eventually switched to the supporting slot when The Who proved to be the more popular attraction. Adverts cite the name The Who, not The High Numbers, for this date.

> **R. & B. Nite at the Trade**
> *(here Watford Junction Station)*
> SATURDAY 18th JULY
> **THE WHO**, plus
> Chris Farlowe and the Thunderbirds
> ADMISSION MEMBERS 4/6
> ● *The Best in Rhythm and Blues every Saturday and Sunday at the Trade*

Sunday July 19
Florida Rooms, Brighton
 Advertised as The High Numbers.

Tuesday July 21
Railway Hotel, Harrow & Wealdstone
 Billed as The High Numbers (formerly The Who), 8 to 11 pm.

Sunday July 26
White Hart Hotel, Acton, West London
 The High Numbers' payment for this show was £12.

Tuesday July 28
Railway Hotel, Harrow & Wealdstone

Friday July 31
Goldhawk Social Club, Shepherd's Bush, West London

The High Numbers played support to The Kinks on this date, the first of three appearances they would play together in the coming month. Their payment for this show was £12.

Saturday August 1
Trade Union Hall, Watford

The High Numbers' fee for this engagement was £30.

Kit Lambert had phoned Chris Stamp in Ireland where Stamp was working on a film, suggesting that his business partner fly back to London *tout suite* to check out the band he'd found. Over the next month Lambert and Stamp ousted Pete Meaden (and Helmut Gorden) as the group's managers.

Sunday August 2
Florida Rooms, Brighton

Billed as an 'All Night Rave', midnight to dawn, sharing the bill with another Mod band from London called The Clique. The High Numbers netted £25 for this show.

Tuesday August 4
Railway Hotel, Harrow & Wealdstone, 8 to 11 pm

Wednesday August 5
The Scene Club, Soho, Central London

Through an arrangement made by Pete Meaden, The High Numbers began a five week residency at the Scene Club, a Mod mecca in Ham Yard, Soho, appearing on Wednesday nights.

Thursday August 6
White Hart Hotel, Southall, West London

The band received £12 for this gig.

Saturday August 8
All Saints Hall, Whetstone

The band's fee here was £30.

Sunday August 9
The Hippodrome, Brighton

The High Numbers were signed up to play support to major acts in a series of Sunday concerts booked by promoter Arthur Howes. (They had auditioned for Howes at the Stork Club back in the spring.) As well as their own brief set, the group backed female singer Val McCullam. The first of the Howes concert appearances starred Gerry and The Pacemakers in two shows: 6 and 8:30 pm.

Tuesday August 11
Railway Hotel, Harrow & Wealdstone

Wednesday August 12
Labour Hall, South Oxhey

This venue is listed on Lambert and Stamp's account sheet for this date along with a payment of £25.

Saturday August 15
Riverboat Shuffle, Central London

This was an afternoon gig aboard a boat for which the High Numbers were paid £35.

Sunday August 16
Opera House, Blackpool

The second of the Sunday concerts, this time for two performances with The Beatles. The Kinks were added to the bill at the last minute.

John Entwistle and Pete's art school friend, Richard Barnes recalled these historic concerts to Andy Neill for *Record Collector* magazine.

Entwistle: "Keith Moon and I got a lift in Kit Lambert's Volkswagen – top speed 80 mph. So we were doing 80 mph up the M1 – very uncomfortable! The Opera House was one of those old-fashioned theatres, with speakers in the dressing room so you could hear the other artists performing. Because of all the constant screaming, nobody could hear what the Beatles were singing anyway. All that was coming through these speakers were the words, and some of them were hilarious. The *Hard Day's Night* film had just come out and Lennon was singing, 'It's been a hard day's night and I've been *wanking* like a dog!" The audience couldn't hear it but we could!

"They wouldn't use our PA, they used the house PA which was useless. I went up to their roadie Mal Evans and asked if I could borrow a guitar lead as mine wasn't working. He brought out Paul's lead and said (adopts Scouse accent) "Don't forget to give it back. It's the only one we've got!" I thought 'they're as bad as we are!' McCartney asked me about the Rickenbacker I was using. I told him the neck was awful and I was getting rid of mine but that didn't stop him getting one later."

Barnes: "I travelled up to Blackpool with Pete in the equipment van, and Keith and I spent some time messing about on Blackpool Tower. He was only just starting to blossom; he was nothing like the 'Moon The Loon' character he became. Seeing the Beatles – or more importantly, the reaction to them – really had an effect on Keith and the rest of the band. The Kinks were also on the show and they made an impression on Pete musically. I remember he and I staring in awe as Ray Davies was brushing his hair, surrounded by these beautiful girls.

"We shared the lift from the dressing room to the stage with the Beatles. McCartney was very polite and genial and Lennon was quite garrulous, reading out the safety regulations in one of those mock voices of his. I was so used to seeing the High Numbers at the Railway, the club I was running at the time, so the band looked and sounded rather ordinary, playing their small stint on such a big stage. The Beatles were using these large Vox amps, which probably only had tiny speakers inside, but they looked massive. I think it was these that made Pete ask Marshall to design the 8x12 cabinets the Who later used.

"What was amazing was the Beatles' getaway. Towards the end of the concert, I noticed loads of bobbies and officials massing together at one of the exits. The minute the Beatles played the last note, the curtain was pulled and these police lit-

erally grabbed the Beatles and led them running through this underground passage and out of the theatre next door to where their car was waiting. The audience, who'd all stood up for the National Anthem, ran round to the stage door thinking the Beatles were still inside. When we left, we had to run the gamut of all these kids. Moon and I had these striped madras jackets which we'd swapped over and I got the sleeve torn off mine. Pete reckoned it was all because the kids mistook Kit Lambert for Brian Epstein."

The Who went on to appear with The Beatles on one further occasion at the 1966 *NME* Pollwinners Concert.

Tuesday August 18
Railway Hotel, Harrow & Wealdstone

Wednesday August 19
The Scene Club, Soho, Central London

Thursday August 20
Majestic Ballroom, Luton
A fee of £25 was received by the band.

Saturday August 22
Trade Union Hall, Watford
The band's fee was £30.

Sunday August 23
The Hippodrome, Brighton
The third of the Sunday concerts, this time supporting Dusty Springfield and Eden Kane for two shows, 6 and 8:30 pm. It was also Keith's 18th birthday!

Tuesday August 25
Railway Hotel, Harrow & Wealdstone, 8 to 11 pm

The High Numbers did not appear here on the following Tuesday, September 1 - the only break in their twelve week residency at the Railway. They were replaced by Gary Farr & The T Bones.

Wednesday August 26
The Scene Club, Soho, Central London

Sunday August 30
Queen's Theatre, Blackpool
The High Numbers played support to The Searchers for two shows, 6 and 8:10 pm. Also on the bill were The Kinks, "hit recorders of 'You Really Got Me' ".

Wednesday September 2
The Scene Club, Soho, Central London
The last of the four Wednesday nights at the Scene. An indication of the kind of performance The Who gave at the Scene Club can be found on the only live tape that survives from this era (mistakenly thought to be from a show at the Marquee Club). The tape is not dated, but is thought to hail from mid-1964. The tracks included are 'I Gotta Dance To Keep From Crying,' 'Young Man Blues,' 'Long Tall Shorty,' 'Pretty Thing,' 'Here 'Tis,' 'You Really Got Me', (Medley:) 'Spoonful', 'Smokestack Lightning', 'Green Onions' and 'Money'.

A solid drum pattern started 'I Gotta Dance To Keep From Crying', a light, breezy and danceable performance which featured good harmony vocals. 'Young Man Blues' was a very laid-back traditional blues song with a cool, jazzy feel. It was very short and vastly different to the song it would later become in The Who's stage act. In

contrast, the stomping 'Long Tall Shorty' was more routine despite the tight playing. Of special note, is the heavy debt Roger's vocals owe to the style of Howlin' Wolf (evident throughout the set). The song incorporated two guitar solos from Townshend which showed a spark of originality with heavy, crashing chords and distortion. The same up tempo energy was displayed on 'Pretty Thing', which started with a fast, hard guitar intro before subsiding into straight R&B with harmonica fills from Daltrey in between the verses. 'Here 'Tis' closely followed the version The High Numbers recorded for Fontana in June.

The remaining songs are much less tightly arranged. A loose version of The Kinks' 'You Really Got Me' followed, with the two–chord guitar riff being repeated with no vocal lines. This was most notable for Townshend's heavily distorted guitar sound. The interpretation was so casual that it sounded like a rough jam or rehearsal until Daltrey added a snatch of vocal. The final medley again resembled a long R&B jam, with Townshend's lacerating metallic guitar riffs to the fore. Only 'Money' featured Roger's , and the separate numbers of the medley tended to merge into one another to the point of obscurity. But the R&B element here, significantly, took a second place to Townshend's experimental feedback and distortion.

Friday September 4
Kelvin Hall Arena, Glasgow, Scotland
In their first Scottish appearance, The High Numbers were included on the bill for *Fab '64 - The Big Beat Show* starring Dave Berry & The Cruisers and Lulu & The Luvvers. Two performances: 6 and 8:15 pm.

Sunday September 6
Queen's Theatre, Blackpool
The fifth and final of the Sunday concerts, this time supporting The Swinging Blue Jeans and The Nashville Teens at 6 and 8:10 pm.

Tuesday September 8
Railway Hotel, Harrow & Wealdstone, 8 to 11 pm

Tuesday September 15
Railway Hotel, Harrow & Wealdstone

Saturday September 19
Trade Union Hall, Watford

Tuesday September 22
Railway Hotel, Harrow & Wealdstone, 8 to 11 pm

The last night of the Tuesday residency the group had been playing at the Railway since the last week of June.

Wednesday September 23
Town Hall, Greenwich, South London

Kit Lambert and Chris Stamp tried to expand The High Numbers' appeal beyond their usual West London stronghold and booked a series of gigs in Greenwich. This was one of four dates at the Town Hall which were eventually terminated because of poor attendance.

Saturday October 10
Olympia Ballroom, Reading

Journalist Virginia Ironside accompanied Kit Lambert to a gig at the Olympia, ostensibly to witness Pete's guitar smashing act but missed the event since she and Kit were chatting in the adjoining bar when he demolished the instrument!

Sunday October 11
Wolsey Hall, Cheshunt

The High Numbers were billed as 'raving R&B'.

Wednesday October 14
Town Hall, Greenwich, South London

Wednesday October 28
Town Hall, Greenwich, South London

Wednesday November 18
Wolsey Hall, Cheshunt

Reverting back to the name The Who, the group made a return visit to Cheshunt. The ad says "Wednesday Scene" but the date listed fell on a Thursday. The gig was actually Wednesday November 18, 8 to 11 pm.

Tuesday November 24
The Marquee, Soho, Central London

The opening night of The Who's residency at the legendary Marquee Club, 7:30 to 11 pm. This Tuesday night residency was set to run for 16 weeks but was extended for another seven weeks as the group eventually broke house attendance records established by Manfred Mann and The Yardbirds.

This first night drew fewer than 30 of the group's most ardent followers; loyal fans who in the past two years had come to innumerable gigs at the Goldhawk, the Railway and the Oldfield Hotel.

It's difficult to describe the impact that the Marquee shows were to have on young people seeing The Who for the first time. Three valuable eyewitness accounts give something of the revelatory nature of being first exposed to The Who at this time.

Pearce Marchbank: "There was this group called The Who, who had a rather smart logo. There were hardly any people in the Marquee and this guy, who I later discovered was either Chris Stamp or Kit Lambert, was walking round giving people whisky. This was to gee up the audience, since they were all there from the Railway Hotel or wherever. What they did on stage then was completely different to their records. Their showstopper was 'Heatwave'; they never played their

MARQUEE

90 WARDOUR ST.
LONDON, W.1

Thursday, November 19th (7.30-11.0):
★ **LONG JOHN BALDRY**
AND THE HOOCHIE COOCHIE MEN
★ **THE NIGHT SHIFT**

Friday, November 20th (7.30-11.0):
★ **THE T-BONES**
★ **HEARTS AND SOULS**

Saturday, November 21st (7.30-11.0):
★ BIG BAND SATURDAY NIGHT
★ **JOHNNY DANKWORTH**
AND HIS ORCHESTRA with BOBBY BREEN
★ **JOE HARRIOTT QUINTET**

Sunday, November 22nd (8.15):
★ **"JAZZ 625"** (B.B.C.-2 TV)
(All tickets for this telerecording featuring ALTON PURNELL and KEITH SMITH have now been allocated)

Monday, November 23rd (7.30-11.0):
★ **THE MOODY BLUES**
★ THE MULE SKINNERS

Tuesday, November 24th (7.30-11.0):
★ THE **"WHO"**
★ THE SNEAKERS

Wednesday, November 25th (7.30-11.0):
★ **HUMPHREY LYTTELTON'S**
JAZZ NIGHT with HUMPH, THE BAND and
★ JOHNNY TOOGOOD'S JAZZBAND

Thursday, November 26th (7.30-11.0):
★ **"AN EVENING WITH
THE BLUES"**
HOWLING WOLF, HUBERT SUMLIN
OTTILIE PATTERSON, CHRIS BARBER
LONG JOHN BALDRY, ROD STEWART
Tickets: Members 7/6, Guests 10/-
IN ADVANCE from The Marquee Club

singles on stage... I gathered they were an art-school band by the look of them."

Dave Goodman: "The first time I came out of my shell was when I saw The Who at the Marquee. I'd never seen anything like it. I couldn't imagine that people could do such things. I went straight out and broke a window, I was that impressed. It broke down so many barriers for me, just that one evening of seeing The Who. The set was so fucking violent and the music so heady it hit you in the head as well as the guts, it did things to you. You'd never heard anything like it. 'Maximum R&B' said the poster... and fuck me, was it!" (Both quotations from *Days In The Life: Voices From The English Underground 1961-1971*, Jonathan Green, 1988).

Mick Farren: "The Tuesday night Marquee was an unreal spectacle of nearly a thousand speeding Mods watching transfixed, packed shoulder to shoulder, bopping and gum chewing, as at deafening volume The Who go through their act to the culmination in an orgasmic ritual of frantic destruction as Keith Moon climbs onto his drums and swings at them with an axe as Townshend drives his guitar into his speakers until it splinters." (quoted in *Watch Out Kids*, 1972)

Wednesday November 25
Florida Rooms, Aquarium, Brighton

The Who appeared here for the next five Wednesdays nights.

Tuesday December 1
The Marquee, Soho, Central London, 7:30 to 11 pm

In contrast with the sparse attendance the previous week, The Who attracted 298 to this show, grossing £57.

Michael Aldred, a compere on ITV's pop programme *Ready, Steady, Go!*, atmospherically described the gig in his column for *The Daily Sketch* (December 5): "The club was packed. Hundreds of fans were swarming round the stage watching 'The Who' at work. Suddenly, somebody jumped up from the crowd and joined singer Roger Daltry (*sic*) at the mike. Someone else from the audience started beating time on a tambourine, and suddenly it seemed half the audience were with the group on stage.

"Adding to the excitement, lead guitarist Peter Townshend weaved to and fro in front of the huge amplifiers, with the volume turned right up. This creates the weirdest note whining from the speakers. A cymbal crashed and the singer grated his mike against the vibrating metal. The overall sound was sensational. The fans were going mad, dancing as if they were hypnotised. What a fantastic sight.

"Like the vast majority in the audience, 'The Who' is a very Mod-looking group. 'But,' says Roger Daltry, 'the Mod scene is dying out. People are running out of ideas.' Then I talked to 'The Who' about their sound gimmick. 'It just developed,' they said. And Peter Townshend explained: 'We bend and distort notes. To us it is now part of the music.' The drummer chipped in with his idea of their highly unconventional sound: 'It's atmospheric music,' he said.

"Well, it's certainly that all right. I wonder if they will capture the same atmosphere on their first record which is due out soon."

Wednesday December 2
Florida Rooms, Aquarium, Brighton

Tuesday December 8
The Marquee, Soho, Central London, 7:30 to 11 pm

Wednesday December 9
Florida Rooms, Aquarium, Brighton

Saturday December 12
Harrow Technical College, North London

Monday December 14
The Red Lion, Leytonstone, East London
The first of four Monday night gigs here.

THE WHO
Maximum R & B
at the
RED LION
High Street
Leytonstone, E.11
Every Monday from
7.30 p.m.

Tuesday December 15
The Marquee, Soho, Central London, 7:30 to 11 pm

Wednesday December 16
Florida Rooms, Aquarium, Brighton

Monday December 21
The Red Lion, Leytonstone, East London, 7:30 pm

Tuesday December 22
The Marquee, Soho, Central London, 7:30 to 11 pm

Wednesday December 23
Florida Rooms, Brighton
The last night of the five–week run at the Aquarium.

Monday December 28
The Red Lion, Leytonstone, East London, 7:30 pm

Tuesday December 29
The Marquee, Soho, Central London, 7:30 to 11 pm
Earning their first notice in the national music press, Nick Jones reviewed this show for *Melody Maker* (9 January 1965).

THE WHO

"THE WHO", appearing each Tuesday at London's Marquee Club, should be billed not only as "Maximum R&B" but as "Far-out R&B."

These four young musicians present their own brand of powerful, stinging rhythm-and-blues which, last Tuesday, quickly stimulated an enthusiastic audience.

"Heatwave" — the Martha and the Vandellas hit number — is given typically fiery "Who" treatment. Another of their outstanding numbers was an instrumental "Can't Sit Down". This performance demonstrated the wierd and effective techniques of guitarist Paul Townshend, who expertly uses speaker feedback to accompany many of his solos.

"The Who", spurred by a most exhilarating drummer and a tireless vocalist, must surely be one of the trendsetting groups of 1965. N.C.J.

The Who began the year that would see them become a chart band with a new single, 'I Can't Explain', set for release on January 15. At the end of 1964, Kit Lambert, desperate to get The Who a recording contract, signed them to a niggardly production deal with the American record producer Shel Talmy, then operating in London and enjoying massive success with The Kinks. The deal empowered Talmy to place The Who's records with whatever record company he chose, always assuming that some company somewhere wanted The Who on their label. This was the first, and probably the biggest, mistake that Kit Lambert would ever make as far as The Who's career was concerned, at least from a financial point of view.

Talmy signed The Who to a production deal, giving them a two-and-a-half per cent royalty. He took their records to American Decca who released them in the UK on the Brunswick label, and who doubtless gave Talmy a royalty substantially in excess of two-and-a-half per cent. By playing both ends against the middle, Talmy came out well ahead. The Who's management, who were themselves taking 40 per cent of The Who's earnings, soon realised how little the band would ultimately receive and persuaded Talmy to increase their royalty to 4 per cent, but this was probably still far less than Talmy was getting. Worse was to come.

After three singles and one album, all of them released in 1965, The Who wanted out – they reckoned they could make better records and more money without Talmy – but he wouldn't budge. To force Talmy's hand, Kit Lambert took the group's next single, 'Substitute', to Robert Stigwood who put it out on his Reaction label (through Polydor). Talmy sued, and in an out-of-court settlement was granted a 5 per cent royalty on all The Who's records and singles for the next six years, up to and including *Who's Next* in 1971. He would thus earn considerably more in royalties from The Who's record sales than the individual members of the band ever did... without so much as lifting a finger. Even today, over 35 years later, Talmy still collects pro rata royalties on every track The Who recorded up to 1971.

But no one cared much about the long–term future in an era when no pop band, not even The Beatles, had established the concept of a sustained career in this field. Pop groups were evanescent in 1965, and no one could have known, or even dreamt, that The Who would still be going strong in six years time, let alone become the kind of million dollar superstar touring rock attraction that they eventually did. So The Who, like so many others, signed away their future in the adrenaline rush to get into the recording studio.

Nevertheless, after two years of non-stop work on the pub, club and ballroom circuit, and getting noticed by the music press at their increasingly successful Marquee residency, The Who were poised to make a name for themselves all over Britain. These were exciting times.

Although they were playing mainly cover songs in their live set, it was the original material that Pete began submitting to the group that was to provide them with a future. In April they recorded an album of mostly R&B covers with only one Townshend composition in the running order, but the entire LP was scrapped. Their first album would eventually contain an even split between covers and Townshend originals.

From their very first hit with 'I Can't Explain', The Who began to attract the interest of critics on the Continent. The European avant-garde set – much less self-conscious of stuffy ideas of "art" than the British establishment – responded to the Pop Art sensibilities of The Who's music and image, and certainly the anti-materialism of the auto-destruction. The French film-maker, Alain de Sedouy, filmed the band in London in February for a documentary, telling the *New Musical Express* (February 25) that he believed The

Who to be "a logical musical expression of bewilderment and anarchy of London's teenagers". The resulting film now seems to have been lost, but before the year was out one of the leading figures of *nouvelle vague* – Michelangelo Antonioni – was planning to include The Who in a big-budget film. The group's second single, 'Anyway Anyhow Anywhere' was released on May 21. Apart from The Beatles' 'I Feel Fine' which opens with a short burst of feedback, 'Anyway Anyhow Anywhere' became acknowledged as one of the first records with sustained feedback as an integral part of the guitar solo. When Talmy sent Decca the master, the record company returned the tape believing it to be defective.

The B-side was Derek Martin's 'Daddy Rolling Stone'. The record appeared in the UK chart on June 5 at number 26 and in the next few weeks climbed steadily to number 10. 'Anyway Anyhow Anywhere' was released in America with a B-side written by Ragovoy- Mimms entitled 'Anytime You Want Me' but like 'I Can't Explain' it failed to chart Stateside.

With a record in the charts, the band were able to play further afield and command higher fees. They played their first Scottish tour in early May and went on to make their début on the Continent in Paris at the beginning of June. The trip was a resounding success and they returned to France later in the year. The group played a couple of outdoor festivals during the summer, starting with the Uxbridge Festival on June 19 and later took part in the Richmond National Jazz & Blues Festival on August 6. The Who undertook their first Scandinavian tour in September. Like the Paris trip in June, the trek was successful enough to warrant a return this time to Sweden for one day only on October 10. They played a matinée in Stockholm and an evening show in Gothenburg, resuming a series of UK dates that week. It was also around this time that Roger was kicked out of the band. Differences over the use of drugs, usually 'leapers' (uppers), particularly with Keith, led to backstage battles which reached a climax in the autumn. Realising just how important The Who were to him, Roger backed down and adopted a more peaceful approach to group relations. He was duly reinstated. Few, if any, rock groups have had a better front man.

In late October, the English music press announced that "a new Pete Townshend protest song, 'My Generation', had been recorded and was due for release in November". The single appeared on October 29 and The Who's début album (of the same name) followed on December 3. Much has been written about 'My Generation', and it remains a quintessential rock record of the Sixties, as well as the most important record The Who ever released – despite the glittering successes that would come their way over the next 10 years. The raw sound and rough-edged performance of the studio version of the track are testimony to the pent–up rage and desperation that was The Who in 1965. The song was initially banned by the BBC because the stuttering effect was deemed insulting to genuine stammerers. Only after constant airplay by pirate stations and the record's immediate effect upon the public did the BBC reverse its decision. Such was the song's authenticity that some who bought the record really believed that Daltrey suffered from a stammer.

Pete Townshend's original demo was much slower, being based on a typical Jimmy Reed riff. Chris Stamp came up with the idea for the stammer and had a hard time trying to persuade the band to adopt it. Acknowledged as an anthem for frustrated youth, Townshend's famous line, "Hope I die before I get old!", has lived to haunt its author to the present day. In America, 'My Generation' was released on the Decca label with 'Out In The Street' as the B-side (from the *My Generation* album). It failed to impress American listeners and climbed no higher than number 74 before dropping out of the charts altogether.

Keith was stricken with whooping cough in mid-December and the group was forced to employ the services of Viv Prince (formerly of The Pretty Things) as a stand-in until he was well again. He recovered in time to appear at the Ricky Tick, Windsor but collapsed again and had to be carried from the stage. Prince was recalled to fill in for two gigs before Keith was able to rejoin for the December 21 gig at the Marquee.

Saturday January 2
Ealing Club, West London

Monday January 4
The Red Lion, Leytonstone, East London
After four weeks here, The Who completed their Monday night residency.

Tuesday January 5
The Marquee, Soho, Central London, 7:30 to 11 pm

Saturday January 9
Club Noreik, Tottenham, North London
The Club Noreik ran 'all-nighter' shows on Saturdays, midnight to 6 am.

Tuesday January 12
The Marquee, Soho, Central London, 7:30 to 11 pm

Wednesday January 13
Wolsey Hall, Cheshunt
A return to Cheshunt by "popular request", 8 to 11 pm.

THE WHO

Here's a group I like immensely, and their absorbing sound matches their gimmick name, The Who. (They were originally the Hi Numbers).
"I Can't Explain" is a pounding shuffle-shaker, with surf-like counter-harmonies behind the main lyric.
It's insidious and insistent, with an arresting backing—a sort of blend of Mersey beat and surfing! Keep your eye on this one.
Even better is "Bald Headed Woman," which starts with a bluesy solo vocal set to a rasping funereal backing with gospel-type chanting—and gradually speeds into a wild hand-clapping raver. On Brunswick.

Sunday January 17
New Theatre, Oxford
The Who appeared on a package show with American singer P.J. Proby topping the bill. Two performances. There would be a 32 year interlude before The Who would appear with P. J. Proby again, when he played the part of the Godfather in the 1997 *Quadrophenia* tour.

Monday January 18
Technical College, Chelsea, Central London

Tuesday January 19
The Marquee, Soho, Central London, 7:30 to 11 pm

Saturday January 23
Corn Exchange, Chelmsford
A 'Saturday Scene' gig. The first of two gigs.

Saturday January 23
Club Noreik, Tottenham, North London
Midnight to 6 am, with The Muleskinners.

Tuesday January 26
The Marquee, Soho, Central London, 7:30 to 11 pm

Saturday January 30
Ealing Club, West London

Sunday January 31
The Marquee, Soho, Central London

Tuesday February 2
The Marquee, Soho, Central London, 7:30 to 11 pm

Tuesday February 9
The Marquee, Soho, Central London
Billed as "The Who London 1965", 7:30 to 11pm.

Thursday February 11
Ealing Club, West London
The first of three consecutive Thursday night bookings at the Ealing Club.
    Billed as 'The Who London 1965', 7:00 to 11pm.

Saturday February 13
Waterfront Club, Southampton.

Tuesday February 16
The Marquee, Soho, Central London
    Billed as 'The Who London 1965', 7:30 to 11 pm.

Thursday February 18
Ealing Club, West London
    Billed as 'The Who London 1965', 7:00 to 11 pm.

Sunday February 21
St. Joseph's Hall, Wembley

Tuesday February 23
The Marquee, Soho, Central London
    Billed as 'The Who London 1965', 7:30 to 11 pm.

Thursday February 25
Ealing Club, West London
    Billed as 'The Who London 1965', 7:00 to 11 pm.

Friday February 26
Lynx Club, Boreham Wood
    In ads that appeared a year later, the venue's name was spelled Links Club.

Sunday February 28
Agincourt Ballroom, Camberley

Tuesday March 2
The Marquee, Soho, Central London
    Billed as "The Who London 1965", 7:30 to 11 pm.

Wednesday March 3
Le Disque A Go! Go!, Bournemouth

Wednesday March 4
Ealing Club, West London

Friday March 5
Granby Halls, Leicester
    Rag Rave, 8 pm – 2 am, with Manfred Mann headlining. Also on the bill were Mike Berry & The Le Roys, More Than Five, The Beatniks, and The Contacts.

Tuesday March 9
The Marquee, Soho, Central London
    Billed as 'The Who London 1965', 7:30 to 11 pm.

Wednesday March 10
Ealing Club, West London

Friday March 12
Goldhawk Road Social Club, Shepherd's Bush, West London

Saturday March 13
Club Noreik, Tottenham, North London
    Another 'all-nighter' session, midnight to 6 am, with The Candles.

Sunday March 14
Starlite Ballroom, Greenford, West London

27

Tuesday March 16
The Marquee, Soho, Central London
  Billed as 'The Who London 1965', 7:30 to 11 pm.

Wednesday March 17
Ealing Club, West London

Friday March 19
Public Baths, Royston

Saturday March 20
Goldhawk Social Club, Shepherd's Bush, West London

Sunday March 21
Trade Union Hall, Watford

Monday March 22
Parr Hall, Warrington

Tuesday March 23
The Marquee, Soho, Central London
Billed as 'The Who London 1965', 7:30 to 11 pm.

Wednesday March 24
Ealing Club, West London

Thursday March 25
Blue Opera Club, Cooks Ferry Inn, Edmonton, North London

Friday March 26
Ealing Club, West London

Saturday March 27
Rhodes Centre, Bishop's Stortford, 8 to 12 pm
  Supported by Cops 'n' Robbers. Interestingly enough, the advert for the gig cites The Who as Decca recording stars and not Brunswick, the UK affiliate of Decca.

Sunday March 28
Kavern Club, Birmingham
  The Who were additionally supposed to appear at the Ritz Club during the afternoon, but as a special afternoon of only Midlands bands was being held, this appears unlikely.

Tuesday March 30
The Marquee, Soho, Central London
  Billed as 'The Who London 1965', 7:30 to 11 pm.

Wednesday March 31
Bromel Club, Bromley Court Hotel, Bromley

Thursday April 1
Town Hall, Wembley, 7:30 pm to 1 am
  Donovan topped the bill of the Harrow Rag Week dance, with Rod Stewart & The Soul Agents and The Who as support acts.

Friday April 2
Youth Centre, Loughton

Saturday April 3
London College of Printing, Elephant & Castle, Central London

Sunday April 4
Plaza Ballroom, Newbury

Monday April 5
Lakeside Club, Hendon, North London

Tuesday April 6
The Marquee, Soho, Central London
Billed as 'The Who London 1965', 7:30 to 11 pm.

Wednesday April 7
Dacorum College, Hemel Hempstead

Thursday April 8
Olympia Ballroom, Reading

Friday April 9
Stamford Hall, Altrincham

Saturday April 10
The Cavern Club, Leicester Square, Central London

Sunday April 11
Majestic Ballroom, Luton

Tuesday April 13
The Marquee, Soho, Central London
Billed as 'The Who London 1965', 7:30 to 11 pm. The set they played included 'Heatwave', 'Motoring', 'Shout And Shimmy', 'Please Please Please', 'I Don't Mind', 'Smokestack Lightin'' and 'I'm A Man' according to Nick Jones who reviewed the show in the April 17 issue of *Melody Maker*.

Wednesday April 14
Il Rondo Club, Leicester

Thursday April 15
Locarno Ballroom, Swindon (cancelled)
A letter of cancellation was packaged as part of the material included in the *Live At Leeds* album in 1970.

Thursday April 15
Victoria Ballroom, Chesterfield

Friday April 16
Goldhawk Social Club, Shepherd's Bush, West London

Saturday April 17
Florida Rooms, Brighton
The Who's 1973 album *Quadrophenia* was dedicated to the audiences at this venue (among others) that the band played to during 1965. It is also possible that this gig provided one of the formative experiences of the Mod/Rocker phenomenon that Pete Townshend later recalled as being an influence on *Quadrophenia*: "We were playing at Brighton Aquarium and I saw about two thousand Mod kids and there were three Rockers up against a wall. They'd obviously just come in thinking that they were going to a party and they really were scared as hell, and the Mods were just throwing bottles at them. I mean, there's no sort of hero in my eyes in something like that. There's no nostalgia. It just moved me to do something to perhaps make the music elevate the people a bit. I know it sounds idealism, but those people who were kicking the Rockers in on the front would come in and listen to our music. So I knew then that I had what felt like a certain kind of power. There were all the tough guys looking at me, waiting to hear what I was about to say." (*New Musical Express*, November 3, 1973).

Sunday April 18
Civic Hall, Crawley
  The band netted £51 for this show.

Monday April 19
Botwell House, Hayes, West London

Tuesday April 20
The Marquee, Soho, Central London, 7:30 to 11 pm

Thursday April 22
Waterfront Club, Southampton

Friday April 23
Oasis Club, Manchester

```
CLUB NOREIK
Sat. April 24th
THE WHO
plus the Jynx Pack
11.30-6 a.m.
```

Saturday April 24
Lynx Club, Boreham Wood
  A double booking on this date, with the group moving on to Club Noreik for a very late (or very early!) set.

Saturday April 24
Club Noreik, Tottenham, North London.
  'All-nighter' 11:30 pm to 6am.

Sunday April 25
Trade Union Hall, Watford

Monday April 26
Town Hall, Bridgwater
  The Who's fee was £200.

Tuesday April 27
The Marquee, Soho, Central London
  The last gig of the legendary Marquee residency. An after-hours party was thrown at the venue attended by Doris Troy, Eric Burdon, Lulu & The Luvvers, The Mojos, Kenny Lynch, Screaming Lord Sutch, and Chris Stamp's actor brother Terence and girlfriend, model Jean Shrimpton. The Who had finally made their mark on the London music scene with their exciting stage act,

and the Marquee was the platform for that live exposure.

Wednesday April 28
Bromel Club, Bromley Court Hotel, Bromley

Friday April 30
Town Hall, Trowbridge
  The band's fee was £200.

Saturday May 1
College of Art & Technology, Leicester

Sunday May 2
Dungeon Club, Nottingham
  The Who arrived very late for this show. Richard Evans (who would later do design work for the Who): "I was a fashion student at Nottingham Art School in 1965 and had got myself on the Social Committee because it meant you could get into the college dances for nothing. We booked The Who for this gig at The Dungeon. I'd just bought 'I Can't Explain' and loved it. I still have that same copy - it's the one on the back of Disc 1 in the box set (*30 Years Of Maximum R&B*). The Who turned up about two hours late to a very disgruntled crowd of pissed-off and drunken art students. Once they started playing

Saturday May 15
Neeld Hall, Chippenham

Neeld Hall was given the moniker 'Top Twenty Club' for this night's performance, 7:45 to 10:45 pm. Billed as "Brunswick recording artists from TV, radio and films, The Fabulous Who." "Leather coats not allowed in the ballroom", added the poster. The Who received £150 for this concert.

Sunday May 16
Town Hall, Stratford, East London

though, they were forgiven. It was worth the wait. I particularly remember Townshend and Moon, but especially Townshend. We thought he was the coolest looking bloke we'd ever seen. I think it was the shoes. I still check him out every time I see him, starting with his shoes. A very snappy dresser."

STRATFORD TOWN HALL SUNDAY CLUB
SUNDAY 16th MAY
THE FABULOUS FANTASTIC
WHO
7.30-11 p.m — 6/-
PLUS DISCS PLUS ★ ★ ★

Monday May 3
Majestic Ballroom, Newcastle

Wednesday May 5
City Halls, Perth, Scotland (cancelled)

Thursday May 6
Two Red Shoes, Elgin, Scotland

Friday May 7
Raith Ballroom, Kirkcaldy, Scotland

Saturday May 8
New Palladium Ballroom, Greenock, Scotland

Sunday May 9
De Montfort Hall, Leicester

The Who appeared on a package show, starring Tom Jones and Marianne Faithfull. Two performances: 5:40 and 8 pm.

Wednesday May 12
The Palais, Bury (cancelled)

Thursday May 13
Public Hall, Barrow-in-Furness

Friday May 14
Civic Hall, Dunstable

Monday May 17
The Pavilion, Bath

Tuesday May 18
McIlroy's Ballroom, Swindon

Wednesday May 19
Corn Exchange, Bristol.
Supported by The Strolling Bones.

Due to an earlier incident involving roadie Cyrano Langston, Roger was attacked on stage by the venue's bouncers before the Who's roadies intervened.

Thursday May 20
Town Hall, Kidderminster

Friday May 21
The Ricky Tick Club, Guildford

The Who were paid £100 or 60 per cent of gross receipts (whichever was higher).

Saturday May 22
Astoria Ballroom, Rawtenstall

Monday May 24
Majestic Ballroom, Reading

des Rockers' promotion, this gig was reviewed in *Disco Revue* (No. 9, June 1965), translated thus: "The British group who are considered most likely to become the triumphant group of 1966... The appearance of The Who seemed to evoke a strange, supernatural presence. The audience understood that a new style of rock was being created, particularly with the song 'Anyway Anyhow Anywhere'. The wild drummer was capable of a lively, forceful rhythm... The singer came over as somewhat overpowering. The audience responded to The Who with ecstatic delirium..."

Tuesday May 25
The Marquee, Soho, Central London

Thursday May 27
Assembly Hall, Worthing

Friday May 28
Ricky Tick Club, Windsor
The Who were paid either £125 or 60 per cent of gross receipts.

Saturday May 29
Pavilion Ballroom, Buxton
The Who played two sets, from 9:10 to 9:40 pm and 10:25 to 10:55 pm.

PAVILION BALLROOM, BUXTON (Saturday, May 29th)	
8.00p.m. to 8.15p.m.	Records
8.15p.m. to 9.05p.m.	Phil Ryan and the Crescents
9.10p.m. to 9.40p.m.	The Who
9.45p.m. to 10.20p.m.	Phil Ryan and the Crescents
10.25p.m. to 10.55p.m.	The Who
11.00p.m. to 11.45p.m.	Phil Ryan and the Crescents

Sunday May 30
Mojo Club, Sheffield

Wednesday June 2
Club au Golf Drouot, Paris, France, 9:00 pm
The Who made their first trip outside the UK on a short but successful visit to Paris. A 'Les Club

Friday June 4
Trentham Gardens, Stoke-on-Trent (cancelled)
The Who were to receive 50 per cent of box office receipts.

Saturday June 5
Loyola Hall, Stamford Hill, North London

Sunday June 6
St. Joseph's Hall, Upper Holloway, North London
The Who's fee was £200.

Monday June 7
The Marquee, Soho, Central London
The Who returned to the Marquee for an unusual Monday night booking, considering their just completed residency had been a run of Tuesday night gigs. Supported by Jimmy James and The Vagabonds, 7:30 to 11 pm.

Tuesday June 8
Public Hall, Wallington
The band were paid £100 or 60 per cent of gross receipts.

Wednesday June 9
Il Rondo Club, Leicester

The band received £100 or 60 per cent of gross receipts.

Friday June 11
Co-Op Ballroom, Nuneaton

There was a session for those under 17 years of age from 5:30 to 8:15pm with the evening show from 8:30 to midnight.

Saturday June 12
Town Hall, Dudley

The band were guaranteed £150 or 60 per cent of gross receipts.

Sunday June 13
Manor Lounge, Stockport

A £90 fee against 60 per cent of gross takings.

Tuesday June 15
Town Hall, High Wycombe, 7:30 to 10:30 pm

The band were paid £125 or 60 per cent of the gross takings.

Wednesday June 16
Town Hall, Stourbridge

The Who were paid a minimum guaranteed of £100 against 60 per cent of takings.

Thursday June 17
Bowes Lyon House, Stevenage

The Who broke the attendance record at this venue. Their terms were £140 or 60 per cent of takings.

Friday June 18
Floral Hall, Morecambe

The band were paid a minimum of £75 or 50 per cent of takings.

Saturday June 19
Uxbridge Blues And Folk Festival, Uxbridge Show, Park Road, Uxbridge

The Who appeared here during the afternoon, sometime between 2:30 and 4:30pm, and then moved on to play the Cavern in Leicester Square that evening. Their fee for the Uxbridge Festival was £150. Among the acts on the bill were Marianne Faithfull, The Spencer Davis Group, American soul singer Solomon Burke, John Mayall's Bluesbreakers, The Birds (with future Rolling Stone Ron Wood) and others.

Saturday June 19
The Cavern, Notre Dame Church Hall, Leicester Place, Central London

Sunday June 20
The Blue Moon, Hayes, Middlesex

Thursday June 24
Town Hall, Greenwich, South London
A return to Greenwich where, less than a year earlier, the group had to cancel a resident booking due to poor attendance!

Friday June 25
Ricky Tick Club, Windsor

Saturday June 26
Town Hall, High Wycombe
The Who appeared here before moving on to Club Noreik for another "all-nighter" session.

> John Entwistle: "We all come from the Shepherd's Bush area. Before I started playing guitar I used to be a trumpeter in a jazz band. But now we all prefer the Tamla-Motown and Zoot Money sound of music. We went to see the Motown show and loved every minute of it!"
> *(New Musical Express, 23 April 1965).*

Saturday June 26
Club Noreik, Tottenham, North London
'All Nighter,' midnight to 6 am.

Sunday June 27
Starlite Ballroom, Greenford, West London

Monday June 28
Manor House Ballroom, Ipswich

Tuesday June 29
Burtons Ballroom, Uxbridge.
Supported By The Mark Four.

Wednesday June 30
Town Hall, Farnborough

Friday July 2
Maple Ballroom, Northampton

Saturday July 3
Gaiety Ballroom, Ramsey

Sunday July 4
Community Centre, Southall, West London

Monday July 5
Assembly Rooms, Tunbridge Wells

Wednesday July 7
The Manor House, North London
The Who appeared at the 'gala opening' of this club, opposite the Manor House Tube station. An all-time record crowd turned out to witness  an explosive set of 'Daddy Rolling Stone,' 'Heatwave,' 'Jump Back,' 'Motoring,' 'Green Onions,' and 'Anyway Anyhow Anywhere'.

It was at this concert that *Melody Maker* reviewer Chris Welch remembered Keith Moon's performance displaying a staggering level of energy. Moon was so exhausted in the fetid atmosphere of the club that, at the end of the set, several roadies had to carry him outside feet first to recover in the cool night air.

The Who definitely are Mods. Their audience is largely of the same faith, but a good sprinkling of show biz personalities always turn up to see the group.

Their manager, Kit Lambert, spent some time in a nearby pub trying to convince me about the group's merits. A very loquacious gentleman who takes great pains to put his points across.

Then we were joined by Who drummer Keith Moon. Keith was wearing an emerald roll-collar shirt and had a lot of black hair worn long.

"We call ourselves Mods, but it's not a disadvantage," he said. "The people who come along identify themselves with us. They look at us on stage and think they're like us.

"But we go down just as well in big Rocker areas."

It was only when we went into the Marquee and saw the Who on stage, that I realised they would be a recording technician's nightmare if they went into a studio and played in their normal manner.

Thursday July 8
Olympia Ballroom, Reading

Friday July 9
Locarno Ballroom, Basildon

Saturday July 10
Winter Gardens, Ventnor, Isle-of-Wight

Sunday July 11
Savoy Ballroom, Southsea, Portsmouth

Tuesday July 13
The Marquee, Soho, Central London

Wednesday July 14
Locarno Ballroom, Stevenage

Thursday July 15
The Ritz, Skewen, Wales

The first of two appearances in Wales – The Who's first concerts there.

Thursday July 15
Glen Ballroom, Llanelli, Wales

Friday July 16
Athletic Ground, Cheltenham

The Yardbirds, Shades Of Blue, and The Hellions were also on the bill.

Saturday July 17
Town Hall, Torquay

The Who acted as replacements for P.J Proby, who was originally scheduled to replace The Walker Brothers. Supported by The Dicers, and The Hunters, 8 to 11:45 pm, this was the group's last engagement for almost two weeks. The Who took a uncharacteristic ten day break from live dates until they resumed gigging on July 28.

Wednesday July 28
The Pontiac, Zeeta House, Putney, South London.

8 pm 'til late', supported by The Drag Set.

Friday July 30
Fender Club, Kenton, Middlesex

For this engagement the band was guaranteed £180 against 60 per cent of the gross receipts.

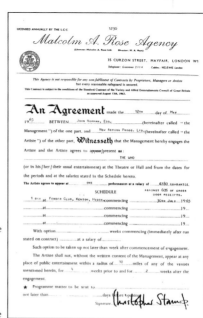

Saturday July 31
Wilton Hall, Bletchley

Sunday August 1
Britannia Pier Theatre, Great Yarmouth

The group was booked for four Sunday performances here, co-starring Donovan, "England's answer to Bob Dylan". The Who, supported by three other acts, including female folk singer Dana Gillespie, closed out the first half of the show. Donovan did not appear on the opening Sunday due to illness.

Wednesday August 4
Witchdoctor Club, St. Leonard's-on-Sea, Hastings

The BBC filmed parts of this gig and 'Heatwave' and 'The Kids Are Alright' were later broadcast as part of the BBC1 TV programme, *A Whole Scene Going* on Wednesday, January 5, 1966.

THE 5th NATIONAL JAZZ &
BLUES FESTIVAL
sponsored by
THE EVENING NEWS & STAR
RICHMOND
ATHLETIC ASSOCIATION GROUNDS
FRIDAY, 6th AUGUST
7.30 - 10.30   Ready, Steady, Richmond !   Tickets 10/-
THE YARDBIRDS • THE WHO
THE MIKE COTTON SOUND
THE MOODY BLUES
Plus Radio Luxembourg recording of the famous Ready, Steady, Radio Show

Friday August 6
5th National Jazz & Blues Festival, Athletic Ground, Richmond

Set-list: 'Daddy Rolling Stone,' 'I Can't Explain,' 'My Generation,' 'Anyway Anyhow Anywhere,' 'Shout And Shimmy.'

Their set during the first evening of this annual outdoor event was an important showcase for the band. 'Anyway Anyhow Anywhere' featured a dramatic extended feedback break, during which Pete customarily smashed a Rickenbacker into his speakers, then threw it to the back of the stage and simply picked up another one to continue. Roger placed his microphone under Keith's ride cymbal which he hit from above with his fist to add to the cacophony. Keith moved to pull the cymbal stand away out of Roger's grasp which he then threw to the ground, in the process, telling the singer to "fuck off". A ragged (and extended) 'Shout And Shimmy' closed the set and was notable for Keith's powerhouse drumming. This was a very loose version of the James Brown number, reduced down to just drums and vocals before Townshend added some heavy, thrashed guitar chords. Chris Welch noted in *Melody Maker* (August 14) that "Keith Moon's drum solo was an

explosive firing on all tom toms. Keith looked like a white tornado, dressed in slacks and tee shirt soaked in sweat."

ABC TV, the American network, aired a special two part *Shindig Goes To London* edition on Saturday December 4 and Thursday December 9. The Who were featured in the second programme performing 'Anyway Anyhow Anywhere,' and 'Shout And Shimmy.' A segment of 'Shout And Shimmy' was used in *The Kids Are Alright*.

Saturday August 7
Loyola Hall, Tottenham, North London

Sunday August 8
Britannia Pier Theatre, Great Yarmouth

Wednesday 11 August
Blue Moon, Cheltenham

Support band The Silence featured Dale 'Buffin' Griffin and Pete 'Overend' Watts, later of Mott The Hoople. Griffin remembers playing Keith's Ludwig kit and that Silence guitarist Robert Fisher blew up the Who's guitar amp he was using. Griffin also recalls Watts sitting on the neck of Pete's Rickenbacker and breaking it!

Thursday 12 August
Dreamland Ballroom, Margate

Friday August 13
Central Pier, Morecambe

Thursday August 26
City Hall, Salisbury

Friday August 27
Town Hall, Torquay (cancelled)

Friday August 27
Rang-A-Tang Club, Basingstoke

Saturday August 28
Matrix Hall, Coventry
The Who's set climaxed with "Anyway Anyhow Anywhere" with Pete smashing his guitar into the amp and kicking it frenziedly.

Sunday August 29
Mojo Club, Sheffield

Monday August 30
Sophia Gardens, Cardiff, Wales
John's Union Jack jacket was stolen backstage.

Wednesday September 1
Top Rank Suite, Hanley

Friday September 3
California Ballroom, Dunstable
Supported by Mike Sheridan & The Nightriders & The Vivas.

Saturday September 4
Spa Royal Hall, Bridlington

Monday September 6
Town Hall, Farnborough

Saturday September 11
Imperial Ballroom, Nelson

Sunday September 12
Oasis Club, Manchester

Friday September 17
Gaiety Ballroom, Grimsby

Saturday September 18
Drill Hall, Grantham

Sunday September 19
Savoy Ballroom, Southsea, Portsmouth

Saturday August 14
The New Georgian Club, Cowley

Sunday August 15
Britannia Pier Theatre, Great Yarmouth

Thursday 19 August
Assembly Hall, Worthing

Friday August 20
The Pavilion, Bournemouth

Saturday August 21
The Palais, Peterborough

Sunday August 22
Britannia Pier Theatre, Great Yarmouth
The closing show of four Sunday concerts with Donovan.

Monday August 23
Corn Exchange, Colchester
The Who play the 'Four Hour Rave' with four other acts (including Sean Buckley & The Breadcrumbs, who were coincidentally produced by Shel Talmy), starting at 8 pm.

Tuesday August 24
Town Hall, High Wycombe

Monday September 20
Studio Bellevue, Hilversum, The Netherlands

The Who performed live in front of TV cameras in a studio for broadcast the following evening at 8 pm on Netherlands II. This TV appearance and the following night's show were arranged by Freddy Haayen, the head of Dutch Polydor, who was impressed by the band. (Haayen later became an executive at Warner Brothers and is still a close friend of Roger Daltrey.)

The Dutch TV technicians, unused to groups as loud as The Who, found it difficult to balance their sound. Microphones went down and instructions through headphones went unheard. At one point Daltrey asked for a bottle of whisky to moisten his throat – he'd caught a cold on the journey – but producer Bob Rooyens refused the request. "You sing or you leave the studio," Daltrey was told. Freddy Haayen endeared himself to the band by going out and buying a bottle of Scotch, then passing it in to them through a toilet window. Pete Townshend later described the show as "a great bore".

Commenting on The Who, the Dutch newspaper *De Telegraaf* drew unfavourable comparisons with Sandie Shaw who had appeared on a rival network the same evening: "The second network brought the umpteenth beat group, two members of which tried to swallow the microphones, to which the first network replied with English female singer Sandie Shaw who at least had some qualities and a freshness that was very pleasant after the foregoing..."

The Who and their entourage spent the night at the Wilhelmina Hotel in Delft.

Tuesday September 21
De Marathon, The Hague, The Netherlands

The Who's second live show outside of the UK took place before 450 fans at a restaurant attached to a roller-skating rink. It was organised by 18-year-old Jacques Senf in association with the newly launched Sunday newspaper *Boulevard*, and The Who were paid 1,000 Dutch gilders. Before the show started, fans watched The Who's TV show from the previous evening.

To reduce expenses The Who had left their amplifiers back in the UK and were obliged to borrow equipment from a group called The Hagues. Unfortunately this was no match for The Who's form of attack and Townshend's amplifier

went down shortly after the show began. Daltrey knocked over microphone stands and bashed Keith's cymbals with a mike-stand. Keith, who had a bottle of gin to drink from, knocked over his drum kit, and after eight songs the group was unable to continue. At this point the audience began to shout for more and the organisers, mindful of the riot that had occurred at a Rolling Stones' show in Kurhaus the year before, persuaded two other groups, The Golden Earrings and The Empty Hearts, to loan their equipment to The Who, which they were understandably reluctant to do.

Jacques Senf later stated: "They are very difficult guys. Very weird and very uncivilised. And they spend as much as fl. 1,000 a day." *Boulevard* magazine reported that at various times in the evening The Who could be found in the bushes outside where "they were in discussion with female fans".

Saturday September 25
Folkets Hus, Helsingor, Denmark

The Who performed their first Scandinavian concert at 9 pm with about 600 fans in attendance. They then rushed back for a midnight set at the K.B. Hallen, 20 odd miles away.

Saturday September 25
K.B. Hallen, Copenhagen, Denmark

Sunday September 26
Aarhus Hallen, Aarhus, Denmark

As was the common practice at the time, The Who played two shows in two different towns on this Sunday. The first performance here was at 8:00 pm.

Although Pete was quoted as saying that this was "the best concert we ever played in Denmark", Svante Borjesson considered it a disaster: "Violence lay in the air of Aarhus Hallen even long before The Who were to perform. They had to do their set rather early in the schedule, to be in time to do their show in Aalborg as well. The thousand strong audience were tearing their chairs apart, and throwing pieces, along with bottles and trash, at the supporting groups on the stage... By the time The Who got on stage, the audience had turned into a riot mob. Again, kids tried to get up on stage. George Mitchew once more tried to push them back. Instead, he was pulled down into the audience where he was beaten and kicked. The Who only played half of one song before the situation got completely out of hand. The kids stormed the stage, took the instruments that were still there and began smashing them. The Who and their management had already escaped through the back exit, once they realised what was happening." This incident resulted in The Who being banned by the Aarhus authorities for five years.

Local reviewer "J.L." commented that The Who... "used all wild and extreme means to change the traditional use of musical instruments... The instruments were used to their limits and the four performers actually seemed to create sounds we'd never heard before... Indeed - The Who is anarchy!" (translation).

Sunday September 26
Fredrikstorv, Aalborg, Denmark

The second performance of the day, a 9:30 pm show in Aalborg. Svante Borjesson: "The concert in Aalborg was something of an anticlimax. Still, The Who played a good concert to almost ecstatic kids." In the local newspaper, a reviewer, failing to understand the nature of distortion and feedback, wrote: "Unfortunately their sound equipment wasn't very good. The last song was drowned in awful noise and static coming from the speakers!"

During the Danish trip, Roger was 'sacked' from the band, or at least asked to reconsider his attitude towards the band and his role within it. In retrospect, so full was The Who's date sheet, so far in advance had dates been booked and so important was it for them to sustain their momentum, that it was foolhardy to contemplate sacking anyone.

Saturday October 2
Agincourt Ballroom, Camberley

Sunday October 3
The Twisted Wheel, Manchester

Wednesday October 6
Kinema Ballroom, Dunfermline, Scotland

Friday October 8
City Halls, Perth, Scotland
Advertised as "their first visit to Perth".

Saturday October 9
Market Hall, Carlisle

Sunday October 10
Johanneshovs Isstadion, Stockholm, Sweden

The Who made a fleeting visit to Sweden, playing in two different cities on the same day. They appeared in Stockholm at 2:00 pm and went on to Gothenburg for two evening shows. Due to a flight mix-up, The Who's equipment had been shipped directly to Gothenburg for the later

With big 'one-way-street' signs on the back of their jackets, the famous instrument-smashing group, The Who, arrived yesterday afternoon in Copenhagen. They didn't seem that awful at the airport and were even quite nice to the 15-20 screaming teenage girls who had come to tear them apart. The Who is part of the new wave of girl-follower groups. Their music and performances are described as so-called Popart. - What do you think of this Popart? we ask the singer Roger Daltrey - I can't explain anything about it, since are Popart! The Who has in any case created their own style which is not only expressed in their music, but in their clothing. They have, for instance, used the English flag to make jackets. Their pop clothes have also become the latest in teenage fashion. The group is known for smashing its instruments during performances and the natural question how they afford it. - We don t, but it's great! - How much are you going to smash during the concert in KB-Hallen tomorrow night? - We're not telling you yet, but we've bought enough equipment anyway!

They sounded awfully loud and awfully much, but why – and how?" (Translation).

Monday October 11
Parr Hall, Warrington (cancelled)

Thursday October 14
Skating Rink, Camborne, Cornwall

Friday October 15
Hillside Ballroom, Hereford

Saturday October 16
Baths Ballroom, Scunthorpe

Wednesday October 20
Top Rank Ballroom, Southampton

Friday October 22
Social Centre, Milford Haven, Wales

Saturday October 23
Rhodes Centre, Bishop's Stortford, 8:00 pm to midnight

show. The gig went ahead with equipment borrowed from the supporting acts The Overlanders, The Mascots and The Moonjacks. Under the circumstances, the band had to curb their more violent tendencies and Monica Tromm wrote: "The pop gala was very boring, all instruments intact."

Sunday October 10
Cirkus Lorensbergsparken, Gothenburg, Sweden
Two shows, 7 and 9 pm, with five other bands on the bill!
Once again, The Who failed to smash any equipment! The newspaper *Goteborgs–Posten* said: "No sensation – they played 'Anyway Anyhow Anywhere' but didn't smash a single guitar...

Sunday October 24
Carlton Ballroom, Slough

Monday October 25
Trade Union Hall, Watford

Thursday October 28
Locarno Ballroom, Swindon

This was the same venue that cancelled a Who appearance for Thursday April 15.

Friday October 29
Starlite Ballroom, Greenford, West London

Saturday October 30
Manchester University

Sunday October 31
Cavern Club, Liverpool

The Who's only performance at the legendary Cavern Club where The Beatles performed over 275 times between 1957 and 1963.

Monday November 1
Baths Hall, Ipswich.

Supported by the Pete Barden Quartet.

Tuesday November 2
The Marquee, Soho, Central London

After a four–month absence, The Who came back to the Marquee for the now prestigious Tuesday night booking, the regular 7:30 to 11 pm session. This Marquee night broke box–office records. Nick Jones found that although "a bit subdued, The Who found their usual fire on the last number, their latest hit 'My Generation', when it all started happening again." (*Melody Maker*, November 13 1965). It was during November 1965 that The Who added to their live set versions of The Everly Brothers numbers 'Love Hurts' and 'Man With Money.'

Wednesday November 3
Locarno Ballroom, Stevenage

Thursday November 4
Queen's Hall, Barnstaple (cancelled)

Over 450 disappointed fans were turned away when The Who missed out on this date because Roger was suffering from a throat ailment. According to Queen's Hall manager Mr Gordon, The Who failed to inform him of their cancellation and he was left to explain to an anxious audience that his star attraction of the evening would not be appearing.

Roger recovered in time for the group's live appearance on *Ready Steady Go!*, performing 'My Generation,' the following evening.

Saturday November 6
St. George's Ballroom, Hinckley

Sunday November 7
Mojo Club, Sheffield

Saturday November 13
La Locomotive Club, Place Blanche, Paris, France

Two shows, 5 pm and midnight.

MARQUEE

90 WARDOUR STREET
LONDON, W.1
Phone: GER 8923

Thursday, October 28th (7.30-11.0)
★ **THE STEAM PACKET**
LONG JOHN BALDRY, ROD STEWART, JULIE DRISCOLL, BRIAN AUGER TRINITY
★ **BO STREET RUNNERS**

Friday, October 29th (7.30-11.0)
★ **GARY FARR and**
★ **THE T-BONES**
★ FELDER'S ORIOLES

Saturday, October 30th (2.30-5.30)
★ **THE MARQUEE SATURDAY SHOW**
Top of the Pops, both live and on disc, introduced by guest D.J.s and featuring star guests

Saturday, October 30th (7.30-11.0)
★ **JIMMY WITHERSPOON**
★ **DICK MORRISSEY QUARTET**
featuring PHIL SEAMEN
★ **RONNIE ROSS QUARTET**

Sunday, October 31st (7.30-11.0)
★ **DEDICATED MEN JUG BAND**
★ **THE LEVEE BREAKERS**

Monday, November 1st (7.30-11.0)
★ JIMMY JAMES and
★ **THE VAGABONDS**
★ **ROSCOE BROWN COMBO**

Tuesday, November 2nd (7.30-11.0)
★ **THE WHO**
★ **MARK LEEMAN FIVE**
(Members' Tickets: 6/-, available in advance on evenings only)

Wednesday, November 3rd (7.30-11.0)
★ Special Students' Rate: 2/6
★ **THE SETTLERS**
★ AL STEWART
★ TOM, DICK and HARRIET
★ Plus Guest Folk Artists

41

Jean-Claude BERTHON & "DISCO REVUE" présentent
DEUX SUPER SOIREES 100 % ROCK EN NOVEMBRE
AU CLUB "LA LOCOMOTIVE", PLACE BLANCHE, PARIS (XVIIIᵉ)

Monday November 15
The Pavilion, Bath

Tuesday November 16
Winter Gardens, Malvern

The Who attracted a crowd of 1,056 fans to the Winter Gardens, the best attendance to date in the 1965 'Beat Sessions'.

Friday November 19
Glad Rag Ball, Empire Pool, Wembley

The Glad Rag Ball was held in the 10,000 seat Wembley Empire Pool, and it was the biggest

● **Glad Rag Ball, Empire Pool, Wembley.** November 19th. All night dancing (9pm-4am). Dress : Odd. Tickets 30/- each, reduction for Radio Caroline Club members. Available from Wembley and from Selfridges, Oxford Street. Ticket enquiries Holborn 2681.

DONOVAN. The Kinks, The Who. Georgie Fame & The Blue Flames. The Hollies. The Barron Knights. Wilson Pickett. John Lee Hooker. Geno Washington & The Ramjam Band. The Birds. The Masterminds. The Golden Apples of the Sun. Ted Heath & His Music. Cathy McGowan. Denny Piercy. The Merseybeats. Radio Caroline Disc Jockeys: Tom Lodge. Ugli Ray Terret.

Organised by London Students Carnival Limited in association with Radio Caroline and with the kind permission of Immediate Records Limited.

indoor British concert The Who had played to date. Running from 9 pm to 4 am, the show was staged by London Students Carnival Limited in association with Radio Caroline, the pirate radio station.

The concert was filmed and broadcast by ATV on Wednesday December 8. The Hollies, Wilson Pickett, Georgie Fame & The Blue Flames and Donovan were among the other acts that appeared. Although listed on the bill, The Kinks failed to appear.

The Who's performance was delayed when Roger Daltrey objected to the poor quality of the PA system provided by the promoters. He refused to sing until The Who's roadies had installed their regular equipment. This incident was, of course, edited out of the ATV broadcast on December 8.

Disc (November 27) reported: "The Who ran into a big storm when lead singer Roger Daltrey stalked off stage at the height of a show last week. It happened when everything was swinging at the London Students' Glad Rag Ball, attended by about 3,000 at Wembley Pool on Friday. There had been an argument over microphones and electric amplifiers. Daltrey was not satisfied with the ones provided. He wanted to use the group's own equipment. After stalking off stage – leaving Pete Townshend, John Entwistle and drummer Keith Moon playing to thousands of fans clustered around the platform – Daltrey said: 'I'm choked off. We dashed here straight from *Ready, Steady, Go!* I tested the mikes before things started. They were no good. We couldn't get the sound we wanted. I wanted to use our amps – with their gear behind them. But they said 'No, use ours and like it!' It was only because we didn't want to disappoint the kids that we went on at all. We thought of jacking in altogether."

Eventually Daltrey returned to the stage. He stood out of sight of the audience while The Who's road managers staggered around the platform erecting amplifiers. The other three kept playing. At one point the fans began chanting: 'Where's the singer?' – and a fusillade of objects came from the audience. A huge amplifier unit was being balanced precariously on top of another and looked in danger of falling onto the fans. Finally Daltrey – his clash with electricians settled – went back to the mike and explained the reason for his disappearance. Their act then got under way again."

Saturday November 20
Florida Rooms, Brighton

Tuesday November 23
Dorothy Ballroom, Cambridge

Wednesday November 24
Town Hall, Stourbridge

Friday November 26
The Palais, Wimbledon, South London

Saturday November 27
London School of Economics, Aldwych, Central London

Sunday November 28
Oasis Club, Manchester

Monday November 29
St. Matthew's Hall, Norwich (cancelled)
This show was cancelled as the band could not reach Norwich due to snowdrifts across the roads. Their van was forced to return to London.

Tuesday November 30
Town Hall, High Wycombe

Wednesday December 1
Wolsey Hall, Cheshunt, 8 to 11 pm

Friday December 3
Goldhawk Social Club, Shepherd's Bush, West London

This night marked the Who's last appearance at the Goldhawk, the band's acknowledged power base for more than two years.

Irish Jack: "The air hummed with excitement as everyone waited for The Who to appear on stage. They hadn't played the Goldhawk for six months but they'd decided to do a thank-you gig for all their Mod followers at the Shepherd's Bush club where they used to play regularly Friday nights. There was a distinct atmosphere of 'the heroes return' about the occasion. For the first time in the history of the Goldhawk (apart from appearances by Adam Faith and Shane Fenton) a huge queue lined the street outside. I'd gone in with their co-manager Kit Lambert which gave me a buzz because it looked like I was his assistant or one of the band's brothers. The last time The Who played the Goldhawk they were paid £50; this time they were on £300.

"I stood on the steps of the stairs that led to the bar. With me were some Goldhawk regulars: Martin Gaish and his brother Lee, Peter Campbell, Tommy Shelley, Joey Bitton, Jez Clifford, his mate Chris and Alan Bull. We stood tier-like on the stairs from where we had a clear view of both The Who on stage and the audience jammed together like sardines on the floor below. They were reaching the end of a pulsating set and the adrenaline reached fever pitch as we anticipated a murderous final assault. They thanked all the Goldhawk Mods for their loyal support which was greeted by hearty cheering and much stamping of feet. Before the cheering died away they launched into a thunderous version of 'The Ox' which was to be the last song The Who ever played at the Goldhawk."

Italian film director Michelangelo Antonioni attended this concert, and as a result offered The Who a key scene in his forthcoming film *Blow-Up*. Sensing that The Who would be perfect for his study of reality and illusion in Swinging London, he was disappointed when Kit Lambert allegedly asked for too high a fee. In any case, Pete had reservations: "Antonioni wanted us for the part but we were too genuine. He likes to manipulate his actors. He wants to make films about himself." (*The Village Voice*, April 6 1967)

Antonioni finally settled on the second–wildest act in London, The Yardbirds (currently sporting their short-lived Jeff Beck/Jimmy Page line-up), with whom he filmed the scene on a set made to resemble the Ricky Tick Club. Some genuine Who ambience was still demanded by Antonioni, who had Jeff Beck smash his guitar. Thus The Who's anarchic early trademark was immor-

> Pete Townshend: "The guy who's singing ('My Generation') is supposed to be blocked. It's reminiscent in a way because Mods don't get blocked anymore. They get drunk or other things. Pills was a phase... No, he's not blocked, he just can't form his words. I wrote it just after I did 'I Can't Explain'. We had loads of rows about doing it. Chris Stamp was all for it, but the others kept wanting to put their own bits in. The ending is a natural progression of what's come before. It's the way it happens on stage. It was meant to get back more to the general theme at the end, but it doesn't." (*Record Mirror*, 6 November 1965).

talised in a film in the hands of another group! (Maintaining the cinema connection, a poster advertising this concert can clearly be seen in a location scene from *The Sandwich Man*, released in 1966.)

Saturday December 4
Corn Exchange, Chelmsford

Sunday December 5
White Lion Hotel, Edgware, North London

Monday December 6
Eltham Baths, Eltham Hill, South London

Keith Moon was taken ill during this week and missed several gigs. The *NME* reported that Viv Prince, formerly of The Pretty Things, joined The Who for this gig and for the rest of the week while Keith recovered. (Prince had left The Pretty Things only the week before.) Moon was expected to return to the group on the following Monday, December 13.

ELTHAM BATHS
Eltham Hill, S.E.9
Monday, December 6th
THE
WHO
8 - 11 p.m. Tickets in advance at Eltham
Baths and S.E. London's leading record stores

Wednesday December 8
Corn Exchange, Bristol

Thursday December 9
Guildhall, Plymouth

Saturday December 11
Southampton University

The Zombies were among the acts on the bill. Keith came back for this show, as Zombies' guitarist, Paul Atkinson remembered: "Keith had bought this gas pistol in Paris and just as we were due on stage, he fired it into our dressing room and shut the door. When we finally got out and walked on stage, we all had tears streaming down our faces!"

The Who/High Numbers had upstaged at the Watford Trade Union Hall back in July 1964.

Thursday December 16
Town Hall, Kidderminster

Friday December 17
Ricky Tick Club, Windsor
   Arriving straight from a TV appearance on *Ready Steady Go!*, The Who had been playing for only half an hour when Keith collapsed onstage. For the second time in less than a week, Viv Prince was called on to fill in until Keith had fully recovered.

Saturday December 18
The Birdcage, Portsmouth

Sunday December 19
Ricky Tick, Guildford, Surrey
   Prince completed his second, short tenure with The Who on this date.

Tuesday December 21
The Marquee, Soho, Central London

Thursday December 23
The Pavilion, Worthing

Friday December 24
The Pier Ballroom, Hastings

Sunday December 12
New Barn Club, Brighton

Monday December 13
Federation Club, Norwich
   This gig made up for the date that the band missed on November 29. Keith was expected to return by this date after a week off due to illness. Viv Prince was still deputising.

Wednesday December 15
Student's Union, University College of Swansea, Wales. 8pm to 1pm
   "Going Down Ball", supported by Chris Farlowe and The Thunderbirds, the group that

After the rapid advances made during the previous 12 months, 1966 seems in hindsight to have been a period of treading water for The Who. This was due partly to the situation with Shel Talmy, which was ultimately resolved at a price that would almost certainly have broken a lesser band, but also to The Who's peculiar character. They were simply too good to be a 'pop group' and 'rock bands' were a thing of the future, so The Who were stuck between eras, seeking a stage that had yet to be built. Their time would come, of course, but this wasn't it. Their situation could probably have been improved by opening their American campaign this year instead of waiting until 1967, but visiting the US required money and, as ever, the destruction of their instruments had left them critically short of cash. A planned US trip in the autumn was aborted at the last minute.

Mod was dying, consumed by media exposure and mass production, so as the year progressed, the group moved away from their raw R&B style towards what can be termed power pop. This was an important and far sighted development in The Who's evolution, enabling Pete (and the rest of the band) to prove themselves among the principal exponents of the possibilities of new 'progressive' rock music.

Litigation with Shel Talmy kept them out of the UK singles charts for nearly six months (an almost certain kiss of death in the mid-Sixties) but they soldiered on. They worked all over Britain in the first three months of the year and revisited France at the beginning of April. Their first full–scale theatre tour of the UK began later that month with The Spencer Davis Group as one of the supporting acts. They also took part in the prestigious *NME* Poll Winners' Concert a month later, on a bill that included The Beatles and The Rolling Stones.

June saw the group return to Scandinavia for a week of shows in Sweden and two concerts in Denmark. The tour was such a success that a second swing through Sweden was planned for the autumn. Ballroom and university gigs took them around England through the summer while Lambert and Stamp struggled to secure a US visit for later in the year.

The Who were to headline a major UK tour beginning in September but the schedule was cancelled after only three dates so that they might make their first promotional visit to the United States. Unfortunately, that trip never materialised so the group concentrated on recording, interspersed with the occasional ballroom or theatre gig.

The Who made yet another Scandinavian junket in mid–October, followed by their first concerts in Germany in early November. Through the summer and autumn they continued work at IBC and Pye Studios on their second album, *A Quick One*, which was released on December 9, and reached number 4 in the UK album charts. It contained songs by all four members of the group and featured Pete's first 'mini-opera' - the title track - which occupied most of the record's second side. It was Pete's first venture into the realms of rock opera, in this case a cycle of six separate songs telling the tale of an unnamed heroine who pines for her absent lover, takes a substitute, regrets her folly when her man returns, confesses her indiscretion and is ultimately forgiven. *A Quick One*, of course, was the precursor to *Tommy*. Critically acclaimed in England, The Who now found themselves among the vanguard of groups creating new and intelligent music, influencing even The Beatles as they began recording their monumental album *Sgt. Pepper's Lonely Hearts Club Band*. There was strong competition, though, particularly with the arrival in England of Jimi Hendrix.

The Jimi Hendrix Experience burst upon the London scene in the autumn of 1966 and quickly earned the respect and admiration of England's top rock musicians. Much of the groundwork that The Who had laid in the past two years was now being snatched from under their feet by this brilliant newcomer, but The Who held their ground. Their long apprenticeship as The Detours, and all that weight of experience, seemed to have insured them against failure, regardless of the obstacles that fate seemed ever ready to place in their path.

Chart success continued to elude the band in the US. However with 'Happy Jack' garnering some airplay in New York (and a few other markets, notably Detroit), the group was poised to make its first assault on the other side of the Atlantic in the spring of 1967.

Saturday January 1
Trade Union Hall, Watford

Sunday January 2
Ultra Club, Downs Hotel, Hassocks

Friday January 7
Mister McCoys, Middlesbrough

Saturday January 8
Jigsaw Club, Manchester

Sunday January 9
Cosmopolitan Club, Carlisle

Thursday January 13
Ritz Ballroom, Skewen, Wales
  First gig of a double booking.

Thursday January 13
Regal Ballroom, Ammanford, Wales

Friday January 14
Municipal Hall, Pontypridd, Wales

Saturday January 15
Two Puddings Club, Stratford, East London
  Another double booking.

Roger Daltrey: "We are all so different and we've all got different points of view. We still don't go around with each other but things aren't as bad as they were. We find friction in the groups helps anyway because we play emotional music. We might take a month arguing about 20 new numbers and end up with four. But we are so busy now we don't get much time for rehearsals. We feel very pleased about our success but wary." (*Melody Maker, 11 December 1965*).

Saturday January 15
The In Crowd Club, Hackney, East London
  This gig was an 'all-nighter'.

Sunday January 16
Agincourt Ballroom, Camberley

Friday January 21
Glenlyn Ballroom, Forest Hill, London

SO I WALKED into The Who's dressing room at the Leigh Beachcomber and there they were—arguing about having the same shirts and trousers. A friendly argument, understand.

Nothing like the wild disagreements which the group are reported to have had from time to time.

So later when the rest of The Who were on stage playing an instrumental I nipped in to speak with Roger Daltry, the singer.

Roger was "narked" when I asked about the group's famous internal disagreements.

"Of course we quarrel," he remarked, "but we don't quarrel more than any other group. It's just that ours are more publicised."

"O.K. then," I said. "Why have you stopped smashing up equipment?" (The Who were notorious at one time for going wild on stage and breaking up guitars and amps).

"Well, we're so skint we stand to go to jail. That's why we don't do it any more," said Roger.

Saturday January 22
The Adelphi, West Bromwich
  For the third time in the month, the group appeared at two clubs on the same date.

Saturday January 22
The Baths, Smethwick
  Another 'all-nighter'.

Sunday January 23
The Co-Op, Warrington

Wednesday January 26
Locarno Ballroom, Stevenage

Friday January 28
Birmingham University, Edgbaston

Saturday January 29
Imperial Ballroom, Nelson

Sunday January 30
Beachcomber Club, Leigh

Monday January 31
Coed Eva Community College, Cwmbran, Wales

Tuesday February 1
Britannia Rowing Club, Nottingham

Friday February 4
Astoria Theatre, Finsbury Park, North London, 6:40 and 9:10 pm
The Who began their first headlining theatre tour, a three date jaunt beginning with two shows at this north London venue. Also on the bill were Screaming Lord Sutch & The Savages, The Merseys, The Fortunes and The Graham Bond Organisation. Advance ticket sales were so successful for these three trial dates that promoter Robert Stigwood booked a full length tour in April.
The Who's set comprised: 'Heatwave', Dion &

The Belmonts' 'Runaround Sue', 'Dancing In The Street', Stevie Wonder's 'Uptight', 'Daddy Rolling Stone', 'It's Not True' and 'My Generation'.
Nick Jones reported for *Melody Maker* (February 12) that "the scene was set for The Who to take Finsbury Park by storm but as often happens, the big occasion was too much. Daltrey's mike seemed to be off all night, and Keith Moon's drums were inaudible, the acoustics only permitting an occasional cymbal crash to get through. Despite these difficulties The Who played immaculately and their 'inverted-hipness' by reviving Dion's 'Runaround Sue' must be admired."

Saturday February 5
Odeon Theatre, Southend-on-Sea, 6:30 and 8:45 pm
A member of the audience, R. Rivetts of Essex, wrote in a letter to *Melody Maker* that, in his opinion, The Who's "twenty minute act was about as exciting as a sick headache". In the same issue it was reported that the group had this week completed recording their new single, 'Circles'.

Sunday February 6
Empire Theatre, Liverpool, 5:40 and 8 pm
The conclusion of the three–date theatre tour.

Monday February 7
Town Hall, Chatham (cancelled)

Friday February 11
The Palais, Wimbledon, South London

Saturday February 12
Dreamland Ballroom, Margate

THE Who's four-week concert tour, which opens on March 25, could well be one of the most successful this year. Six trial concerts were held at the weekend—two each at London, Southend and Liverpool.

Although the first night at Finsbury Park Astoria was plagued by gremlins — like mikes not working and curtains not closing—the Who got a thunderous reception, almost loud enough to drown the noise they made!

They opened on a darkened stage with "Heatwave" and although many of their subsequent numbers were indistinguishable through the barrage of noise, I managed to identify "Runaround Sue," "Dancing In The Street," "Up Tight," "Daddy Rolling Stone" and "It's Not True," before they closed with "My Generation."
The Who's first bill-topping concert appearance was quite impressive. Lead singer Roger Daltrey (dressed in patriotic red, white and blue shirt), moved well, but guitarists John Browne and Pete Townshend could rehearse a few more stage actions.

Sunday February 13
Community Centre, Southall, West London
   Prior to playing, Keith dressed in a nun's habit and walked incognito among the audience!

Monday February 14
Liverpool University
   The Who appeared at the University's Panto Ball dance.

Tuesday February 15
Esquire Club, Sheffield

Thursday February 17
Club A Go-Go, Newcastle

Friday February 18
Volunteer Hall, Galashiels, Scotland

Saturday February 19
Memorial Hall, Northwich

Sunday February 20
Oasis Club, Manchester

Monday February 21
Beachcomber Club, Preston

Thursday February 24
Victoria Ballroom, Chesterfield (cancelled)
   Roger came down with laryngitis and missed the next three gigs in Wellington, Boston and Eltham.

Friday February 25
Majestic Ballroom, Wellington

Saturday February 26
Starlight Ballroom, Boston

Monday February 28
Eltham Baths, Eltham Hill, South London

Wednesday March 2
Wolsey Hall, Cheshunt, 8 to 11 pm

Thursday March 3
Victoria Ballroom, Chesterfield
   Rescheduled show from February 24.

Friday March 4
Social Club, Pontypool, Wales

Saturday March 5
Marcam Hall, March

Wednesday March 9
Town Hall, Farnborough

Thursday March 10
Ram Jam Club, Brixton, South London

Friday March 11
The Cavern, Central London

Saturday March 12
The Birdcage, Portsmouth

Sunday March 13
Starlite Ballroom, Greenford, West London

Also added to The Who's live set on occasion around this time were versions of the Lovin' Spoonful's 'Do You Believe In Magic?' and its B-side 'On The Road Again', both of which were sung by John Entwistle.

Friday March 18
Locarno Ballroom, Basildon

> **Keith Moon:** "We've got forty-eight 12-inch speakers, which is about 600 watts worth of power and with my drums it makes ú3,000 worth of equipment on stage every night. That's why we have three road managers to get the stuff erected. In some clubs we have to turn the speakers sideways to get them all on stage."
> *(New Musical Express, 18 March 1966).*

Saturday March 19
King's Hall, Stoke-on-Trent

Wednesday March 23
Tower Ballroom, Great Yarmouth

The Who Fan Club Newsletter reported that road manager Neville Chesters joined the band onstage to sing a version of Crispian St. Peters current hit, 'You Were On My Mind'.

Thursday March 24
Starlight Ballroom, Crawley

Friday March 25
Corn Exchange, Hertford

Saturday March 26
St. George's Ballroom, Hinckley

Sunday March 27
Central Pier, Morecambe

Pete wrecked one of his amps so badly that Marshall's had to work overtime to have it repaired in time for the Who's Paris trip.

Saturday April 2
La Locomotive Club, Place Blanche, Paris, France

Two shows, matinée and midnight performances. The Who flew back to London on Sunday April 3.

Monday April 4
The Who were originally booked to appear at the Majestic Ballroom, Reading, on this date. The Mike Cotton Sound appeared instead.

Friday April 8
Queen's Hall, Leeds

Saturday April 9
Pavilion Ballroom, Buxton

Thursday April 14
Gaumont Cinema, Southampton. Two shows, 6:15 and 8:40 pm

Opening night of the Who's first proper theatre tour of England, booked in association with Robert Stigwood. The complete line-up included The Spencer Davis Group, The New Generation, Hamilton, The Jimmy Cliff Sound and Paul Dean. The Merseys, also managed by Lambert and Stamp, had been listed in the music papers to appear as part of the package but did not perform at this concert.

DAVIS GROUP AND WHO IN WILD STAGE SHOW

By Norrie Drummond

SO you think you've seen it all? Then, brother, you haven't until you've seen the Who-Spencer Davis tour, which opened last Thursday at Southampton Gaumont.

The Who closed the second half, with Pete Townshend ramming his guitar into his amplifier and Keith Moon kicking his drum kit around the stage as he tossed his drum sticks to the audience. Singer Roger Daltrey bounded about the stage like some kind of blond demon, and John Browne stood around like an unemployed undertaker.

The Who appeared on a darkened stage and, as the lights went up, they dashed, smashed and hammered their

The Who's set was: 'Barbara Ann', 'My Generation', 'I Can't Explain', 'Substitute' and 'Dancing In The Street'.

Friday April 15
Fairfield Halls, Croydon. Two shows, 6:45 and 9 pm

At the second show, Roger kicked the mike stand into the audience, Pete punctured his amps and Keith threw his bass drum and cymbals to the front of the stage.

Saturday April 16
Odeon Cinema, Watford. Two shows, 6:30 & 8:45 pm

"The Who have pulled their socks up at last," wrote Nick Jones (*Melody Maker,* April 23). "They didn't let up and haven't played as well – or as hard – for some time... a fast-moving, powerful show." The group were mobbed midway through 'My Generation' during the second house, when fans broke through a cordon of attendants and swept onto the stage. Keith was dragged from his stool, Roger was pulled to the ground, John was knocked sideways and Pete protected himself by circling his arm in front of his guitar.

Sunday April 17
Regal Cinema, Edmonton, North London. Two shows, 6 and 8:30 pm.

Part of The Who's evening set: 'Heatwave', 'Barbara Ann', 'Substitute', 'My Generation'.

Roger Simpson covered this gig for the *Tottenham And Edmonton Weekly Herald* (April 22): "The Who, probably the wildest group on the scene at present, crashed onto the stage and led into 'Heatwave', a Martha & The Vandellas number. Keith (the loon) Moon, wearing a white tee-shirt with a printed medal on it, went crazy on the drums, throwing his drumsticks high into the air and crashing them down onto the skins. Their version of The Beach Boys' recent hit 'Barbara Ann' was a disappointment, but their present top ten number 'Substitute' was well done. They ended the act with 'My Generation', lead guitarist Pete Townshend bringing out every conceivable weird sound from his guitar."

Tuesday April 19
Town Hall, Walsall

This was a regular gig and not part of the theatre tour.

Thursday April 21
Locarno Ballroom, Stevenage

This was a regular gig and not part of the theatre tour. A planned fan club get-together at the town's Roebuck Hotel scheduled for the previous day had fallen through, so this gig was ample compensation for some of The Who's most ardent fans.

Friday April 22
Odeon Cinema, Derby

The Who resumed the theatre tour with two shows in Derby, 6:15 and 8:40 pm.

Saturday April 23
Odeon Cinema, Rochester

Two shows, 6:15 and 8:45 pm.

Sunday April 24
Birmingham Theatre, Birmingham

Two shows, 5:30 and 8:00 pm. The final shows on the Spencer Davis Group tour.

Monday April 25
The Pavilion, Bath

Tuesday April 26
Links Club, Boreham Wood, 7:30 to 11 pm

building up into a drum climax which finally resulted in the whole drum kit disintegrating and falling into the audience which left Keith drumming on a single drum. The original symbolic drummer – at an execution."

Tuesday May 3
Winter Gardens, Malvern (cancelled)

This gig was cancelled because the band's car broke down coming out of London. A crowd of about 1,000 people had come to the hall, and when told that The Who were unable to appear, a small gang of disgruntled fans smashed windows at the Winter Gardens and Festival Theatre as well as the neighbouring Dorothy Café and The Sports Depot pub. A group called The Deep Feeling replaced The Who for the evening.

Roger missed the next two gigs in the Midlands.

Wednesday May 4
Town Hall, Stourbridge

Thursday May 5
Town Hall, Kidderminster

Friday May 6
Top Hat Ballroom, Lisburn, Ireland, 9 pm to 1am

Thursday April 28
The Witchdoctor, Savoy Rooms, Catford, South London

Friday April 29
Tiles Club, Oxford Street, Central London, 7:30 to 11:30 pm

Saturday April 30
Corn Exchange, Chelmsford

Sunday May 1
NME Poll Winners' Concert, Empire Pool, Wembley

The Who made their one and only *NME* Poll Winners' Concert appearance on this date. The annual concert event was video–taped and broadcast on ITV over two Sundays, May 8 and 15 between 3:50 and 5 pm.

The complete line-up featured the crème de la crème of English pop: The Beatles, The Rolling Stones, The Yardbirds, The Small Faces, The Spencer Davis Group, Dusty Springfield, Herman's Hermits, Cliff Richard, Sounds Incorporated, The Alan Price Set, Crispian St. Peters, The Overlanders, The Seekers, Dave Dee, Dozy, Beaky, Mick and Tich, The Shadows, The Walker Brothers and The Who, as well as American Roy Orbison.

Kit Lambert recalled: "At one concert at Wembley, Keith more or less stole the show by

The Who visited Ireland for the first time, playing three dates and opening with a gig in the town of Lisburn, Northern Ireland, just southwest of Belfast. Supported by local act The Oceans.

Saturday May 7
National Stadium, Dublin, Ireland

According to a newspaper report, the Irish Republican Army threatened to blow up The Who with bombs planted under the stage if they appeared wearing their Union Jack jackets. Police searched but found no bombs and the group went on to perform for 2,500 fans in jackets made up with the colours of the flag of Ireland, green, white and gold. The jackets were specially made at Dublin's only boutique.

This was the only time in their career that The Who played in Dublin.

Sunday May 8
Arcadia Ballroom, Cork, Ireland, 9 pm to 2 am

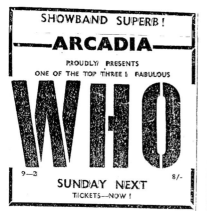

The Who's one and only visit here. Michael O'Callaghan, then a local musician, borrowed ten shillings from his parents to see The Who. He recalls: "It was eight shillings to see them so I had two shillings for cakes and minerals. At the time I was still at school and going to see The Who was an unforgettable event. I was known as Mick the Mod around town because I was one of the few who had all the right clothes and I had big feet

and a big nose like Pete Townshend. I also had a Fender Telecaster. I couldn't believe it when, at the end during 'My Generation' Townshend began to bang his guitar off the railings around the high stage. It was cool and irresponsible and brilliant!"

Before the show 'Irish' Jack's mother Anna and cousin Joey went to the local Intercontinental Hotel and met Pete Townshend and Kit Lambert. 'Irish' Jack did not travel to Cork for this show.

Wednesday May 11
Corn Exchange, Bristol

Thursday May 12
The Pavilion, Worthing

Friday May 13
The Palais, Wimbledon, Southwest London

Roger missed this and the following gig in Bury.

Saturday May 14
The Palais, Bury

Friday May 20
Ricky Tick Club, Newbury

Controversy surrounded this date when an incident on stage was splashed across the pages of the music trade papers. Although there are conflicting reports, it appears that Keith and John arrived late, by which time Pete and Roger had played a short set with the supporting group, The Jimmy Brown Sound. When The Who finally

53

went on stage there was menace in the air, and during the destructive finale in 'My Generation', Pete lost his grip on his guitar as he was slamming it into his amps and Keith was hit in the head with the instrument. Keith received a black eye and badly bruised face and also required three stitches in his leg. The next day Pete went to Keith's house in Wembley to apologise but Keith refused to open the door.

KEITH: black eye

"Then I swung out with my guitar not really meaning to hit Keith. I lost my grip of the instrument and it just caught him on the head.

"At the weekend, I went to Keith's home in Wembley to apologise but he wouldn't answer the door.

"It's over and done with now and there's no suggestion that we might break up because of what happened."

Saturday May 21
Floral Hall, Southport

Without Keith; an unknown deputy drummer filled in.

Monday May 23
Locarno Ballroom, Blackburn

Without Keith.

Thursday May 26
Locarno Ballroom, Ashton-under-Lyne

Without Keith.

Friday May 27
Granby Halls, Leicester

Without Keith.

Saturday May 28
South Pier, Blackpool

In two houses (6:15 & 8:30 pm), The Who were supported by The Rockin' Vicars, The Birds, and Reaction label-mate, Oscar. Keith returned to his place behind the drums.

The Who had connections with both support groups. The Birds featured future Faces and Rolling Stone guitarist Ron Wood and during 1965, The Birds released a single of 'Leaving Here', based upon The Who's arrangement of the song.

Earlier in the year, the Rockin' Vicars (featuring Lemmy on guitar, later famous as bass player of Hawkwind and Motorhead) had released a cover of 'The Kids Are Alright' –re-titled 'It's Alright'. The Birds were one of Lemmy's favourite groups and Motorhead – in turn – recorded a version of 'Leaving Here' in the late Seventies. Incidentally, Lemmy always cited John Entwistle as rock's greatest bass player, bar none!

Sunday May 29
Winter Gardens, Morecambe. Two shows - 6:15 and 8:30 pm

Supported by The Merseys with The Fruit Eating Bears, Mike Berry & The Innocents, Philip Tait & The Stormsville Shakers, 'The Glamorous All Girl' She Trinity, and singer, Oscar.

Pete was involved in a six–car accident on the M1 motorway on his way back to London. His car was the fourth in the pile–up and sustained some damage but he escaped without serious injury. Radio stations in The Netherlands, Germany and France received inaccurate information and reported that Roger had been killed! Although the story was obviously wrong, the Polydor Records offices were inundated with phone calls from anxious fans.

Monday May 30
Sincil Bank Football Ground, Lincoln

The Whit Monday, all-day outdoor Pop Gala Festival. Some of the acts on the massive bill were Georgie Fame and The Blue Flames, The Kinks, Screaming Lord Sutch, The Small Faces and The Yardbirds. Admission was only £1, including a programme!

Thursday June 2
Grona Lund, Stockholm, Sweden

Set: 'Heatwave', 'Dancing In The Street', 'Barbara Ann', 'Daddy Rolling Stone', 'Uptight', 'Daddy Rolling Stone' (reprise), 'A Legal Matter', 'Substitute' and 'My Generation'.

This outdoor concert at the Tivoli Gardens was

the highpoint of the tour. Quite early on in the set, Pete broke a string and threw down his Rickenbacker, and a roadie handed him a second guitar. The Motown songs 'Heatwave' and 'Dancing In The Street' were tightly played and the band's harmonies sounded good and true, with Townshend playing a heavy solo spot at the end of 'Dancing...'. Keith Moon took the lead vocals for 'Barbara Ann'. A long, loose version of 'Daddy Rolling Stone' led directly into a fine interpretation of Stevie Wonder's 'Uptight', before returning to the first song again. Townshend had to re–tune his guitar before taking the lead vocal on 'A Legal Matter', which sounded somewhat ramshackle. 'Substitute', which followed, was hard and energetic. John Entwistle then introduced 'My Generation' while Townshend changed his guitar. This version of the song was as towering as could be expected and degenerated into noise and feedback.

This is the first known gig where Keith played a double bass drum kit. He had probably made the transition from a small–size kit to the new nine–piece set–up sometime in late May.

Friday June 3
Liljekonvaljeholmen - Club 66, Uppsala, Sweden

Recalling the show, Magnus Sjostedt, wrote: "They burst into 'Heatwave', an unexpected opening... In one hour, in that small far-away place, in front of a small Swedish audience (1500?) they went for it. Yes – Pete blew the fuses, furiously stabbing the loudspeakers, Keith really kicked hell out of his drums in 'The Ox', until they appeared to explode, Roger tossed the mike into space and screamed his lungs out and John acted cool..."

Friday June 3
Kungsparken, Kungsor, Sweden

The 30-minute outdoor show was reviewed in Eskilstuna *Kuriren* (June 4): "The sound effects presented by previous bands on the stage in Kungsor seemed like whispers compared to Friday night's English guests. The stage was packed with amps and speakers... The band used to smash a guitar or two during their wild shows, but this evening there were no fights between the members. Apart from a fallen drum and a cymbal that fell to the floor, they were very gentle with their instruments." (Translation). 'Barbara Ann' was also remembered as having been played.

Saturday June 4
Berget, Soderhamn, Sweden

Another outdoor venue, and the band opened with 'Substitute'. "The Who gave an impressive performance," wrote Hempo Hilden, "and we were amazed how the small Selmer amplifier could produce Roger Daltrey's vocals over the massive wall of sound coming from the Marshall stacks... and during the instrumental feed-back parts, like on the end of 'My Generation', he held his mike over the cymbals of Keith Moon. It made a lot of noise. I also remember being surprised by the fact that they did a cover version of The Beach Boys' 'Barbara

Ann' with Keith Moon singing the top vocal harmony... We were also impressed by John Entwistle's cool stage attitude while his fabulous bass riffs were thundering over this little town."

Saturday June 4
Hogbo Bruk, Sandviken, Sweden

"The English band succeeded very well in getting the 3000 Mods into something that could be described as ecstasy with their pling-plong music and leg-rattling... The Who were a rather advanced band, they performed the songs with good musical quality," ran the bizarre review (translation) from Sandviken's *Tidningar* (June 7).

Sunday June 5
Club Nycklen 65, Nykoping, Sweden

The first show of the day with a total of ten groups on the bill! The concert began at 3 pm here and moved on to Orebro in the evening. A crowd of almost 2,500 fans turned out in Nykoping.

Anton, reviewing this show for Sodermanland's *Tidningar*, wrote: "After having watched pop galas indoors and out, I thought I'd heard everything. But after listening to The Who I have to admit, I was wrong. Their speakers managed several decibels more than I thought possible..."

Sunday June 5
Club Nycklens, Orebro, Sweden

The Who headlined a massive pop gala here with 11 other groups on the bill, the event running from 3 to 10 pm. This date concluded the Swedish leg of the tour, and the group flew on to Denmark on Monday June 6.

As The Who began their set very late, the audience rushed the stage and the police in attendance started to panic, unable to control the excited crowd. A few songs into the act, the chief of police decided to cut the power until order was restored. With the stage lighting and amplifiers now dead, Pete Townshend furiously stormed over to the power supply room of the building ready to tackle both the police and stagehands. The power was soon restored, however, and the concert continued with Who roadies defending the mains power switch. But the police once more intervened, cut the electricity for a second time and the concert continued with Keith Moon offering an improvised drum solo. Soon tiring of the solo, Moon joined Townshend and threatened the policemen guarding the power switch but they soon realised that nothing more could be done and The Who withdrew after an aborted set, swearing never to play in Sweden again! But they returned in October, of course.

Tuesday June 7
Tivoli Hit House, Copenhagen, Denmark

In the Danish paper *Politiken* (June 7) "O.J." wrote: "England's most extreme beat group The Who arrived yesterday in Copenhagen... It is said that they nowadays have ceased to smash their instruments and limit themselves to play on them. This was unanimously denied by the young performers in Tivoli yesterday. The group's leader Pete Townshend said he wants to avoid thrusting his guitar into the amplifiers, but that the audience's enthusiasm sometimes makes him lose control. The drummer Keith Moon added: 'We would also like to go further than just smashing our instruments – maybe the whole building.' The four musicians rate the success of their performance entirely on the response from the audience. They are also fully aware that the more instruments they smash, the more publicity they get and the more money they earn." (Translation).

Tuesday 7 June
Fyens Forum, Odense, Denmark

Thursday June 16
Hull University

The size of The Who's PA system stuck in the memory of Ched (a local Hull musician) who recalled (*Where* No.6 December 1991): "I remember walking down Newland Avenue afterwards and my hearing had gone completely! My ears were ringing for days!" Ched also remembered The Who smashing up all their equipment at the end of the set after 'My Generation'. "What happens on stage is all spontaneous," Keith Moon told the *Hull Times* after the show. "We are extroverts and it's a form of expression. When the audiences go mad I can't really believe it's directed at us... We get on much better now as people. It was dreadful at one time. We have learned to accept each other. It's better to be amicable, otherwise life's just miserable..."

Friday June 17
City Halls, Perth, Scotland

Saturday June 18
Market Hall, Carlisle

Sunday June 19
Britannia Pier Theatre, Great Yarmouth
The Who were scheduled to appear at this show – the first of nine Sunday appearances, stretching to August 28 (except August 7 and 14 when they were set for a two week vacation). The Merseys, also managed by Lambert and Stamp, headlined this show, with The Who not joining the package until June 26.

Monday June 20
Gay Tower Ballroom, Birmingham

Tuesday June 21
Winter Gardens, Malvern
This date made up for the show The Who missed back on Tuesday May 3. It was reported that an American film crew covered this concert and that footage was later shown on *CBS Reports*.

Thursday June 23
University Refectory, Leeds

The Who played the University Rag Ball on a bill with John Mayall's Bluesbreakers, Wayne Fontana, The Alan Price Set and The Swinging Blue Jeans. Eric Clapton had just left Mayall's band to form a new trio called Cream with Jack Bruce and Ginger Baker.

Friday June 24
Salisbury University

Saturday June 25
College of Further Education, Chichester
The Who's equipment van was stolen from outside the venue while the group were playing. Fortunately, the vehicle was recovered the following day.

> **Keith Moon: "If we are playing somewhere for the first time, or at a big date, we make sure we give a spectacular performance to win over the audience. Once they have got over the initial shock, we concentrate more on what we are playing. It means we have to play harder at first. I've got to play louder than the guitars. Naturally, it means I have to hit the drums harder than the normal pop drummer and the equipment breaks sooner."** *(Hull Times, June 1966).*

Sunday June 26
Britannia Pier Theatre, Great Yarmouth
It seems that The Who's act was considered unsuitable family entertainment for the summer crowds. This second gig of the nine scheduled Sunday shows was the last that went ahead. All remaining gigs were cancelled.

Tuesday June 28
South Pier, Blackpool (cancelled)

Wednesday June 29
Sheffield University (cancelled)

Friday July 1
Winter Garden, Eastbourne

Monday July 4
Marina Ballroom, Ramsgate

Thursday July 7
Locarno Ballroom, Streatham, South London

shirted and intense, bashed his drum skins with unrelenting savagery. Pete Townshend, the most soberly dressed of the four, looked sadly at his audience when not weaving interesting patterns and half-circles with his arms."

Friday July 15
Starlite Ballroom, Greenford, West London

Saturday July 16
Civic Hall, Barnsley, 7:30 to 11:30 pm

Supported by Pythagoras Square and Fourth and a Fifth.

Thursday July 21
Locarno Ballroom, Bristol

One fan who attended this gig remembers that Keith arrived armed with house bricks to help demolish his drum kit!

Friday July 22
Central Pier, Morecambe

Saturday July 23
Spa Royal Hall, Bridlington, 8:30 to 11:45 pm

Supported by The Mandrakes (who included a very young Robert Palmer). The 21st Century were also on the bill.

Wednesday July 27
Flamingo Ballroom, Redruth

Friday July 8
Top Rank Ballroom, Cardiff, Wales

Saturday July 9
Technical College, Westminster, Central London

Parts of this show were filmed by the CBC network (Canada) and broadcast as *Take 30 In London*. Set included 'Baby Don't You Do It' (featuring an extended solo from Pete incorporating feedback and power chords, as well as the riff from The Rolling Stones' 'Satisfaction'), 'See See Rider' (featuring John on vocals), 'Substitute' and 'My Generation'.

Thursday July 14
Liberal Hall, Yeovil

"D.F." was present at this concert, and reported in *Melody Maker* (July 27) that "The Who have a kind of bizarre science-fiction appeal – electronically violent, deafeningly strident, all rather removed from reality. There is no other group on the current scene remotely like them... the correct technical balance was never achieved. Words were hardly ever caught, melody was blasted out of existence. True there was a sort of sensual excitement about the performance – this in spite of the group's doleful, deadpan expressions. Occasionally, one detected a pleasant and unexpected sense of vocal harmony. Keith Moon, tee-

Thursday July 28
Queen's Hall, Barnstaple

Friday July 29
Tiles Club, Oxford Street, Central London, 7:30 to 11:30 pm
The supporting group was The Blue Aces.

Saturday July 30
Sixth National Jazz & Blues Festival, Windsor Racecourse
The Who were the star attraction on this evening's programme of the weekend festival, moved to Windsor from Richmond because of complaints about the behaviour of the crowds at previous festivals.

The supporting bill included The Vagabonds, Chris Barber, Gary Farr, Louis Nelson, The Move, Kid Martyn, Alex Welsh, The Summer Set and Julian Covey. After this performance, The Who had a 17-day break from live dates but continued recording.

Their set in the open air included: 'Barbara Ann', 'I Can't Explain', 'Anyway Anyhow Anywhere', 'Heatwave', 'Substitute', 'Dancing In

The Street', 'See See Rider', 'A Legal Matter', 'I'm A Boy' and 'My Generation'.

Photographs show Pete Townshend in a formal dinner suit and bow tie. The auto-destruction was still startling enough to cause a headline in *Melody Maker* (August 6): "The Who enjoyed themselves smashing footlights, kicking over amplifiers, breaking guitars, demolishing drums, throwing buckets of water at the audience, and managed to squeeze in 'Barbara Ann', 'Heatwave' and 'My Generation' in between... As well as pushing their own amplifiers and drums over, and smashing guitars, singer Roger Daltrey kicked in footlights. Microphones went flying and the stage was left in utter chaos when they finished the evening. A bucket of water went flying when flames appeared at one point, and a dry ice-machine was used to create smoke. Said one eye-witness: 'The group weren't going down all that well so in the end they pulled all the stops out. Then the crowd went wild.' A small section of the crowd responded to The Who by breaking up chairs and damaging canvas screens..."

*Guitar destroyed: Rickenbacker Rose Morris Model.

Monday August 1
The group had a two–week break from gigs, August 1 to 14, during which they worked on their next single, 'I'm A Boy' and other tracks at IBC Studios.

Thursday August 18
The Palace Ballroom, Douglas, Isle of Man

Saturday August 20
Town Hall, Torquay, 8 to 11:45 pm
Support groups were the Stagger Lees, The Hunters and The Empty Vessels.

Sunday August 21
Pier Ballroom, Hastings

Tuesday August 23
Sherwood Rooms, Nottingham

Wednesday August 24
Orchid Ballroom, Purley

Thursday August 25
Dreamland Ballroom, Margate

Monday August 29
Ultra Club, Downs Hotel, Hassocks (cancelled)

Thursday September 1
Locarno Ballroom, Coventry
The Who were scheduled to appear at 9:15 during this four–hour dance.

Friday September 2
Locarno Ballroom, Basildon

Saturday September 3
Drill Hall, Grantham
After the gig, Pete was attacked by a bouncer after he had accidentally toppled his speaker stack onto the man.

Sunday September 4
New Elizabethan Hall, Belle Vue, Manchester

Tuesday September 6
The Palais, Ilford, Essex

Roger Daltrey: "It's a kind of relief, smashing things up. And it's not as bad as you think. Most of the equipment can be repaired again - in fact we've got everything from amplifiers to guitars all covered in patches. They sound exactly the same. And our two road managers are geniuses at putting them back together again. It's only Pete who permanently damages things, and that's because some of his guitars are so fragile... he started it when he used to play about with amplifiers and pull them and everything for feedback sounds. It just developed. It makes us feel much better to do it. The rest of the act is for the audience. But the smashing up bit is for us." *(Record Mirror, 17 September 1966).*

Wednesday September 7
Locarno Ballroom, Stevenage

Friday September 9
Pier Pavilion, Felixstowe
This gig, filmed by a French television network, was aired later on a show called *16 Millions Des Jeunes*. Set included: 'Heatwave', 'So Sad', 'I'm A Boy', 'Substitute' and 'My Generation'.

PIER PAVILION   FRIDAY
FELIXSTOWE   SEPTEMBER 9
7 p.m. to midnight
COME AND BE SMASHED BY
THE WHO   The Who?   THE WHO
PLUS THE SULLIVAN JAMES BAND AND TOP RADIO D.J.
Tickets available from Mannings Music Centre, Ipswich; Phillips, Newsagents, Felixstowe, and at Pier Pavilion Booking Office.
PRICE 1/6

Saturday September 10
Corn Exchange, Bedford

Sunday September 11
Ultra Club, Downs Hotel, Hassocks

Thursday September 15
Gaumont Cinema, Hanley, two shows - 6:35 and 9:00 pm
The Who began what was to have been their second theatre tour of Britain in 1966 but only two dates were completed and eleven dates were cancelled. One of the supporting acts for this date was the new trio Cream.

Friday September 16
Odeon Cinema, Derby
The supporting bill was The Merseys, M.I.5, Oscar (Pete had written a single for the singer entitled 'Join My Gang') and comedian Max Wall.
The set: 'Heatwave', 'Dancing In The Street', 'Barbara Ann', 'Substitute', 'I'm A Boy' and 'My Generation'.
This was the last date played of the proposed autumn tour with two shows – 6:15 and 8:40 pm. All subsequent dates were cancelled so the group could finish their second album and then make a promotional tour of America. They never went, and ended up playing sporadic gigs around Britain interspersed with studio sessions for *A Quick One*, known in the US as *Happy Jack*.

Saturday September 17
Odeon Cinema, Cheltenham (cancelled)

The remaining cancelled tour dates were at De Montfort Hall, Leicester (September 18), Glasgow Odeon (22), Dundee Caird Hall (23), Sunderland Odeon (24), Manchester Palace (25), Portsmouth Guild Hall (30), Birmingham Hippodrome (October 2), Luton Odeon (6), Walthamstow Granada (7), Southend Odeon (8) and Bournemouth Winter Gardens (9).

Thursday September 29
Town Hall, Maidstone (cancelled)

Saturday October 1
Imperial Ballroom, Nelson

A hastily organised gig, booked as replacements for The Kinks.

Saturday October 8
The Palais, Peterborough

The Who's concert was reported in the local papers as being "the final test" to determine whether it was worthwhile continuing to hold Saturday dances at the Palais.

Monday October 10
The Pavilion, Bath

American network CBS-TV filmed this gig for later broadcast on the programme *CBS Reports*.

Wednesday October 12
Club 192, Casino Oberbayern, Scheveningen, The Hague, The Netherlands, one show, 10.45pm

Set included: 'Heatwave', 'Dancing In The Street', 'Barbara Ann', 'So Sad About Us', 'Substitute', 'On The Road Again', 'It's Not True', 'A Legal Matter', 'Man With Money', 'I'm A Boy', 'My Generation'.

Jacques Senf, who had promoted the Who's first visit to The Netherlands in September 1965, had tried to arrange a second Dutch tour for them in May 1966 but the band were unable to obtain work permits in time. By the time this show was arranged The Who's fee had risen to 7,000 Dutch gilders, excluding travel and hotels. Eventually their friend Freddy Haayen of Dutch Polydor intervened and arranged this show. The group arrived on a Channel Airways plane at

Zestienhoven Airport near Rotterdam and stayed at the Scheveningen Europa Hotel where they celebrated the recent success of 'I'm A Boy' by drinking champagne.

Unlike the first time The Who played in Holland, they had brought their own equipment on this occasion and when it became clear that the 2,000 capacity hall was only going to be half full, Chris Stamp proposed that fans be let in for free and that The Who would waive their fee. Jacques Senf didn't agree to this proposal and, probably out of frustration, The Who smashed their equipment, Townshend apparently switching his expensive Rickenbacker for a cheaper guitar just in time for the mayhem.

● KEITH MOON

RSG! gives sixteen minute spot to Who's stage act

A POP "happening" is to be televised in Britain for the very first time!

On Friday, October 21 Rediffusion's Ready Steady, Go! will devote half of their show — sixteen minutes — to the Who's stage act — an act, "based on the 'Theatre Of The Absurd' ideas that the Who have," said Kit Lambert, the group's co-manager.

Friday October 14
Queen's Hall, Leeds

Due to public demand, The Who headlined shows here and in Chelmsford on this weekend. The first was an all-night dance and barbecue! The Who were advertised as "Number 1 in this weeks charts"!

Saturday October 15
Corn Exchange, Chelmsford

Sunday October 16
Starlite Ballroom, Greenford (cancelled)

Thursday October 20
Herlev Hallen, Copenhagen, Denmark

The Who flew to Denmark on Wednesday October 19 for the opening of their fourth Scandinavian tour. Joining The Who in Denmark was Chris Hutchins of the *New Musical Express* (October 28): "Over 2,000 Danish fans screamed and yelled as they went through numbers like 'Heatwave', 'Barbara Ann', and 'Substitute'. At this point Pete spotted a few empty chairs in the centre of the auditorium and suggested people from the back came forward to fill them. Chaos followed as more than a thousand fought for those few seats. Order was never restored and no one sat down again! It was like The Beatles all over again as the stage filled with burly protectors ejecting fans left, right and centre. The four took no notice but stormed through 'Legal Matter' and 'I'm A Boy'. Finally they reached 'My Generation' and Townshend tried hard to smash his new guitar through an amplifier. Hysteria prevailed even after they had returned to the dressing room."

This trip to Europe necessitated The Who cancelling scheduled concerts in the UK in Ashton-under-Lyne (October 20), Scotland (21-23), and Newcastle Mayfair Ballroom (26). In fact, the contract for Newcastle had already been signed and the band's fee was to have been £350.

Friday October 21
Liseberg Konserthallen, Gothenburg, Sweden, two shows - 7 pm & 9 pm

"Ear-bending – but a very professional noise – was the main impression given by The Who," wrote Gosta Hansson, reviewing one of the shows. "Liseberg stopped the show for some strange reason when The Who had played eight songs, among them the brilliant 'Substitute' and 'My Generation'. But also some from their forthcoming album... like 'Barbara Ann' and 'Heatwave'. They struck 'Konserthallen' with an almost unendurable volume. I can't help wondering whether or not the band members are deaf by now – perhaps they use ear-plugs?"

Saturday October 22
Gislovs Stjarna, Simrishamn, Sweden
Early show.

Saturday October 22
Jagersbo-Hoor, Hoor, Sweden
Late show. Mats Malmsstrom recalls obtaining a rare souvenir at Hoor: "The show started. It was a fantastic feeling and my first pop-concert ever. Keith broke several drumsticks and threw them into the audience. I stood right below Pete, when something suddenly came rolling along the scene. I grabbed it immediately and put it in my pocket. After a short while I picked it up and looked at it – it looked like some kind of 'control'. I looked around and noticed there was a knob missing on Pete's guitar. And I still have it in my possession. When Roger told the audience that it was time for the last song, Pete picked up another guitar. A green rather shabby one. The last song was 'My Generation'. During the song Pete tore one string after another. When the last string broke he took the guitar off and banged it to the floor several times. Then Keith laid back, aimed and kicked his drums to the audience. It was a show to remember for life."

Sunday October 23
MFF-Stadion, Malmo, Sweden

The set: 'Heatwave', 'Dancing In The Street', 'Barbara Ann', 'So Sad About Us', 'The Kids Are Alright', 'Substitute', 'I'm A Boy' and 'My Generation'.

The half-hour set impressed *Fuzz*, whose review appeared the day afterwards (*Sydsvenskan*, October 24): "Expectations were high, and no one was disappointed. The four band members were in an excellent playing mood... What was really impressive was the proficiency the four band members displayed. Keith Moon, for example, must be the most dynamic and skilled drummer the pop world can offer: after only a few songs, he looked as if he had just come out of a shower. The group's guitarist and brain, Pete Townshend, kept up the action, as well did the singer Roger Daltrey. In contrast to the others, the bass player John Entwistle stays calm, an observer almost indifferent to what is happening on stage. The only complaints about the group's performance was that the loud sound from the guitars drowned the vocals."

Sunday October 23
Fyens Forum, Odense, Denmark

The second gig in the second country of the day, this one at 8pm. The curtain was closed while The Who were still playing which provoked Townshend into pulling down the entire curtain!

Fans rushed the stage and the performance came to a chaotic conclusion.

Monday October 24
Folkparken, Halmstad, Sweden

A local reviewer (unknown) reported that: "During the last song, which was performed with the help of lots of kilowatts, things started to look scary. Smoke began pouring out from a big speaker and panic struck the stage. The musicians became worried, amplifiers fell apart, the gigantic drum kit collapsed. Everything seemed chaotic. The young listeners wanted to join in with the band on stage, or at least steal a drumstick, but were stopped by the guards. The smoke and total havoc were part of The Who's finale. After that, it was all over."

Tuesday October 25
Club Nalen, Stockholm, Sweden

Set: 'Heatwave', 'Dancing In The Street', 'Barbara Ann', 'So Sad About Us', 'Substitute', 'The Kids Are Alright', 'I'm A Boy' and 'My Generation'.

The Who launched straight into 'Heatwave' with a careering, manic energy that ten years later would be called punk, and followed directly with 'Dancing In The Street' which built up to a fierce power-chord climax. 'Barbara Ann' featured Keith Moon's comically off-key falsetto vocals, which added to the charm and audacity of the choice of song, which remained tight and fast. The audience might have wondered why the first four songs of the set were all unavailable on Who records at this point. 'So Sad About Us' and 'Substitute' gave a more up-to-the-minute impression of The Who's sharp power pop. 'I'm A Boy' stayed close to the recording in its arrangement, and the delicate middle section was handled very skilfully by the band, with all vocal harmonies intact. The unrelenting drive of 'My Generation' brought the show to its close with a long descent into chaos and noise, with only John Entwistle's bass riffs holding the rhythm together to the bitter end.

Friday October 28
Palais d'Hiver, Lyon, France

With Screaming Lord Sutch and The Stormsville Shakers.

Sunday October 30
Sportpalast, Berlin, Germany

Each member of The Who had flown into Berlin the same day from either France or London. The following day, they returned to London.

Friday November 4
Venue unknown, Kassel, Germany (probably cancelled)

Saturday November 5
Messehalle 10, Saarbrüken, Germany, one show at 8 pm

Because of it being Guy Fawke's Day in England, The Who let off Roman Candles on stage, with John attaching a Catherine Wheel to his amplifier.

Sunday November 6
Kongresshalle, Cologne, Germany, two shows - 4 and 8 pm

Monday November 7
Rheinhalle, Dusseldorf, Germany

On their return to London, the band continued work on their second album, tentatively titled *Jigsaw Puzzle*, and a single, 'Happy Jack'.

Saturday November 12
Duke of York's Barracks, Kings Road, Chelsea, London

The Who were filmed performing five songs live for US television. These were aired on the *Today* show (7 to 9 am EST) on Tuesday November 15 on the NBC network. This day's programme was entitled "Swinging London" and included interviews with various celebrities and a look at English Mod fashion. It is not known how much of The Who's performance was used in the broadcast.

Richard Evans: "I'd skived off art school for a long weekend down in London and was staying in a friend's bed-sit in Walpole Street, close to the Barracks. When The Who started playing it was *so* loud but instantly recognisable as The Who. I grabbed my coat and ran out of the house following the noise up the street. It was a cold, foggy November morning but I stood at the railings and watched The Who play off and on for about an hour."

Thursday November 17
Locarno Ballroom, Glasgow, Scotland

Friday November 18
City Halls, Perth, Scotland

Saturday November 19
Market Hall, Carlisle

Pete's Rickenbacker guitar was stolen from the group's dressing room after the show but later recovered in Scotland.

Thursday November 24
The Pavilion, Worthing

Saturday November 26
Spa Royal Hall, Bridlington

Tuesday November 29
Winter Gardens, Malvern

Thursday December 1
Town Hall, Maidstone (cancelled)

Saturday December 3
Midnight City, Birmingham

With The Family.

Friday December 9
Drill Hall, Dumfries, Scotland

Pete recovered his guitar (stolen in Carlisle on November 19) here.

Saturday December 10
Empire Theatre, Sunderland

Two shows – 6 pm & 8:30 pm. Supported by Dave Berry and an all–female band called She Trinity.

Thursday December 15
Locarno Ballroom, Streatham, South London

This was soundman Bob Pridden's first gig with The Who. Pridden would become The Who's most loyal retainer, virtually the fifth member of the band, mixing their sound from the side of the stage until The Who disbanded in 1983. He's been back with them since they've reformed, and he continues to work on various projects with Pete and Roger to the present day.

Saturday December 17
Imperial Ballroom, Nelson

Money was so light in The Who's kitty that the group asked to be paid in cash at this gig instead of a cheque being sent to the office.

Wednesday December 21
Upper Cut Club, Forest Gate, East London

The Who played the gala opening night of this club, run by British boxer Billy Walker. The set

Bob Pridden: "I was on my way to get a job with the Easybeats and I met John Wolff at the station. He asked me what I was doing and I told him I was looking for a gig. He said 'Well, I'm going into the office. Are you interested in a job with The Who?' So I said sure. I went to their office and met several people and then Pete turned up. He said to me 'I hear you're going to be our new roadie' and he poked me in the forehead with his finger. Vey strange.

That night I went for a drink with John and Keith and apparently I sealed my employment by buying them a drink. They thought that was marvellous. The first gig I ever did with them was the Streatham Locarno in December, 1966. We reheared for the afternoon and that night they went on stage and I couldn't believe it! I'd never seen anything like it in my life! Pete came onstage looking very hip, John was dressed well too but didn't move all evening. Roger twirled mikes around and Keith's sticks were going everywhere. At the end they just smashed everything to pieces. I thought 'Oh, my God!' I was in a state of shock. They walked off stage and Roger turned to me and said 'Bobby, get it all fixed for tomorrow!'"

more. Keith grinned and shouted 'My Generation – yeah!' and the group roared into the old favourite with gay abandon and a riff that sounded suspiciously like 'Knees Up Mother Brown', ending in a violent, vicious climax. Keith Moon kicked his seven-drum kit off the stage and Pete vanished behind a cloud of smoke as he smashed his guitar into speakers."

'Irish' Jack recalls: "I can't exactly remember going to this gig with Pete but I remember the show and later when we went back to the dressing room there was a tense atmosphere because Pete was complaining that the band shouldn't do these kind of gigs - whether it was the fact that there were so many non-Who fans in because of all the celebrities or the fact that it wasn't a sell-out, I can't be sure."

After appearing at the Upper Cut, Pete, John and Roger adjourned to Blaises, one of the 'in' night-clubs in London, to watch the Jimi Hendrix Experience. The club featured acts between 10 pm and 4 am.

included: 'Barbara Ann', 'See My Way', 'Substitute', 'I'm A Boy', 'Whiskey Man', 'Happy Jack' and 'My Generation'.

Amid a celebrity audience from the worlds of showbiz and sport, Chris Welch witnessed The Who as they "exploded in a whirlwind of flying drums and clouds of smoke" (*Melody Maker*, December 31). "Keith Moon looked like a tiny demon in a red T-shirt, battering his drums into submission, while Pete in a sloppy jersey grinned evilly as they roared through numbers like 'Barbara Ann', 'See My Way', 'Substitute' and 'I'm A Boy'. John Entwistle sang 'Whiskey Man', his own LP composition, and Roger leapt about and sang with happy joy 'Happy Jack', and many

Friday 30 December
Baths Hall, Cheam

New roadie Bob Pridden recalls having to pay for a new guitar out of his own pocket when Pete's was stolen backstage.

Saturday December 31
The Roundhouse, Chalk Farm, North London

Billed as "Psychedelicamania" and a Giant Freak-Out All Night Rave, this was The Who's first genuine Underground promotion, though not a particularly good performance. Pink Floyd were considered to have played the best set of the evening, originating a long friendship between themselves and The Who. At the end of the show, Townshend – obviously pissed off and determined to make an impact - went crazy and scared the audience beyond any expectations, sending people running away from the stage in fear of their safety.

John Piner of Hammersmith was in the audience and wrote to *Melody Maker* (January 14, 1967): "I don't mind Pete Townshend wrecking his gear as part of The Who's act, but I don't want my head knocked off by bits of flying electronic shrapnel. Do I get compensation if I'm hurt by an amplifier on my ever loving head, or if I get electrocuted?... After a depressing Who performance, Pete went really wild. He smashed an old amp box and demolished what looked like a new one. Then waving his guitar over the audience's heads, making me and my bird flinch, he stomped off. I think The Who are too good to need all this."

Piner wasn't the only person who felt this way. In the same issue of *Melody Maker*, Bill Montgomery made a similar point: "Pop stars are renowned for their moody temperament, but Pete Townshend went too far at the excessively violent climax to The Who's act... He went into unparalleled frenzy and using the guitar as a sledge hammer sent amplifiers toppling across the stage amidst clouds of smoke, sending hangers-on scurrying for cover. The whole audience reared back from the stage in absolute terror. Excitement on stage, yes, but violence which threatens to involve fans – no thanks!"

Much has been written about what is still rather quaintly termed "The British Invasion", in which a dozen or more UK pop groups, ably led by The Beatles and The Rolling Stones, suddenly became immensely popular in America in 1964–5, simultaneously turning the hitherto insular US record industry on its head. The Who were not a part of this, but they were certainly the leaders of another kind of British Invasion that occurred three years later, one that from an artistic and commercial point of view was far more significant and long lasting. During 1967, as they made their first forays into America, The Who ceased to be a 'pop group' and became a 'rock band', one of the first and certainly one of the best. In time Americans would take rock bands to their hearts with a collective enthusiasm which turned rock into a billion dollar industry that can be traced directly to The Who.

In time the group's American fans would come to cherish The Who more than any others in the world. It might seem unusual that this most British of bands, who wore Union Jack jackets and sang about Mods, a very British youth cult, would find so much success in America, but The Who's popularity there had nothing to do with gimmicks or fashion. It was due entirely to their competence, to the simple fact that The Who became incredibly good at performing on stage, and unlike so many of their peers, seemed prepared to do it often and everywhere. American rock fans have always appreciated stagecraft and hard work, as other touring giants who followed, from Led Zeppelin and Bruce Springsteen to U2 and R.E.M., would find out.

The Who's love affair with America began in 1967. In the beginning their reputation spread by word of mouth, the best form of publicity there is, and not through radio play or record sales. They made four trips across the Atlantic in little more than eight months, the opening salvo in a campaign that would ultimately see them become one of the highest grossing concert attractions in the world. America was their salvation, and the country's importance in The Who's story, especially their live history, cannot be overemphasised.

The Who were busy elsewhere during 1967 too. They undertook European and Scandinavian junkets in the first half of the year and eventually made a UK theatre tour in late October and November. They played a few widespread gigs around England in January, culminating with a prestigious show at the Saville Theatre with the up–and–coming Jimi Hendrix Experience who had been signed to the new Track Records label formed by Lambert and Stamp. By the end of February the Who had made their first trip to Italy, returning to England to record 'Pictures Of Lily'. The record entered the UK chart at number 16 and peaked at number 4 on May 20. In America, due largely to its subject matter having offended radio stations, 'Pictures Of Lily' climbed no further than number 51.

Despite this limited chart success, the group made their concert début in America at the end of March, appearing on DJ Murray The K's shows at the RKO 58th Street Theatre in New York. They performed alongside Cream, Mitch Ryder, Wilson Pickett and The Blues Project. The Who's performances during the nine-day run left audiences stunned in disbelief by the visual onslaught and instrument destruction. Without question, The Who left an indelible impression on their first American audiences.

The band returned to England in the first week of April, only to leave again after a few days for a two–week German tour, and an eight–day Scandinavian jaunt. During 1967, The Who played in more countries than ever before – or ever again. May found the group recording tracks for their third album, provisionally entitled *Who's Lily?*. Recording and gigs were affected by an injury to John Entwistle's right hand - self-inflicted by punching the picture of "a well known pop star" on the dressing room wall backstage at the Stevenage Locarno. Less than a week later, Keith pulled stomach muscles while throwing his drums around at the Pembroke College May Ball in Oxford. This further delayed recording and dashed any hopes of completing the album before the group left for a mini–tour of the US in mid-June. They also missed out on a major concert in Paris on June 1 and had to use other drummers to fill in on a handful of UK gigs in the early part of the month.

The Who's appearance at the tiny Fifth Dimension Club in Ann Arbor, Michigan, on June 14 opened a whirlwind trip that took them to the Monterey Pop Festival, the all important showcase for 'new music' emerging in the Summer of Love. Psychedelia was in full bloom and, although peace and love were the bywords of the day, The Who tore through a six–song set with their customary energy and impetuosity. They shocked the largely unsuspecting assembly with a savage display of guitar smashing and general mayhem, making sure no one would forget them when the Jimi Hendrix Experience took the stage later that evening. The running order had been decided by the toss of a coin backstage, and The Who had lost the toss. Both acts proved to be two of the most memorable of the whole three–day event.

Back in England Mick Jagger and Keith Richard had been arrested on drugs charges and it seemed likely that they would serve terms of imprisonment. The actual offences were very minor and it was widely believed that the jail terms merely reflected the Establishment's disapproval of their music and lifestyle. The Who rallied to their support, releasing versions of 'Under My Thumb' and 'The Last Time', and indicated that they would continue to record Stones songs until the issue was resolved. Pete overdubbed the bass track since John was on his honeymoon and the record was in the shops by Friday June 30. In the event, Jagger and Richard won their appeal and were released from prison before The Who could record any other material from the Stones catalogue.

The Who's first major American tour began on July 13 in Calgary, Canada. Unlikely as it may now seem, especially after their triumph at Monterey, they were the opening act for Herman's Hermits, a Manchester pop group fronted by a gap-toothed teenybop hero who had enjoyed 11 US Top ten hits in three years. This kind of package tour was commonplace in 1967, and the two groups, supported by a New York band called The Blues Magoos, spent eight weeks travelling around America together. Some shows were in the large arenas of major cities while other gigs were booked into theatre–size auditoriums. The Who played for about 30 to 40 minutes on most dates, concluding their set with smashed guitars and smoke bombs leaving audiences either stunned or ecstatic. The group never returned to many of the towns visited on this tour but despite the circumstances they were beginning to make a name for themselves as a live act across America.

Just after the end of the tour, The Who appeared on *The Smothers Brothers Comedy Hour* promoting their latest single, 'I Can See For Miles' for a nationwide audience. While on the road they had spent time in studios in New York, Nashville and Los Angeles recording tracks for *The Who Sell Out*. Returning to England on September 16, they settled into completing the album, recording at IBC Studios, De Lane Lea and Kingsway (where most of the jingles were done).

On October 28, The Who began a 12–date UK tour, ending on November 10 in Slough. Just four days later the group embarked on their fourth and final American tour of the year, playing a varied and widespread series of gigs from coast to coast. They headlined most shows on this tour, solidifying their reputation in the US as one of the most exciting bands around. Two notable concerts on this trek were at the Cow Palace in San Francisco and the Hollywood Bowl in Los Angeles, where they were added to a multi-act bill starring The Association, The New Animals and The Everly Brothers. A few gigs took the group into high–school gymnasiums where they usually attracted two to three thousand people a night.

Back in England by early December, The Who had been booked to play Christmas On Earth Continued at the Kensington Olympia Grand Hall but missed out on the gig because Pete injured one of his fingers the previous week and couldn't play. The group ended the year with a date at the Hastings Pier Pavilion on the 30th. By the end of the year Swinging London had now moved into a more serious phase with the emergence of the Underground/psychedelic movement. Jimi Hendrix and Pink Floyd were at the forefront of a counter-culture trend (led by the publications *Oz* and *IT*) which advocated revolution via drugs, sex, youth and rock'n'roll – a credo also recently adopted by The Beatles and The Rolling Stones. The Roundhouse and UFO Club in London became the bases for many a "freak out" or "happening". Groups had to adapt or die in a climate that increasingly derided blatantly commercial music. For The Who, however, it seemed like the rest of the pop world had finally caught up with them.

Pete Townshend, in particular, was heralded as a leader and visionary by the Underground movement, and he made various appearances at the UFO, Roundhouse and 14 Hour Technicolor Dream (in the process discovering The Crazy World of Arthur Brown – perhaps Britain's definitive psychedelic weirdo, whom Track would later sign). He also took LSD, and The Who's music developed into psychedelia (partly with 'I Can See For Miles' but more convincingly with songs like 'Relax' and 'Armenia City In The Sky' written by John 'Speedy' Keene).

Friday January 6
Marine Ballroom, Central Pier, Morecambe

Pete did not appear with The Who at this gig as he was involved in a car accident on the M6 motorway. In need of a substitute guitarist, Roger approached Mike Dickinson of The Doodlebugs, one of two supporting groups on the night. Dickinson agreed to sit in and quickly ran through a selection of songs with John. It was agreed to stick with rock standards.

'Boris The Spider' was performed twice during the set and even possibly 'The Ox' from The Who's first album! One of the most unusual performances in all Who history!

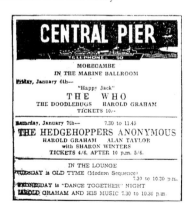

Friday January 13
Festival Hall, Kirkby-in-Ashfield

Curiously advertised as "definite appearance prior to WORLD tour and only British date this month." In fact, the band had already played the previous Friday in Morecambe and were set to play two theatre gigs by the end of the month.

Wednesday January 18
Orchid Ballroom, Purley, 7:30 to 11 pm

Saturday January 21
Leeds University

A Leeds college magazine article clearly states that The Who did not play this university dance because Pete showed up an hour late after his car had run out of fuel on the A1. However, Peter Vernon-Kell, from one of the support groups, The Hamilton Movement, states that he stood in for Pete, during The Who's first set, and that Pete borrowed (and damaged) his guitar to finish the gig.

Wednesday January 25
Kingsway Theatre, Hadleigh, Essex, two performances, 6:15 and 8:45 pm

Other acts on the bill were The Roulettes, Sounds Around, She Trinity and The Sovereigns. The Who's set list was: 'I Can't Explain', 'So Sad', 'Barbara Ann', 'Run Run Run', 'Don't Look Away', 'Substitute', 'I'm A Boy', 'Happy Jack' and 'My Generation'.

Thursday January 26
Locarno Ballroom, Bristol

Saturday January 28
Toft's Club, Folkestone

THE WHO FAIL TO APPEAR AT HOP

"WHO the hell do they think they are?"

This was a typical reaction of Union members when The Who failed to appear at the Hop last Saturday.

Ents. Secretary Godfrey Claff explained that they were due to appear at 9.30, and that their equipment had arrived at 7.00. "They decided at 10.20 that they would have to cancel their performance; Pete Townshend appeared soon afterwards and still expected to play."

CONCERNED

Jerry Howarth, who talked to Pete Townshend, said, "He was very concerned about it all. His car ran out of petrol on the A1 and he even offered his guitar as surety as he had no money to pay.

"He went to a police station and managed to raise money by ringing up home, but it was too late by the time he got here.

'EXPENSES PAID'

"He offered to appear again when the Union wanted and he said he would pay the group's expenses."

"I am afraid that this might spoil my Leeds image, and I didn't want this," said Townshend.

SAVILLE
TEM 4011
BRIAN EPSTEIN PRESENTS
THIS SUNDAY, 29th JAN.
6.00 & 8.30 p.m.
THE WHO
JIMI HENDRIX EXPERIENCE
THE KOOBAS
Compere : MIKE QUINN
Tickets 20/- 15/-, 10/-, 6/-

Sunday January 29
Saville Theatre, Central London, two shows, 6 and 8:30 pm

As The Who had recently begun to use Brian Epstein's NEMS Enterprises as a booking agency, they gained this date at the newly relaunched Saville Theatre for a "Sunday Soundarama" presentation. The Jimi Hendrix Experience were added to the bill at the last minute, giving The Who some hot competition. The show was opened by The Koobas, then Hendrix played, and finally The Who.

Chris Welch wrote in *Melody Maker* (February 4) that The Who were as "wild and unpredictable as ever. They played their best for months". During the show John Entwistle kicked to pieces a miniature mechanical doll (a theatrical trick later used by both Frank Zappa and Alice Cooper). Keith Moon sang 'Barbara Ann', John sang 'Boris The Spider' and the set was concluded with 'A Quick One, While He's Away'. The band used no smoke bombs or auto-destruction and still matched Jimi Hendrix. It would seem that this show was the first ever live performance of the 'A Quick One' mini-opera. Welch played up the rivalry between The Who and Jimi Hendrix: "It was a close battle... and fans will be arguing about the winners. Either way, two of Britain's most exciting groups thrilled the crowds with hard-hitting sights and sounds."

Tuesday January 31
Palais Des Danse, Ilford

Thursday February 2
Locarno Ballroom, Coventry

Saturday February 4
The Birdcage, Portsmouth
   Supported by the Jimmie Brown Sound and Legs.

> **THREE LITRE WHOVER! WHO?**
> Britain's wildest, woolliest, hippiest band! Welcome back, Jack and the boys! The Who! Birdcage! Saturday!
>
> **PEOPLE TRY TO PUT US DOWN!** But, we're gonna raise a wild whopee at the Birdcage, Saturday! The Who! Jimmy Brown sound! Ex-Brady!

Sunday February 5
Unknown venue, Southampton (cancelled)

Friday February 10
Gaiety Ballroom, Grimsby

Saturday February 11
Royal Links Pavilion, Cromer, 8 to 11:45 pm
   Supported by The Money Spiders and Alex Wilson's Sect

Sunday February 12
Starlite Ballroom, Greenford, West London
   The Who appear to have taken a week off here although The Who Fan Club Newsletter noted provisional bookings for Hull (February 17), Carlisle (18), Newcastle (19), and Cardiff (20). These were not played. The same bulletin also noted four Scottish concerts (February 24-27) which were later cancelled to make way for the Italian trip.

Tuesday February 21
Town Hall, High Wycombe (cancelled)

Thursday February 23
Palazzetto dello Sport, Turin, Italy
   The Who began their first Italian tour with two shows in this northern city.

Friday February 24
Palazzetto dello Sport, Bologna, Italy, two performances, 4 and 9:15 pm

1967

Saturday February 25
Palalido, Milan, Italy; one performance at 4:30 pm.

Saturday February 25
Piper Club, Milan, Italy.
   An evening show at 9:15 pm.

Sunday February 26
Pallazo dello Sport, Rome, Italy
   One concert at 4:30 pm with no fewer than eight other acts on the bill!

Sunday February 26
Piper Club, Rome, Italy
   An evening show at approx 10:30 pm. The Who returned to England the next day.

Thursday March 2
The Marquee, Soho, Central London
   The Marquee was used as the location for filming of Radio Bremen TV's *Beat Club aus London*, broadcast on Saturday, March 11. Songs performed live included 'Happy Jack', 'So Sad About Us' and 'My Generation'. Just as 'My Generation' was driving to its climax, the power failed, silencing both Pete and John's amplifiers. Pete looked annoyed but gave up the effort and didn't smash his guitar.

   The other groups that appeared on the show were The Jimi Hendrix Experience, Cliff Bennett & The Rebel Rousers, Geno Washington & The Ram Jam Band, and The Smoke. The Who were introduced by English DJ Dave Lee Travis.

Saturday March 4
California Ballroom, Dunstable

Friday March 10
Top Rank, Swansea, Wales
Supported by The Herd, The Rubber Band, The Neat Change and Ronnie Keane.

Saturday March 11
King's Hall, Stoke-on-Trent (cancelled)

Monday March 13
Granby Halls, Leicester
Supported by The Alan Price Set, Zoot Money and Dick Morrissey.

Friday March 17
Exeter University

Saturday March 18
Forum, Devonport

Monday March 20
The Pavilion, Bath (cancelled)
Two days later, on Wednesday March 22, The Who flew to New York for the first time.

Saturday March 25
RKO 58th Street Theater, New York
The Who made their American début, opening a nine-day season at the 1,500-seat venue. The series of concerts, billed as 'music in the fifth dimension', was produced by legendary DJ Murray The K.

Rehearsals began on Thursday March 23 in preparation for the opening show. There were five shows a day, starting at 10:15 in the morning and running continuously until late in the evening. The Who were paid $5,000 for their nine-day stint. Folk singer Phil Ochs was added to the opening night's performances.

The Who's set for all these shows seems to have been two or three songs: 'Happy Jack' and/or 'Substitute' and finally 'My Generation'.

The bill also included Wilson Pickett, Cream, The Blues Project, Jim & Jean, The Chicago Loop, Mandala, Jackie & The 'K' Girls (a fashion show staged by Murray The K's wife) and the comedy troupe, The Hardly Worthit Players. Special guests were added on various other days of the week.

In his book *Backstage Passes*, Al Kooper, keyboard player with The Blues Project, wrote: "They (The Who) were chosen to close the show and wisely so. The first day everyone in the cast stood in the wings to see what all the talk was about. They launched into 'My Generation' and you could feel it coming. Keith Moon flailed away on those clear plastic drums, and it seemed like he had about twenty of them. It was the first time any of us colonists had seen the typical English drum kit. He had huge double bass drums, one of which said THE, and the other of course, WHO. Moon just beat the shit out of them for twenty minutes non-stop. Pete Townshend leaped in the air, spinning his arms wildly and just being the most uninhibited guitar player ever seen in these parts. Roger Daltrey broke a total of 18 microphones over the full run of the show. And John Entwistle would just lean up against his amp taking it all in. They reached the modulation part of the instrumental and Townshend spun his guitar into the air, caught it, and smashed it into a Placebo amp. No cracks in his Stratocaster so he aimed for the mike stand. Whackkkk! Crack number one. Then the floor. Whommmmmpppp! The guitar is in three or four pieces and he's still got a signal coming out of it. All of a sudden Moon kicks his entire drum kit over and the curtain rings down in a cloud of artificial smoke."

Among those in the audience for several of the shows was premier American Who fan, 'Binky'

72

Phillips: "I was totally flabbergasted," he would later write in *Record World* magazine. "I've never seen anything so loud and brutal. They were the absolute epitome of flash. Townshend dressed in white, with pants up to his chest, Daltrey's hair was all puffed up – they were gorgeous. Townshend would throw his Stratocaster twenty feet up into the air and catch it. When he was tired he would let it slam on the floor. Such a gas! They had a film behind them for the first day which was incredible. They were sitting around in a hotel smoking joints, and there's a knock on the door. It opens and in walks the cops. The Who are armed with custard pies and they slam them in the cops' faces."

Sunday March 26
RKO 58th Street Theater, New York

Smokey Robinson & The Miracles were billed to appear on the Saturday and Sunday shows but cancelled with no explanation.

Monday March 27
RKO 58th Street Theater, New York

Simon & Garfunkel were due to appear for the evening performances on this date only. In addition, The Mitch Ryder Show was brought in for the entire week.

Tuesday March 28
RKO 58th Street Theater, New York

The Blues Magoos played the evening shows on this date. Later in the year they would join The Who and Herman's Hermits for a summer–long national tour.

The short set on this day was witnessed backstage by Richard Goldstein, who mentioned the final song being 'My Generation' and the auto-destruction: "The Who has built a reputation, not on their compositions or arrangements, but on their ability to attack a song... Close your eyes to The Who and open your ears... onstage, The Who are stylistic labourers." (*Village Voice*, April 6)

Wednesday March 29
RKO 58th Street Theater, New York

Mitch Ryder and The Detroit Wheels were again on the bill.

Thursday March 30
RKO 58th Street Theater, New York

Contrary to reports elsewhere, The Who did not appear on Murray The K's *Coliseum* television show on this date or any other date.

Friday March 31
RKO 58th Street Theater, New York

Saturday April 1
RKO 58th Street Theater, New York

Sunday April 2
RKO 58th Street Theater, New York

The Young Rascals played the afternoon and evening shows on this closing date of the nine–day stand. It was later reported that during their New York engagement, The Who lost 22 microphones, five guitars, four speaker cabinets and a 16–piece drum kit.

Having made a lasting impression on their first American audiences, The Who flew back to London on Monday April 3.

Saturday April 8
Messehalle, Nuremberg, Germany, 11pm

Less than a week after their return from America, The Who flew to Germany for the opening date of a 12–day tour there. John's Children, recently signed to Track Records, were the support act for the first four dates. Marc Bolan, later to form T. Rex, was the guitarist with the band.

Sunday April 9
Thalia-Theater, Wuppertal, Germany

Monday April 10
Jaguar Club, Herford, Germany, 10:30pm

The Who were paid £500, plus DM175 to cover travelling expenses.

Tuesday April 11
Rheinhalle, Düsseldorf, Germany, one show at 8 pm

Wednesday April 12
Friedrich-Ebert Halle, Ludwigshaven, Germany, one show at 8 pm

John's Children's final gig as support act when audience reaction turned violent with fans beginning to destroy the wooden chairs in the arena. Police stepped in to quell the riot and The Who's performance was nearly cancelled.

Thursday April 13
Circus Krone-Bau, Munich, Germany, two shows - 5:15 and 8:30 pm

Some or all of this show was filmed in colour, and the final moments can be seen during the closing credits of the film *The Kids Are Alright*, where an inactive John Entwistle is actually sitting on a seat in front of his speakers!

Friday April 14
Münsterland Halle, Münster, Germany

Saturday April 15
Siegerlandhalle, Siegen, Germany, early show

Saturday April 15
Rhein-Main Halle, Wiesbaden, Germany, late show

Sunday April 16
Oberschwabenhalle, Ravensburg, Germany, early show

Sunday April 16
Donauhalle, Ulm, Germany

The Who performed for 1,400 fans at this, the second of two gigs in two different cities on the same day.

Wednesday April 19
Stadhalle, Bremen, Germany

Six thousand marks were stolen from the group's dressing room. This was the last date on the German tour and the group flew back to England the following day.

Friday April 21
The Dome, Brighton

The Who played at the Arts Festival with Cream and The Merseys among the supporting acts. One show at 8 pm.

Monday April 24
The Pavilion, Bath

Tuesday April 25
Town Hall, High Wycombe

Saturday April 29
14 Hour Technicolour Dream, Alexandra Palace, London (cancelled)

The Who were originally billed to play at Britain's prime psychedelic 'happening', but cancelled probably because of their commitment to tour Scandinavia from the following day. Later adverts for the event billed Pete Townshend as a celebrity guest, but it is unclear whether any other members of the band attended.

Sunday April 30
Ice Hall, Helsinki, Finland, one show at 8pm

The group flew to Helsinki for the first gig of an eight–date Scandinavian tour. Footage of their arrival can be seen in the *Thirty Years of Maximum R&B* video, released in 1994. Also included in the *Thirty Years…* video is footage of 'Substitute' and 'My Generation' from the concert. This was the Who's one and only appearance in Finland.

Tuesday May 2
Njardhallen, Oslo, Norway, one concert at 8 pm

Mit Schall und Rauch ging das Finale der „Who" zu Ende. Auf der Bühne seh es aus wie

Wednesday May 3
Lorensbergsparken Cirkus, Gothenburg, Sweden, two performances, 7 and 9:15 pm

The set: 'Substitute', 'Summertime Blues', 'Run Run Run', 'I'm A Boy', 'Boris The Spider', 'Bucket T', 'Happy Jack' and 'My Generation'.

"Why the volume?" asked Gosta Hansson. "My ears are still ringing as I write this. The Who play enjoyable music – so why not let people enjoy it? Now it's painfully loud."

*Guitar destroyed: Fender Stratocaster - sunburst finish.

Thursday May 4
Masshallen, Norrkoping, Sweden

The first of two shows on this date was a concert at 4 in the afternoon. The set: 'Substitute', 'Pictures Of Lily', 'Run Run Run', 'Boris The Spider', 'Happy Jack', 'I'm A Boy', 'My Generation'.

The audience response at this show was uncharacteristically cool until Pete attacked an amplifier at the end of 'My Generation'. Lotta reported *(Norrkopings Tidningar)* that "the sweaty drummer threw his drums all over the stage. When the havoc was complete, the four Englishmen left both a delighted and confused audience behind. The Who will probably never forget the 'ice-cold' audience in Norrkoping."

Thursday May 4
Rigoletto, Jonkoping, Sweden

The evening show at 8 pm seen by about 1,700 fans.

The verdict by K. Hultin *(Jonkopingsposten)*: "When The Who started, (the audience) gathered on the dance-floor. The room was filled to the limit with fantastic electronic sound-waves. But, unfortunately the small stage didn't allow a real

'Who-show' with smashed instruments. Nevertheless, everyone was more than satisfied anyway."

Friday May 5
Sporthallen, Eskilstuna, Sweden, one performance at 7 pm

This was one of the less satisfactory shows of the tour due to the unsuitability of the venue. When Pete Townshend first saw that The Who would have to play on a tiny extended balcony metres above the audience, he stormed out and threatened to cancel the show. Heated negotiations then ensued: the security guards were fearful of a riot and the promoters threatened to withdraw the band's cash. The Who reluctantly agreed to play and offered a less-than-enthusiastic five songs, culminating in a token demolition of some speaker cabinets. The audience left somewhat disappointed.

Saturday May 6
Kungliga Tennishallen, Stockholm, Sweden, one show at 6 pm

The inappropriate choice of venue again caused problems at this show, with poor acoustics dampening the performance. Ludwig Rasmussen reported that "The Who started out with their speakers on full power trying their best to surprise the audience, which was successful at first. But after a while the concert turned lame... Keith's drumming was brilliant. For long periods, he was the central point, sometimes unintentionally, as the speaker system made the others hard to hear. The indispensable final number 'My Generation' became the most destructive The Who has presented in Stockholm. Roger swung his microphone into the drums. Pete hit his guitar into another microphone so it broke. Keith pushed out his entire set of drums. Speakers and amps fell, Townshend's guitar was smashed to pieces. Luckily, the finale was chaotic, otherwise the audience probably would have been disappointed..."

Sunday May 7

Sommarlust, Kristianstad, Sweden

The Who wound up the last day of the tour with two shows, the first in the afternoon in Kristianstad as part of an eight–hour event, the second in the evening at Malmo.

"The Who presented a violent sound," reported *Kristianstadbladet*. "Twelve speakers on full power were more than any other band had ever dared. In the last song, a microphone stand served as a bow to the guitar, that was later rudely thrown to the floor. Speakers were kicked down, as were the drums."

Sunday May 7
MFF-Stadion, Malmo, Sweden

An evening show at 7 pm concluded The Who's fourth Scandinavian tour. They flew back to England on Monday May 8.

With audience reaction at fever pitch from the first riff of the opening 'Substitute', this show was a battle ground between the fans attempting to storm the stage and 30 or so frantic policemen. Many fans were carried from the stadium unconscious as the crowd surged back and forth beneath the stage. The Who played on regardless through to 'My Generation', and as the equipment was smashed a full-scale riot ensued with fighting between the police and the audience. The Who's final tour of Sweden ended here: it had

been a trip fraught with problems, varied audiences, and the band sensed their time of triumph in Scandinavia had now passed. They didn't return for five years.

Wednesday May 10
Top Rank Ballroom, Swansea, Wales (cancelled)

Saturday May 13
Shoreline Hotel, Bognor Regis (cancelled)

This show was cancelled because the venue's stage was too small for all of the band's equipment.

Wednesday May 17

Pete Townshend discovers singer

WHO's Pete Townshend is raving over a new British singer, Arthur Brown, he discovered at the recent Alexandra Palace "Technicolor Dream."

"He has a fantastic voice and I hope to use him in the opera I am writing," Pete told Disc.

Pete is recording Arthur for Track Records, but it is not yet decided whether his recording debut will be on a single or an album.

"I'm so enthusiastic about Arthur that possibly an album will be best suited to his talent," said Pete.

Locarno Ballroom, Stevenage

It was reported that John had broken a finger on his right hand when he punched a picture of "a well known pop singer" on the dressing room wall backstage. This mishap delayed the recording of *The Who Sell Out* which Kit Lambert had hoped to complete before the group left for America in mid-June.

Thursday, May 18
Locarno, Bristol

There seems to be some confusion as to whether this gig actually took place. Logically, bearing in mind John's injury fresh from the night before, it would have been presumably cancelled. However, no apology appeared in the local paper.

An eyewitness account, from Chris Powel, posted on the "Hypertext Who" concert website, read as follows: "The Bristol Locarno concert was definitely 18 May 1967... I do remember The Who coming on very late that evening, and the audience was getting very restless with the delay. From where I was sitting, you could just see backstage, and it was obvious that Roger Daltrey was there from about (7 pm), but the group didn't come on until (10 pm). All of the group were totally stoned, and it was during the height of them smashing all of their equipment - not much remained after the hour that they played. Unfortunately with the passage of time, I cannot remember the play list, but I do know they started with 'My Generation.'"

Saturday May 20
Third Annual Wolu Festival, Brussels, Belgium
The Who didn't play in Belgium again until August 16, 1972.

Saturday May 27
Pembroke College May Ball, Grand Marquee, Oxford
The Who were obviously bemused by the whole situation where their audience was dressed in formal dinner suits and ball gowns. John Entwistle later derided the undergraduates for trying to dance to The Who (an inappropriate and

near-impossible activity!). Other distressed-looking students were seen with their hands on their ears watching Townshend's speakers in horror as feedback spewed forth! Pete's guitar was stolen from the Grand Marquee after they had finished their set. It is not known if it was ever recovered.

The following day at a recording session, Keith strained his stomach muscles while throwing his drums around. Keith's injury caused him to miss some live dates and, along with John's broken finger, delayed recording sessions for *The Who Sell Out*.

Monday May 29
Locarno Ballroom, Glasgow, Scotland
The Who employed the temporary services of drummer Julian Covey while Keith was recuperating from his hernia operation. Covey, a friend of Roger's, could only sit in for one gig as he had commitments with his own group, The Machine.

Saturday June 3
Floral Hall, Southport
Supported by The Sound Five. This was The Who's first visit to Southport since May 21, 1966 when, by a strange coincidence, Keith Moon had also been unable to play! The Who employed the services of Chris Townson, of John's Children.

Sunday June 4
Guildhall, Southampton (cancelled)

Monday June 5
Top Rank Suite, Swansea, Wales (cancelled)

Thursday June 8
Ulster Hall, Belfast, Ireland, two shows, 7:45 & 10:30 pm.
With Chris Townson on drums.

Friday June 9
Magilligan Golden Slipper Ballroom, Derry, Ireland
Chris Townson drummed at The Who's last ever appearance in Ireland.

Saturday June 10
Palace Ballroom, Douglas, Isle Of Man
With Sounds Incorporated. Chris Townson's last gig deputising for Keith.

Monday June 12
Christ Church College Ball, Cambridge

The group played this Summer Ball event along with The Moody Blues, Georgie Fame, The Herd, and French singer Françoise Hardy.

The Who left for America on June 13 to begin their mini–tour, culminating at the Monterey International Pop Festival.

A concert at the University Of Sussex, Brighton, on Friday June 16 was unfulfilled. Cream played instead.

Wednesday June 14
The Fifth Dimension Club, Ann Arbor, Michigan

This was The Who's first US appearance outside New York. They played two shows in this small club.

Thursday June 15
The Cellar, Arlington Heights, Illinois, 7 to 11 pm

Supported by H.P. Lovecraft. This gig was advertised as a 'Special Benefit Show' in conjunction with the Mount Prospect Junior Women's Club! It's unlikely that The Who waived their fee for this date since these few club dates were supposedly arranged to help pay their expenses for

the trip to the Monterey Pop Festival.

Friday June 16

Fillmore Auditorium, San Francisco, California

The Who's first dates for America's pre–eminent rock promoter, Bill Graham, with whom they continued their working relationship right up through 1989's *The Kids Are Alright* tour. The group played two nights at this famed venue on their début in San Francisco. Supported by The Carlos Santana Blues Band as a last–minute replacement for Loading Zone.

Pete was actually more excited at the prospect of playing at the Fillmore than at the Monterey International Pop Festival. He later said: "We played two 45-minute spots each night. It was a gas. It was like going back to the Marquee Club. We were immediately thrown into panic by not having enough numbers but we got by. Ended up rehearsing in our hotel! And the amplification at the Fillmore is too much. It's a great pity that England doesn't take pop as seriously as those American guys do. The bloke who runs the Fillmore really worried about what we thought of his place and whether the amps were OK... The vibrations you pick up are incredible. [The audiences] want to listen. They want to hear what you're playing. At the Fillmore I was going to make an announcement but I couldn't think of anything to say and I just stumbled about. Suddenly they all applauded. They understood what was happening and I didn't really need to say anything anyway because it's there in the music." (*Melody Maker*, July 1)

Saturday June 17
Fillmore Auditorium, San Francisco, California

Due to a last–minute schedule change, The Carlos Santana's Blues Band replaced Loading Zone as the support act for this date as they had the night before.

Sunday June 18
Monterey County Fairgrounds, Monterey, California

The Monterey Pop Festival was the cornerstone rock gathering that exemplified the multi-date, multi-act festivals for years to come. It also captured the essence of the "Summer of Love", the idyllic vision of the youth movement in America and Europe. The afternoon concert was devoted entirely to the music of Ravi Shankar, Indian sitarist and friend of Beatle George Harrison. Amid this haven of hippie celebration, The Who arrived on stage to blast their way through a brief set which was concluded with an especially enthusiastic display of equipment destruction.

A heated discussion had occurred between Townshend and Jimi Hendrix as to who would follow whom; Hendrix lost and The Who opted to play first. Without their regular Marshall gear, The Who were sonically hampered from the outset by weak Vox amplifiers but they injected a fierceness into their playing that made up for any technical setbacks. Eric Burdon introduced them as follows: "This is a group that will destroy you completely in more ways than one, this is The Who, this one."

Starting with 'Substitute', they sounded ragged and disjointed but managed to infuse enough enthusiasm into their playing to make an impact. Pete was clearly dissatisfied with the guitar sound, although the band looked exactly right for the moment. Pete was wearing a gold, multi-shade satin jacket, Roger a fringed shawl, and Keith wore a red shirt with a tooth necklace. After 'Substitute', Roger said: "Thank you. It's great to be here at Monterey from us. Here's an old rock-'n'roll number now, one of Eddie Cochran's old ones, one called 'Summertime Blues'." A fuzz box on the guitar was used extensively by Pete on the block chords of this song, which went over much more powerfully than the opener. Roger then introduced Keith: "I don't know if you can hear this... This is Keith Moon, if you can see him behind there..." Keith then took the mike and said: "This one is our last record in England. We've come over to, sort of, promote it... It's called 'Pictures Of Lily'." Onstage, this song lacked the finer qualities of the single version, but it held together fairly well.

The American crowd – almost all of them seeing The Who for the first time – were undoubtedly impressed, and the next song – 'A Quick One, While He's Away' – seemed elaborate and demanding. Roger introduced it rather grandly: "Thank you very much. This is a group of numbers off our LP, written by Pete. It was part of an opera he wrote. It's a bit shorter than it was supposed to be... It's one called 'A Quick One'." After this song Pete and John tuned their guitars and Pete, speaking for the first time and sounding none-too-happy said "You ever had that feeling it's all going to stop?" Daltrey then introduced the next song, a routine version of 'Happy Jack'.

"This is where it all ends," said Pete, knowing the last song would really hit home. "This one's called 'My Generation'," said Daltrey. It was a fast, hard performance, far and away the best song of the set. Entwistle's bass solo was as dazzling as ever, and at the end of the song, the smoke bombs drifted on to the stage and Pete began to dismember his guitar. Unfortunately, after much abuse, he didn't manage to coax any screeching feedback from the speakers, which was usually an integral part of the auto destructive routine. The audience was dumbfounded and shocked. Pete battered his guitar until it splintered, then set about the amplifiers with the

Who's that girl . . . ?

WHO's John Entwistle, pictured with his childhood sweetheart, 20-year-old secretary Alison Wise, after their marriage last Friday at Acton Congregational Church. They met six years ago at the same school in Acton.

● Who's Pete Townshend has bought an antique shop in Harefield High Street, Middlesex, which is being run by his parents. "I've bought it for them—it's not security or anything like that," he told Disc.

Who are currently continuing work on their next album, "Who's Lily?" in the hope of having it completed before the opening of the American tour at Portland, Oregon on July 14.

broken guitar neck. The sound engineers and stagehands became worried and attempted to retrieve the microphones before the stage disintegrated. During the destruction, John and Keith kept playing the riff over and over until finally Pete and Roger had finished and walked off the stage. Keith then kicked over his drum kit and followed them. Along with the Jimi Hendrix Experience, it was the most unusual and dynamic set of the festival, and was critically acclaimed by most of the music critics present, although the guitar smashing did not find favour with everyone.

D.A. Pennebaker's film *Monterey Pop* appeared in 1968, and included 'My Generation', while the Who's set finally appeared on the *Monterey Pop Festival* box set in 1992. Excerpts can also be seen in both *The Kids Are Alright* and *Thirty Years Of Maximum R&B* Live.

Also on the bill for the evening's performances were The Blues Project, Big Brother and The Holding Company (in a repeat of their previous set), Buffalo Springfield, Tommy Smothers, The Grateful Dead, The Jimi Hendrix Experience and The Mamas and The Papas.

*Guitar destroyed: Fender Stratocaster - sunburst, maple neck.

Friday July 7
Malibu Beach and Shore Club, Lido Beach, New York
The Who played two dates in the New York City area just prior to joining the extensive, summer-long Herman's Hermits tour. This gig took place on Long Island, just east of the city.

Saturday July 8
The Village Theater, New York, one performance at 9 pm
The Who sold out this 2,400-seat theatre for a gross of $11,200. Supported by The Blues Project and Richie Havens, Chrysalis, plus "an amazing 4-dimensional audio visual presentation" called After The 3rd World Raspberry.

Thursday July 13
The Calgary Stampede Corral, Calgary, Alberta, Canada, two shows, 2:30 & 8:30 pm.
The opening date of The Who's first full-scale American tour, 58 days on the road opening for Herman's Hermits, with fellow support act, The

Blues Magoos.
Calgary was listed on Keith's itinerary (with the amount he'd received written next to it) but there was no review in the local press.

Friday July 14
Memorial Coliseum, Portland, Oregon

Saturday July 15
Center Coliseum, Seattle, Washington, one performance at 8 pm

The Who's basic set list for the tour was: 'Substitute', 'Pictures of Lily', 'Summertime Blues', 'Barbara Ann', 'Boris The Spider', 'A Quick One', 'Happy Jack', ' I'm A Boy' and 'My Generation'.

Sunday July 16
Memorial Auditorium, Sacramento, California
"The guitarist threw his instrument to the floor, then picked it up and threw it down some more. Next, the drummer broke about a dozen sets of sticks, knocked over his cymbals, made faces, then kicked over his drums. Not to be outdone,

the lead singer kicked down an amplifier, threw his microphone to the floor while smoke bombs went off like gangbusters... If you caught the show, man – what a deal!" wrote Karen Vitlip in the *Sacramento Union*.

Monday July 17
The Agrodome, Vancouver, British Columbia, Canada

This was the band's first concert in Canada and one of only five appearances they ever made in this city. A near sell-out crowd of 4,200 fans attended, 600 seats short of a full house.

Wednesday July 19
The Lagoon Terrace Ballroom, Salt Lake City, Utah

Two shows, a concert at 7 pm and a 'show and dance' at 9 pm.

A local band was added to the bill for the second performance.

Friday July 21
Oklahoma State Fair Arena, Oklahoma City, Oklahoma

Saturday July 22
Sam Houston Coliseum, Houston, Texas, one show at 8 pm

COLISEUM SAT., JULY 22

The Houston Post Presents: 8:00 PM

ALL IN PERSON DIRECT FROM ENGLAND

HERMAN'S HERMITS

THE WHO   LARRY KANE, MC

SPECIAL GUEST STARS THE BLUES MAGOOS

TICKETS: $2.50-$3.25-$4.00

BOND'S 811 MAIN—CA 8-9904
BOND'S NORTHLINE, SHARPS-
TOWN, MEMORIAL, GULFGATE

Sunday July 23
Memorial Auditorium, Dallas, Texas, one concert at 8 pm

Set: 'Substitute', 'Summertime Blues', 'Pictures Of Lily', 'So Sad About Us', 'Love Hurts', 'Boris The Spider', 'Happy Jack', 'I'm A Boy', and 'My Generation'.

A surviving tape seems likely to be from this show, revealing a female MC introducing the band as follows: "I would like to introduce to you now the most explosive group ever to come out of England, The Who!" Roger complained about problems with the microphone, and later went on to introduce "an old Roy Orbison number called 'Love Hurts'", which The Who played as an up tempo rocker.

The tour took a two–day break after this gig.

Wednesday July 26
Redemptorist High School Football Stadium, Baton Rouge, Louisiana

One performance at 7 pm with all seats priced at five dollars!

Friday July 28
Garrett Coliseum, Montgomery, Alabama

Saturday July 29
Auditorium, Birmingham, Alabama

Six more acts were added to the bill for this concert! As if this were not enough, there were three shows, the only such gig of the entire summer tour. A total of 15,000 fans turned out for performances at 2, 6 and 9 pm.

The complete line-up was: Herman's Hermits, The Who, The Blues Magoos, Sam The Sham & The Pharaohs, Lou Christie, Jim 'Harpo' Valley, Every Mother's Son, Billy Joe Royal and The Rockin' Rebellions.

Sunday July 30
Miami Beach Convention Hall, Miami, Florida

Monday July 31
Bayfront Center, St. Petersburg, Florida
One performance seen by about 5000 people.

Tuesday August 1
Mississippi State Coliseum, Jackson, Mississippi

The Who had joked since mid-1966 of playing a version of Nancy Sinatra's 'These Boots Are Made For Walkin'', with John Entwistle on vocals! And in the same spirit they played at this concert a version of Nancy Sinatra and Lee Hazelwood's recent hit 'Jackson' – a one-off and utterly unique Who performance. This unlikely occurrence was confirmed by Kit Lambert, who told *Beat Instrumental* (December 1967) the following: "... in Jackson, Mississippi, they rehearsed, the day before, a version, a rock version of the Nancy Sinatra song... ." The fans delighted in Roger singing "I'm going to Jackson... ."

The Who finished their set with the usual equipment destruction before a stunned audi-

ence. They never appeared in Jackson again.

Thursday August 3
Dane County Coliseum, Madison, Wisconsin
A single performance at 8 pm with about 6000 fans in attendance.

Friday August 4
Rosenblatt Stadium, Omaha, Nebraska
One show at 7:30 pm in this minor league baseball park.

Saturday August 5
International Amphitheatre, Chicago, Illinois
One show at 8:30 pm.

Monday August 7
Herman's Hermits appeared at the Westbury Music Fair, Long Island for two shows on this date but neither the ads nor the review make any mention of The Who appearing. The group were at Talentmasters Studio, during their free time in New York, working on tracks for *The Who Sell Out* album.

Wednesday August 9
Maple Leaf Gardens, Toronto, Ontario, Canada, one concert at 8 pm
Only 4000 people turned out for the show in this 17,000–seat venue.

Friday August 11
Civic Center, Baltimore, Maryland, one performance at 8:30 pm

Saturday August 12
Convention Hall, Asbury Park, New Jersey, two shows, 8 and 10:15 pm

Sunday August 13
Constitution Hall, Washington, DC., two performances, 3 and 8 pm

Monday August 14
Rhode Island Auditorium, Providence, Rhode Island
The entourage flew south to Tennessee after this show but had to make an emergency landing at Nashville Airport due to loss of oil in the aeroplane engines. A foamed runway helped avert disaster and the aircraft landed safely.

The band spent two days in Nashville during a break from the tour, recording at Decca's studio Bradley's Barn where, in 1956 Buddy Holly and The Crickets recorded 'Rock Around With Ollie Vee' and several other songs.

CIVIC CENTER
201 W. Baltimore Street

TOMORROW
One Performance Only : 8:30 P.M.

All in Person

Direct from England

herman's hermits
the who

SPECIAL
GUEST
STARS

the blues magoos

TICKETS NOW ON SALE!
JERMAC TICKET AGENCY
Civic Center Lobby
All Seats Reserved
Prices: $1.75—$2.50
$3.50—$4.50

Thursday August 17
Memorial Auditorium, Chattanooga, Tennessee

Neil Diamond was added to the bill for the shows here, at 6 and 9 pm, seen by a total of 6,626 fans.

Friday August 18
The Big Moose Showcase, Lorain, Ohio (cancelled)

Adverts for the show mention The Who only, a separate booking away from the Hermits tour, but the band did not appear. It was reported that Dick Clark, the American pop music impresario, did not want The Who to appear in the Cleveland area just prior to their August 31 appearance at the Public Music Hall with the Hermits.

Although the tour had two scheduled free days, Friday August 18 and Saturday August 19, The Who may have played their own gigs on these dates. It's also possible that they returned to Nashville to continue recording sessions for the *Sell Out* album at Bradley's Barn.

Sunday August 20
Civic Auditorium, Fargo, North Dakota

A 2:30 pm performance to accommodate an

> The Who, an English group with not much of a reputation around here, was very good. They highlighted their show by drop kicking over three expensive amplifiers and completely demolishing a guitar.

evening show in Minneapolis. The Fargo concert attracted 2,200 fans.

Sunday August 20
Minneapolis Auditorium, Minneapolis, Minnesota

In the Sixties, package tours were routinely scheduled to play two cities on the same day. The Hermits '67 summer tour made three such stops and these gigs were the first of those bookings. A crowd of about 4,000 attended the 7:30 pm concert.

Monday August 21
New Edmonton Gardens, Edmonton, Alberta, Canada

Over 8,000 people saw this performance, one of the best–attended gigs of the entire tour.

Tuesday August 22
Winnipeg Arena, Winnipeg, Manitoba, Canada

Some 7,000 fans turned out for the single performance at 8 pm.

Wednesday August 23
Atwood High School Stadium, Flint, Michigan

This is a legendary date in The Who's history, the occasion of Keith's 21st birthday party at the local Holiday Inn. After the show, which was poorly attended, Keith was presented with a five-tier birthday cake paid for by Decca Records and Premier Drums. By all accounts, the party was in full swing when, close to midnight, the hotel manager arrived to inform all present that the party would have to end at midnight. "I knew that wasn't going to sit well with anybody," recalls Tom Wright, an American friend of Pete's from art college who was now a roadie with the band. "I told him we'd wind it down and so on and he left. At one minute after twelve he comes running back and says 'Godammit, this sounds more like a revolution than a birthday party. We're having complaints and you can't do this and you can't do that' and he was just about to go into a big deal when Keith just picked up what was left of the five-tiered cake and just shoved it into this guy's face. Everybody in the room just went silent, including this guy. All this stuff like, just, drips. And you can't even laugh because it's so shocking."

What happened next is the subject of much Who mythology and the absolute truth is difficult to establish. What appears beyond any doubt is that the manager, cake dripping from his face, left the room, entered the reception area, picked up a phone and put out an all-points Holiday Inn bulletin which effectively banned The Who from its entire American chain for an indefinite period. Keith left the room, grabbed a fire extinguisher and sprayed cars in the parking lot with foam. The police were called and Keith, fleeing from a sheriff, tripped and knocked out a couple of teeth. Moon's teeth required the immediate attention of a dentist who had to pull out what was left without the benefit of anaesthetic since Keith had consumed so much alcohol, and he was held in police custody overnight. Next day the rest of the entourage departed for Philadelphia but Keith missed the flight and had to charter a plane.

When the dust finally settled Lambert and Stamp received a bill for $5,000 (£18,000 in 1967).

Thursday August 24
Civic Center Convention Hall, Philadelphia, Pennsylvania

About 4,000 fans, out of a capacity of 13000 thousand, saw the single show at 7:30 pm.

Friday August 25
Kiel Opera House, St. Louis, Missouri, two concerts, 5:45 and 8:40 pm

Some 1,541 people saw the first show and 1,862 attended the later performance.

Saturday August 26
Fort William Gardens, Fort William, Ontario, Canada

The *News-Chronicle* reported that there had been a bomb scare at the finale but, fortunately, the concert ended without incident. About 2,000 people attended this 2 pm performance.

Saturday August 26
Duluth Arena, Duluth, Minnesota

Not just a double booking but two gigs in two countries on the same day! The Duluth concert was at 8:00 pm.

Sunday August 27
Music Hall, Cincinnati, Ohio, two shows, 3 and 8 pm

Monday August 28
Sioux Falls Arena, Sioux Falls, South Dakota; one performance

Tuesday August 29
Municipal Auditorium, Atlanta, Georgia, two shows, 4 and 8:30 pm

Wednesday August 30
War Memorial Auditorium, Rochester, New York

Gross gate receipts were $21,000. Keith's lead vocal on 'Barbara Ann' prompted a smattering of scream-

ing from the teeny-bopper element in the audience.

The set: 'Substitute', 'Pictures of Lily', 'Summertime Blues', 'Barbara Ann', 'Boris The Spider', 'A Quick One, While He's Away', 'Happy Jack', 'I'm A Boy', 'My Generation'.

Thursday August 31
Public Music Hall, Cleveland, Ohio, two shows, 6:30 and 9:30 pm

Local act, The Choir, opened both shows.

Friday September 1
Indiana Fairgrounds Coliseum, Indianapolis, Indiana, two shows, 4 and 8:30 pm

7,551 people attended the evening show with a take of $21,511.

Saturday September 2
Ohio State Fairgrounds, Columbus, Ohio

The tour made a three–day stop in Columbus. There were two shows on this first day at 1 and 4pm. The afternoon concert, on Sunday September 3, enabled the troupe to play in Pittsburgh that evening, then return to Columbus for two shows on Monday, September 4.

Sunday September 3
Ohio State Fairgrounds, Columbus, Ohio, two shows, 3 and 5 pm

The Avco Broadcasting Company was set to telecast 60 hours of events at the State Fair and produce three half–hour specials for later broadcast. NBC TV aired *In Concert With Herman's Hermits* on Tuesday January 9, 1968 (7:30 pm EST) with footage taken at the Ohio State Fair but The Who were not included in the programme. It is unknown if they were actually filmed during the fair.

The entourage travelled 184 miles to Pittsburgh for an evening show at the Civic Arena, returning to Columbus on Monday for the final performance there.

instrumentation by playing a double-necked 6 and 12 string guitar, but he switched to a more conventional guitar before their destructive finale. Townshend and Entwistle splinter their instruments by battering them against the stage during the ending of 'My Generation' while Daltrey flung cymbals and microphones about and a cloud of dry ice vapour shrouded the area."

For both Pete *and* John to smash their guitars was most unusual. This show was extended to an hour–long performance (twice the normal length) "in response to their fervid reception".

Sunday September 3
Civic Arena, Pittsburgh, Pennsylvania, an 8 pm performance

Monday September 4
Ohio State Fairgrounds, Columbus, Ohio

Two performances, 1 and 4 pm. The tour took a three–day break after these shows in Columbus. The next day, The Who flew to Los Angeles to continue work on tracks for the *Sell Out* album and complete their next single, 'I Can See For Miles' at Gold Star Studios.

Friday September 8
Anaheim Convention Center, Anaheim, California

The set included 'Substitute', 'Pictures Of Lily', 'A Quick One', 'I Can't Explain', 'Boris The Spider', 'Run Run Run', 'Barbara Ann', 'Happy Jack' and 'My Generation'. Pete Johnson covered this gig for the *Los Angeles Times* (September 11): "Moon's animated drumming is excellent and violent. He shattered 20 or so drum sticks during their set. Townshend added flexibility to their

Saturday September 9
Honolulu International Center Arena, Honolulu, Hawaii

The final concert of the mammoth tour supporting Herman's Hermits and the only time The Who ever played in Hawaii.

The two daily papers gave quite opposing opinions of the show with the *Honolulu Star Bulletin* declaring that "The Who earns a place in rock'n'roll's who's who" while the *Honolulu Advertiser* disagreed, commenting they "were bad to begin with". The band had a few days off while on the island of Oahu, a well deserved rest after the hectic ten week tour with the Hermits.

Friday October 6
Ballerina Ballroom, Nairn, Scotland

Saturday October 7
Beach Ballroom, Aberdeen, Scotland

Sunday October 8
Kinema Ballroom, Dunfermline, Scotland

Saturday October 21
New Century Hall, Manchester

Sunday October 22
Saville Theatre, Central London, two performances, 6 and 8:30 pm

It was advertised that this show would feature the band "presenting the 45- minute act which staggered Herman's Hermits' fans in the USA". At the second show, Pete wore a dazzling Pearly King suit that had been created by his girlfriend Karen

Astley, while Keith wore a full court jester's outfit. Chris Welch reported (*Melody Maker*, October 28) that "The Who eschewed ye olde violence. No freak-outs, but plenty of 'Substitute', 'Pictures Of Lily', 'Summertime Blues', 'Shakin' All Over', 'My Generation' and 'A Quick One'. Pete played double-necked guitar, Keith galvanised his nine drum kit, Roger and John sang and played with drive and enthusiasm. It was a welcome return to Britain for The Who..."

This was the first report of Johnny Kidd's 'Shakin' All Over' being reintroduced into the set since The Detours/High Numbers days. *Record Mirror* (October 28) also covered the gig and Derek Boltwood wrote: "The magnificent Who were magnificent – they proved to me that they are worth every inch of their reputation, plus a few inches for good measure... They ran through most of their hits with the audience going absolutely wild... definitely a knockout."

Supported by American group Vanilla Fudge.

Saturday October 28
City Hall, Sheffield

It had been more than a year since the band had undertaken a UK tour but they finally arranged a theatre tour for October and November. On this opening night there were two performances at 6:20 and 8:50 pm. Support acts on the tour were Traffic, The Herd, The Tremeloes, Scottish group Marmalade and compere Ray Cameron.

Due to the logistics of playing on a large bill, The Who found that they had only been allotted sufficient time to complete two numbers at this concert. The band's tempers were pushed to the limit and Roger Daltrey and Pete Townshend had a disagreement on stage that ended in a scuffle. The concert finished with Pete kicking his speaker cabinets over onto the theatre manager who had ordered the act to be curtailed. Pete then grabbed the manager by the throat and dragged him across the stage!

later that their act had been cut down to only two numbers and having the curtain lowered on them "was just too much".

Reviewing the show for the *Coventry Evening Telegraph* (October 30), Ken Hillman wrote: "Townshend shouted for the curtain to be raised, threw his guitar on the stage and kicked angrily at the footlights. Then he picked up a footlight and used it to hammer the floats. Finally he swung at the lights with a microphone stand... Despite being cut short, The Who played most of their hits and threw in some exciting revivals of rock 'n' roll numbers like 'Summertime Blues' – though the late Eddie Cochran would hardly have recognised it. It was thrilling, violent music even without the light-smashing episode."

Sunday October 29
Coventry Theatre, Coventry, two shows, 6 and 8:30 pm.

The first performance ended in the destruction of the theatre's footlights as well as Pete's guitar when the curtain was lowered during The Who's set. Amplification problems had delayed the show by about 20 minutes with only 10 minutes before the second show was due to start. As a result, the tour manager ordered the curtain be brought down. Pete and Roger were left in front of the curtain and 'God Save The Queen' was played over the house PA system. Pete shouted for the curtain to be raised, threw his guitar on the stage and began his assault on the footlights. Pete explained

❝I find I can't go to sleep unless I've smashed the gear up❞

Monday October 30
City Hall, Newcastle, two shows, 6 and 8:30 pm

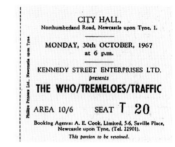

CITY HALL,
Northumberland Road, Newcastle upon Tyne, 1.

MONDAY, 30th OCTOBER, 1967
at 6 p.m.

KENNEDY STREET ENTERPRISES LTD.
presents

THE WHO/TREMELOES/TRAFFIC

AREA 10/6   SEAT T 20

Booking Agents: A. E. Cook, Limited, 5-6, Saville Place, Newcastle upon Tyne. (Tel. 22901).
This portion to be retained.

Wednesday November 1
Empire Theatre, Liverpool, two shows, 6:15 and 8:35 pm
Pete's guitar lead malfunctioned during the late house. Thinking it was the guitar at fault, he smashed it to pieces over his knee, then had to sheepishly borrow a guitar from one of The Tremeloes to finish the show.

Friday November 3
Granada Cinema, Kingston-on-Thames, two shows, 7 and 9:10 pm

Saturday November 4
Granada Cinema, Walthamstow, two shows, 6:30 and 9 pm

Sunday November 5
Theatre Royal, Nottingham, two shows, 5:30 and 8 pm

Monday November 6
Town Hall, Birmingham, two shows, 6:30 and 8:45 pm

Wednesday November 8
Granada Cinema, Kettering, two shows, 7 and 9:10 pm

Thursday November 9
Granada Cinema, Maidstone, two shows, 6:20 and 8:30 pm

Friday November 10
Adelphi Cinema, Slough, two shows, 6:40 and 8:50 pm

This was the closing night of the British tour.

Saturday November 11
Imperial Ballroom, Nelson

Supported by Michael's Angels and The Beathovens. The Who left England on Wednesday November 15 to embark on their fourth US visit of the year.

Friday November 17
Shawnee Mission South High School Gymnasium, Overland Park, Kansas City

The Who opened their fourth American tour with this date in a high school gym playing support to The Buckinghams, a Chicago pop group with a string of successful singles. The show drew an estimated 3,500 people. "Usually we just sort of show up, do the gig and split," Pete told *Rolling Stone* (January 20, 1968), "but the most fantastic thing happened in Kansas City. There were 500

kids at the airport. They all had our records and were making the point of 'We remember you when…' But at the concert that night they were stone cold."

*Guitar destroyed: Gibson Les Paul Special, Modified with three pickups.

Saturday November 18
The Cow Palace, San Francisco, California

The second night of the tour found the group as "special guest stars" in the "Festival of Music" in the 13,000–seat Cow Palace. The hall was only half–full for the 8pm show and The Who, by all accounts, were the most exciting act of the evening. They stormed through 'I Can See For Miles', 'Summertime Blues' and 'A Quick One, While He's Away', ending with the guitar–smashing finale of 'My Generation'.

"The Who are impressive," wrote Ralph J. Gleason (*San Francisco Chronicle*, November 26). "Lead singer swinging his hand mike like he's not even afraid of dropping it. Lead guitar looks like Ichabod Crane in drag. Bass guitar looks like Les Crane in drag. And the drummer. This guy is obviously past putting on. Way past. The Who do 'Miles And Miles', 'Summertime Blues', a long medley of theatrical bits ['A Quick One'] and then the finale to the first half of the show, 'My Generation'. In case you didn't know, this is an artistic response to 'War Games'. However, it has long ceased being nuclear, with conventional smoke bombs and crushed guitars."

Other acts on the bill were The Association, The Everly Brothers, Eric Burdon and The New Animals, Sopwith Camel and The Sunshine Company.

*Guitar destroyed: Gibson ES 335, dot neck.

Sunday November 19
The Hollywood Bowl, Los Angeles, California

Intermittent downpours kept attendance "down" to about 12,000 fans who saw a varied, multi-act bill almost identical to the previous night. Supported by The Association, The Who again proved to be the most exciting group of the day, outpacing the other acts with two emotionally charged sets. Townshend spared his Gibson Les Paul Jr. in the afternoon show but broke it up at the end of the evening performance.

According to Keith in his then-current *Beat Instrumental* monthly column, the promoters had

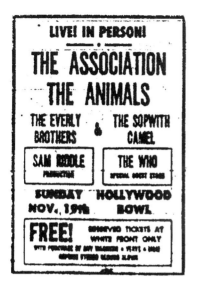

LIVE! IN PERSON!

THE ASSOCIATION
THE ANIMALS

THE EVERLY BROTHERS & **THE SOPWITH CAMEL**

SAM RIDDLE PRODUCTION **THE WHO** SPECIAL GUEST STAR

SUNDAY HOLLYWOOD NOV. 19th BOWL

FREE! RESERVED TICKETS AT WHITE FRONT ONLY

---

occasions (including the week of the show).

The show was not without incident as The Who and the supporting band, a local act by the name of The Unbelievable Uglies, were accused by the Mayor of inciting the audience and were banned from ever appearing in Fargo again. According to a member of The Uglies, about $75 dollars worth of damage was done to the washroom "by a few sub-teen ingrates". As if this was not offence enough, local police reported that several teens were seen openly smoking cigarettes!

Wednesday November 22
Southfield High School Gymnasium, Southfield, Michigan

This show was taped by a fan in the audience and Pete smashed an Epiphone guitar in the finale. One performance at 8 pm.

Thursday November 23
The New Barn, Lions Delaware County Fairgrounds, Muncie, Indiana

This date was a 'dance' concert from 7:30 to 11 pm.

Friday November 24
The Swinging Gate, Fort Wayne, Indiana

Another club gig on a tour of varied venues. The Who went on to New York immediately after this show.

asked the group to forego using smoke bombs and fireworks during the show's conclusion, so Keith compensated by throwing his floor toms into the water jets surrounding the stage, sending them rocketing skywards!

The Who were described as possessing "a solid driving and sharp-edged sound," by Michael Rudd (*Los Angeles Times*, November 22). "They forced themselves through the artificial situation... and led the audience through emotionally charged songs. 'A Quick One, While He's Away', a medley of loosely connected ballads, the ending a church-like chorus. 'You Are Forgiven' ironically preceded 'My Generation', a hard-driving piece closing in symbolic destruction of their instruments."

*Guitar destroyed: Gibson Les Paul JR.

Tuesday November 21
Civic Auditorium, Fargo, North Dakota

The Who's second appearance in Fargo in almost exactly three months with 2,200 people in attendance for one show at 7:30 pm. Their latest single 'I Can See For Miles' was very successful in this area, actually topping the local chart on four

Saturday November 25
The Village Theater, New York, two shows, 8 and 10:30 pm

This venue was later to become the famous Fillmore East, operated by Bill Graham. The Rich Kids, and The Vagrants, featuring lead guitarist Leslie West who later went on to play with Mountain, supported.

Sunday November 26
The Village Theater, New York, one performance at 3 pm

Wednesday November 29
Union Catholic High School Gymnasium, Scotch Plains, New Jersey

The third high–school gym gig of the tour and another successful turnout with attendance reported at 2,200 people.

*Guitar destroyed: Coral Model

Friday December 1
Long Island Arena, Commack, New York, one show at 8 pm

Vanilla Fudge opened.

*Guitar destroyed: Sonic blue Fender Stratocaster

The Who returned to London on December 3.

Wednesday December 6
Hull University

Friday December 8
Durham University

Monday December 18
The Pavilion, Bath

Friday December 22
Olympia Grand Hall, Kensington, London (cancelled)

The Who did not play the gig although they were billed to appear as part of an impressive line-up, advertised as "Xmas On Earth Continued". Jimi Hendrix, Pink Floyd, Eric Burdon and The Animals and others played during this all–night extravaganza. The Who missed out because, according to The Who Fan Club Newsletter, "Pete had cracked one of his fingers that week and couldn't play."

Saturday December 30
Pier Pavilion, Hastings

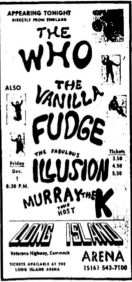

APPEARING TONIGHT
DIRECTLY FROM ENGLAND

THE WHO

ALSO

THE VANILLA FUDGE

THE FABULOUS
ILLUSION

Friday
Dec.
1
8:30 P.M.

Tickets
3.50
4.50
5.50

MURRAY THE K
YOUR HOST

LONG ISLAND ARENA

Veterans Highway, Commack

TICKETS AVAILABLE AT THE
LONG ISLAND ARENA

(516) 543-7100

Pete Townshend: **"We've got some ideas to try and get the English pop scene on it's feet again. The drag is that kids over here have seen so much... In a few months we'll be ready with something a bit different - something that's going to give them their money's worth and make them appreciate what we're doing."** *(Melody Maker, October 14, 1967).*

This was a critical year for The Who, and one in which progress stalled in much the same manner as it had in 1966. Although they had become a force to be reckoned with in America, the ritual of equipment destruction was sinking them deeper and deeper into debt, and talk of disintegration was rife within the group, specifically the departure of John and Keith to form a new band, possibly with Jimmy Page.

Unlike today, when three years or more often lapse between albums by major acts, this was an era when top bands were expected to produce an album a year, and no new Who album was forthcoming during 1968. There were no hit singles either, but, by the end of the year, salvation was at hand. Pete was immersed in a project that would elevate the group to superstar status and solve their money problems for good; enter the deaf, dumb and blind kid. Nevertheless, there was much hard work ahead.

The band joined up with The Small Faces and Paul Jones (formerly of Manfred Mann) for a tour of Australia and New Zealand that began in late January. Even their most charitable supporters would be hard pressed to describe the tour as a critical success, and The Who found themselves pilloried on all sides by the local media. They pledged that they would never play there again and, to date, they never have.

A much more encouraging reception awaited them in America when they kicked off their first headlining US tour on February 21 in San Jose, California. Guitar demolition and Keith's hotel antics kept expenses high but the band was getting through to American audiences, mainly because they were performing on the new circuit of psychedelic ballrooms that had been born out of the counterculture movement. It was the perfect stage for a group like The Who to present themselves to an audience eager for a performance and not just a pop concert of predictable hits for screaming teenage girls. The tour was extended into the first week of April, taking the group to Bill Graham's famous Fillmore East for a two–night engagement. Dr Martin Luther King Jr. was assassinated in Memphis on April 4 and riots erupted in big cities all across the country. The Fillmore remained open in the wake of the civil disorder, possibly as a place for people to gather

under happier circumstances, perhaps as a plea for sanity and stability. Whatever the reasons, the shows were sparsely attended. The tour ended in Toronto on April 7 and the band returned to England for a short rest. They played two gigs at the Marquee Club on April 15 and April 23 - a Tuesday night, no less - and Pete smashed two guitars for the occasion!

The Who played a number of college shows before setting out on a two–month American tour, opening in Los Angeles on June 28 and working their way east and then west again, concluding the trek back in California at the end of August. The group enjoyed a well–deserved three–week rest when they returned to England, before recording sessions commenced at IBC Studios for a new album. Pete had been talking about writing a "rock opera" for some time and had already produced one long, thematic piece in 'A Quick One', from the album of the same name, back in 1966. The new album was to be a full–scale work, with a central figure and supporting characters following a storyline realised through music played by The Who. It was an all–or–nothing proposition. The group might have continued as a novelty in rock'n'roll, known for their on-stage excitement, breaking up their equipment and releasing the occasional catchy single, but their future would have been uncertain at best.

As work on the album continued, the group played weekend gigs at universities. A full–scale British tour was set for late October since the band had been away from England for much of the year. Joe Cocker, The Small Faces and other acts joined The Who for the opening concert at the Walthamstow Granada on November 8. The group had never sounded better and Pete even went back to smashing his guitar on some dates. Visual evidence of The Who's performing prowess can be seen in The Rolling Stones *Rock & Roll Circus*, as they blaze their way through 'A Quick One, While He's Away'. The proceedings were filmed on December 11, with the intention of a television special, but those plans weren't realised until October 1996 when the film was seen at special screenings in London and New York and released on video shortly after. The Who performed with an energy that most bands could only dream of.

The Who returned to the Marquee one last time

on December 17, billed as "The Who's Christmas Party". The legendary club at 90 Wardour Street would see many more greats cross its stage but not The Who. (Foolishly demolished in 1989, it is now the site of a stylish, over-priced Italian restaurant.) Throughout the autumn and winter the group continued work on the "rock opera" album which would be released in May of 1969.

Wednesday January 3
Bal Taberin Club, Downham Way, Bromley

Saturday January 6
Civic Hall, Nantwich

Monday January 8
Silver Blades Ice Rink, Bristol

Tuesday January 9
Brave New World Club, Southsea, Portsmouth

Thursday January 11
Assembly Hall, Worthing

Friday January 12
The Royal Ballroom, Tottenham, North London

"The Who give an all-round powerful act which for those unprepared can be a nerve-shattering experience," wrote reviewer Roger Simpson (*Tottenham & Edmonton Weekly Herald*, January 19). "On one number Keith Moon, having mercilessly battered his nine-piece drum kit, took a hammer and crashed it down on to a cymbal... Daltrey repeatedly threw his microphone at Moon's drums, while Moon kicked part of his drum-kit off the stage. Townshend pushed the amplifiers to the ground and bounced his guitar on the fallen equipment. But for all the violent actions and assaults on their equipment they were doing minor damage. Gone are the days when The Who totally smashed equipment running into thousands of pounds in value. They no longer find it necessary to be so destructive (or can afford it) and their music is valuable as it stands."

By this time the group had largely dispensed with guitar destruction in England, except on rare

occasions. Included in their 50–minute set were 'Substitute', 'Pictures Of Lily', 'Summertime Blues', 'Tattoo', 'Shakin' All Over', and a finale of 'My Generation'.

Saturday January 13
Dreamland Ballroom, Margate

Saturday January 20
Festival Hall, Brisbane, Australia, two concerts at 6 and 8:45 pm.

The Who's one and only tour of Australia and New Zealand, with fellow performers Paul Jones and The Small Faces, began in this east coast Australian city, with a total of 8,000 fans attending both shows.

WHO   SMALL FACES

'Ban these scruffy urchins once and for all...'

The Who had arrived in Sydney the day before after a laborious flight, accompanied by road manager John 'Wiggy' Wolff and sound engineer Bob Pridden. For economy reasons the bands brought no amplification equipment, relying upon the services of the local promoters to provide all amplifiers, speakers and microphones. Each concert of the tour was billed as 'The Big Show'. The plane was greeted at the airport by a host of screaming girls and reporters. The bands were very weary after an uncomfortable flight and in no mood to deal with the reception that awaited them. A reporter immediately asked, "How do you feel now that the pound has been devalued?" and, apparently, Pete Townshend, without answering, just hit the reporter. Based on this incident, the Antipodean media immediately took an hysterical and antagonistic attitude against 'The Big Tour', expressing their distaste at the idea of good Aussie dollars being sucked out of their ailing economy by delinquent money-grabbing long-haired Pommie scruffs.

Taking the stage the following day in Brisbane, The Who were greatly dismayed by the dire quality of the PA system that had been provided. Andy Neill wrote: "The result, at each of these acoustically disastrous halls, was a murky din which Daltrey fought, in vain, to hear himself above. Added to this was that Aussie teenagers still thought it *de rigeur* to shout, scream and throw party streamers at the bands, which must have only added to their bewilderment. The Who's set list consisted of tried and trusted hits and stage 'faves' that they'd been playing over the previous year, namely: 'Substitute', 'Summertime Blues', 'Happy Jack', 'I'm A Boy', 'Pictures Of Lily', 'Shakin' All Over', 'Tattoo', and 'Relax' from the new album, *A Quick One*, 'Boris The Spider' and the auto-destructive 'My Generation'. The band had already started to drop the equipment smashing antics in Britain, but felt obliged to resurrect them, to win over new audiences, particularly here in Australia where their reputation for this preceded them. Besides this there was good reason for the band smashing their equipment on this tour, as it was, quite simply, piss poor."

Monday January 22
Sydney Stadium, Sydney, Australia, two concerts, 6 and 8:45 pm

By their fourth day in Australia, The Who had experienced at first hand the inadequacies of the local hotels. Andy Neill: "Townshend found how backward Australian hotel room service was when, phoning down for breakfast one morning, at what he considered a reasonable hour, he was laughed at by the desk: 'This is Orstraylia, mate, we get out of bed in the morning here.' Pissed off, he decided to take matters into his own hands! Visiting a local supermarket he purchased a large box of cornflakes and a gallon of milk. Returning to his room he poured the contents into the sink and after sampling a few mouthfuls of his breakfast delicacy, he left the rest to solidify into the sink like concrete before checking out of the hotel."

The actual concert at Sydney Stadium also held in store a hilariously disastrous incident, as Andy Neill explained: "They played Sydney Stadium, a massive old structure with a revolving stage, that used to host boxing matches. During the first 6 pm show the revolving stage stuck during The Small Faces' set... Things didn't improve when The Who turned up late and played to a section of the crowd who could only see the backs of their heads! Despite considerable manpower being employed underneath the stage, to coax it into revolving, it still refused to budge for the late

show." Paul Jones, alone, was singled out for praise in the *Sydney Morning Herald*: "His professional act doesn't rely on the contrivance of electronic gimmickry unlike the other acts who shout above their own cacophony to make themselves heard."

Tuesday January 23
Sydney Stadium, Sydney, Australia, two concerts, 6 and 8:45 pm

Thursday January 25
Festival Hall, Melbourne, Australia, two concerts, 6 and 8:45 pm

Moving on to another of Australia's centres of cultural excellence, the bands found a posse of local rednecks permanently hanging around the Southern Cross Hotel entrance in the hope of picking a fight with members of the groups who had diverted the attentions of their girls for the night! Keith Moon and Steve Marriott narrowly avoided a fight with these youths.

Friday January 26
Festival Hall, Melbourne, Australia, two concerts, 6 and 8:45 pm

Adverts urged fans to "book now for the wildest show ever".

Saturday January 27
Centennial Hall, Adelaide, Australia, two concerts, 6 and 8:45 pm

Some 2,000 fans attended the first show and 3,000 the second. The Who took the stage about

50 minutes late due to the absence of Pete Townshend who had missed his flight from Melbourne. The next day, the tour ran into trouble on the flight from Adelaide to Sydney. Someone in the entourage had been drinking beer and was told to stop by a flight attendant. They did not stop drinking, tempers flared and words were exchanged. Other passengers said they overheard "offensive language" used towards senior flight attendant Lexie Hobson. She summoned Captain L. Jacobs to help restore order but, according to passengers seated nearby his appeals went unheeded. The Ansett pilot, Captain Douglas Way, radioed ahead to Essendon Airport where the whole 19-man entourage was ordered off the plane and delayed for three hours in the reception lounge until arrangements were made for them to continue on to Sydney. They were escorted to their 4:15 pm flight to Sydney by four security men, two of whom made the flight with them. John made reference to the episode in his song 'Postcard' on the *Odds and Sods* album, released in October 1974.

Monday January 29
Town Hall, Auckland, New Zealand, two concerts, 6 and 8:30 pm.

The second show actually started at 9:15 as stagehands attempted to replace five microphones The Who had smashed during the first concert. Problems with the PA system were not resolved by the second show when two more mikes were damaged and Pete smashed his guitar.

"If the bands thought New Zealand PA systems would prove superior to Australia's," wrote Andy Neill, "they were in for a shock. Having not bothered to soundcheck (most bands didn't in those package show days), The Who found the PA to be the worst they'd yet encountered. After a muffled 'Substitute', Daltrey spat in contempt 'I guess they gave us these mikes because they heard we smash them up!', before sending anoth-

er one spinning to its crackling death on the stage floor. 'Summertime Blues' concluded with Townshend declaring 'It just seems pointless us continuing'. While Pridden bravely stepped in to find some half decent replacements, the band played on to placate the fans, who despite being restless with the abysmal sound, were sympathetic to the band's plight. The sound problems were improved slightly for the 8.30 pm show (which ran late), but still left a lot to be desired.

Andy Neill also quoted an eyewitness account of the second show, from someone who took his seat as the hall was still full of smoke from the end of the first show. "I remember the DJ's from Radio Hauraki (the N.Z. equivalent to pirate radio) introducing them and on they ran. Townshend was wearing a gold spangly jacket, Moon, crushed red velvet trousers and white shirt, Daltrey in a Regency blue outfit, complete with frilly shirt, whilst Entwistle was dressed in the most bizarre suit – pinstripes one side and polka dots the other! From the opening note they were deafeningly loud. I can't remember every song they played, but 'My Generation' at the end, I'll never forget. Townshend stuck his arms out and let his Fender Strat feed back, while all these smoke bombs were going off behind the amps. Daltrey swung his mike full force into Moon's cymbals, then flung the mike stand against his kit. Entwistle just stood there watching, in *that* suit. By now Townshend was flinging the Strat high into the air, catching it before it narrowly missed Daltrey's head. After a while he got bored with this and just let it crash onto the stage, picking it up and bashing it against the stage and amps before the neck finally gave way. He kicked the amps over, as Moon kicked his 'Pictures Of Lily' Premier drum kit, sending it rolling over the stage. As the smoke dispersed, the band had left the stage while the roadies scuttled on to grab anything that could be saved. An unforgettable night."

The Who concluded their only Australian/New Zealand tour in Wellington with two concerts at 6 and 8:30 pm as controversy continued to plague the tour.

Arriving in Wellington on January 30, the entourage was set to celebrate Steve Marriott's 21st birthday on their free evening. The ongoing festivities in various parts of Wellington (the hotel had banned a big birthday bash for Marriott) had culminated and the police and army being alerted to contain the wild men of pop from becoming too wild. The first batch of police cadets sent to calm the event merely joined the party and started drinking! Order was finally restored, apparently, at gun point by the army.

Andy Neill: "The next evening (the 31st) the final two concerts, at the Wellington Town Hall were, quite probably, a blur in the minds of the musicians, who were just happy that it was the end of the tour. The shows were notable for two reasons. Firstly, the compere, radio DJ Paddy O'Donnell, was so appalled by the groups' behaviour that he refused to introduce them, after being threatened by Roger Daltrey. A compromise was eventually reached where he introduced them from offstage. Secondly, Marriott had bought a brand new Gibson guitar, as a 21st birthday present to himself. While his back was turned, it was spray painted pink, with gold 'MARRIOTT' lettering for effect. Unable to bring himself to hold, let alone play, such a hideous looking instrument, the ever style-conscious Marriott gave it to Pete Townshend to smash on stage that night!"

The Wellington paper *Sunday News* (February 4) headlined with the story of The Who's departure: "Ex-fans of The Small Faces and The Who sighed 'Good Riddance' when the riotous rockers left New Zealand on Thursday night, leaving behind them an Australasian tour-trail of bashed mikes and guitars. And after last week's stormy Auckland concert it's extremely unlikely the groups will EVER return."

Paul Rodgers contributed his much-quoted condemnation of The Who in *New Zealand Truth* (February 6): "They took nearly 8,000 teenagers for $2.60 to $3.60 each. All the kids got for their money was an ear-splitting cacophony of electronic sounds that was neither musical nor funny... the two Wellington performances turned out to be the most hopeless flops ever staged there. Without the aid of recording technicians, this bunch of long-haired boors were worthless. They had no idea of public presentation. From start to finish the shows were a mixture of amateurish bungling, jarring off-pitch guitar chords, inane drum-thumping and thunderous amplification... I'm ashamed to have come from the same country as these un-washed, foul-mouthed, booze-swilling no-hopers. Britain can have them."

The bad publicity continued even after the groups had left. The Australian paper *The Showman* called for a ban on "these scruffy, guitar-twanging urchins once and for all" because a four–letter word had allegedly been used by one of The Small Faces on stage at Sydney Stadium on January 22. Another paper accused both acts of "behaving like animals onstage". Chris Stamp denied that The Who had used any four–letter words on stage and pointed out that they had, in fact, already been invited back by promoters due to the success of the tour.

Rampaging Pop Group Jeered By Teenagers

AUCKLAND, Today, (PA).—"The Who" pop group damaged seven microphones and ruined several guitars during two acts at the Town Hall last night.

At the end of their first act five microphones lay on the stage and a jeering, slow-handclapping audience of teenagers had to wait 45 minutes while technicians worked feverishly to replace the equipment in time for the second show which was due to start at 8.30pm.

In fact, it started at 9.15 pm. At one stage during the first act, it seemed likely that the four-man group would walk out on the show.

Throughout they complained about their sound equipment—and threatened not to continue unless something was done to replace the microphones.

The microphones were replaced for the second show, but the crowd was forced to wait for 45 minutes. Again in the second act, "The Who" complained bitterly and their stage act was interspersed with bitter comments from both Townshend and Daltry.

At the climax of this act, two more microphones were damaged and Townshend closed the show by smashing his guitar repeatedly to the floor.

After the show, Mr P T Stebbing, managing director of Stebbing Sound Ltd, which provided much of the equipment, surveyed the stage and complained about the antics of the group.

Saturday February 10
Essex University Hexagon, Colchester, England

Supported by The Shell Shock Show, Yum Yum Band and Exploding Orange, The Who were the star attraction at the Valentine Ball with over 100 people turned away at the door. Booked to perform a 40 minute set during the 9 pm to 4 am show, they played for an hour and 10 minutes, including 'Pictures of Lily', 'Shakin' All Over' and 'Run Run Run'.

Sunday February 11
Starlight Ballroom, Crawley, Sussex

Supported by Jo-Jo Gunne.

Tuesday February 13
Glen Ballroom, Llanelli, Wales (cancelled)

Thursday February 15
University, Hull, Yorkshire (cancelled)

Friday February 16
Sheffield University

Supported by the Bonzo Dog Doo-Dah Band.

Saturday February 17
College of Technology, Manchester

The group was recording this week just prior to their departure for America on February 20. They had been working at De Lane Lea Studios and got carried away during the proceedings. They 'went to town' on the studio equipment although Kit Lambert told engineer Mike Weighell to "send me the bill" for the damages. Sound Techniques and City of London studios reported similar incidents with The Who. The group never again worked in any of those studios!

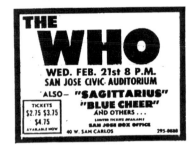

Wednesday February 21
Civic Auditorium, San Jose, California

Opening date of the band's first American tour of 1968, supported by Sagittarius and Blue Cheer The set: 'Substitute', 'Pictures Of Lily', 'Summertime Blues', 'Tattoo', 'Relax', 'My Way', 'Happy Jack', 'I'm A Boy', 'A Quick One', 'Boris The Spider', 'Shakin' All Over', 'My Generation'.

One of the highlights of this opening concert was 'Shakin' All Over', prior to which Pete paid tribute to Johnny Kidd & The Pirates. On this song, 'My Generation' and 'Relax', the band expanded the soloing into an improvised jam that lasted up to 10 minutes each. During these sections The Who's sound was exploited to the full with feedback, distortion and contrasting loud and soft passages. Eddie Cochran's 'My Way' was played along with the more familiar 'Summertime Blues'.

Before the final song, Roger Daltrey said: "I think we've come to the last one tonight. No doubt you know what number it is. We'd like to thank you all for coming, you've been a great audience... And we only came over yesterday and it's a bit awkward for us to get adjusted." Townshend then said "No it isn't!" Daltrey continued: "... and it's been great to play here. So this one's the last one tonight..." Pete interjected, shouting at Roger "hold on, hold on, hold on, hold on, hold on, hold on..." "Got his old guitar," said Daltrey, referring to Pete changing over to the guitar to be smashed. Pete responded with: "Whaddya mean 'old guitar'? It's a guitar, innit?... Sounds all right, don't it? It's made of cardboard, innit, cardboard guitar! Has to be in tune before I can bounce it properly..." The show then climaxed with a long version of 'My Generation'.

Thursday February 22
Fillmore Auditorium, San Francisco, California

Supported by jazz artist Cannonball Adderley and The Nice (featuring future ELP organ virtuoso Keith Emerson) replacing the advertised Vagrants. The first of three nights in San Francisco, one show at the Fillmore and two nights in the larger Winterland Auditorium.

John and Pete both played the Fillmore in 1996, John in March with his touring band and Pete on April 30 in a two–man show.

Friday February 23
Winterland Auditorium, San Francisco, California

Due to ticket demand, The Who's shows were moved into the larger Winterland. Kit Lambert had arrived in San Francisco the day before to personally supervise the recording of these shows but, for whatever reason, the tapes were never used and they remain unissued to this day.

Saturday February 24
Winterland Auditorium, San Francisco, California

This show was also recorded for a proposed live album. During a five–day break from gigs, The Who booked studio time at Gold Star Studios, in Los Angeles. Tracks recorded here included 'Call Me Lightning', an unreleased song 'Do You Want Kids, Kids' and the completion of 'Little Billy', the latter pair commissioned by the American Cancer Society.

Friday March 1
The Agrodome, Vancouver, British Columbia, Canada

Live gigs resumed with this performance and Roger celebrated his 24th birthday as the band made their way across Canada and the United States by tour bus.

*Guitar destroyed: Fender Stratocaster - sunburst.

Saturday March 2
New Edmonton Gardens, Edmonton, Alberta, Canada

A four-and-a half hour extravaganza, seen by about 6,000 fans for a gross of almost 14,000 Canadian dollars. After the show, Keith and John were thrown out of a bar for having long hair, an

incident that inspired John Entwistle to write the song 'What Are We Doing Here' which appeared on his first solo album. "It was an English pub in a hotel," he recalls. "We had pretty short hair and I was wearing a suit and a white shirt, but I still got thrown out for being a stinking hippie."

Friday March 8
Metropolitan Sports Center, Bloomington, Minnesota

Saturday March 9
The Grande Ballroom, Dearborn, Michigan

One show supported by The Electric Prunes (who had played the Grande the previous night).

Sunday March 10
Youth Building, Exposition Gardens, Peoria, Illinois

One show from 3 to 6 pm with local acts Suburban 9-5 and The New Coachman also on the bill. 'My Generation' from this gig was filmed by English producer Tony Palmer for *All My Loving*, a television special that was aired in Britain on November 3 on BBC1 's *Omnibus* programme. Footage from this gig was used in *The Kids Are Alright*, as was film taken while the band travelled to Peoria from Dearborn.

The same BBC film crew caught Jimi Hendrix in Worcester, Massachusetts five days later.

Friday March 15
Municipal Auditorium, San Antonio, Texas, one concert at 8pm

Saturday March 16
City Auditorium, Beaumont, Texas, two shows, 3 and 8 pm

Sunday March 17
Music Hall, Houston, Texas, two shows, 2:30 and 7:30 pm

Three local bands were on the bill: The Dream Machine, The Tornadoes and Avalon.

Friday March 22
Curtis Hixon Hall, Tampa, Florida
*Guitar destroyed: Gibson Firebird VII - reverse body, sunburst.

Saturday March 23
Code 1, Fort Lauderdale, Florida
A local group called Bridge was the opening act.
*Guitar destroyed: Fender Stratocaster

Sunday March 24
Orlando Coliseum, Orlando, Florida

Wednesday March 27
The Forum, Montreal, Quebec, Canada
The Who made their début in Montreal with this concert at 8 pm. The Troggs, making their first North American appearance, were also on the bill.

Friday March 29
Baldwin Gymnasium, Drew University, Madison, New Jersey
One show at 8 pm with Orpheus as the supporting act.

Saturday March 30
Westbury Music Fair, Long Island, New York
The Who received a $10,000 fee for their performance here at 8:30 pm.

Sunday March 31
Constitution Hall, Washington D.C.
One concert at 8 pm with The Troggs, Orpheus and The Beacon Street Union on the bill. "Smashing Guitar Concert's High Note", headlined the *Washington Post* (April 1), and reviewer Jim Hoagland was most impressed by Pete Townshend: "the tremendously talented and exciting lead guitarist". Hoagland's was a distinctly intellectual response to the music: "The Who have already established through their playing the abrasive nihilism that is the key to electronic rock... The Who's approach is a paradigm of the drug-state, distorted music that dominates pop music today. This approach is tearing down the old linear concept of music."

mented to the audience that it was a song that the band always used as a warm-up number in the dressing room, and that so far it had never sounded as good on the stage. The band turned in a tremendous version of the song, with Cochran's acoustic rockabilly guitar figures being replaced by Townshend's bone-crunching power-chords. Another new addition to the set at this concert was 'Fortune Teller', one of the few remaining R&B songs from their earlier years. The Who's arrangement slowed down the first two verses, then speeded up for the remainder, utilising harmony vocals throughout.

Linda Eastman (Paul McCartney's future wife) photographed the group at the Fillmore concerts - both on stage and off.

*Guitar destroyed: Fender Stratocaster - white.

Wednesday April 3
Fillmore North, Canada

This venue was not owned by Bill Graham but it appears to have been named after his famous auditoriums. The *Melody Maker* named the location as Vancouver but it's highly unlikely that The Who returned to this city since they had played there on March 1. The exact city has yet to be determined due to insufficient data.

Friday April 5
Fillmore East, New York

The first of a two–night stand in New York. The Who were the first English band to headline over two nights at the Fillmore East. The assassination of Dr Martin Luther King Jr. in Memphis on the night of April 4 caused widespread violence in cities across America. Many New York nightspots closed down in the wake of the unrest but the Fillmore remained open and combined the two scheduled shows into one performance each night. Buddy Guy was the opening act and B.B. King guested on two songs in Guy's first set.

The set: 'Substitute', 'Pictures Of Lily', 'Summertime Blues', 'Fortune Teller', 'Tattoo', 'Little Billy', 'I Can't Explain', 'Happy Jack', 'Relax', 'I'm A Boy', 'A Quick One, While He's Away', 'C'mon Everybody', 'Shakin All Over', 'Boris The Spider', 'My Generation'.

An uncompromisingly powerful concert with the band on top form and brimming with energy. One highlight was a rare version of Eddie Cochran's 'C'mon Everybody'. Townshend com-

Saturday April 6
Fillmore East, New York

The two shows were again combined into one, offering the audience a five–hour–plus concert. The Who played for more than 90 minutes with Buddy Guy as supporting act. Both nights were recorded for a proposed live album which never happened, although bootleg tapes eventually surfaced.

The set: 'Substitute', 'Pictures Of Lily', 'Summertime Blues', 'Fortune Teller', 'Tattoo', 'Little Billy', ' I Can't Explain', 'Happy Jack', 'I'm A Boy', 'Relax', 'A Quick One, While He's Away', 'My Way', 'Shakin' All Over', 'Boris The Spider', 'My Generation'.

The band were pleased to be playing at the Fillmore East and mentioned that in its previous incarnation as the Village Theater they had considered it a "pisshole"! These Fillmore concerts were also the only confirmed occasions when The Who performed 'Little Billy', their anti-smoking anthem. Pete told the audience: "The song arose when the agency that manages our publicity contract also manages a contract for the American Cancer Society. They asked us, after hearing the 'Odorono' commercial on the (*Sell Out*) album, if we could write a song to discourage youngsters from smoking tobacco. So we said yes, and we tried it out… we were a bit sceptical at first, we don't want to dictate to anyone what to smoke! But you should be hearing it on the radio soon, it's about a boy who doesn't smoke and doesn't die of obesity even though he is very fat, and ends up looking after all the children of the parents who died of cancer. The guy's name is Little Billy…"

Some tuning problems were experienced by Pete during this show and 'I Can't Explain' and 'Little Billy' suffered slightly for it. 'Summertime Blues', however, was exceptionally strong, with a colossal block of noise thrusting out of the speakers. 'Relax' and 'Shakin' All Over' featured much extended soloing, during which Moon, Entwistle and Townshend pushed their instruments to the limit, feeding off each other's musical ideas with a unique empathy. This is a technique which The Who never attempted in the studio, but which was mesmerising in concert with the Fillmore's oil lamps swirling around the back of the stage. 'Boris The Spider' suffered a lapse when Roger and John simultaneously sang different verses. "I've got to admit I'm kinda' down tonight over several things," Townshend told the audience towards the end of the show. "Most of it is being kicked out of three hotels in one day… Get stuffed! We've been kicked out of three, right?… Anyway, that's loading luggage all day and playing guitars. Same thing really, loading luggage and playing guitars. But this one… THIS is gonna be different! This is a very long and grooooovy ver-

sion… and I'm staying with friends now… and it's called 'My Generation'." The band played an outstanding version of this song which moved into an extended instrumental passage in which Pete played some fine guitar solos.

Sunday April 7
CNE Coliseum, Toronto, Ontario, Canada

This date, with The Troggs and The MC5 as the opening acts, concluded the first North American tour of 1968 and The Who flew back to England the following day. By now the group had solidified their reputation in America as the most exciting live group on the circuit. An extensive summer tour was already being planned.

Monday April 15
The Marquee, Soho, Central London

The Who's first gig on their return from America was an unadvertised visit to the old familiar surroundings of the Marquee, supported by the Bonzo Dog Doo-Dah Band. "The Bonzo's drummer, Legs Larry Smith hung these old rotting fish around the Marquee," remembered fan Dave Stark, "and totally stank the place out."

Tuesday April 23
The Marquee, Soho, Central London.

Supported by up and coming group Jethro Tull, and The Gun, featuring singer Jon Anderson (who joined Yes later that year) and the Gurvitz Brothers, Paul and Adrian, who had a UK Top 10 hit that year (as Gun) with 'Race With The Devil'. For the second, advance-advertised Marquee gig, Pete, wearing a Fair Isle pullover and bow tie, smashed two guitars.

* Guitars destroyed: Gibson ES 345 Stereo, Coral Model.

Monday April 29
Top Rank, Watford

Supported by Geno Washington's Ram Jam Band and The Free Expression.

Friday May 3
Hull University

Originally a booking for Jimi Hendrix (who pulled out due to recording commitments in New York), the promoters asked for The Crazy World of Arthur Brown and finally ended up with The Who. Six billed supporting acts for this "Pre Rag

Ball" had whittled down on the night to just Michael Chapman and The Amboy Dukes (not Ted Nugent's band). The University student magazine *Torchlight* reported: "'Masher' Townshend brought his boys on about two o'clock in the morning... The Who put in an hour's hard work... Keith Moon broke several pairs of sticks, Pete Townshend kicked somebody off the stage (great, man, great!) and sexy Rog Daltry [sic] (we could see he had no vest on) threw his mike into the audience. All good, clean, healthy fun and we were all so intent on not getting a mike in the mouth that we forgot we'd paid twenty two shillings and sixpence for an hour of The Who and a small plate of savoury."

Saturday May 4
Mountford Hall, Liverpool University
The group began playing longer sets than their contracts required and, at this gig, played from 10:15 to 11:20 pm.

Saturday May 11
Strathclyde University, Scotland

Sunday May 12
Locarno Ballroom, Wakefield, Yorkshire (cancelled)

Friday May 24
City University, Clerkenwell, Central London

Friday May 31
Manchester University

Tuesday June 11
St. John's College Ball, Cambridge (cancelled)
The group were reportedly preoccupied making a promo film for their latest single, 'Dogs'. The gig, promoted by future Who tour organiser, Peter Rudge and featuring The Scaffold and Spooky Tooth, went ahead with an unknown replacement.

Friday June 14
Leicester University
With P.P. Arnold supporting.

Saturday June 15
London College of Printing, South London
With the Alan Bown! supporting. Singer Jess

Roden came back on to sing 'Magic Bus' which had just recently been recorded.

Friday June 21
Durham University
Supported by Status Quo, The Nashville Teens, and Ray McVay & His Orchestra.

Friday June 28
Shrine Auditorium, Los Angeles, California, 8 pm to 2 am
The Who began their summer American tour with two nights in Los Angeles. Originally planned to last three weeks, it was extended to more than two months as the group gained momentum in the States. Support acts here were Fleetwood Mac and The Crazy World of Arthur Brown on Friday joined by The Steve Miller Band on Saturday only.

Saturday June 29
Shrine Auditorium, Los Angeles, California
Los Angeles Times reviewer Pete Johnson summed up the show as follows (July 2): "Advertisements for this event billed The Who as monsters of pop, and that description is in both senses of the word monster, although theirs is a kind of benign grotesqueness. The British quartet had made its reputation by specialising in a violently iconoclastic variety of hard rock... They are great fun to watch, even aside from the widely publicised instrument smashing ending of their act, which has become somewhat of a cliché. The three instruments and their four voices (they are capable of good harmonies) create an overwhelming feeling of excitement which makes up for their sometimes blurred lyrics."

*Guitar destroyed: Fender Stratocaster - sunburst, maple neck.

The group enjoyed an eight-day break in Los Angeles where they may have spent some time at Gold Star Studios. A concert date on the original itinerary on Wednesday July 3 in Albuquerque, New Mexico, never took place.

Monday July 8
Memorial Auditorium, Sacramento, California
According to the *Sacramento Union*, the show was attended by "a surprisingly mediocre-sized crowd of about 2,000 persons". Iron Butterfly and The Neighbourhood Children were the opening

acts. *The Sacramento Union* also commented: "The obvious highlight of The Who's rebellion against blasé band business was the closing number, 'My Generation', Daltrey's stuttering song that shouts out for youth. While the lights throbbed, destruction ensued and The Who boldly and blatantly attacked, toppled and beat equipment in the glorious manoeuvres of close combat for which they are renowned."

Tuesday July 9
Exhibition Hall, Regina, Alberta, Canada

This date was probably cancelled. The local paper reported that nobody had confirmed that The Who would perform in Regina that evening. The local promoter couldn't confirm the date either as he had not booked the hall even though it was available.

Wednesday July 10
Calgary Stampede Corral, Calgary, Alberta, Canada

A combined total of more than 4,000 came to two shows here at 2 pm and 8:30 pm. This was the second–best attendance for a single event at the 1968 Stampede.

Thursday July 11
Saskatoon Arena, Saskatchewan, Canada

The music trade paper *Amusement Business* reported that the group drew an estimated 1,600. The show got off to a late start due to a delay in the arrival of their equipment from Calgary. Saskatoon was supposedly the place where a bored Keith Moon chopped up every piece of furniture in his hotel room with an axe!

THE
**WHO
?**

One of the most incredible stage acts and sounds to come from Britain. Pop Art music that is excitingly different. Also featuring Graham and the Wafers.

STAMPEDE CORRAL
WED., JULY 10th
2 p.m. and 8:30 p.m.

TICKETS
$5.00, $4.00, $3.00, $2.00

CORRAL BOX OFFICE
Daily 10 to 5 p.m. and for each performance.

DOWNTOWN
Stampede Ticket Office 100 yeards east of Husky Tower in CPR Station Building. Daily 9 a.m. to 5 p.m.

Friday July 12
Indiana Beach Ballroom, Monticello, Indiana

Two performances, 8:45 and 10:30 pm

FLEETWOOD MAC
RHYME THURS JULY 11 NO AGE LIMIT
PINK FLOYD
RHYME FRI JULY 12 JAGGEDGE
SAT 13 JULY WHO TWO SHOWS
FROST 6-9PM PSYCHEDELIC STOOGES 10-1AM
GRANDE BALLROOM

Saturday July 13
Grande Ballroom, Dearborn, Michigan

The Who attracted a sell-out crowd for this date, grossing $6,500 for two shows. A review in a local underground paper mistakenly noted that the band played on Friday; the show was positively on Saturday, July 13.

*Guitars destroyed: Fender Stratocaster - custom colour and an unknown instrument.

Sunday July 14
Music Carnival, Cleveland, Ohio

Attendance was about 2,400 people for one show at 7 pm. Fans rushed the stage during 'Magic Bus', causing a short delay in the proceedings but the group returned to finish their performance, the first sell-out for a "teen rock show" in the tent-in-the-round venue, as reported by *Billboard* magazine. This show was also recorded from the stage on reel–to–reel tape.

The Who followed a support act called Cyrus Erie, opening with 'Substitute'. During the fifth song 'Magic Bus' (during which soundman Bob Pridden, nicknamed 'Ben Pump' by Steve Marriott of The Small Faces, apparently joined in on backing vocals and claves), Townshend began to break up his guitar and amplifiers in a spontaneous act which caused such excitement that the fans overran the stage and the band were forced to retreat to the dressing room until order had been restored. Finding his guitar too damaged to continue Pete managed to borrow gear from the support act to complete the show. During the show, both Daltrey and Townshend had their clothes and passports stolen from the dressing room (which caused problems for the next show when

Wednesday July 17
Auto Stade, Montreal, Quebec, Canada, two shows, 2 & 7 pm

The third successive and final Canadian date of the summer tour grossed a $6,700 gate.

Thursday July 18
Rhode Island Auditorium, Providence, Rhode Island

One show at 8:30 pm supported by jazz-rock group Blood, Sweat and Tears.

the band landed in Toronto). *Billboard* (July 27) noted: "The Who run amok at Cleveland rock concert... the concert had everything from early pandemonium and an unexpected intermission to a road manager singing along with drummer Keith Moon."

Monday July 15
Memorial Centre, Kingston, Canada

The Who arrived at Kingston two hours late and eventually played this show before 1,300 fans in the early hours of Tuesday morning. Although the band were scheduled to be on stage at 10.00pm, three local support acts kept the audience entertained. Trouble started for The Who when they landed en route to Toronto. With Daltrey and Townshend now without passports, the customs officials demanded a $20,000 bond to release the band's equipment, among other formalities. James McCormick, the promoter, chartered two aircraft to fetch The Who and entourage from Toronto after the customs had been satisfied, but the equipment stayed behind. McCormick supplied instruments and equipment from a local source, although this didn't stop Pete smashing a 1958 vintage Fender Stratocaster. According to McCormick, The Who "put on a wonderful show". Incidentally, the restored guitar is now owned by Mike Moore of Calgary.

Tuesday July 16
Civic Center, Ottawa, Ontario, Canada

Despite difficult conditions from excessive heat and technical delays, The Who electrified an appreciative crowd of well over 6,000 fans. Supported by The Troggs, The Ohio Express and 5D "with orchestra" (?) for one performance at 8 pm.

Saturday July 20
Civic Center, Virginia Beach, Virginia

Two shows at 8 and 10:30 pm with The Troggs as opening act.

The venue was also known locally as The Dome.

Sunday July 21
Oakdale Music Theatre, Wallingford, Connecticut; one performance at 8 pm

Tuesday July 23
The Mosque, Richmond, Virginia

Two shows, 7 and 9:30 pm with The Troggs on the bill, although neither performance in the 3,730–seat hall was a sell-out.

*Guitar destroyed: Fender Jazzmaster.

Wednesday July 24
JFK Stadium, Philadelphia, Pennsylvania; one show at 8 pm

A series of concerts were staged at this venue during the summer of 1968, and The Who took part in this evening's "English Invasion" show with Pink Floyd and The Troggs on the bill. All advance tickets were one dollar!

Friday July 26
Saint Bernard Civic Auditorium, Chalematte, Louisiana

Two shows with support by The People.

Saturday July 27
Orlando Sports Arena, Orlando, Florida; one show at 8:30 pm

The WHO

Recently Featured on 2 Pages in LIFE
AND "The People"
ARE COMING TO

ORLANDO SPORTS STADIUM

JULY 27th at 8:30

Advance sale tickets 3.00 at Bill Baer Stores, Southern Music. Decor on the Mall in Colonial Plaza, and Orlando Sports Stadium. Tickets at door 3.50. Mail order to P. O. Box 5295, Orlando 32805.

CALL 277-8000

Supported again by The People, the show attracted about 1000 fans.

Sunday July 28
Marine Stadium, Miami, Florida; one show, 7:30 to 11:30 pm

Supported by The Ohio Express and The People. According to *The Orlando Evening Star* review, The Who "mastered their hit 'I Can See For Miles'".

Monday July 29
Tamarack Lodge, Ellenville, New York

The Who played before a predominantly older audience at this venue, a summer vacation lodge in the Catskill Mountains of upstate New York.

Wednesday July 31
The New Place, Algonquin, Illinois

This venue was actually a converted barn located two miles north of Algonquin, a north-western suburb of Chicago. The hall held up to 1,000 people but burned to the ground on December 20, 1968.

Thursday August 1
The 'Lectric Theatre, Chicago, Illinois

Shows here ran from 8 pm to 3 am!

Friday August 2
The Singer Bowl, Flushing, New York

The Who played as supporting act for The Doors with a third act, The Kangaroo, opening. The set: 'Heaven And Hell', 'I Can't Explain', 'Summertime Blues', 'Fortune Teller', 'Tattoo', 'A Quick One, While He's Away', 'Magic Bus', 'Shakin' All Over', 'My Generation'.

John Entwistle's newest song 'Heaven And Hell' was used to open the set, a hard rock song structured to display Townshend's power-chord technique, along with a simultaneous guitar and bass solo. 'Summertime Blues' was introduced by Pete, somewhat curiously, as a "song recorded by the Blue Cheer". (Blue Cheer had recorded a heavy rock arrangement of 'Summertime Blues' on their 1968 LP *Vincebus Eruptum*, and although this may have made The Who seem like copyists, Townshend was a Blue Cheer fan.) The version played at the Singer Bowl was frenzied and exciting, and was probably the highlight of the set. Townshend preceded 'A Quick One' (now referred to as the mini opera) with a corny and long-winded joke that because Ivor is an engine driver "he never comes on time", which produced groans from the audience. Much extended and vastly different from the single was 'Magic Bus', during which Townshend played a few excellent bursts of guitar soloing. Unusually, however, the version of 'Shakin' All Over' which followed was comparatively short, omitting the extended solo.

'My Generation' concluded an excellent performance with the customary guitar and drum

Tuesday August 6
Music Hall, Boston, Massachusetts; two shows, 7:30 and 9:30 pm

Even though this was the group's sixth visit to America, these were their first appearances in Boston. Local band Quill served as the opening act. The second show featured a five–song set and Keith's particularly brutal destruction of his Premier drum kit.

Wednesday August 7
Wolman Skating Rink, Central Park, New York

The set: 'Substitute', 'Heaven and Hell', 'I Can't Explain', 'Magic Bus', 'Young Man Blues', 'Shakin' All Over', 'My Generation'.

Although shorter than usual, a loud, intense and dynamic set was delivered at this show, which formed part of the annual Schaefer Music Festival sponsored by Schaefer Brewery. A mix-up on 'I Can't Explain' occurred towards the end of the song where Daltrey lost track of the guitar and bass, probably a result of inadequate monitoring. With some of the slower songs omitted, this show was a constant barrage of fever-pitched hard rock, with the extended 'Magic Bus' being a highlight. 'Young Man Blues' was relatively laid-

destruction. After The Who had left the stage, the compere began his address to the audience saying: "After we've picked up the pieces of guitar...". The audience was restless throughout The Who's set, and the atmosphere was not abated by Townshend's guitar smashing. As The Who came off, Pete warned Jim Morrison that the audience was potentially dangerous, though Morrison – in a belligerent mood – didn't much care, and treated the audience with some degree of disrespect. Disputes between The Doors and The Who over the former's equipment being on stage during The Who's act resulted in some Doors equipment being damaged.

The Who had performed with the house lights on but these were turned off for The Doors. According to *Variety*, this date grossed $75,000 from a near sell-out crowd of 16,000. As The Doors ended their set there was a melee in the audience and at least one girl was injured in the fracas. The incident inspired Pete to write 'Sally Simpson', a song from *Tommy*.

Saturday August 3
Majestic Hills, Lake Geneva, Wisconsin

Sunday August 4
Melody Fair, North Tonawanda, New York

One concert at 8:30 pm in a summertime tent venue in this suburb of Buffalo.

The Schaefer Music Festival in Central Park

Monday, August 5, 8:00 & 10:30 p.m.
Lou Rawls/Joe Keyes
Wednesday, August 7, 8:00 & 10:30 p.m.
The Who/The Mandala
Friday, August 9, 8:00 p.m.
George Shearing/Amanda Ambrose
Saturday, August 10, 8:00 & 10:30 p.m.
Flip Wilson/Anthony & The Imperials

back and bluesy, while 'My Generation' completed the show in the usual guitar-splintering manner.

New York Times music critic Robert Shelton gave The Who one of the most scathing reviews ever after witnessing the evening's second show. "A capacity audience watched and cheered as Peter Townshend broke up his electric guitar. Whether Mr. Townshend was having a breakdown or being a showman was not discernible. Perhaps he thought, as have some other pop musicians recently, that the demolition of his instrument was making a statement. If so, it is the sort of statement that is populating our mental hospitals."

Back in the UK, Pete told Chris Welch of *Melody Maker* of a nerve-wracking encounter with one of New York's finest. "A superintendent of police saw me smash my guitar on stage. He came into our dressing room, took out a gun, aimed it at my head, fired an inch from my skull and said if I smashed my guitar in the second half, he would blow my head off. He could have killed me but he probably went home to his wife and kids and thought nothing about it." Whether this incident actually happened or not, Pete has never confirmed or denied in subsequent years, but it remains doubtful.

Friday August 9
Illinois State Fairgrounds Cavalcade of Music Stage, Springfield, Illinois

The Who were on the bill with The Association, the same American pop group they had appeared with at the Hollywood Bowl the previous November.

Saturday August 10
The Jaguar, St. Charles, Illinois

Another psychedelic ballroom, this was located in a town about 40 miles west of Chicago.

The set: 'I Can't Explain', 'Fortune Teller', 'Tattoo', 'Heaven And Hell', 'Young Man Blues', 'Daddy Rolling Stone', 'Summertime Blues', 'Magic Bus', 'Boris The Spider', 'A Quick One, While He's Away', 'My Generation'.

Following the first number, Daltrey commented to the audience that the ceiling of the venue was very low, and that the sound balance would need some adjustment. The intimate venue showed The Who in their best light, however, and they revived their old favourite 'Daddy Rolling Stone' for the occasion.

Pete and Keith played the introduction to 'A Quick One' for laughs, and the following exchange occurred:

Pete: "And now we'd like to play a mini-opera... the story of which is quite complex and I know a lot of faces in the audience so I know a lot of you have heard the story before. But for those of you who haven't heard the story..."

Keith: "Here it is for the first time!"

Pete: "I'm gonna tell it again. The mini-opera is something which takes six different themes of music and it's just one story and we believe it's one of the first efforts of its kind in that direction and we're gonna try and make our next album very much like it. The story is all about a campfire girl who was seduced..."

Keith: "Take off your knickers!"

Pete: "Afterwards. Later..."

Keith: "Aha! It was only geezers clapping then!"

Pete: "And, uh, yeah... Geezers don't like taking their knickers off. Anyway, he s-s-s-seduces her and, er, this is while the campfire girl's boyfriend is away working and when he finds out about it...you see, he rushes in right in the middle of it..."

Keith: "Trouble!"

Pete: "Trouble.'Cause he rushes in right in the middle of it and the reason for this is because the seduction takes much longer than it should because Ivor, because he's an engine driver, doesn't come on time... Thank you. Anyway, when her boyfriend finds out about it, Ivor the engine driver looks like a very big person... he's a very big person indeed and so he forgives them..."

Keith: "Cause he likes watching!"

Pete: "Cause he likes watching... "

Tuesday August 13
The Fillmore West, San Francisco, California

The opening show of a three–night stand. Supporting acts were The James Cotton Blues Band and Magic Sam. Bill Graham had opened this venue on July 5, the site of the old Carousel Ballroom at the corner of Market and Van Ness streets, and renamed it the Fillmore West.

Wednesday August 14
The Fillmore West, San Francisco, California
The set: 'Substitute', 'Heaven And Hell', 'Fortune Teller', 'Tattoo', 'Summertime Blues', 'Young Man Blues', 'Boris The Spider', 'Relax', 'A Quick One, While He's Away', 'Happy Jack', 'Magic Bus', 'Shakin' All Over', 'My Generation'.

An energetic concert but one dogged by tuning problems and a broken guitar string. Townshend referred to 'Summertime Blues' as "one of our favourite songs of all time". 'Young Man Blues' featured 20 minutes of improvised soloing from Townshend and Entwistle, incorporating feedback and an overkill of power-chording, propelled by Keith Moon's frenzied drumming. The problems began with 'Boris The Spider' by which time the guitar was out-of-tune and had broken a string. (Given how roughly Pete handled a guitar, he very rarely sounded out of tune, compared to Jimi Hendrix, for example.) Townshend offered his excuses, and was left holding the guitar lead while the road crew took his guitar away for restringing: "This is a guitar cord, and on the end of it should be a guitar in order for us to play the next number. And I do carry spare guitars but one string has broken on each guitar, because you see these days, guitars don't like me! Not like they used to. I walk into a guitar shop and they all blush... Anyway, the reliable, faithful roadie is getting it together – aren't you, reliable, faithful roadie?... In New York there's a music shop called Manny's, and it's very famous and he gives me lots of bargains 'cause I often buy guitars in there sometimes. And one day I was going in and buying my 144th guitar, and he said to me: 'As it's your 144th guitar, I'm going to give you a present!' What's it gonna be?..." Pete then held up his guitar pick for the audience to see. Laughter broke out among the audience. "Actually, it proves very handy," Pete concluded.

Thursday August 15
The Fillmore West, San Francisco, California
The last night in the newly relocated venue.

Friday August 16
Selland Arena, Fresno, California
One show at 8:30 pm, supported by Quicksilver Messenger Service.

Saturday August 17
Tempe Diablo Stadium, Phoenix, Arizona; one show at 8:30 pm
The Who's debut in Arizona at an outdoor venue in the middle of the summer!
Again supported by Quicksilver Messenger Service

Sunday August 18
Kelker Junction Concert Hall, Colorado Springs, Colorado

Thursday August 22
Music Hall, Kansas City, Missouri
A single performance seen by 2,000 fans.

Friday August 23
Wedgewood Village Amusement Park, Oklahoma City, Oklahoma
One show at 8:15 pm.

Saturday August 24
Wedgewood Village Amusement Park, Oklahoma City, Oklahoma
Two shows, 3:15 and 8:15 pm. Based upon an existing recording thought to be from this gig, the 3.15 show featured 'Substitute', 'I Can't Explain', 'Boris The Spider', 'A Quick One, While He's Away', 'Magic Bus' and 'Shakin' All Over'. Played in an outdoor setting in the blazing summer heat at the height of the afternoon, the sun shone directly into the eyes of the audience prompting Pete to comment: "Actually, despite the fact that the sun is bearing down on the back

The James C. Pagni Company Presents

THE WHO
with
QUICK SILVER MESSENGER SERVICE
FRIDAY, AUGUST 16
8:30 PM – SELLAND ARENA
Mail Orders acceptable: $2.50, $3.50, $4.50
Enclose self addressed, stamped envelope to The Who
700 "M" St., Fresno, Calif. Call 235 6501 for information

of our necks, I just realised it's also bearing down
in your eyes and it's very difficult to see. Sorry
'bout that, you can thank Uncle Morris for that..."
'Boris The Spider' was introduced by Pete as "one
of our most requested songs that we do on stage."

Throughout the show the audience response
was somewhat restrained. Roger Daltrey introduced 'Magic Bus' and said: "I'd like to introduce
you to Ben Pump our roadie. Let's have a hand
for Ben." As at Cleveland, Bob Pridden sang
backing vocals on this song, as he probably had
been doing for the whole tour. The set seemed to
finish without playing 'My Generation', as if the
band were saving the equipment to smash up
during the later set at 8.15.

Monday August 26
Civic Auditorium, San Jose, California

Tuesday August 27
Community Concourse, San Diego, California
For their début in San Diego, The Who deliv-
ered a riveting performance for 3,000 enthusiastic
fans.
*Guitar destroyed: Fender Stratocaster.

Wednesday August 28
Civic Auditorium, Santa Monica, California
Ticket sales were so poor for this date that the
two scheduled performances were combined into
one! The James Cotton Blues Band was the open-
ing act.
*Guitar destroyed: Fender Stratocaster -
Olympic White.

Tired Who cut tour to come home to Britain

The Who . . . life on the road is hell!

Thursday August 29
Earl Warren Showgrounds, Santa Barbara, California
The end of the summer tour that further solidified the group's reputation in the US. The next
time The Who arrived on these shores they would
bring *Tommy* with them.

Saturday October 5
The Roundhouse, London
An 'all-nighter', running from 10:30 pm to
dawn, with Blossom Toes and The Fox.

Friday October 11
York University
Supported by Spooky Tooth.

Saturday October 12
Sheffield University
Supported by the Crazy World Of Arthur
Brown.

Friday October 18
The Lyceum, The Strand, Central London
Supported by The Crazy World of Arthur
Brown, the Alan Bown!, Elmer Gantry's Velvet
Opera and Skip Bifferty, and set to run to 7 am,
this concert was promoted by Brunel University
Students' Union. Chris Welch reported in *Melody
Maker* (October 26) that "The Who's comeback to
the British scene continues to be one of the most

BRUNEL UNIVERSITY STUDENTS' UNION

MIDNITE RAVE

Friday Night, Oct. 18th/19th, 12.30 to 7 a.m., at the LYCEUM, Strand, W.C.2

WHO

CRAZY WORLD OF ARTHUR BROWN

ALAN BOWN ● ELMER GANTRY ● SKIP BIFFERTY, etc.

Bars till 3 a.m.

Limited tickets available 18/- in advance, send S.A.E. and money to Social Sec., BRUNEL UNIVERSITY STUDENTS' UNION, Woodlands Avenue, Acton, W.3. One guinea on night (S.U./Club Cards). Tickets at door not guaranteed. Dress anyhow — now you can enter Mecca in your hippiest gear!

pleasing surprises of Autumn '68. Playing like men possessed, they are more together than during their entire career. Roger Daltrey, looking splendid in a fringed jacket, naked chest and glittering cross, has perfected his microphone swinging stage movements, and sang better than I have ever heard him. Peter Townshend's guitar hurling caught the audience's breath on 'Generation' and Jess Roden [singing earlier with the Alan Bown!] sat in on 'Magic Bus'. Apart from the time-honoured demolition job involving Peter toppling a battery of speaker cabinets, The Who achieved an excellent sound and displayed a professionalism in the more serious numbers proving they are not [sic] one of the world's best playing groups." (An unfortunate typo had a "not" slip in here!)

Saturday October 19
California Ballroom, Dunstable

Friday October 25
Granby Halls, Leicester

Joe Cocker and The Grease Band and Family were the supporting bands on the bill. 7:30 pm to 1 am.

Wednesday October 30
Eel Pie Island, Twickenham, Middlesex

Supporting acts were East of Eden, Proteus, and David Booth.

Friday November 8
Granada Theatre, Walthamstow, London

Two shows, 7:00 and 9:10 pm. This was The Who's last theatre tour and (due to it being promoted by Lambert and Stamp) the most satisfactory, with a supporting cast of The Crazy World Of Arthur Brown, The Mindbenders, Joe Cocker and The Grease Band. Some dates also featured The Small Faces (who, by this time, were on the verge of disintegrating), Free, and Yes.

Ray Tolliday wrote: "The Who ended the show by proving they have lost none of their excitement. They tore into their first record 'I Can't Explain'. Then a tremendous arrangement of 'Summertime Blues' which should have had the Rockers everywhere spinning in their shallow graves. During their mini- opera, 'A Quick One' Pete Townshend proved he is still one of the most exciting guitarists, despite the 'left hand' purists. The show finished with 'Magic Bus' and chaos. The management closed the curtains as the group were still playing, but The Who kept blasting. The audience didn't know whether to go or stay, then someone opened the curtains again to reveal The Who taking part of their ritual immolation scene. A great show ended as the curtains closed, the lights went up and there was nowhere to go." (*Melody Maker*, November 16).

The Walthamstow Gazette noted that The Who's act "put the other 'one hit wonder' groups firmly into the second class compartment of the Magic Bus".

Apparently, the house manager at Walthamstow had been disgusted with the destruction, and the booking manager for the Granada circuit, John Arm, issued the following statement: "I closed the curtains because I get a bit tired of violence on stage. It's not necessary. I've told The Who before. They say violence is a big part of their act in America, but I said what they do in America is one thing, and what they do in England is entirely different." It is most likely that this incident (and Arm's statement) were the main rea-

sons why The Who chose never again to play at a Granada venue.

Saturday November 9
Adelphi Cinema, Slough, two shows, 6 and 8:30 pm

Sunday November 10
Colston Hall, Bristol, two shows, 5:30 and 7:45 pm

The Alan Bown! replaced Joe Cocker for these performances.

In the Bristol *Evening News* (November 11) James Belsey was more than impressed: "The happy, noisy confusion of The Who and the satanic disturbing sight of Arthur Brown linked last night for the best pop show Bristol has seen in months... The Who built up to a climax of decibels which would have caused Jericho a second thought about the safety of the walls and the whole show worked perfectly... The Who were loud, tough and powerful. They had vivid vocal attack, an exciting guitarist in Pete Townshend and the spontaneous stage presence... The group played lip service to teenage fans by quickly singing a medley of hits, but then switched to a wilder, freer music that they have never used on record building up to a deafening climax."

Friday November 15
The Roundhouse, Chalk Farm, London, 10:30 pm till dawn

Another "all-nighter" extravaganza with Joe Cocker, The Small Faces, The Crazy World of Arthur Brown, The Mindbenders, Yes and DJ Jeff Dexter on the bill.

Saturday November 16
The Roundhouse, Camden Town, London

Another 'all-nighter' gig from 10:30 pm till dawn. Joe Cocker and Yes did not appear at this show as The Mindbenders and a group called Tea & Symphony appeared instead.

Sunday November 17
Birmingham Theatre, Birmingham, two shows, 5:30 and 8 pm

Joe Cocker and The Grease Band did not appear.

Monday November 18
City Hall, Newcastle, two shows, 6:15 and 8:30 pm

Joe Cocker and his band rejoined the tour here.

Tuesday November 19
Paisley Ice Rink, Glasgow, one performance only at 8 pm

Wednesday November 20
Empire Theatre, Liverpool, two shows, 6:15 and 8:35 pm

The British tour ended here with Kenney Jones of The Small Faces joining Keith on drums for 'Magic Bus'.

Friday November 22
City Hall, St Albans

Roger Daltrey: "You have to tour for at least six weeks over there (United States). The first three weeks pays your fares and all the expenses. The fourth week pays for your road managers. The fifth pays for your manager. The sixth is profit for us… And please don't think we've forgotten about Britain. We all love working here, but what is the point with the tax we pay? It's stupid. We pay 18s 3d in the pound so it's hardly worth working. At the moment we are just doing two gigs a week, mainly at universities." *(Melody Maker, June 15, 1968).*

Saturday November 23
Corn Exchange, Devizes

Tuesday November 26
Southampton University
In this Southampton University Students Carnival the support acts included the Freddie Mack Show, The Savoy Brown Blues Band, Chris Shakespeare and The Globe.

Saturday November 30
Manchester University

Saturday December 7
Bristol University

Monday December 9
The Pavilion, Bath

Wednesday December 11
Stonebridge House Studios, Wembley
The Who spent all this day (and the previous day in rehearsal) taping what was planned as a TV special, *The Rolling Stones' Rock'n'Roll Circus.*

A real circus tent was built inside the studios and a stellar line up of talent was assembled including John Lennon and Yoko Ono, Eric Clapton, Jethro Tull, Taj Mahal, Marianne Faithfull, The Who and, of course, The Rolling Stones in the grand finale. Unfortunately the production involved endless hours of waiting around and by the time the Stones went on at around one o'clock in the morning of the following day, the excitement of the occasion had long since evaporated. Earlier The Who had somehow found the energy to offer a stunning rendering of 'A Quick One' which was arguably superior to anything else performed.

Not until October 1996 was the filmed event made available to the public, in a TV special and on video. It has long been rumoured that the reason why the Stones refused to sanction the proposed TV special or allow a subsequent video

release was because The Who turned in a superior performance.

The Who's segment can also be seen in the original version of *The Kids Are Alright.*

Thursday December 12
Reading University
The Who received a fee of £475 for this date. Jess Roden joined them onstage for 'Magic Bus'.

Saturday December 14
Bubbels Club, Brentwood, Essex, supported by The Kult.

Tuesday December 17
The Marquee, Soho, Central London
'The Who's Xmas Party' was the band's last performance at the Marquee. Supporting was Yes, "a great new group". Who fan Nigel Cornthwaite joined the band on stage for 'Magic Bus'.

Thursday December 19
The Pier, Worthing

Saturday December 21
Gaiety Ballroom, Ramsey

1969

This was the year of The Who's great triumph, just reward for all the hundreds of shows they'd performed together since Roger first assembled the group back in 1962. The band that started out as The Detours from Shepherd's Bush, who at one time had seen fit to play trad jazz and country and western numbers to satisfy their audiences, now bestrode the rock world like a colossus. No rock band in the world was performing better. No rock band in the world dared follow them on stage. With The Beatles unable to perform live any longer and the Stones hampered by having to introduce a new guitarist into their ranks, The Who, erstwhile bronze medallists in the Sixties British Pop Olympiad, thus shot through the gap to lead the field. For a brief shining moment – three years actually – they became the greatest of Britain's premier league rock bands, and certainly the most exciting live act in the world.

The years 1969 and 1970 were dominated by the release of *Tommy* and the tours performing the work, virtually in its entirety, to audiences throughout Britain, the US and Europe. The record received overwhelming critical acclaim and, in conjunction with the constant touring, the group achieved superstar status.

The introduction of *Tommy* into the live act coincided with a period when The Who had established a formidable system of amplification and on-stage sound. They could now vary their PA system to cover outdoor festivals and small college ballrooms and always deliver a trademark ear-splitting level of volume. But unlike a whole legion of heavy metal bands who took their cue from their pioneering "bigger-louder-wall-of-Marshall's" approach, The Who's sound always had depth, clarity and musical muscle within the decibel output. The skills of sound-engineer Bob Pridden and a commitment to developing and investing in new technology meant The Who always sounded better than all other groups. (Significantly, when most established groups were using Marshall amplifiers – which The Who had helped to develop – the band switched to a different system involving Hi-Watt, Sunn and WEM equipment.)

Pete Townshend had by now settled into using Gibson SG guitars and Hi-Watt amplifiers and speakers (two 100W amps plus one as a spare and four 4 x 12" speaker cabinets). Unlike many guitar heroes, Pete used no special effects or gadgets at all apart from a fuzz pedal: he achieved a massive range and tone of sound simply through varying the volume of the guitar pick-ups and through his unorthodox but masterly playing technique. John Entwistle took a similar approach to Pete. His bass sound also involved distortion and a high treble attack and on occasion – the introduction of 'Pinball Wizard' for instance – his bass sound actually incorporated controlled feedback. John's bass sound was so powerful, melodic and full that new listeners sometimes thought that what they were hearing was being played by Pete on the guitar. (One of John's secrets was to play every single concert with a new set of wire-wound strings to obtain the maximum twang!)

The free-form solos that were played during 1967 and 1968 as part of songs like 'Relax', 'Shakin' All Over' and 'My Generation' were phased out. Many bands were now stretching material out in this way and the novelty of a 30-minute solo/jam (of the kind most directly associated with Cream) had largely given way to boredom among audiences, although this didn't stop most rock acts continuing with this laboured approach. The Who, as ever, evolved something different. They retained one song which included a free-form solo improvisation ('Young Man Blues') which was devastating in effect, but towards the end of their shows (on songs like 'My Generation' or 'Magic Bus'), Townshend would work through a whole sequence of melodic variations and riffs, contrasting some beautifully delicate and quiet arpeggio work with some of the most powerful guitar riffs and themes ever played. These improvisations were exciting and fresh because Townshend often played them without any prior consideration or rehearsal. They seemed to be instant expressions of his musical thoughts as they were occurring.

The intuition of Keith Moon and John Entwistle was so attuned to Pete's playing that they were actually able to join in after Pete had played his phrase only once. Even Daltrey began to add vocals to these improvisations. Some of these themes grew into whole songs, such as 'Naked Eye', while others were played once when the mood took them and never repeated. 'My

Generation', from the (1970) *Live At Leeds* album, gives a perfect example of this unique approach. Show after show incorporated these improvisations – often different each night – and some of the most memorable are referred to in this text as 'improvisation', although this hardly does justice to such an inventive and inspired musical approach.

The band finished recording *Tommy* during the early part of 1969, interspersed with weekend gigs at universities and ballrooms around England. A brief foray of gigs in the north of England and Scotland ended on April 28 at Sunderland. *Tommy* was premiered on the tiny stage of Ronnie Scott's club in Soho on May 1. This was a press preview and the British music trade papers were virtually unanimous in their praise. None of the group's trademark intensity was lost but now it was focused on a coherent musical work rather than a selection of hit singles, a smattering of album tracks and various cover songs.

One week after the London début, the group began their first *Tommy* tour in the US. They opened at the Grande Ballroom just outside Detroit, and thereafter astounded audiences as they worked eastwards through the Midwest and out to California. At one show in Columbia, Maryland, they even blew opening act Led Zeppelin off the stage, the only time the two bands shared a bill.

Pete got into trouble with the law when he booted a plainclothes policeman off the stage at New York's Fillmore East on May 16. The supermarket next door had caught fire and police entered the theatre to announce that the auditorium must be evacuated. His appearance onstage was uninvited and unwanted, prompting Pete to kick him off with some assistance from Roger. They were arrested for the assault and appeared at a preliminary hearing on May 27. Released on bail, they were able to continue the tour on to the west coast before a second court appearance set for June 20.

Within a week they were back in England, playing the Royal Albert Hall on July 5 as part of the Pop Proms Programme. July and early August were spent playing various venues around Britain until the group departed again for America for just two dates, one of which was the Woodstock Festival in upstate New York. The weekend festival became a world event but the gig itself was a shambles of delayed performances, inadequate supplies and financial manipulation. Some groups were paid months in advance but The Who had to demand payment of their contracted fee just before they went onstage.

The group played at the Isle of Wight Festival on August 30 and worked around the UK through the rest of September, culminating with a superlative performance at Fairfield Halls, Croydon just southeast of London. A one-off show in Amsterdam followed, officially recorded for radio broadcast. Eleven days later the group were back in America to begin a five–week tour of theatres, colleges and ballrooms.

The second US and Canadian *Tommy* tour opened in Boston on October 10, and moved on to Dearborn, Michigan for two nights. Then The Who played an unprecedented six–night series at the Fillmore East from October 20, selling out all seats 30 days in advance. They became the first group to play to capacity houses mid–week. Clearly, they were fast outgrowing the ballroom circuit. The year ended with a five–date UK mini–tour which closed in Newcastle on the 19th.

Friday January 17
Great Hall, King's College, The Strand, London (cancelled)

This concert was originally listed in The Who Fan Club Newsletter.

Saturday January 18
Civic Hall, Nantwich

113

Sunday January 19
Mothers Club, Erdington, Birmingham

Friday January 24
Civic Hall, Wolverhampton

Saturday January 25
Middlesex Borough College, Isleworth, Middlesex
    Supported by five other acts, the group took part in this belated New Year's Ball. 8:00 pm to 'late'.

Saturday February 1
Union Ballroom, Newcastle
    Supported by Free and The Love Affair.

Sunday February 2
Coathams Hotel, Redcar
    On returning to his home in Twickenham, Pete Townshend learned of the death of Meher Baba, his spiritual guru.

Friday February 7
Top Rank Ballroom, Bristol
    A Bath University social.

Saturday February 8
Central London Polytechnic, London
    Supported by Family.

Friday February 14
Lanchester College, Coventry

Saturday February 15
Dreamland, Margate (cancelled)
    This concert was listed in The Who Fan Club Newsletter.

Friday February 21
Kinetic Circus, Birmingham
Birmingham University Social, supported by The Idle Race and The Honeybus.

Saturday February 22
Liverpool University

Sunday February 23
The Roundhouse, Chalk Farm, London
    An eight–hour extravaganza, 4 pm to midnight, with Cat Stevens, Pete Brown's Battered Ornaments, Third Ear Band, Occasional Word Ensemble on the bill with "many guests" cited to appear.

    The Who were on stage at 9:00 pm. According to Gary Herman (in his book *The Who*), the group reportedly destroyed a cardboard replica of the gates during the show's climax, in recognition of the students who had recently torn down the real gates being used to keep them out of the London School of Economics buildings on Houghton St.

Saturday March 1
Mothers Club, Erdington, Birmingham
    "We queued and grabbed the two best seats in the house," recalled John Woffinden (*Generations*, number 6). "It was an incredible show. We were so close we were literally dodging Roger's microphone when he twirled it. We smoked in those days and Keith Moon kept coming round the drums between numbers to scrounge cigarettes. He made a few disparaging remarks about the fact we could only afford Player's No.6 but he still had them. It was, of course, Roger's (25th) birthday and he actually started the wrecking when his microphone packed up. He smashed it with the mike stand and threw it at Bob Pridden,

who seemed used to such things. Townshend soon followed, rocking the stacks until the top one fell down and his guitar and feet went through it. And we all know when Roger and Pete start breaking things, Keith could become very careless. People have often said to me about the stupidity and waste of The Who smashing things up. All I can say is that this gig was the nearest I ever came to seeing The Who on auto-destruction and it was just about the most wonderfully exciting thing I've ever seen on stage, but don't expect me to be rational or logical about it. It was just incredibly exciting and you just get lost in the music and the mayhem."

Friday March 7
Technical College, Headington

Friday March 14
Corn Exchange, Cambridge

Wednesday April 2
Pavilion Ballroom, Bournemouth
Originally scheduled for Sunday March 2. Supported by The Third Ear Band and The Embers.

Monday April 7
Alexandra Palace, London (cancelled)
This concert was provisionally listed in The Who Fan Club Newsletter.

Tuesday April 22
Institute of Technology, Bolton
This is believed to be the very first public performance of *Tommy*, although some sources claim it as Glasgow three nights later.

Thursday April 24
Mayfair Ballroom, Newcastle (cancelled)

Friday April 25
Strathclyde University, Glasgow, Scotland
Supported by Jimmy James and The Vagabonds and Fred's Jazz Band.

Saturday April 26
Community Centre, Auchinleck, Scotland
Supported by The Merry Macks and Pure Greed..

Sunday April 27
Kinema Ballroom, Dunfermline, Scotland
Supported by The Shadettes.

Monday April 28
Bay Hotel, Whitley Bay, Sunderland

Thursday May 1
Ronnie Scott's Club, Soho, Central London
This press preview was a simple but effective way to launch *Tommy* before an audience of invited journalists, and guests such as Marc Bolan, Dave Dee and Ian McLagan (of the recently disbanded Small Faces). Such previews were standard practice in the world of cinema and theatre, but uncommon among rock bands. The Who gave a live performance of most of the songs from the new work, which impressed those present despite claims that the volume was excessive. The show gave a clear indication of how much better *Tommy* sounded on the stage, although at this point no one had yet heard the recorded version.

Townshend introduced *Tommy* to London for the first time from the small stage: "There is a story to the music," he said. "It's the story of Tommy... a boy who is born normal, just like you and me. Tommy is born and with the advent of war, his father goes off to fight. Tommy's mother, meanwhile, gets randy and takes a lover. One day, Tommy sees something he shouldn't and is told to keep quiet about it. He witnessed a murder. The shock causes him to go deaf, dumb and blind." Some journalists then jokily suggested

that this was sick, echoing Tony Blackburn's sentiments on the BBC. "No, it's not sick, ha, ha," continued Pete. "Contrary to what one hears on Auntie. I think Auntie is the sickest thing in this country... The next scene introduces Tommy to Gypsy the Acid Queen, who declares that she will take him into a room for a while and make a man out of a boy. He is later raped by his uncle and

> And in a generous, unprecedented hour long show for the press and pop industry held at London's Ronnie Scott Club, the Who gained an excited reaction from critics.
>
> The group played selections from their controversial opera, which has been branded as "sick" in some quarters.
>
> As enormous speaker cabinets were piled high along the walls of the club and hummed ominously at the assembled throng, Pete drily explained the story line.
>
> "It's about a boy who is born normal, just like you and me. Then he witnesses a murder and becomes deaf, dumb and blind."
>
> "He is later raped by his uncle and gets turned on to LSD as has been explained in various in-depth interviews.
>
> "It's not sick — contrary to what one hears on Aunty. I think Aunty is the sickest thing in this country" (Applause).

gets turned on to LSD... Following this episode, Tommy becomes renowned as a Pinball Wizard and becomes the hero of the younger generation."

Lon Goddard reported in *Record Mirror* (May 10) that "The Who gave us a good solid hour's worth of quality listening and excellent showmanship." And Chris Welch wrote of the occasion in *Melody Maker* (May 10) that "as enormous speaker cabinets were piled high along the walls of the club and hummed ominously at the assembled throng, Pete dryly explained the story line... In the confined space of Ronnie Scott's club which is more accustomed to the refined rhythms of jazz, the overwhelming intensity of The Who's

performance left scores of people literally deaf... Despite the discomfort of those nearest the speakers, nobody wanted to miss a minute of the group's riveting rave-up, which included their classic versions of 'Shakin' All Over' and 'Summertime Blues'... As a playing group The Who seem to be at their best ever with a sudden spurt of activity in recent months almost amounting to a Renaissance... Some might call Keith's playing destructive and tasteless and their volume crippling and cruel. Both are vital ingredients to The Who, a group who must surely be hailed as one of the mainstays of British pop. They may be loved or hated. We can't do without 'em.'"

Friday May 9
The Grande Ballroom, Dearborn, Michigan
    The Who's embarked on their first *Tommy* tour, opening with a three–night stand in Dearborn. The first night saw a 90 minute show with Joe Cocker & The Grease Band in support. Pete's old friend, former Ealing Art College room mate and one time Who road–manager, Tom Wright, was now the manager of the Grande.

Saturday May 10
The Grande Ballroom, Dearborn, Michigan
    The Who broke all previous attendance records during the three–night stand at the Grande.

Sunday May 11
The Grande Ballroom, Dearborn, Michigan

Tuesday May 13
The Boston Tea Party, Boston, Massachusetts
    The Who's first appearances at the city's premier 'underground' ballroom. Jazz artist Roland Kirk was the supporting act for the three gigs here.

Wednesday May 14
The Boston Tea Party, Boston, Massachusetts

Thursday May 15
The Boston Tea Party, Boston, Massachusetts

Friday May 16
The Fillmore East, New York
    The Who returned to New York in sensational fashion for a three night stand at the Fillmore

East. At about 10:30 pm during the first of two shows on Friday, a fire started in the neighbouring Lion Supermarket which completely gutted the store and a five story apartment building. When the fire broke out Fillmore East promoter Bill Graham was informed and he prepared to make a low-key announcement. At this point The Who were about half-way through their first set when from out of nowhere a man wearing a sports coat and slacks suddenly appeared on stage and tried to commandeer one of the microphones. Assuming he was a heckler, Pete and Roger quickly booted him off the stage.

It turned out that the man was Daniel Mulhearn, a plainclothes member of the elite Tactical Police Force, who had been sent into the Fillmore building to warn the crowd about the fire. Thanks to Pete and Roger the announcement was never made – if it had there might have been a potentially disastrous panic – and the show was completed as normal, though the second performance was cancelled as a safety precaution. Around midnight the police turned up backstage to form a line-up for officer Mulhearn to identify his 'assailants'.

The next day, Kit Lambert turned up at the 9th precinct to explain to the police what had happened. They were unsympathetic and wanted to charge Pete and Roger with felonious assault, and Lambert spent until showtime that day arguing their case. (It is amusing to consider Lambert, a chain-smoking English eccentric with an exaggerated Oxford accent, arguing with street-wise cops in one of New York's busiest precincts!) Finally Roger was released without charge but Pete faced charges of third degree assault and was arraigned for a court appearance on May 27.

About', 'There's A Doctor', 'Go To The Mirror', 'Smash The Mirror', 'I'm Free', 'Tommy's Holiday Camp', 'We're Not Gonna' Take It', 'See Me, Feel Me'), 'Summertime Blues', Shakin' All Over', 'Magic Bus'.

Heralded by the tremendous guitar extravaganza of 'Heaven And Hell', in which Pete played some brilliant solos, and a non-stop charge through the bulk of *Tommy* – which most of the audience hadn't yet heard – The Who were back in New York with a vengeance. Long-time Who admirer Fred Kirby commented in *Billboard* (May 31): "A remarkable, dynamic group whose electricity never lets up. Roger Daltrey's vocals are as strong as anyone's in the field, whilst Townshend still is a formidable challenger to the title of the most exciting guitarist around. Moon, at times a comic performer-conductor, ranks among the upper echelon of rock drummers. John Entwistle, not as animated as his three colleagues, is one of the steadiest of bass guitarists... Moon's remarkable ending brought the large audience to its feet. Half of his drum set fell over, but he kept playing. He carried one snare drum onto the stage and played it. Before the show ended, this drum and cymbal were sent flying... The Who is unique in today's musical scene."

Sunday May 18
The Fillmore East, New York

The group played the first of two shows at 3 pm, a make-up gig for Friday night's postponement of the second show caused by the fire in the building next door. Jimi Hendrix was in the audience to hear *Tommy* for the first time. The Fillmore itself sustained only a scorched marquee so there was no interruption to other scheduled shows.

England's the Who suggests feeding time at the zoo

Saturday May 17
The Fillmore East, New York, two shows, 8 and 11:30 pm

Set: 'Heaven And Hell', 'I Can't Explain', 'Young Man Blues', *Tommy*: ('It's A Boy', '1921', 'Amazing Journey', 'Sparks', 'Eyesight To The Blind', 'Christmas', 'Acid Queen', 'Pinball Wizard', 'Do You Think It's Alright', 'Fiddle

Monday May 19
The Rockpile, Toronto, Ontario, Canada

An audience of 2,500 fans saw the first of two shows in Toronto. Set: 'Heaven And Hell', 'I Can't Explain', 'Young Man Blues', 'It's A Boy', '1921', 'Amazing Journey', 'Sparks', 'Pinball Wizard', 'Substitute', 'I'm A Boy', 'Shakin' All Over', 'Magic Bus', improvisations.

A short set was played on this occasion, including only the first half of *Tommy*. 'Heaven And Hell' seemed to fall apart during the guitar solo, probably due to bad sound monitoring. Someone in the audience shouted "happy birthday" to Pete, who was celebrating his 24th birthday. Later in the show, Pete made a few sarcastic comments about The Guess Who, claiming that they (The Who) had taught the Canadian band 'Shakin' All Over' (with which The Guess Who had had a hit), but Pete conceded that they were "nice guys really". The most impressive and unusual part of the set was 'Magic Bus', which began with a long succession of improvised guitar riffs, and continued in this unorthodox mode throughout, ending with Townshend de-tuning his guitar and inducing feedback. The guitar improvisation during this unconventional show was recklessly breathtaking.

Wednesday May 21
Capitol Theatre, Ottawa, Ontario, Canada (cancelled)

The Who missed this date, the result of Keith's bout with bronchial pneumonia and their equipment having failed to arrive from Toronto.

Friday May 23
The Electric Factory, Philadelphia, Pennsylvania

Saturday May 24
The Electric Factory, Philadelphia, Pennsylvania

Sunday May 25
Merriweather Post Pavilion, Columbia, Maryland

Set included: 'Heaven And Hell', 'I Can't Explain', 'Fortune Teller', *Tommy* (17 songs, as May 17), 'Summertime Blues', 'Shakin' All Over', 'Magic Bus', improvisation.

A capacity crowd jammed this outdoor amphitheatre near Washington DC. to see The Who steal the show from the then up-and-coming Led Zeppelin.

This was undoubtedly one of the best concerts of the tour, with the band rocking hard and furiously from the moment they hit the stage at 10.15 pm. Pete told the audience: "It's been a good evening... This is a good place to play. And we're going to finish up tonight with... It's been long enough, it'll keep you away from the restroom... It's a song which kind of works out better on the stage than it did on record. Before we go we'd like to remind you of Led Zeppelin, remind you what they did to you this evening... spitting all over the place and all that mess. Anyway, it's not meant to insult anybody. This is 'Magic Bus'." This concluding song moved into the three-chord coda that would later be incorporated into 'Naked Eye', and then Pete smashed his guitar.

Richard Cowan witnessed the show and wrote in the *Washington Post* (May 27): "The Who performed to a packed hall, field and parking lot. *Tommy*... is beautiful. Pete Townshend is a writer of such talent that might only be overshadowed by his luxurious excellence on the guitar. Though not possessed of a blues background, he is forceful on stage and on plastic... It was this and the cooperation of Daltrey, Moon and Entwistle which stole the show on Sunday, not the Armageddon of the finale."

Guitar smashed: Gibson SG

Thursday May 29
The Kinetic Playground, Chicago, Illinois

The Who combined their two scheduled shows into one, giving a 90 minute performance of *Tommy* on this first night in Chicago. The show was deemed "one of the best at the Playground, or anywhere, in a long time". The two billed shows were lumped into one because, according to Pete "not enough of you **** [expletive unknown!] showed up", quoted Lew Harris in his review in the *Chicago Tribune* (May 30). Harris went on to say that "everything about their performance was remarkable. Peter Townshend... had better control of his guitar than almost any other performer we've seen... They had remarkable control. And remarkable knowledge of what they were doing at every second".

In the days of booking an eclectic mix of artists on the same bill, Buddy Rich & The Buddy Rich Orchestra and Joe Cocker & The Grease Band were the supporting acts. According to the *Chicago Tribune*, Rich and his orchestra "got two much deserved standing ovations" and Rich's drum solo "was interrupted four times by ovations".

Friday May 30
The Kinetic Playground, Chicago, Illinois
The same bill also appeared on this night.

Saturday May 31
The Kinetic Playground, Chicago, Illinois
Joe Cocker & The Grease Band were joined by a local band called Soup on the last night in Chicago.

Sunday June 1
Kiel Auditorium, St. Louis

Thursday June 5
The Fillmore East, New York; two shows, 8 and 11:30 pm
The "new revised schedule" brought The Who back to the Fillmore East for two nights, supported by Chuck Berry and bluesman Albert King.

Friday June 6
The Fillmore East, New York, two shows, 8 and 11:30 pm
The Detroit Fifth Estate listed The Who to appear with The Crazy World of Arthur Brown and Dr. John at the Detroit State Fairgrounds at 3 pm on this day but The Who were definitely in New York for their second night at the Fillmore.

Billed as the "triumphant return of The Who, the 8 pm set included 'Heaven And Hell', 'Substitute', 'Eyesight To The Blind', 'Christmas', 'Acid Queen', 'Magic Bus', improvisations. The 11.30 pm set included 'Young Man Blues', 'It's A Boy', '1921', 'Amazing Journey', 'Sparks', 'Pinball Wizard', 'We're Not Gonna Take It', 'See Me, Feel Me', 'Substitute', 'Summertime Blues', 'Shakin' All Over'.

Before the first set, Pete said how happy he was to share a bill with Chuck Berry and Albert King, then declared that – in contrast – The Who played "English rock music". During the intro to 'Magic Bus', Townshend played a few Chuck Berry-style guitar figures as a tribute to one of his heroes. This song emerged as the tour-de-force of the evening, moving into a variety of improvised riffs.

"Tommy" is another story in itself. It is about a deaf, mute, and blind child who lives in an electric experience, and tries to share his experience with the masses, who refuse it. That is, of course, a vast oversimplification. The feeling and the sounds created by the opera must be learned first hand.

The second set prompted many calls from the audience for *Tommy*. Townshend introduced this by saying: "If there's anything that we miss from the album – sorry! But we're trying to concentrate the energy into the juicy little lump that we're gonna play you, and get it to mean the same thing, we hope. We obviously can't play the whole thing because we don't know it all, you see!" More bizarrely, a member of the audience was heard to shout out "Led Zeppelin sucks, chaps!" (Led Zeppelin had played at the Fillmore East the previous week).

Saturday June 7
Majestic Hills Theater, Lake Geneva, Wisconsin

The group returned to southern Wisconsin to appear at this outdoor venue where they had first appeared in August 1968.

Sunday June 8
Tyrone Guthrie Theater, Minneapolis, Minnesota

WALKER ART CENTER PRESENTS

THE WHO

ROGER DALTREY — Singer
PETE TOWNSHEND — Guitar
KEITH MOON — Drums
JOHN ENTWISTLE — Bass

ALSO

KOERNER, RAY AND GLOVER

TWO PERF. SUNDAY
JUNE 8, 7 & 9:30 P.M.

GUTHRIE THEATRE

TICKETS: $5.15-$4.15-$3.10
at Dayton's, Discount Records
in Dinkytown, Guthrie.

The Who played an abbreviated show here in the second of two appearances, performing for a mere 45 minutes (and only six songs from *Tommy*). After this date, the tour took a four-day break.

Friday June 13
'The Magic Circus', Hollywood Palladium, Los Angeles, California

Set: 'Heaven And Hell', 'I Can't Explain', 'Fortune Teller', 'Tattoo', 'Young Man Blues', *Tommy* (17 songs, as May 17), 'Substitute', 'Summertime Blues', 'Shakin' All Over', 'Magic Bus'.

Opening a new venue, Roger Daltrey commented that it was good to play in Los Angeles, especially at the Shrine, which had now closed down. The full 17 song version of *Tommy* was here unveiled on the West Coast for the first time, and The Who dazzled the audience of 6,000 with a lengthy segment, playing for well in excess of two hours. Opening acts were country rock group Poco and The Bonzo Dog Band.

Tuesday June 17
The Fillmore West, San Francisco, California

The group played a shortened set in the first show (about half an hour!) but came back in the second show and included massive segments from *Tommy*. Also on the bill were Woody Herman and The New Third Herd, the famous big band of the Forties, who according to newspaper reports, "won over the Fillmore crowd in the first show, receiving a final cheer considerably longer than The Who whose abruptly brief initial showing had annoyed everyone, including producer Bill Graham".

Wednesday June 18
The Fillmore West, San Francisco, California

Set: 'Heaven And Hell', 'I Can't Explain', 'Young Man Blues', 'Fortune Teller', 'Tattoo', *Tommy* (17 songs, as May 17), 'Summertime Blues', 'Shakin' All Over', 'Magic Bus'.

The first part of this show wasn't quite as together as usual, causing Townshend to comment that "we came on the stage the wrong side of bed!", prior to playing *Tommy*. After the rock opera, The Who played a few raw rock'n'roll songs to show that the band hadn't moved away from their roots and that *Tommy* wasn't the sum

Thursday June 19

The Fillmore West, San Francisco, California

Set: 'Heaven And Hell', 'I Can't Explain', 'Fortune Teller', 'Tattoo', 'Young Man Blues', *Tommy* (17 songs, as May 17), 'Boris The Spider', 'Summertime Blues', 'Shakin' All Over', 'Magic Bus', improvisations.

Before the Who commenced playing the last of the three nights at Fillmore West, Pete stepped to the microphone: "Before we start, but it will be a complete... set!" 'Young Man Blues' was an early highlight, having by now lost its jazzy feel to become a blistering heavy rock extravaganza, featuring some of Pete's most breakneck guitar soloing. Following this, Townshend introduced *Tommy*: "We'd like to play our latest album now... and we'd like to apologise for any tracks anybody particularly came to hear which we don't play. We play most of it. We don't play 'Sally Simpson' or the 'Overture' but we play a sensible, generous amount..." *Tommy* was performed very well, with good singing and instrumental work, followed by the high energy rock-'n'roll of 'Summertime Blues' and 'Shakin' All Over'. A fine version of 'Magic Bus' was played – a hypnotising Bo Diddley boogie building into a prolonged thrash of total noise. Roger Daltrey added some excellent mouth-organ playing, concluding with the guitar figure that would later become 'Naked Eye', with Pete improvising on vocals.

At the end of the concert, Townshend explained why the band couldn't play an encore: "When we were last at the Fillmore in New York we had a bit of a problem with an alleged police officer and tomorrow morning at 9 o'clock we've got to be in court in New York." The audience called for more music. "No way," said Pete. "We've gotta catch a plane at 11:30. We've really gotta go. Thanks very much."

Allan McDougall wrote in *Melody Maker* (June 28): "The Who gave perhaps the performance of their lives... they are great, great musicians and singers. The love between them and San Francisco is reciprocal." So ended a triumphant tour that had seen only one smashed guitar and no performances of 'My Generation'.

Roger and Pete made a mad dash for the airport right after the show and flew all night to reach New York in time for a 9 am court appearance over the scuffle on stage at the Fillmore East

---

The Who is still one of the most exciting rock bands.

For three or four years now, the British group has been known for its cataclysmic stage act that ends with the destruction of guitars and drums in a burst of electronic thunder. They seldom do this now, but they still crash on. Take for instance, their Friday concert at the Fillmore East. The drummer, Keith Moon, beats away double-time, sweating and gulping air like a beached guppy. The lead singer, Roger Daltry, waves arms and twirls the mike over his head; and Peter Townshend, who blasts feedback and other distortions, while doing high lead riffs on guitar, sounds like two or three people playing at once. Add to this his much-imitated movement of swinging his arm in a full circle, hitting the strings on the way around, making sudden splits and leaps into the air—all without missing a note.

The only sedate bit comes from the bassist, John Entwistle, who just stands to one side and plays, barely moving his fingers, vaguely amused by it all, while his friends fly around.

---

total of the band's vision of rock music. As Pete explained from the stage while introducing 'Summertime Blues': "We're gonna play some music which isn't really what the opera is all about. The opera's an optimistic view, and what we're talking about is a pessimistic view – this is rock'n'roll. Youth... A song written by the original teenybopper Eddie Cochran." The concluding 'Magic Bus' was preceded by an amusing tale by Keith Moon about how he came to get the two blocks of wood that form the percussion for the first part of the song.

on May 16. Charges against Roger were dropped but Pete was fined $75.

Saturday July 5
The Pop Proms, Royal Albert Hall, London

The Who's first appearance at this world famous venue, sharing the bill with Chuck Berry for two performances, 5:30 and 8:30 pm. These concerts concluded the seven–day 'Pop Proms' series that had opened on Sunday June 29 with Led Zeppelin.

> Saturday, July 5th, at 5.30 and 8.30 p.m.
>
> # THE WHO
> # MR. CHUCK BERRY
> ## BODAST
>
> Tickets:
> 5.30 p.m. 25/-, 20/-, 15/-, 10/-, 5/-
> 8.30 p.m. 30/-, 25/-, 21/-, 15/-, 10/6, 5/-

Chuck Berry had questioned The Who's top billing above him (he had already topped the bill himself at the previous Pop Prom the night before) and was allowed to close the early show. As this date coincided with The Rolling Stones' famous free concert in Hyde Park in the afternoon, a large number of teddy boys and Rockers had turned up for the final show at the Albert Hall to catch Chuck Berry. This small but vocal minority made clear their hostility towards The Who as old memories of Mod/Rocker rivalries lived on. The Who came onstage for the final set and Townshend – appreciating Berry's act – said "we'll be reliving our past too".

As the music began, the Rockers started to throw beer cans, sharpened pennies and other missiles at the stage, and became more incensed. The Albert Hall management (sensing that a riot was incipient) called the police. Townshend appealed to the disruptive elements in the crowd to be less narrow-minded: "Listen, we dig Chuck Berry too. Yeah, we dig Chuck. Now you dig us!"

The majority of the audience applauded this comment. Meanwhile, dozens of policemen appeared in the aisles and were watching carefully. "My favourite piece of rock'n'roll," Pete said. "This is American music played in an English manner" and in order to eliminate the imagined divisions in music, The Who launched into 'Summertime Blues'. The heavy police presence prevented any serious violence but the show had a very menacing and uneasy atmosphere, and the stage was almost overrun by unimpressed, drape-jacketed, DA'd greasers.

Richard Neville, the editor of *Oz*, recollected in *Play Power* (1970): "Accompanied by an overdose of decibels, megacycles and multi-kilowatts, The Who screamed into action... In genuine rage, Townshend smashed his guitar, pummelled the giant amplifiers, and finally stormed off stage." However, Valerie Wilmer writing in *Down Beat* (January 22, 1970) claimed otherwise: "Fortunately The Who have given up the destruction ritual which would in the past have had Townshend battering his guitar wilfully into an amplifier for the finale. Instead they gave us a fine extended version of 'Magic Bus', complete with free improvisation from the arms-whirling-like-a-windmill Townshend and Moon's cheery tornado... in my book they are second only to The Beatles when it comes to originality. They have their bad days, but at this particular concert they were not far from their best."

FIRST LONDON GALA POP FESTIVAL 1969 ROYAL ALBERT HALL OFFICIAL SOUVENIR 1'6

Reviewing the show for *Melody Maker* (July 12), Tony Wilson wrote: "The Who played some excellent music. Most of their act was taken up with their pop-opera *Tommy* which must rank as one of the finest pieces of progressive rock ever written, standing musically head and shoulders above a lot of what is misguidedly called 'progressive' today."

Saturday July 19
Mothers Club, Erdington, Birmingham

The Who's third appearance at this 'underground' club in a little over seven months. Keith collapsed due to the oppressive heat inside the packed club and was taken backstage to recover. After about an hour, the show continued.

Sunday July 20
Pier Ballroom, Hastings

Sunday July 27
Coathams Hotel, Redcar

Monday July 28
Bay Hotel, Whitley Bay, Sunderland

Saturday August 2
Winter Garden, Eastbourne

Following this gig The Who travelled the length of England for one gig in Carlisle and then all the way back down again for a gig in Bath.

Sunday August 3
Cosmopolitan Ballroom, Carlisle

Monday August 4
The Pavilion, Bath

Thursday August 7
Assembly Hall, Worthing

Saturday August 9
Plumpton Racecourse, Lewes, Sussex

The Who headlined the third night of the four-day annual festival. Among the supporting acts were Chicken Shack, Fat Mattress, Yes, Aynsley Dunbar's Retaliation, and King Crimson during the evening performances, 7:30 to 11:30 pm.

Set included: 'Heaven And Hell', 'I Can't Explain', 'Fortune Teller', *Tommy* (17 songs, as May 17), 'Summertime Blues', 'Shakin' All Over', 'My Generation'.

This was The Who's third (and final) appearance at the National Jazz And Blues Festival (also known as the Marquee Festival and soon to become the Reading Festival) and their first outdoor appearance in the UK since 1966. They delivered a powerful set and proved themselves able to handle large outdoor festivals with ease, having a huge, loud sound and a commanding stage presence.

Casually dressed in blue jeans and a T-shirt (instead of his white boiler suit), Pete introduced *Tommy* as follows: "At this time we'd like to play the majority of the tracks from our latest album called *Tommy*. It's our rock opera thing and it takes about three quarters of an hour to wade through and then you can catch your last buses to East Grinstead! Seriously, is this the last day? Anyway, despite the fact that this isn't the last day, I'm sure you've all had a nice time. I know they had to dig Keith up from a trench somewhere out in the borders because he came a bit too early and had a bit too much 'fun'! He seems to be all right now, though. Anyway, this is *Tommy* and this is the life of the deaf, dumb and blind boy, things that happen to him when he's a kid, and the good things that happen to him when he gets a little bit older and what happens to the people that love him and that kinda scene. It's something which should be very much clapped when we've finished... I'd like to just co-ordinate myself with the bass player over there... Oh, incidentally, John, your flies are undone... Chicken Shack told me to tell you, 'fuck the amplifiers!' This is *Tommy*, thank you." 'My Generation' had been reintroduced into the act during the past few British gigs.

Richard Green noted in *New Musical Express* (August 16): "They are still one of the world's loudest groups. It's quite possible that the villages around Plumpton Racecourse could have sat in their living rooms and listened to the group. But the loudness did not disguise the quality of the playing which has increased tremendously... All the guitar smashing and mike throwing was included and The Who looked pleased with the way things were going – both musically and visually. The visual bit got even better when a girl in a revealing dress came on stage during 'Summertime Blues' and began cavorting about... An unqualified hit."

Guitar smashed: Gibson SG

Tuesday August 12
Tanglewood Music Shed, Lenox, Massachusetts

The Who flew to America for two gigs only - Tanglewood and the Woodstock Festival. The first was this outdoor show, staged by Bill Graham as part of a new Contemporary Trends series of concerts. More than 23,000 people saw a performance that included much of *Tommy* in the set. The show closed with 'Summertime Blues' and 'My Generation'. Said Fred Kirby in *Billboard* (August 23): "The Who built excitement as they got into the *Tommy* selections. By the time they reached the single 'Pinball Wizard', they were devastating in effect. Townshend's guitar playing, as usual, was top notch and joined with Roger Daltrey in the effective lyrics."

Bluesman B.B. King played the opening set while The Who took the middle slot before headliners Jefferson Airplane.

Sunday August 17
Woodstock Music & Arts Fair, Max Yasgur's Farm, Bethel, New York

Set: 'Heaven And Hell', 'I Can't Explain', *Tommy* (17 songs, as May 17), 'Summertime Blues', 'Shakin' All Over', 'My Generation', improvisation.

The Who appeared at the legendary Woodstock Festival which seemed to signal the end of the Aquarian Age rather than its beginning. The group were scheduled to perform on Saturday night, August 16, but did not actually take the stage until about 4 am on Sunday August 17. While waiting to take the stage they had inadvertently sipped drinks that were spiked with LSD, and were in a foul mood as a result. Such matters were not detrimental to their set which was widely regarded as the one of the highlights of the festival. It ended as the sun came up, providing a perfect setting for Pete's climactic gesture - casually tossing his guitar into the crowd (which was apparently later retrieved by a member of the stage crew.)

Taking the stage in darkness, Pete immediately kicked film director Michael Wadleigh off the stage, thinking him to be some tardy stage hand. John Morris then announced: "Will you please warmly show your appreciation... A group who came to us specially for this festival. Please warmly welcome… The Who!" A shortened set was offered, played well-enough, and Pete certainly warmed up during 'Sparks', but the gig lacked the intimacy and vitality of their usual concerts. The band made few attempts to talk to the audience, and immediately following 'Pinball Wizard', Abbie Hoffman stepped up to Townshend's microphone, yelling "I think this is a pile of shit while John Sinclair rots in prison." Townshend then smashed Hoffman in the head with his guitar, and he fled the stage pouring with blood. "I can dig it," Pete sarcastically offered, to jibes from the audience.

After the next song, Townshend issued a warning while tuning up: "The next fucking person who walks across this stage is going to get fucking killed! You can laugh. I mean it!" Although this aggression went against the spirit of the event, good vibes were restored by the sun rising to coincide with 'I'm Free' and the end of *Tommy*. 'Summertime Blues' restored a manic intensity and 'Shakin' All Over' positively throbbed with energy, with John's bass riffs matching the guitar for distorted sonic power. The group returned for an encore ("we knew we were gonna come back and do it!" Pete said arrogantly) with the concluding 'My Generation' ("This is kinda our hymn," said Pete. "It's a song about you and me, we're getting a bit older now"), which went into the 'Naked Eye' riffs which Townshend ended with a passage of feedback and soloing before bashing his guitar several times onto the stage. He then unplugged it, threw it into the audience and the group walked off. The Who had contributed a rare and unadulterated shot of high-energy British rock'n'roll to an event that smacked of American diversity and (in some cases) indulgence. They flew back to New York City by helicopter immediately after the show.

The documentary film *Woodstock* appeared a year later and The Who were featured with 'See Me, Feel Me' (also on the soundtrack album) and 'Summertime Blues'. *The Kids Are Alright* included further footage of 'Pinball Wizard' and 'Sparks'. Finally, the 1993 television series *Woodstock Diary* added 'My Generation' to the canon.

In the notes that accompanied *Thirty Years Of Maximum R&B*, The Who's 4-CD retrospective box set released in 1994, Pete commented on the Abbie Hoffman incident (which, it appears, wasn't filmed): "What Abbie was saying was politically correct in many ways – the people at Woodstock really were a bunch of hypocrites claiming a cosmic revolution simply because they took over a field, broke down some fences, imbibed bad acid and then tried to run out without paying the band. All while John Sinclair rotted in jail after a trumped-up drug bust. My response was reflexive rather than considered. Later I realised his humiliation on that occasion was fatal to his political credibility."

In subsequent interviews over the years, all of The Who, especially Townshend, would make disparaging remarks about Woodstock and their contribution to it. "Fucking awful," was their most common observation.

Friday August 22
Music Hall, Shrewsbury

Saturday August 23
Grays Festival Marquee, Brentwood Road, Grays, Essex (cancelled)

Although this event went on as planned, Keith had broken his foot in a fall at home and was unable to play. The Who went to the event to apologise to the crowd for not being able to perform.

Friday August 29
The Pavilion, Bournemouth

Set: 'Heaven And Hell', 'I Can't Explain', 'Fortune Teller', 'Tattoo', 'Young Man Blues', *Tommy* (17 songs, as May 17), 'Substitute', 'Summertime Blues', 'Shakin' All Over', 'My Generation'.

Slotted in en route to the Isle of Wight, this booking at nearby Bournemouth was a handy warm-up show that attracted those festival-goers who didn't make it to the island. 'Young Man Blues' featured improvised soloing that stretched out to 10 minutes. Introducing *Tommy*, Pete said: "It's quite an ordeal, particularly for people who don't like it 'cause it's quite long. And for those of you who like it, it's very nice..." *Tommy* was followed by a great version of 'Substitute', which was received with wild applause, and the concluding 'My Generation' extended into some extravagant guitar soloing from Townshend.

Saturday August 30
Isle of Wight Festival

The Who gave a triumphant performance at the second Isle of Wight Festival supporting the first major appearance in three years by Bob Dylan & The Band. The following year they were headlining the Festival. Among the other acts on this day's bill were Joe Cocker & The Grease Band, Family, Marsha Hunt & White Trash, Aynsley Dunbar's Retaliation, The Pretty Things, Blodwyn Pig, Gypsy, Free, Blonde on Blonde, King Crimson and the Edgar Broughton Band. Keith had to have a painkilling injection in his ankle to play the drums, and by all accounts, gave an incredible performance in spite of his broken foot.

The set: 'Heaven and Hell', 'I Can't Explain', 'Fortune Teller', 'Tattoo', 'Young Man Blues', 'It's A Boy', '1921', 'Amazing Journey', 'Eyesight To The Blind', 'Christmas', 'Acid Queen', 'Pinball Wizard', 'Do You Think It's Alright', 'Fiddle About', 'There's A Doctor', 'Go To The Mirror', 'Smash The Mirror', 'I'm Free', 'Tommy's Holiday Camp', 'We're Not Gonna Take It', 'Substitute', 'Summertime Blues', 'Shakin' All Over', 'My Generation', 'Naked Eye'.

The PA system was the largest that had ever been assembled at that point and Pete joked that it was built from Meccano. For The Who's set, signs were erected on the speakers warning people to keep at least 15 feet away. The band played a fine version of *Tommy*: tight, hard and frantic. At one point, Townshend asked the audience: "Has Joe Cocker played yet? Well, I can tell you something. There's a change taking place and I should imagine that he's gonna be very, very, very exciting to you all. We played a couple of times with him in the States on our last tour and I mean he was absolutely incredible and I think he will probably be the high spot of the evening. Anyway, keep your eyes and ears open for Joe Cocker."

Throughout the set, various members of the audience were yelling at the band to tell other members of the audience to sit down, pleas to which the band did not respond. Prior to *Tommy*, Pete told the audience: "You look quite a lot from the air, you know. There's quite a lot of you from the air. Probably more of you from the air than there is, 'cause you can see all the tents an' all. Our manager hired a nice helicopter for us to ride in and when it landed it did something terrible to its rear end. My faith in the aeronautic world rapidly dwindled and I think I'll swim home."

Saturday September 6
Kinema Ballroom, Dunfermline, Scotland

Supported by Alan Jordan and The Shadettes.

Sunday September 7
Cosmopolitan Club, Carlisle

Saturday September 13
The Belfry, Sutton Coldfield

TOWNSHEND: wild

John Woffinden recollected that "The Herd were on the same bill... and when they'd finished my mate and I decided to go for a walk and get some fresh air. We stepped outside and were run into by Keith Moon! The Who were coming straight on, and we finished up next to Pete's speaker stack. Deafened for a week but a great view!" (*Generations*, number 11, January 1994).

Sunday September 21
Fairfield Halls, Croydon

Set: 'Heaven And Hell', 'I Can't Explain', 'Fortune Teller', 'Tattoo', 'Young Man Blues', 'A Quick One, While He's Away', 'Substitute', 'Happy Jack', 'I'm A Boy', *Tommy*: ('Overture', 'It's A Boy', '1921', 'Amazing Journey', 'Sparks', 'Eyesight To The Blind', 'Christmas', 'Acid

> AN OPERA at a pop concert? It seems hard to believe, yet The Who managed to get away with it at the Fairfield Hall, on Sunday.
>
> But then The Who have grown up, and the opera was their "Tommy" album—said to be their best-ever long-player.
>
> The group's performance was far more professional than in the past. It was also less wild.
>
> Of course Roger Daltrey hurled his microphone around; Keith Moon managed to splinter a few drumsticks, and Peter Townshend thrashed his guitar about his body; John Entwistle was very placid—he is usually the quietest of the four anyway.
>
> But when they wearily trekked away from the bright lights to their dressing rooms, all their instruments had survived. Apparently they have realised there is no need to smash up their equipment.

Queen', 'Pinball Wizard', 'Do You Think It's Alright', 'Fiddle About', 'Tommy Can You Hear Me?', 'There's A Doctor', 'Go To The Mirror', 'Smash The Mirror', 'Miracle Cure', 'Sally Simpson', 'I'm Free', 'Tommy's Holiday Camp', 'We're Not Gonna Take It', 'See Me, Feel Me'), 'Summertime Blues', 'Shakin' All Over', 'My Generation', 'See Me, Feel Me', improvisations, 'Magic Bus'.

Playing in a renowned classical music venue without, for the first time a support act, The Who stretched out their performance to an incredible length, including a comprehensive survey of their past triumphs, and even included 'A Quick One' as the acknowledged forerunner of *Tommy*, to which four songs had now been added. During 'Young Man Blues', Daltrey injected some topical lines about the Piccadilly squatters. "I hope you won't be bored," said Pete, before launching into the 'Overture' for the first time on stage. Tommy was also embellished with back projections of the album sleeve graphics behind the stage. These occasionally missed their cues.

The rich acoustics of the hall – most famously used for recording symphony orchestras – resulted in a superb sound quality, courtesy also, of course, of the unparalleled skills of Bob Pridden at the mixing desk. A standing ovation brought the group back on stage for 'Magic Bus'.

Townshend rated this show as his favourite ever performance of *Tommy*. He recalled: "The best performance of all was at Croydon, Fairfield Hall. It was the first time we played it including 'Sally Simpson' and a few other things we did specially. The sound in that place – oh, Croydon, I could bloody play there all night... It is just a good acoustic. It's as though the whole place was designed so that you could hear the conductor banging on his rostrum and not the orchestra. It's a freak but it's great for rock." *Zigzag* (number 44, August 1974.)

Elton John was present in the audience and noted in his diary that The Who were "excellent". K.A. in the *Croydon Advertiser* (September 26) wrote: "An excellent evening, with far more professional entertainment than offered by the average pop concert. It was made even more enjoyable by the sophisticated behaviour of the enthusiastic audience." In *Melody Maker*, Alan Lewis gave the group one of their greatest write-ups (September 27): "Forget the supergroups. The

matic start to the rock opera. Pete explained from the stage that The Who had decided to give *Tommy* its opera house premiere in Amsterdam simply because the band thought it a great city and more representative of a European capital than London. 'Amazing Journey' was wonderfully charged and powerful, and Roger provided some fine singing. This moved into the instrumental 'Sparks' at a furious pace, with John Entwistle providing some manic bass lines.

The audience response, perhaps befitting the venue, consisted of polite applause rather than overt cheers and whistles. "We want to thank you very kindly and we'd like to play for you as our going away present, a song from the past that we still really mean," said Pete, before the final number. 'My Generation' was newly conceived as a 15-minute medley offering a short 'history' of the band in a seamless flow of music from the 1965 anthem to the reprise of *Tommy*, followed by several improvised passages, snatches of 'Pinball Wizard' and 'The Ox', the latter prompted by a furious drum roll from Keith Moon, climaxing with screeching guitar solos and crashing riffs. Also during this medley, Pete played several beautiful and delicate passages of guitar to link the various sections, although much of this song was entirely spontaneous and at several points John Entwistle and Keith Moon seemed to lose track of what Pete was playing. The riff that was later incorporated into 'Naked Eye' was presented very distinctly as 'So Very Long' (an assumed title) which Roger sang as a farewell message.

The two-hour show that The Who presented at this time took the band's performance to new heights of excitement and excellence. Yet it wasn't a show rehearsed to the point of sterility - it sounded raucous and fresh, despite the fact that the band were capable of turning in performances this good night after night.

Who are now the band against which the rest of rock must be judged. Their two-hour concert... was a shattering tour-de-force. It was exciting, moving, frightening – and musically brilliant... Their message is excitement and the violent beauty of their performance said everything about youth, rock and revolution. This was surely their finest appearance to date. The acoustics were perfect, the sound came over with stunning clarity, and the group were so together they seemed to be sharing the same nervous system... if they never play another note they have earned their place as the most dynamic group of them all."

Monday September 29
Concertgebouw, Amsterdam, the Netherlands
The Who's first performance of *Tommy* for a European audience - professionally recorded for Dutch radio broadcast.

Set: 'Heaven And Hell', 'I Can't Explain', 'Fortune Teller', 'Tattoo', 'Young Man Blues', 'A Quick One, While He's Away', 'Substitute', 'Happy Jack', 'I'm A Boy', *Tommy*: (21 songs, as September 21), 'Summertime Blues', Shakin' All Over', 'My Generation', 'See Me, Feel Me', improvisations, 'Sparks', improvisations.

This was the first *Tommy* performance at a hitherto all-classical/opera venue, and a very prestigious occasion for The Who – this show also fulfilled many of Kit Lambert's ambitions for serious recognition for *Tommy*. The band turned in a superb performance. 'Overture' emerged as a fine instrumental and was an appropriate and dra-

Friday October 10
Commonwealth Armoury, Boston, Massachusetts; one show at 8:30 pm
The Who returned to America for a lap of honour, opening their second US *Tommy* tour in this National Guard facility.

Saturday October 11
The Grande Ballroom, Dearborn, Michigan
Supported by Alice Cooper and Sky.

THE WHO. THE FLOCK. Friday.
8:30. Commonwealth Armory. Tickets. $2. $3. $4.

SPIRIT. ELVIN BISHOP GROUP.
SHA-NA-NA. Boston Tea Party.
Lansdowne St.. Thursday. Friday.
Saturday. Admission. $3.50

Sunday October 12
The Grande Ballroom, Dearborn, Michigan

Supported by Sky. One of the members of Sky was Doug Fieger who later went on to fame with The Knack who topped the charts in 1979 with their hit 'My Sharona'.

Tuesday October 14
CNE Coliseum, Toronto, Ontario, Canada

About 4,000 people packed the barn-like Coliseum as Pete apologised to the crowd for "having to play in this garbage can for your sake more than ours".

Wednesday October 15
Civic Centre, Ottawa, Ontario, Canada, one show at 8pm

Supported by M.R.Q. The set included 'Heaven And Hell', 'I Can't Explain', 'Fortune Teller', 'Tattoo', 'Young Man Blues', *Tommy* (21 songs, as September 21), 'Summertime Blues', 'Shakin' All Over', 'My Generation'.

Townshend apologised for The Who missing the booking in Ottawa on May 21, concluding "we love it here, we just got kicked out of our hotel!" The absolute highlight of this concert was a stupendous seven-minute version of 'Young Man Blues' in which Townshend played the most awesome guitar solo. Moving from chunks of rhythmic chord work into the most lyrical and dextrous finger work high up the fretboard and even including more delicate passages of jazz-influenced phrases, his guitar just sang its way through this number. (Luckily, this performance was recorded and preserved and can be found on a bootleg CD entitled *Pure Rock Theatre*.) Prior to the song, Pete pointed out to the audience that Mose Allison was a figure very much revered by British musicians, even though the 'cool school' of laid-back jazz artists like Allison was no longer very fashionable.

The sheer power and excitement of this show stands as a testament to the dizzy heights of capability and inspiration The Who had achieved: this was no one-off exception but an absolutely typical concert of the era.

Friday October 17
Holy Cross College Gymnasium, Worcester, Massachusetts

Saturday October 18
State University of New York (SUNY) Gymnasium, Stonybrook, New York, one show at 8pm

Set included: 'Heaven And Hell', 'I Can't Explain', 'Fortune Teller', 'Tattoo', 'Young Man Blues', *Tommy* (21 songs, as September 21), 'Summertime Blues', 'Shakin' All Over/Spoonful', 'My Generation', improvisations.

Since this was the first time the band had played at Stonybrook, they were caught unawares by the acoustics of the hall. As Pete commented during the show: "I'm a little bit surprised by the echo actually. We come dancing up here, happily dancing, merrily dancing up on the stage only to be an audience to a group at the other end who seem to play that two seconds after we do. I'll repeat that! (I'll repeat that!) We'll beat 'em. This is a gym. We're gonna make an athletic performance tonight." This show featured a very loose jam based on Howlin' Wolf's 'Spoonful', a song (written by Muddy Waters) which became a regular feature of the act from this point on as part of 'Shakin' All Over'.

Sunday October 19
The Electric Factory, Philadelphia, Pennsylvania, two shows, 4 and 8pm

4 pm set: 'Heaven And Hell', 'I Can't Explain', *Tommy* (21 songs, as September 21), 'Summertime Blues', 'My Generation', 'See Me, Feel Me', improvisations.

8 pm set: 'Heaven And Hell', 'I Can't Explain', 'Young Man Blues', 'Summertime Blues', *Tommy* (21 songs, as September 21), 'My Generation', 'See Me, Feel Me', improvisations.

After the first two numbers of the evening set, Pete said: "We'd like to play a song now written and originally recorded by Mose Allison called 'Young Man Blues', which will appear, we hope, on a live album about mid-November. We've recorded all the shows on this particular tour – including both shows tonight – so it could be tonight's, it could be any other show, you know. We'll pick the best bits... I just thought you'd like to know we've got our [recording equipment] running at the back here..." 'Summertime Blues' was played early on in the set instead of after *Tommy*: "We're changing the shape of our show a little bit tonight, for various reasons... as a special bonus," joked Pete.

Monday October 20
The Fillmore East, New York

The Who returned to New York in triumphant style with an unprecedented six–day stand at the Fillmore East. They became the first group to sell out the Fillmore 30 days in advance as well as the first to play to capacity midweek, reported *Amusement Business*, the American music trade paper. Each night *Tommy* was performed just four songs short of its entirety.

Taking the stage at 8 pm, the group gave one performance each night, Monday through Thursday, and two shows each night at 8 and 11:30 pm on Friday and Saturday. The eight shows grossed $75,000 of which The Who received 70%. It was the first time any major group had played the theatre for more than two consecutive days and it was the first time that the Fillmore management had allowed an act to use its own sound system. The Who set up a total of 45 speakers in the hall!

The opening–night set included 'Tattoo', 'Happy Jack', 'A Quick One, While He's Away', *Tommy* (21 songs, as September 21), 'Summertime Blues', 'Shakin' All Over', 'My Generation'.

Fred Kirby of *Billboard* (November 1) said: "Rock had one of its greatest nights at Fillmore East... Townshend, one of the most sensational of performers, was at his most exciting best as he pounded his guitar, leaped, dropped to his knees and did almost everything else to emphasise the hard rock material. His theatrical presence, however, never detracted from his superior musicianship. Lead singer Roger Daltrey, another exciting performer, whether beating tambourines, twirling his microphone or just singing, also was completely with it. In many ways drummer Keith Moon is the wildest of all. During the opening part of *Tommy*, when the drums were not in use, Moon approached mime as he used expansive stick gestures and expressive face effectively. Bass

NEW YORK—Rock had one of its greatest nights at Fillmore East on Oct. 20, when the Who opened a one-week stand with a set of well over two hours centering on "Tommy," the group's rock opera, which was composed by guitarist Peter Townshend.

The inspired performances also included an extensive amount of the Decca Records group's other top material, including many selections not heard here in some time, such as the hit single "Happy Jack" and "Tattoo."

guitarist John Entwistle, the only seemingly placid member of the quartet, was strong instrumentally as usual... The Who again showed themselves one of a kind by sustaining the excitement of so lengthy a continuous program – and for a full week."

Following the opening night's performance, Bill Graham hosted a party at Max's Kansas City, a New York night-club. Led Zeppelin had just seen the show and met up with The Who for the festivities. The two groups spent the rest of the night in long discussion.

Tuesday October 21
The Fillmore East, New York, one show

Wednesday October 22
The Fillmore East, New York, one show
Set: 'Heaven And Hell', 'I Can't Explain', 'Fortune Teller', 'Young Man Blues', *Tommy* (21 songs, as September 21), 'Summertime Blues', 'Shakin' All Over/Spoonful', 'My Generation', 'See Me, Feel Me', improvisations.

Bill Graham introduced The Who as follows: "On bass guitar and vocals, Mr John Entwistle. On vocals, tambourine smacking and microphone twirling, Mr Roger Daltrey. The mad master of the skins, Keith Moon. On lead guitar and vocals, Mr Peter Townshend. It's a great pleasure to welcome you to an evening of pure rock theatre with our good friends The Who..." (This introduction can also be heard on the *Pure Rock Theatre* bootleg CD.)

Halfway through the opening song 'Heaven And Hell', during the guitar solo, one of Pete's amplifiers blew out, causing him great frustration, and he stopped playing entirely for some bars of the final verse while the roadies hooked up his spare amp. As the song finished, he yelled abuse at the ailing equipment and roadies, adding: "Always goes in the same number, funny isn't it?" Daltrey introduced 'Fortune Teller', which was a particularly fine performance, full of subtle nuances beneath the power.

Prior to 'Young Man Blues', Townshend revealed his feelings: "For those of you that make up my nightmare, which is walking out on the stage and seeing the same 400 people in the first six rows, maybe I ought to tell you now that it is a nightmare. It really is. And it's a real one – every day the same dream, and in the first number in

every show so far – we've only played three [at the Fillmore East] – in the first number, in the guitar solo, the same amplifier has always blown up and at that rate by Saturday we'll have no amplifiers left. So we're hoping that maybe tonight will be the end of the nightmare and we'll get down to some hard facts... We normally play a lot of bullshit before *Tommy* to get ourselves into it and get you into it. We're gonna play one song tonight and then play the thing and then maybe we'll get our arses out of our earholes..." Townshend's guitar never seemed to recover fully from the early set-back and the *Tommy* 'Overture' suffered from being slightly out-of-tune.

The long *Tommy* introduction by Pete was as follows: "We'd like to play for you a song originally recorded and written by The 'Oo. It's quite a long one, it's what we normally wait a little while to play. We're gonna play it now because we feel in the mood to play it now, a long, long, long, long song called *Tommy*. This is a bit unprecedented in our career but we played it one way and didn't like it, so we're playing it another way and maybe we'll like it better... We miss out a couple of songs but there'll still be no intermission tonight and I'd like you to look behind us because it's something unfortunately we can't do. We'd like to be able to play with our arses facing you and our heads facing the Joshua Light Show, but unfortunately we've got to look at you lot. You can get the best of both worlds and see us and the Joshua Light Show, but unfortunately we've got to look at you lot. You can get the best of both worlds and see us and the Joshua Light Show both at once and maybe when you're applauding us at the end you'll give them a thought and sling some pennies in the Joshua Light Show benevolent fund box, which is up by the door... We've arrived, folks!"

The concert concluded with the towering 'My Generation' medley, introduced by Pete as follows: "For those of you that are still here, God help you, we'd like to play The Who hymn for him and for her, and for them, and for all of those of you that are under 90 years of age..."

John's bass solo during 'My Generation' as played here (and all other concerts during 1969 and onwards) had grown in speed and distortion into a breathtaking display of virtuosity. Unlike the rhythm sections of other bands (especially Cream), neither Entwistle nor Moon would have a specific featured solo spot, and all their best playing was incorporated into the body of The Who's material. Moreover, the 'solos', as such, were often taken simultaneously by Townshend, Entwistle and Moon, with devastating results on songs such as 'Heaven And Hell', 'Young Man Blues' and 'Shakin' All Over'. These were not

rehearsed note for note in advance (as they were with many lesser heavy rock bands) but entirely spontaneous. This sometimes resulted in an untogetherness, but more often it would be overwhelmingly forceful.

Thursday October 23
The Fillmore East, New York, one show

Friday October 24
The Fillmore East, New York, two performances 8 and 11:30 pm

Saturday October 25
The Fillmore East, New York, two performances 8 and 11:30 pm

Sunday October 26
Syria Mosque, Pittsburgh, Pennsylvania, one show at 8 pm

Supporting group was The James Gang whose guitarist Joe Walsh would strike up a lasting friendship with Pete and John. After this date, The Who took a four-day break from the tour during which Pete went to Florida to relax. The tour resumed on Friday October 31.

Friday October 31
The Kinetic Playground, Chicago, Illinois

The Who put on a magnificent show, playing well over two hours. Supported by The Kinks and Liverpool Scene.

Early in the show, Pete said: "In the old days, we used to dream about opening for The Kinks. So it's come to this." He paused, glanced to his right and then continued: "Well, this show's for them."

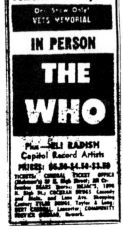

It was ironic that the roles had been reversed by 1969, especially since The Kinks had released their own concept album, *Arthur*, a few weeks earlier. The Who had first played support to The Kinks at the Goldhawk Road Social Club back in 1964.

Saturday November 1
Veterans Memorial Auditorium, Columbus, Ohio, one concert at 8:30 pm

"Twas a beautiful day in Columbus when the fences fell," wrote Pete in 1971 on 'Put The Money Down' released on *Odds And Sods* three years later. The Who's appearance in Columbus inspired the line, but exactly what the incident was remains a mystery which only Townshend can explain!

Sunday November 2
McDonough Gymnasium, Georgetown University, Washington, DC

Set included: 'Heaven And Hell', 'I Can't Explain', 'Fortune Teller', 'Tattoo', *Tommy* (21 songs, as September 21), 'Summertime Blues', 'Shakin' All Over/Spoonful', 'My Generation'.

The addition of the 800 gate-crashers produced a very tense and uneasy atmosphere, although this didn't adversely affect the performance. With much jostling and brawling, and an unsubtle approach by the security staff, Pete finally said: "Before we go back to England we'd just like to say why don't all you fuckers who wanted to cause trouble – and that includes the cops – why don't you go back to Washington 'cause this is a rock'n'roll concert. We're here to play you music and we're going to finish off playing you music. Why don't you relax?... 'Cos we know our job and we do our job and we do it right. SO WHY DON'T YOU FUCKING SIT DOWN??' 'My Generation'."

According to *Washington Post* reviewer William C. Woods: "The Who stupefied 5,000 in the 4,200 person capacity gym," putting on a two–hour show that by even modest estimate was the most electrifying performance he had ever witnessed.

Monday November 3
Westchester County Center, White Plains, New York

One performance at 8:30 pm.

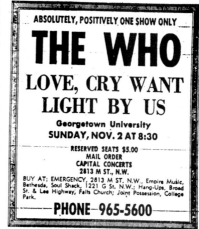

Tuesday November 4
Bushnell Auditorium, Hartford, Connecticut, one show at 8 pm

Thursday November 6
Livingston Gymnasium Indoor Track, Denison University, Granville, Ohio

The group played the opening night of the Raccoon Creek Rock Festival, taking the stage at 9 pm in the university gymnasium.

Friday November 7
Ohio State University, Athens, Ohio

The Who ran into accommodation problems when the local motel refused rooms for "long haired hippie entertainers that smoke marijuana and cause trouble in their establishment". The campus entertainment committee, who had booked the show, eventually found them lodging in nearby Lancaster, Ohio.

Saturday November 8
Kiel Opera House, St. Louis, Missouri

The show drew a capacity crowd of 3,400 people.

Monday November 10
Palace Theater, Albany, New York

The Who in Tommy Gun Attack

The show was sponsored by The Big Brothers and Big Sisters of Albany. Attendance was about 2,200 people for one 8 pm performance.

Tuesday November 11
The Boston Tea Party, Boston, Massachusetts

The group returned to Boston for a two–night stand at the Tea Party. Tony Williams' Lifetime, a jazz fusion group, was the opening act on both nights.

Set: 'Heaven And Hell', 'I Can't Explain', 'Fortune Teller', 'Tattoo', 'Young Man Blues', *Tommy* (21 songs, as September 21), 'Summertime Blues', 'Shakin' All Over', 'My Generation', 'See Me, Feel Me', improvisations, 'Sparks'.

During the 'Overture', Pete played some fine passages of unaccompanied guitar improvisation. The spontaneity of this, and other parts of the Boston concert (particularly the 'My Generation' medley) gave an inspired edge to The Who that other bands often lacked. Townshend always led the way and his guitar figures were startling in their variety and originality. Each audience at every show was treated to something different. Entwistle, Moon and Daltrey would often be left to pick up what Pete was playing by ear in order to contribute, and invariably they managed it every time.

Wednesday November 12
The Boston Tea Party, Boston, Massachusetts

Thursday November 13
New York State University Gymnasium, New Paltz, New York, one show
Set: as Boston, November 11.

Friday November 14
Public Music Hall, Cleveland, Ohio, one concert at 8:30 pm

Saturday November 15
Kleinhans Music Hall, Buffalo, New York, one show at 8:30 pm

Sunday November 16
War Memorial Auditorium, Syracuse, New York

The Who ended the second *Tommy* tour in Syracuse. The group took a well–deserved two weeks off when they returned to England.

Thursday December 4
The Hippodrome, Bristol, England

The first date in a short theatre tour of England. Set: as Croydon (September 21). The opening show of the tour left no-one disappointed, although the proceedings were interrupted by a drunken heckler. *Tommy* sounded as strong as ever, and during the repeated guitar phrase that forms the bridge section in the middle of 'Acid Queen', Pete played some fine inventive variations in the notes. 'Sally Simpson' – the weakest link in *Tommy* – was somewhat hesitant, and during the delicate intro to 'See Me, Feel Me', a smoke bomb was thrown onto the stage by the aforementioned heckler from a balcony, affecting Roger Daltrey's voice.

Both Townshend and Daltrey were glad that Tommy was well-received, despite the interruptions. Moon was comically wearing an ill-fitting pair of dungaree trousers, hitched up over his knees! Pete offered an explanation: "After adjusting Keith's bra, we'd like to carry on... Actually, what happened tonight, the reason why Keith is wearing this particular attire – unorthodox attire – is because he arrived today without any stage clothes, and so he had to wear some of mine. And this is my current attire, I've got good working clothes..." At this point the heckler began shouting at the stage. Pete immediately responded to him: "Was it that loud mouth over there that threw up that smoke bomb? 'Cos it wasn't ours, honest! We haven't used a smoke bomb for a long, long time. We would like to carry on... We'd like to thank you very much for your applause and carry on now with a song..." (Further interruptions occurred from the heckler in the box). "Oh, dear," yelled Pete, "... a song called 'Summertime Blues', which will definitely drown you out!" Perhaps distracted by the heckler, the following 'Shakin' All Over' was marred by some mistakes.

The heckler, however, struck again as Pete was announcing the 'My Generation' medley. "I'll tell you what," shouted Keith towards the man, "you just go ahead and we will watch." More abuse was hurled at the stage and the man finally showed his bared arse over the edge of the balcony. "We'd like to play a song now," said Pete, "which is our signing off song. It's all about people like you and me, and the people in the box up there... And him over there, we're all scum, all of us. Particularly up there in that box, and did you see the pimples?!" at which the audience laughed. 'My Generation' was followed by 'See Me, Feel Me', and 'So Very Long', which concluded with an extravagant flourish of soloing. The medley seemed to lose some momentum during the next improvisation and 'Sparks' suffered as well, diminishing into a repeated one-note riff which in turn led into another improvisation before the finale.

Richard Williams wrote in *Melody Maker* (December 13): "The Who are coming into their own and when they've finished their current tour of Britain they should have dispelled all doubts about their stature... I'm quite convinced that they are quite simply the best performing R O C K band in existence... the performance was masterful... It had been a very good opening night, and as The Who thrive on adversity they managed to weather the bombs and bottoms with praiseworthy equanimity."

Friday December 5
The Palace, Manchester, one concert at 7:30 pm

Wednesday December 10
Venue unknown, Paris, France

According to a *Melody Maker* news report, The Who were due to pay a three –day visit to Paris for television promotion and possible concerts. However, it's probable the trip didn't eventuate, considering the group played two Paris concerts the following month. A recording of a show in Paris has been attributed to this December 1969 date, although it may well be from January 16, 1970.

Pete commented that it was the first Who appearance in Paris for some years, and the first time 'A Quick One (While He's Away)' had been played in the city, let alone *Tommy*. 'Substitute' as played at this show sounded particularly strong.

Set: as Croydon (September 21).

Friday December 12
Empire Theatre, Liverpool

Sunday December 14
The Coliseum, Covent Garden, Central London

This concert sold out in an hour when the box office opened on Friday November 14. The gig was filmed, and 'Young Man Blues' and 'Happy Jack' from this show can be seen in *The Kids Are Alright* and the *Thirty Years...* video respectively. Set: as Croydon (September 21).

This was the first time that the Coliseum had been host to a rock act, and the audience found the venue too strict and traditional. When a freak began to idiot-dance at the foot of the stage, he was forcibly reseated by the security staff. Before the final medley, Townshend asked – sarcastically – if the seats were comfortable enough, to which Moon interjected, to the annoyance of the theatre management: "Riddled with lice, them seats!" Pete's speech after *Tommy* was as follows: "A few isolated requests over there... don't know how lovely you sound... You don't go to the opera and shout out! You reserve it all for the end... We'd like to thank you for rolling up tonight and thank you for your friends who never got in for making our lives a misery asking us for tickets what we never had, because it did sell out real frast [*sic*], real frast it sold out. And maybe this is indicative of something... that we could play this kind of thing seven nights a week as a nine-to-five job, regular like. So starting tomorrow we're chucking out the proper opera and we're putting in us! And it'll be much cheaper than the normal thing 'cause by the end of the week all the seats will be covered in chewing gum and all the binoculars will be gone. So it won't be half as classy but it'll be comfortable and if you fancy some amusements you can always look down in the pit and watch the orchestra... Mustn't feed 'em! We'd like to thank the Coliseum for lending us their nice place even though I did feel fantastically uncomfortable and I much prefer to be down the Lyceum!"

The Who gave a towering performance, the like of which the Coliseum had never heard before. The band had hoped to include the live footage from this show in a forthcoming film of *Tommy* but the quality was too rough for that purpose, and in any case the film was finally postponed. After the reprised 'Sparks' section of the 'My Generation' medley, the band played a dramatic rising chord progression before concluding with a fast riff (which could finally be heard closing the 'My Generation' medley on the *Live At Leeds* LP). This seemed a fittingly bombastic end to the show.

Underground paper *Friends* (January 31 1970) reported: "Two and a half hours of The Who with virtually no breaks made a great concert. They did more than fill the seats and sit back. Audiences are much more discerning these days, but The Who still get as good a reaction as ever." *The Times* (December 15) said: "A most exhilarating concert... *Tommy* is much more impressive musically in a live performance. The effect is more bold because the group dares more than on the records; but one can see as well as hear their technical accomplishments... and appreciate the harmonic subtleties and moments of compassion..."

"The Who are the best live rock band in Britain," said Royston Eldridge in *Melody Maker* (December 20): "Any doubts to the contrary were dispelled by their performance at London's Coliseum on Sunday night... Tremendous."

Friday December 19
City Hall, Newcastle

The Who wrapped up their most successful year to date with the last of five theatre appearances. The show was billed as a two–hour nonstop concert, starting at 7:30pm.

With the world at their feet, The Who consolidated their position throughout 1970, taking *Tommy* everywhere they went. "Assemble the musicians," Pete would say as the band geared itself for 'Thomas', as he liked to call it. Keith would tap the rim of his snare like a conductor would tap his baton on a music stand. "Stop laughing," he'd yell from behind his drums. "This is serious. It's a fucking opera, ain't it?"

And off they would go, crashing into the 'Overture' and sticking at it until the final 'Listening To You' chorus of 'We're Not Going To Take It' almost an hour later. It was a marathon performance, something never attempted by any rock band before or since, and those fans who caught it in its glorious prime were indeed fortunate. By 1970 The Who had achieved a degree of perfection and fluency that must have surprised even them. It had certainly turned Roger Daltrey into a rock god, all golden curls, bare chest, tight jeans and tassels. On stage Roger somehow became Tommy, the embodiment of the character that Pete had created. Townshend, in contrast, chose to play down the rock superstar image and wore white boiler suits and Doc Marten boots – his "work clothes", as he was prone to describe them. John dressed in a variety of colourful tailored outfits, some of them unusually flamboyant, while Keith, the tornado behind the drum kit, always wore white jeans and T-shirt.

The Who's stage attire helped define an image for them, just as *Tommy* gave them a stage show that everyone wanted to experience. But as 1970 wore on it started to become a millstone around their necks, and by the end of the year The Who had pretty much tired of the opera. As John Entwistle muttered in disgust, "Some people think the band's called *Tommy* and the album's called The Who."

As an antidote to suggestions that a rock opera

was the height of pretentiousness, it was decided to record a back-to-basics live album which would demonstrate that The Who's real strength was still gut-wrenching rock'n'roll. Accordingly, after visits to prestigious European opera houses in France, Denmark, Germany and The Netherlands, the group set off for dates at Leeds and Hull universities on February 14 and 15. The result was the electrifying *Live At Leeds* album, released in May, still regarded by many as the best live album by any group ever. The Who were at the peak of their powers at Leeds, the world's best rock'n'roll band recorded on an extremely good night.

A new 'non-album' single, 'The Seeker', was released in March and the band took a rest from live dates until spring, before playing eight shows in England, ending on May 15 at Lancaster. They had also begun recording songs for the next studio album, working at Pete's home studio in Twickenham. 'Water' was one of the tracks from these sessions, and it was soon featuring in the set on the band's upcoming US tour which began on June 7 at New York's Metropolitan Opera House. This unprecedented engagement in one of America's most hallowed halls of serious music brought The Who to the attention of the 'straight' press – not that they liked or even understood what they saw and heard. The Who played two performances in one day at the Met to accommodate the overwhelming demand for tickets and, as fans cheered for more at the end of the second show, Pete appalled the high-brow sections of the crowd by refusing to play an encore after the second show and swearing on stage.

They then went from one extreme to another, heading for Denver where, denied the use of the Red Rocks Amphitheatre, they were booked into Mammoth Gardens, a gymnasium–like downtown ballroom. The city did not allow concerts by rock groups at the famous outdoor venue at the time although the barn–like Denver Coliseum was available for shows. The Who added a sec-

ond night at Mammoth Gardens, a gracious gesture to the fans of a city not on the original itinerary.

The tour moved west to California for four shows. A Sunday afternoon concert was set for June 14 at Anaheim Stadium, a sort of 'mini–festival' event with Blues Image, John Sebastian and, in his first solo appearance, Leon Russell. The group moved on to the Bay Area to appear for two nights at the Berkley Community Theatre, booked by Bill Graham. On the first night The Who devastated the capacity house, giving the finest show the Bay Area had ever seen. Reviews of this show were universal in their praise. The trek continued through the south and Midwest, ending on July 7 at Tanglewood Music Shed in Lenox, Massachusetts. Having completed their most successful American tour to date, they flew back to England on July 8.

Despite the band's fame, in the UK it was still possible to see The Who at your neighbourhood town hall or college. Their next gig was on July 25 at Dunstable Civic Hall and there were dates in Sutton Coldfield and Wolverhampton in August. At the end of August The Who were again booked to appear at the Isle of Wight Festival where, typically, appearances fell way behind schedule and they did not take the stage until the small hours of August 30. In spite of the ungodly hour, they tore through a superb set, finishing well after 5 am. Two songs from this performance, 'Young Man Blues' and 'I Don't Even Know Myself', were seen in the *Thirty Years Of Maximum R&B* home video, and in 1996 The Who's complete set was released, both on video and CD.

The group began a six–date European swing in Münster, Germany on September 12. There were two concerts in The Netherlands as public demand for tickets went unsatisfied when the group played at the Concertgebouw in Amsterdam back in January. The junket closed in Offenbach, Germany on September 23.

In contrast to the increasing size of the venues played in America, The Who undertook a ballroom and theatre tour of Britain in October. Two–thirds of the way through the schedule, Roger came down with laryngitis and two shows had to be postponed. The tour ended on October 29 at the Hammersmith Palais, although the band played sporadic gigs around Britain through November and December. At a charity show at the Roundhouse in north London on December 20, the support act was a relative newcomer called Elton John, to whom that evening's performance of *Tommy* was dedicated. Apart from the reunion tour of 1989, that was the final performance of *Tommy* in its entirety, and a collective sigh of relief could be heard in The Who's dressing room that night.

Friday January 16
Champs Elysées Theatre, Paris, France

The Who set off on a prestigious tour of European opera houses in the New Year, beginning with two concerts in Paris.

Set: 'Heaven And Hell', 'I Can't Explain', 'Fortune Teller', 'Tattoo', 'Young Man Blues', 'A Quick One, While He's Away', *Tommy* (21 songs, as September 21), 'Summertime Blues', 'Shakin' All Over', 'My Generation', 'See Me, Feel Me', 'So Very Long', improvisation, 'Sparks', improvisation.

On taking to the stage, Townshend began playing some random, laid-back, jazzy chords to warm up – in a style totally different to his usual manner – before the distortion and power-chording of 'Heaven And Hell' changed the mood to one of raw power. Introducing 'Young Man Blues', Townshend explained that Mose Allison sounded so pure on the original version (called 'Back Country Suite: Blues') that many people didn't believe he was white! Pete concluded by remarking on the irony of the song being written while Allison was 40 years old. During the performance, great applause followed the apt line "you know nowadays, it's the old man who's got all the money..." Moon's drumming during this performance was rock solid, although imaginative and lithe, and the range of sounds emanating from Townshend's guitar was astonishing, from crashing noise to purely lyrical phrases. 'A Quick One' was played with good humour and affection as pure entertainment. Pete commented that "in its time [it] was considered quite revolutionary... a story all about a Girl Guide, who was seduced by an engine driver called Ivor", while Keith Moon provided suitable sound effects in the background!

Pete's pre-*Tommy* speech: "Now that we've given you the opera-mini, we'd like to go onto the opera-major... the opera-magnificent... If there's anything in your programme about *Tommy*, disregard it because it's probably rubbish... I haven't read it – it might be very good – but if there's any words in it, for example... they're probably taken out of the album sleeve in which case it's the words to the record, and not the words to what we do on the stage... There's a few songs that are on the record which we don't play on the stage and the reason is not because it would make it go on too long, or because we can't play them. The stage performance of *Tommy* is a completely different thing to the record. It's emerged differently, and it's progressed differently, and they just don't fit. So if there's anything that you miss that you particularly like, then hard luck! You'll have to listen to the record... We begin as all good operas – or for you serious music critics, cantatas – begin, with the 'Overture'."

As always, *Tommy* was faultless, despite the weak 'Sally Simpson'. Prior to 'My Generation', Pete noted that this song was "probably in its time much bigger in impact in its two minutes and 15 seconds or however long it lasted, than *Tommy* in its 75 minutes."

N.B: This concert may have taken place on January 17 – see entry for December 10, 1969.

Saturday January 17
Champs Elysees Theatre, Paris, France

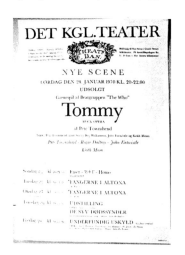

Saturday January 24
Det Kunglige Teater, Copenhagen, Denmark

The first Scandinavian *Tommy* performance - a two–hour concert, 8 to 10 pm, at the 'new scene' in the Theatre Royal. 'The Staerekassen' held only 1,100 people and sold out easily.

Set: 'Heaven And Hell', 'I Can't Explain', 'Fortune Teller', 'Tattoo', 'Young Man Blues', 'A Quick One, While He's Away', 'Substitute', 'Happy Jack', 'I'm A Boy', *Tommy* (21 songs, as September 21), 'Summertime Blues', 'Shakin' All Over', 'My Generation' 'See Me, Feel Me', 'So Very Long', improvisations, 'Sparks', improvisations.

Pete mentioned that the last Who concert in Denmark (in 1966) was at an open air venue and suffered from the rain. John Entwistle had to tune his bass repeatedly between the first few numbers of this show, and 'Substitute' suffered some guitar mistakes. Bearing in mind the climate of the country and the season of the year, Pete wittily announced a new variation on his rock opera: "Here in real life, *Tommy* On Ice!" In all other respects, this concert was the usual triumph.

Monday January 26
Stadt Opera House, Cologne, Germany

The Who donated the proceeds of their three German concerts to the Save The Children Fund. A reception was held in the band's honour by German President Heinemann and Chancellor Willie Brandt. (Heinemann was Chairman of the 1970 Save The Children Fund.)

Tuesday January 27
Stadt Opera House, Hamburg, Germany

Wednesday January 28
Deutchland Stadt Opera House, Berlin, Germany

Friday January 30
Concertgebouw, Amsterdam, the Netherlands

This midnight concert was the last known date of the European tour.

Saturday February 14
University Refectory, Leeds

Set: 'Heaven And Hell', 'I Can't Explain', 'Fortune Teller', 'Tattoo', 'Young Man Blues', 'Substitute', 'Happy Jack', 'I'm A Boy', 'A Quick

One, While He's Away', *Tommy* (21 songs, as September 21), 'Summertime Blues', 'Shakin' All Over/Spoonful', 'My Generation', 'See Me, Feel Me', 'So Very Long', improvisations, 'Sparks', improvisations, 'Magic Bus'.

Another legendary night in Who folklore. Recorded on the eight-track Pye Mobile Studio, this concert yielded the first live material that The Who ever released, and the resulting *Live At Leeds* LP was so good that the band never felt the need to release any further live albums during their working career (despite certain concerts being recorded for consideration). The reissue of the remixed and remastered *Live At Leeds* was released on February 14, 1997 - 25 years to the day of the original concert. It excluded the *Tommy* material, (bar two tracks, 'Amazing Journey' and 'Sparks'), and the full concert was not released until 2001. This show was an absolutely typical night for The Who, and not merely an exceptional one-off that just happened to be recorded. There is little point elaborating on the concert because words fail to do justice to what can be heard on the CD. Pete's introduction to *Tommy* was as follows: "We'll go into a rendition of Thomas, the pot opera, pop opera, rot opera, rock opera, the rock otter, the rop otterer. Assemble the musicians... We're all here, it's all right. We begin with the 'Overture'..." Keith then yelled "It's an opera, init? A bleedin' opera!" Then Pete replied with "How should we bloody know what it is?" The performance of *Tommy* is very good, although the intensity tends to flag from about halfway through, and some minor flaws were apparent.

'Spoonful' was played during 'Shakin' All Over" (but edited out of the *Leeds* album and subsequent re-issues), and Townshend's comments prior to 'My Generation' explain why the medley came about: "We'd like to say goodbye now. There's a long time to go yet, in actual fact. We do a number now which is kinda little bit of everything. It's mostly the 'Oo, and it's mostly the 'Oo of about three years ago, and probably mixed in are little bits of The Who today and this is some-

thing which is more or less our hymn. And the reason we reprise *Tommy* in it – in other words we repeat a bit of it – is to mix all the bits of our history together into one great huge deafening din! And this is dedicated to you, really, because you've been really incredibly kind and nice and friendly and that. No, really, considering..." Pete then put on a phoney mid-Atlantic 'showbiz superstar' accent: "It's really wonderful to be back in Leeds!... A special long drawn–out version of 'My Generation'."

Patrick Dean wrote in the *Yorkshire Evening Post* (February 23): "The long awaited live LP by The Who has at last been recorded – at Leeds University. Students packed the refectory to see and hear The Who roar through over two hours of the best music I have heard... The music of The Who comes rushing out in a solid wall of sound. They are loud, very loud, but they use volume as a catalyst for their musical effect, not like many groups as a bolster for lack of talent. Volume is an intrinsic part of The Who's music, and always has been, but it is not abused... It is a tribute to the magic of their performance that not so much as a cough disturbed the mood they conjured up... For all those who were fortunate enough to be there on this memorable night, it will be a constant reminder that pop music has reached standards that five years ago would have been unthinkable."

Pete commented on the show a couple of months later in *Rolling Stone* (May 14): "It just happened to be a good show, and it just happened to be like one of the greatest audiences we've ever played to in our whole career, just by chance. They were incredible and although you can't hear a lot of the kind of shouting and screaming in the background, they're civilised but they're crazy, you know, they're fantastic. And we played it in their own hall. And the sound is all right, it's a good atmosphere."

Roger: "There was hardly anything dubbed on it - there were more things taken off than put on. Two backing voices were added, but that was only because the mike fell over. The whole thing is as it happened."

The plain packaging of the original *Live At Leeds* album was designed to resemble a bootleg, and within it were contained facsimiles of items of Who memorabilia, including old gig and accounts sheets, a receipt for fireworks, hand-written lyrics, a court summons over an unpaid guitar bill and even the Woodstock contract.

Richard Evans: "Over the years The Who's manager, Bill Curbishley has received many phone calls from people who have 'discovered' these documents and believing them to be the original copies have '... wondered if Mr. Curbishley would, ahem, like to have them returned... for a modest fee, of course.' One such persistent gentleman managed to get a meeting with Bill at the old Trinifold offices in Wardour Street one afternoon. When he turned up Bill had plastered his office with piles of these documents from dozens of *Leeds* albums. 'Now, how can I help you?' said Bill in his most sincere voice."

Sunday February 15
City Hall, Hull

The adverts for this show had stated that "the whole concert will be recorded live for The Who's new LP". The 1,800 fans who attended rated this show highly and it was considered locally to be the finest concert ever held at the venue. One unusual variation was that Pete began playing 'Magic Bus' on an acoustic guitar – the only time he ever used an acoustic on stage prior to 1989. The Who played for a flat fee of £1,000. Barry Nettleton, the concert promoter told the local *Hull News*: "Group members were surprised that both the acoustics and the audience were so good, and said that the event had been well organised. They did not even have to tune up on stage. They were really nice people, the nicest group I've met."

This concert was also recorded for possible use for the live album, but in the event this was unnecessary since the *Leeds* show was exceptional. Years later, while researching unissued live

"FANTASTIC." That was the verdict of Barry Nettleton on Sunday evening's concert in the City Hall by "The Who."

material for the *Thirty Years Of Maximum R&B* box set, producer Jon Astley discovered that the bass signal from this show failed to record.

Tuesday March 17
Royal Albert Hall, London (cancelled)

John Lennon had planned to stage a benefit concert, including The Who, at the RAH on behalf of the National Council for Civil Liberties and Release, a drug offenders' organisation, but the management of the Royal Albert Hall refused to host the event. No other venue was selected and the show never took place.

Saturday April 18
Leicester University

The Who returned to live work with a number of university gigs around England. This concert, which attracted 1,600, is now entirely remembered for the near-riot in the audience rather than the musical content. In fact, in the post-Altamont atmosphere of the times, it seemed to raise serious questions about the future of rock concerts.

In short, the show was curtailed when Pete Townshend's head was badly cut by a flying bottle, courtesy of a Hell's Angel. *Melody Maker* (April 25) reported: "The Who are one of the few groups of their stature who go on the road to play for their British fans and it would be a tragedy if such sub-human behaviour deterred them." But Pete Townshend affirmed that this would not happen: "No, we won't stop doing gigs but after the loss of Keith Moon's chauffeur recently and now this incident, we shall have to take more precautions... We were playing in a small hall at Leicester University and there were a load of Hell's Angels idiot–dancing all over everyone. It got to the point where they were causing such uproar we had to stop playing *Tommy*. It wasn't worth it, so to give the rest of the crowd some enjoyment we went into 'Shakin' All Over'. The Angels tried to get on stage and one threw a bottle of Newcastle Brown Ale which hit me on the head. The team of rugby players who were supposed to be the bouncers vanished."

Apparently, as Pete retired hurt with blood pouring from his head, fans kept asking him when he was going to finish the set! He was taken to hospital and had eight stitches. Over a year later, Pete elaborated on the incident in *Zigzag* (number 24, March 1972): "I had an argument with a Hell's Angel on the stage at Leicester once, and got bottled... a road manager and I had to have eight stitches apiece, but even so, I think that if I had not been quite so pissed and quite so bloody, I would have got stuck in a lot further and probably got a lot more badly hurt. Because I got hit on the head, and it bled a lot, I thought I'd better get to a hospital, but I was really wild; I broke my guitar across some geezer's collarbone but it didn't seem to do much to him – he had a ring in his nose, I remember."

Saturday April 25
Nottingham University

With a capacity of only 800, this was one of the most intimate Who concerts of the era.

Monday April 27
Civic Hall, Dunstable

Supported by Writing On The Wall.

Friday May 1
University Great Hall, Exeter

Attendance at this show was 1,800. Supported by Mighty Baby.

Saturday May 2
Sheffield University

Friday May 8
Eliot College, Canterbury University

Supported by Genesis.

Saturday May 9
Manchester University

A small hall with a sell-out capacity of 1,200. Progressive rock act Jan Dukes De Grey were the support act.

Friday May 15
Lancaster University

Billed as "the greatest social weekend in the history of Bailrigg" (the site of the University campus), The Who became the first major rock group to play in Lancaster before 1,600 fans, in a six–hour concert, supported by Quintessence, Hammer, and Pink Custard.

Saturday 16 May
York University

Supported again by Jan Dukes De Grey.

THE WHO are to be the first, and apparently also the last, pop group to play one of the world's most famous opera houses, the Metropolitan in New York.

The group are to give the last performance of their opera, "Tommy," at the Met. on June 7, the opening date of their American tour which runs until July 7.

Their press officer, Brian Sommerville, told the MM: "The management of the Met say that the Who are not only the first rock band to play there but they will be the only one. They have accepted them because they were impressed with 'Tommy' as a serious piece of music written and performed as an opera.

Sunday June 7
Metropolitan Opera House, New York

The Who kicked off their 1970 American Tour with two performances of *Tommy* in this prestigious 3,788–seat venue. Gross was $55,000.

1st Set: 'Heaven And Hell', 'I Can't Explain', 'Young Man Blues', 'The Seeker', 'Water', *Tommy* (21 songs, as September 21, 1969), 'Summertime Blues', 'My Generation', 'See Me, Feel Me', 'So Very Long', 'Naked Eye', 'Sparks', improvisation, (encore) 'Shakin' All Over/Spoonful', improvisation.

2nd Set: 'Heaven And Hell', 'I Can't Explain', 'Water', 'The Seeker', 'Young Man Blues', *Tommy* (21 songs, as September 21, 1969), 'Summertime Blues', 'Shakin' All Over', 'My Generation', 'See Me, Feel Me', 'So Very Long', improvisations, 'Naked Eye', improvisations, 'Sparks', improvisation.

A Bill Graham/Nat Weiss co-promotion and

"**TOMMY** is rock's first formal masterpiece. **LIVE AT LEEDS** is the definitive hard-rock holocaust. It is the best live rock album ever made."

The New York Times
Nik Cohn, March 8, 1970

the last and most famous of the opera house shows, with the tickets being sold at the Fillmore East. Rudolph Bing, director of the Met Opera Company, initially wouldn't book The Who – he didn't much like the idea of a loud, rowdy rock-'n'roll group at his prestigious Lincoln Center concert hall – but he was invited to listen to the *Tommy* LP and this changed his mind and the booking was accepted for the loudest and rowdiest rock group of all. The concerts were promoted as being the last ever performances of *Tommy*. The audience and the Met didn't mix too well, however, and Bill Graham himself was on hand to quell any potential disruptiveness. Both concerts

received standing ovations of over ten minutes and VIP's present included Warren Beatty and Julie Christie.

At the first show, every line of 'Young Man Blues' was cheered by the audience, as if in vocal agreement with the sentiment of the song. The new song 'Water' received its first airing in concert (at least in the States – it might have already been played in the UK). As Townshend commented: "In a way we feel that we have to play something new because it's a special occasion. We haven't really altered our act radically since the last time we played. This is one that's appearing on our new album..." Daltrey sang 'Water' with great power and commitment, it being a perfect vehicle for The Who's onstage style. The highlights of *Tommy* during this performance (and others) were 'Overture', 'Sparks', 'Pinball Wizard' and the moving 'See Me, Feel Me'. With the "opera" dispensed with, the band ploughed straight into the frenzied rock'n'roll of 'Summertime Blues' and the 'My Generation' medley, which included the second new song 'Naked Eye'. This was still rather rough in its structure, and although Pete Townshend sang the second verse (as on the final recording), the third verse was omitted and it moved into further improvisations.

As he returned to the stage for a rare encore, Pete joked with an ecstatic Kit Lambert, "You really book us on some bum gigs, man!" 'Shakin' All Over' moved into a bludgeoning riff that became the basis for a wild, improvised instrumental, featuring a drum solo and some impromptu slide guitar playing (with the mike stand) from Townshend, forming one of the most unusual and exciting improvisations that the Who ever played. Pete finally threw his guitar about the stage, before casting it into the audience. It was caught by long-term Who fanatic – and later rock musician – Binky Phillips.

Phillips later recalled the show vividly: "It was the best show I had ever seen. Pete came out there and showed everyone he didn't give a damn about the opera. They were so violent and vicious. They sounded like the old Who. That was the night I caught Townshend's guitar, which was the culmination of everything for me... Townshend walked to the tip of the stage with his busted guitar and looked at me as if to say 'Are you ready?' I stood up and all my friends stood back. They all wanted the guitar as badly as I did but they stepped back. It was like a Joe Namath pass over the 30–foot orchestra pit. It just fell right into me." (from *The Who* by John Swenson, 1979.)

The second set was witnessed by many who had been present during the first show and had doubled up on tickets. Prior to *Tommy*, Townshend explained that the show was hopefully to be the last performance of the work, although he must have had doubts that the act could survive its loss so abruptly. 'My Generation' moved from 'So Very Long' into a few lines and guitar figures from 'Water' before moving into 'Naked Eye', and an improvisation which had been released already on *Live At Leeds*. The band didn't return for an encore this time,

and the discontented crowd wouldn't disperse until Townshend reappeared alone, to face booing: "After two fucking hours, boo to you too..." and he threw his mike stand into the crowd.

Reviews were ecstatic. Albert Goldman said in *Life* (July 10): "Rock music may have reached its all-time peak with the recent performance at the Metropolitan Opera of *Tommy*... From the moment the boys walked on stage, it was obvious they were determined to give their greatest performance. Flashing their tawdry show tricks, they worked the Met as if it were a grind house in Yorkshire... Having outclassed the competition by miles and miles, The Who ought to be honoured at this point with a splendid award. I propose an architectural competition. The theme? The world's largest opera house for the world's smallest opera company."

Fred Kirby wrote in *Billboard* (June 20) that The Who were as "dynamic as ever... While the two hours stretch may have been too much for many in the audience, The Who continue in a class by themselves when it comes to hard work."

Twenty years later, Roger Daltrey rated these two concerts as the finest The Who ever played, though at the time *Rolling Stone* thought that a rock act playing at the Met was merely a gimmick. Ever the non-conformist, Pete Townshend considered the Met shows "dire" (see later entry for Coventry, November 28).

Tuesday June 9
Mammoth Gardens, Denver, Colorado

The band played the first of two shows in a poorly ventilated, privately owned ballroom. The Who were denied use of Red Rocks Amphitheatre by the City of Denver at the time because of a ban on hard rock shows at the famous outdoor venue. Jimi Hendrix had played there only two years earlier and, of course, many acts have performed there since.

Another new song, 'I Don't Even Know Myself' was introduced to the set on this night. The set included: 'Heaven And Hell', 'I Can't Explain', 'Young Man Blues', 'The Seeker', 'Water', 'I Don't Even Know Myself', *Tommy* (21 songs, as September 21, 1969), 'Summertime Blues', 'My Generation', 'Naked Eye'. 'Sally Simpson' was played here for the final time, and all *Tommy* performances for the remainder of the Who's career (apart from 1989) omitted it.

Wednesday June 10
Mammoth Gardens, Denver, Colorado

The band added a second show in Denver, a city they had almost skipped on this month–long tour. The two concerts grossed $45,000. The initial itinerary had set June 9 in Seattle and June 12 in Fresno, California.

Saturday June 13
Convention Hall, San Diego, California; one performance at 8 pm

The concert grossed $24,000.

Sunday June 14
Anaheim Stadium, California

Over 30,000 paid $120,000 to see The Who play a 90–minute set in this baseball park. Opening acts were John Sebastian (formerly with the Lovin' Spoonful), Blues Image and, "in his first solo appearance", Leon Russell.

Set: 'Heaven And Hell', 'I Can't Explain', 'Young Man Blues', 'Water', 'The Seeker', *Tommy* ('Overture', 'It's A Boy', '1921', 'Amazing Journey', 'Sparks', 'Eyesight To The Blind',

'Christmas', 'Acid Queen', 'Pinball Wizard', 'Do You Think It's Alright?', 'Fiddle About', 'Tommy Can You Hear Me?', 'There's A Doctor', 'Go To The Mirror', 'Smash The Mirror', 'Miracle Cure', 'I'm Free', 'Tommy's Holiday Camp', 'We're Not Gonna Take It', 'See Me, Feel Me'), 'Summertime Blues', 'Shakin' All Over/Spoonful', 'My Generation', 'See Me, Feel Me', 'So Very Long', improvisations, 'Sparks', improvisations, 'Naked Eye', 'Magic Bus'.

In use for the first time as a rock venue, the Anaheim Baseball Stadium served in lieu of a Los Angeles date on the tour. *Tommy* benefited from the loss of 'Sally Simpson', and Townshend sung 'Tommy's Holiday Camp' with a manic glee. During the 'My Generation' medley, Daltrey sang the first two lines of 'I Don't Even Know Myself' but the whole song was omitted from the set. 'Naked Eye' was beautifully performed.

Robert Hilburn reviewed the concert for the *LA Times* (June 16): "On stage, the group radiates power, showmanship and sensuality. Townshend, on lead guitar, punctuates everything The Who does with a fierce, uncompromising, almost machine gun–like musical style... It was a dazzling display of rock at its highest level. The audience, generally, was at the same level."

Monday June 15
Berkeley Community Theatre, Berkeley, California

Set: 'Heaven And Hell', 'I Can't Explain', 'Young Man Blues', 'Water', 'The Seeker', 'Substitute', *Tommy* (20 songs, as June 14), 'Summertime Blues', 'Shakin' All

Over/Spoonful', 'My Generation', 'See Me, Feel Me', 'So Very Long', improvisations, 'Sparks', improvisations, 'Naked Eye', improvisations.

In direct contrast to the Anaheim Stadium show, the two nights in Berkeley, promoted by Bill Graham, were in the smallest venues of the tour. Immediately after 'Water' during the first night, Townshend began playing 'The Seeker' in the wrong key, and realising his mistake, suddenly stopped, causing great laughter before starting it again properly. He later made an amusing allusion to a Cole Porter track he had recorded solo for a Meher Baba LP *Happy Birthday*: "If you're not especially good, if you're not really good and kind, I'll sing 'Begin The Beguine'..." With this threat abated, the band responded with a requested version of 'Substitute', which was more restrained than usual. While tuning up, Pete introduced *Tommy*: "I'd like to introduce you now to a young man who's not yet been to many parties. He's not had many girls. It's a young chap called Thomas, and Keith Moon here is going to assemble the orchestra for that record that's soaring high in the charts now..." Moon then began his parody of a conductor attempting to call his musicians to attention. During 'See Me, Feel Me', powerful spotlights were shone onto the audience from behind the band, creating a very vivid and unsettling effect, which the band retained at all future shows. Daltrey continued to joke about the title of *Live At Leeds*, pronouncing "live" as in "living" or "residing".

Tuesday June 16
Berkeley Community Theatre, Berkeley, California
    Set: 'Heaven And Hell', 'I Can't Explain',

'Young Man Blues', 'Water', 'The Seeker', 'I Don't Even Know Myself', *Tommy* (20 songs, as June 14), 'Summertime Blues', 'Shakin' All Over/Spoonful', 'My Generation', 'See Me, Feel Me', 'So Very Long', improvisations, 'Sparks'.

The audience appreciated Roger Daltrey's impromptu analysis of the American political scene when he injected into 'Young Man Blues' the following lines: "You got Nixon, you got Agnew, you ain't got nothing in the world these days..." Soon afterwards Pete broke a string, and while the roadies were rectifying the problem, Keith Moon gave a prolonged and amusing introduction to 'The Seeker'. Also at this show, the newest song 'I Don't Even Know Myself' was again played, with Roger on harmonica. The performance was a little uneven, being a song of varying tempo and rhythm, and it certainly wasn't in the band's classic rock mould, having a country tinge. Later in the show, during 'Overture', Townshend teased the audience with the sheer unpredictability of his rhythmic guitar figures that formed the solo. The band were well pleased with the audience and the venue, but they knew it would become increasingly difficult to play such intimate gigs in the future. San Francisco critics praised them for not playing the Cow Palace, but at many of the following gigs on this tour, such as Detroit and Philadelphia, they had little option but to book the biggest arenas available.

Pete Townshend commented about this gig: "The show at Berkeley... was the best we did in the States that tour. The sound was great, if a little loud for such a small place, and the crowd just super-aware and alive. I could smell a lot of dope, but I think a good many people are beginning to

realise that it is a bit of a risk getting high to watch The Who. Keith Moon might do something terrible. After the show, I met a lot of Baba-friends... and it goes without saying that they allowed me my pop star exhilaration that night as Keith and I and the gang destroyed what was left of our minds and bodies and hotel rooms that night." (*Rolling Stone*, November 26 1970)

Richard Barnes commented in *Maximum R&B*: "As the band moved across the country they left a wake of mind-blown, disbelieving Who concerts. In San Diego, San Francisco, Los Angeles (where in front of 30,000 people they became the first band to perform at the Anaheim Stadium), Dallas, Philadelphia, Cincinnati, Cleveland, Chicago and Detroit the press reviews were almost competing with themselves for superlatives to describe The Who live. After the show at the Berkeley Community Theatre, the *San Francisco Examiner* said "They had just heard the finest two hour concert of contemporary music of their lives. They knew it. The Who knew it... Exaggeration? I cannot exaggerate perfection!"

Not to be outdone the *San Francisco Chronicle* reported "The Who show at the Berkeley Community Theater was absolutely staggering in its emotional and musical power... writing about their music is something of an exercise in futility. It need not be explained to those who were there. It cannot be explained to those who were not. If a single word can sum it up, that word would be 'shattering!'"

Two nights in Berkeley grossed $34,000.

Friday June 19
Memorial Auditorium, Dallas, Texas

Set included 'Heaven And Hell', 'I Can't Explain', 'Water', 'The Seeker', *Tommy* (20 songs, as June 14).

Prior to 'The Seeker', Roger Daltrey made some interesting comments about the release of this song on single: "We'd like to carry on with a number that you may have heard before. It was our latest single, and we like to think of it as our sort of pet elephant, you know, 'cause that's how it went up the charts – like an elephant climbing a ladder! It's written by Pete again, released perhaps in a bit of haste but we still like it..." Following this, Keith Moon did his conductor routine, assembling the mock orchestra.

Gate receipts in Dallas totalled $45,000.

Saturday June 20
Hofheinz Pavilion, University of Houston, Houston, Texas

The concert attracted 11,000 fans. Set included 'Heaven And Hell', 'I Can't Explain', 'Young Man Blues', 'I Don't Even Know Myself', *Tommy* (20 songs, as June 14).

Townshend mentioned the erroneous "last Tommy performance" billing at the Met and said "there's very little else we want to play at the moment". Prior to Keith Moon's conductor routine, Pete introduced him to the audience as "Sir Malcolm Moon", a reference to the British conductor, Sir Malcolm Sargent.

Sunday June 21
Ellis Auditorium, Memphis

The Who's début in Memphis before an audience of 4,500. Set: 'Heaven And Hell', 'I Can't Explain', 'Young Man Blues', 'Water', *Tommy* (20 songs, as June 14), 'Summertime Blues', 'My Generation', 'See Me, Feel Me, improvisation, 'Sparks', improvisation.

As The Who began playing 'Heaven And Hell', a number of photographers at the front were standing taking photographs of the band. After

KILT AND CONCERTS WEST PRESENT

The WHO
SUPER GROUP of ENGLAND

UNIVERSITY OF HOUSTON
HOFHEINZ PAVILION
SATURDAY — JUNE 20

TICKETS – BROOK-MAYS MUSIC STORES
HOUSTON TICKET SERVICE

the song, Townshend said: "Well, that one was for the photographers, now how about some for the audience? Why don't you all sit down?" Again, *Tommy* was heralded with the comment from Pete that "we really can't do without him at the moment. If we didn't play it we'd only have about three numbers to do... It's really extremely important you hear it. As all good operas start, so *Tommy* starts with an 'Overture'."

This was a tight, powerful concert throughout, the highlight of which was the concluding extended medley. This incorporated passages of calm and thunder from Townshend's guitar, where the improvisations included some of the most unusual chord variations ever heard in the rock vocabulary – ample enough evidence of Pete Townshend's instrumental genius.

Monday June 22
Municipal Auditorium, Atlanta, Georgia

The band arrived late in Atlanta as a result of an offhand comment by Pete on board an Eastern Airlines flight preparing to take off from Memphis. He said he thought the sales of *Live At Leeds* were "going a bomb in New York", a comment misinterpreted by a flight attendant. She notified the captain who turned the aircraft around and called the authorities. Passengers and baggage were off loaded and inspected before the flight was allowed to proceed. Townshend was detained for further questioning causing a long delay in Atlanta.

Wednesday June 24
The Spectrum, Philadelphia, Pennsylvania

The Who grossed $65,700 for this show from a capacity crowd of 19,000, supported by The James Gang. "Unbelievable! Remarkable! Outstanding!" screamed the *Maryland Democrat*, "... or anything else you want to call better than the best was The Who concert at The Spectrum... "

Thursday June 25
Music Hall, Cincinnati, Ohio; one show each night at 8:30 pm

Supported by The James Gang, The Who played to 3,600 fans each night, at one of the smaller venues on the tour.

Friday June 26
Music Hall, Cincinnati, Ohio

Saturday June 27
Music Hall, Cleveland, Ohio

In addition to The James Gang, James Taylor, then high in the charts with 'Fire And Rain', was added to the bill.

Monday June 29
Merriweather Post Pavilion, Columbia, Maryland

A return to the site of the incredible 1969 concert. On this visit the group performed before 15,000 people, grossing $53,000 at the gate. Set included 'Heaven And Hell', 'I Can't Explain',

'Young Man Blues', *Tommy* (20 songs, as June 14), 'Summertime Blues', 'My Generation', improvisations.

Support band was Ten Lucy. According to a review in the Baltimore *Morning Sun*, Townshend announced 'I Don't Know Myself' but decided not to play it "because I'm too stoned to tune up". Unusually, 'My Generation' as played here began very loosely out of some random guitar playing from Pete, as the structure of the medley was altered. The high standards of the recent concerts were otherwise effortlessly maintained in Columbia.

Wednesday July 1
Auditorium Theatre, Chicago, Illinois

When Pete announced at this Chicago show "... something we've done 40 or more times and swore never to perform on the stage again" there was such a roar of anticipation and delight from the audience, it could only be quietened down by Keith standing up and shouting into the mike "It's a bloody opera! So sit down and shaddup!" The *Chicago Tribune* commented "I'll bet there wasn't a person in the Auditorium Theatre last night who won't tell you that this was probably the best concert that Chicago has ever had. Even those that have seen Janis and Cocker and Blood Sweat & Tears. In *Tommy* alone there were five, six, seven, maybe eight standing ovations."

Thursday July 2
Freedom Palace, Kansas City, Missouri

Set: 'Heaven And Hell', 'I Can't Explain', 'Water', 'Young Man Blues', 'I Don't Even Know Myself', *Tommy* (20 songs, as June 14), 'Summertime Blues', 'Shakin' All Over/Spoonful', 'My Generation', 'See Me, Feel Me', improvisations.

A heatwave had spread over the Midwest, reaching its hottest at this concert, which the band completed despite the extreme conditions. The Freedom Palace was a community-oriented, non-profit venue with which The Who were impressed. However, this feverish performance suffered from the overpowering conditions inside the venue, the power cut out several times mid-song, and – although the concert had its fair share of high points – the band were adversely affected. The 'My Generation' medley lost some momentum at the end of the reprise of 'See Me, Feel Me'

but the improvisations took off with a beautiful sequence of chords (see Tanglewood, July 7) and concluded with a bout of alternating guitar solos and drum rolls which resembled 'Dogs Part 2', a song not otherwise played on the stage.

Three months later, Pete told the audience in Offenbach (September 23):

"... in an incredible heatwave, we played one place owned by the people, run by the people in Kansas City. And it was a good gig with lovely people, and the temperature was 117 degrees with 99 per cent humidity. The electricity kept failing, but we didn't, and neither did the kids. And we played them ['Water'] and we threw water over them all to sing it, a song about a drought..."

While in Kansas City, Keith Moon bought a highly unusual completely transparent drum kit.

Friday July 3
Minneapolis Auditorium, Minnesota; one show at 8 pm

9,000 fans attended this show.

Saturday July 4
Auditorium Theatre, Chicago, Illinois
One concert at 8:30 pm for the second date in Chicago.

Sunday July 5
Cobo Arena, Detroit, Michigan
The James Gang was back as the opening act on this date. Set included: 'Heaven And Hell', 'I Can't Explain', 'Water', 'I Don't Even Know Myself', 'Young Man Blues', *Tommy* (20 songs, as June 14), 'Summertime Blues'.

From the start of the show the band sensed a potential crowd control problem from the ecstatic response they received. Daltrey said to the 12,000-strong audience, referring to the first proper Who concert in the States in Ann Arbor in June 1967: "It goes without saying, the first place we ever played in the States was Detroit, and it seems like one of the wildest crowds still, as it was then. Here's a new song for you, written by Pete, which we've sort of just recorded before we came away on a new album which we recorded in Pete's garage..." A lengthy version of 'Water' followed, and the song, ostensibly a two-chord jam, had by this point in the tour developed subtle nuances throughout. Townshend had to change his guitar for 'I Don't Even Know Myself', which required a capo, while Moon said: "This is another song written by Pete, this is also on the new album – as yet unfinished, and we'll start work on that as soon as we get back..." Townshend once more explained that *Tommy* would be played, contrary to reports in the media. "We're not ready to do a show without it," he said. Moon then repeated his conductor joke.

During 'Summertime Blues' the audience leapt to its feet and caused concern for the security staff, who informed the group of the problem.

Tuesday July 7
Tanglewood Music Shed, Lenox, Massachusetts
The final date of the 1970 US tour and the band's last American appearance for a year. Set: 'Heaven And Hell', 'I Can't Explain', 'Water', 'I Don't Even Know Myself', 'Young Man Blues', *Tommy* (20 songs, as June 14), 'My Generation', 'See Me, Feel Me', improvisations.

Pete Townshend: "We'd like to say what a real pleasure it is to be in Tanglewood again. We were only here last August, last time with Jefferson Aeroplane [sic], this time with another really fine English group, Jethro Tull." Townshend also optimistically mentioned that The Who's new album "will be released very shortly". 'Water' was an early highlight and by this time had developed into a thoughtful, mature but energetic song. After 'Water', Roger said: "I'd like to hand you over to a very quiet English gentleman who sits in the background all night, a very quiet lad indeed, Keith Moon on drums." Keith then took Roger's mike and said: "Thank you, Roger. After that tremendous effort I'd like to introduce you to our guest speaker for this evening..." He then held up a battered 12-inch speaker cone. "And the guest speaker and I would like to play..."
Pete: "For God's sake, sit down!"
Keith (talking with his mouth behind the speaker): "'I do not even know myself'. It's on our new album that's coming out soon as we've finished it, recorded in Pete's garage. Thank you, you can leave the stage now!" Moon threw the speaker cone back to a roadie, then continued: "A song that Pete wrote in his garage, 'I Don't Even Know Myself'..."
Introducing 'My Generation', Pete said that the song was "very, very right for this particular

18,784 Jam Tanglewood Rock Session

"We've just been told," said Daltrey after the song had finished, "that if you don't keep it together and sit down, they're going to stop it. Let's fucking get it together... and we'll keep going." Pete Townshend then said: "If you can all take to your seats, and we'll start to play... you can't find your own seat, sit on somebody's lap. Try to get the aisle clear." The concert resumed but the ruling on seating restrained the audience unduly.

moment... We're going back to England – in many ways we're happy, in many ways we're very sad. It's been one of the finest times we've ever had... the most enjoyable tour we've done in this country..." During the final medley, 'See Me, Feel Me' was immediately followed by the same sequence of beautiful, moody guitar figures which had been played a few days earlier at Kansas City, before breaking into a more characteristic, aggressive riff, followed by even further improvisations. Finally, Pete bashed his guitar about, but without the pure anger that he usually displayed. A magical concert overall.

This show was produced by Bill Graham and professionally videotaped for television broadcast which was never aired. Bootleg copies which show The Who at the peak of their performance before 18,784 paying customers have long since circulated among collectors. Three songs from this show, 'Heaven And Hell', 'I Can't Explain' and 'Water', can be seen in the video compilation *Thirty Years of Maximum R&B Live*.

Having completed their most successful tour to date, the band flew back to England on Thursday July 9.

Saturday July 25
Civic Hall, Dunstable, England

Fresh from their US tour, the band "almost lifted the roof off this architectural marvel as they pounded away for nearly two hours," according to Chris Charlesworth's *Melody Maker* (August 1) review. Townshend wore his tie-dyed multi-coloured boilersuit. Charlesworth noted the disappointment in the audience when Pete told them that he wasn't going to smash his guitar. The bright lamps at the back of the stage were used on the audience during 'See Me, Feel Me' for the first time in the UK at this show. The Who had begun to be billed as "the most exciting stage act in the world" around this time, and Charlesworth said that they "lived up to their name". He went on to say that "The Who are unique in the excitement they manage to create – and this is almost entirely due to Pete Townshend's leaping and jumping as he treats guitar and amps with little or no respect..."

Supported by Wishbone Ash, Axe and Lee's Plastic Sounds.

Guitar destroyed – Gibson SG.

Saturday August 8
The Belfry, Sutton Coldfield

Saturday August 15
Yorkshire Jazz And Blues Festival, Krumlin, Barkisland, Halifax (cancelled)

The Who had been widely advertised to top the bill of this potentially huge outdoor festival but issued a press statement a week beforehand emphatically stating that they would not be playing and that they had never been contracted to play. It seemed the promoters jumped the gun and went ahead with a high-profile publicity campaign before the bill was finalised. As it turned out the festival was attended by only 10,000 people, a third of the number expected, and plagued by poor organisation and foul weather.

Monday August 24
Civic Hall, Wolverhampton
Supported by Trapeze.

Saturday August 29
3rd Annual Isle of Wight Festival, Freshwater Farm, Isle of Wight

Set: 'Heaven And Hell', 'I Can't Explain', 'Young Man Blues', 'I Don't Even Know Myself', 'Water', *Tommy* (20 songs, as June 14), 'Summertime Blues', 'Shakin' All Over/Spoonful/Twist And Shout', 'Substitute', 'My Generation', improvisations, 'Naked Eye', 'Magic Bus'.

Although the band preferred to play smaller indoor venues, they couldn't turn down a repeat performance at the final Isle of Wight Festival, especially as they were reputed to have been paid £10,000 for the show. They were co-billed alongside The Doors to headline on the Saturday. The concert was a triumphant homecoming, although really nothing but a larger rerun of the 1969 gig. The PA for the whole festival was provided by The Who, whose WEM system designed by Bob Pridden was the biggest available. The festival

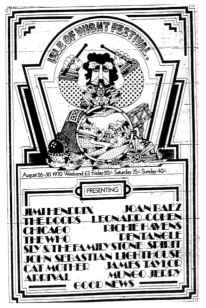

ISLE OF WIGHT FESTIVAL.

August 26-30 1970 Weekend £3 Friday 20/- Saturday 35/- Sunday 40/-

PRESENTING

JIMI HENDRIX   JOAN BAEZ
THE DOORS LEONARD COHEN
CHICAGO   RICHIE HAVENS
THE WHO   PENTANGLE
SLY & THE FAMILY STONE SPIRIT
JOHN SEBASTIAN LIGHTHOUSE
CAT MOTHER   JAMES TAYLOR
ARRIVAL   MUNGO JERRY
GOOD NEWS

like to play for you now something which we played over the other side of the island when we were here last year – wearing the same clothes, carrying the same guitars, with the same personnel, and the same road manager and all the groups using our PA same as last year. Driving over in the same cars, it's all the same this year as it was last year..."

Following a strong version of 'Spoonful', the band played 'Twist And Shout', which was well sung by John Entwistle, with backing vocals from Pete and Roger. 'My Generation' was followed by some long, spontaneous jams, a few lines and chords from 'Water' before concluding with a tremendous version of 'Naked Eye' in which the audience were bathed in white light from behind the stage. The post-*Tommy* part of the set was brilliant and few of the audience would refute that The Who had provided the best two hours of the festival.

With full justification, the set was lavishly praised by the critics: "Probably the most magnificent set I have ever seen..." wrote John Coleman in *Friends* (October 2-15), "certainly the best live band ever, they were happy, they were together, and they were amazing... Sometimes you really do come across an experience that will not allow

attracted a colossal 600,000 fans and was much criticised for its high ticket prices and heavy security presence. It was organised – once more – by Fiery Creations, a supposedly underground non-profit set–up which was held under some suspicion by those involved. Fiery Creations were determined to cover the whole event on film. In fact, a crew even filmed the organisation and planning of the festival months beforehand. In the event, this film was not completed until 1995, released as the documentary *Message For Love* (which featured The Who playing 'Young Man Blues' and 'Naked Eye').

The band were in a comparatively relaxed mood and tended to sound a little ragged at times, but they were so in tune with the huge crowd that their performance was a masterpiece of mass-communication and emotional power. Pete said before *Tommy*: "And the best is yet to come! Why tune up in the dressing room when you can tune up with an audience? It's so much more fun y'know, you bore them all to tears. We'd

itself to be said in just a few words on paper. For me they played what could only be the best set that they've ever done..." The review in *IT* simply concluded "fucking amazing".

Long delays meant that the band took the stage in the small hours and finished around 5 am, just as they had done at Woodstock a year earlier. 'Young Man Blues' and 'I Don't Even Know Myself' from this gig can be seen in the home video, *Thirty Years Of Maximum R&B Live*, and the whole IOW set was made commercially available in 1996.

John wore his famous skin–tight skeleton outfit for this gig, and backstage before the show Keith had somehow got his hands on a box of eggs which he kept breaking into people's drinks – "Go to work on an egg, dear boy" – but a more sensitive side to Moon The Loon was also in evidence that day. When he heard that Melanie was too nervous to take the stage before the huge crowd, Keith spent over an hour with her, boosting her confidence with his inimitable humour to make her forget her nervousness. He succeeded, too.

Saturday September 12
Münsterlundhalle, Münster, Germany

Set: 'Heaven And Hell', 'I Can't Explain', 'Young Man Blues', 'I Don't Even Know Myself', 'Water', *Tommy* (20 songs, as June 14), 'Summertime Blues', 'Shakin' All Over', 'Twist And Shout', 'My Generation', improvisation.

A lengthy introduction by a German compere preceded this performance. 'Water' was described as "a song about a heatwave", and it tended to meander on for slightly longer than it needed. Moon performed his conductor routine, the comedy of which was somewhat lost on many of the German audience. 'Twist And Shout' lacked the responding backing vocals, and 'My Generation' stretched out into a loose jam followed by improvisations, one of which developed through some magical chord progressions from Townshend. (One wonders why such inspired guitar riffs weren't developed into a whole song, they were that good!)

Sunday September 13
Orberrheinhalle, Offenbach, Germany

Set: 'Heaven And Hell', 'I Can't Explain', 'Young Man Blues', 'I Don't Even Know Myself',

'Water', *Tommy* (20 songs, as June 14), 'Summertime Blues', 'Shakin' All Over', 'Twist And Shout', 'My Generation', improvisations, 'Naked Eye', improvisation, 'Magic Bus'.

Keith Moon introduced 'Young Man Blues', which went through an uncharacteristic delicate passage during the solo. Pete announced that the next Who album would be called "6 ft Wide Garage, 7 ft Wide Car": "All the best rock'n'roll music comes out of garages, and so will our next album. We've put our own studio together... got good sounds in our opinion..." Prior to 'Water', Pete made the aforementioned reference to the Kansas City show.

Wednesday September 16
De Doelen Halle, Rotterdam, the Netherlands; one performance at 8:15 pm

Set: 'Heaven And Hell', 'I Can't Explain', 'Young Man Blues', 'I Don't Even Know Myself', 'Water', Tommy (20 songs, as June 14), improvisation, 'My Generation', 'Naked Eye'.

During this show, Keith Moon mentioned that 'I Don't Even Know Myself' was "recorded in Pete's garage", referring to Eel Pie Sound Studios. Following *Tommy*, and in time with the handclaps of the audience, Pete launched into a resounding riff for several bars before leading into 'My Generation', which took on a new shape towards the end. 'Naked Eye' was climaxed with some machine-gun riffing that culminated in feedback.

Thursday September 17
Concertgebouw, Amsterdam, the Netherlands; one show at 8:15 pm

WOENSDAG 16 SEPTEMBER
8.15 UUR IN DE DOELEN - ROTTERDAM
DONDERDAG 17 SEPTEMBER
8.15 UUR IN CONCERTGEBOUW - AMSTERDAM
PAUL ACKET PRESENTEERT I.S.M. NEW ACTION Ltd.

THE WHO
IN CONCERT
TELEFONISCHE INLICHTINGEN: (070) 244455 (INTERTEL)

Friday September 18
De Doelen Halle, Rotterdam, the Netherlands

FALKONERCENTRET

Sondag 20 sept k 20

DMC præsenterer

THE
WHO

Billetter
City Billetburoau PA 4531

ENESTE OPTRÆDEN

Sunday September 20
Falkoner Center, Copenhagen, Denmark; one performance at 8 pm

Set: 'Heaven And Hell', 'I Can't Explain', 'Young Man Blues', 'I Don't Even Know Myself', 'Water', *Tommy* (20 songs, as June 14), 'Summertime Blues', 'Shakin' All Over', 'Twist And Shout', 'My Generation' improvisation, 'Magic Bus'.

Sensing the fact that they had played almost the same set in Copenhagen in January, Townshend told the audience that this per-

Monday September 21
Vejlby Rissov Hallen, Aarhus, Denmark; one concert at 8 pm

Set: As at Copenhagen (September 20). Daltrey amended the lyrics of 'Water' to make direct reference to the Kansas City heatwave. 'Summertime Blues' was a particularly good version, accompanied by frantic audience handclaps. The post-*Tommy* section of this concert was particularly exuberant, and in all this was a brilliant performance.

Tuesday October 6
Sophia Gardens, Cardiff, Wales

Opening night of the 1970 UK tour. The 2,000–seat Sophia Gardens was sold out a week in advance. American trio The James Gang opened on all dates except October 29 at the Hammersmith Odeon.

The band's set was shortened for the British tour by reducing the *Tommy* section, although it is not known which songs were omitted. This rare Welsh concert was reviewed in the *South Wales Echo* (October 10) by Neil Hughes. "The Who, though not perhaps the best rock group in the world (as many would claim) must surely rank among the top two or three... As a journalist, I've learned to dislike and distrust superlatives, and yet to review Tuesday's show without them is impossible." The Who played for two hours and the atmosphere, according to Hughes, was "electric", and the volume "ear-shattering".

Songs mentioned were 'Young Man Blues', 'I Don't Even Know Myself,' and 'Water', climaxing with 'My Generation' and 'Magic Bus'. Visually, the band were typically energetic: "Through it all, Roger Daltrey cavorted about onstage, swinging his mike through the air like a lasso, and even doing something resembling a backward roll

The Astounding Who: Perfection

formance of 'Summertime Blues' was "absolutely, definitely" the last time that The Who were going to play it on stage. This was patently untrue as it was played the very next evening! The improvisations following 'My Generation' were lengthy and featured much virtuoso guitar soloing before leading into a fast-paced 'Magic Bus'.

across the stage into an amplifier... Townshend provided choreographic balance to Daltrey's gymnastics, performing little ballet-like leaps all the time while beating hell out of his guitar". Moon "bashed away for nearly two hours on an incredible set of completely transparent drums, stopping only to make occasional wisecracks to the audience or the group".

Hughes was obviously impressed with Townshend, who "in a white jumpsuit, provided musical balance to Daltrey's powerful voice with his own searing and imaginative guitar work". Apparently, Entwistle "was his usual, reserved self" and sported his joke-shop skeleton outfit. Of course, the band played their usual truncated version of *Tommy*, which "couldn't be faulted". This was the last Welsh Who concert for six years.

Pete had decided to undertake the British tour in his motor caravan, giving him a taste of gypsy life and later giving him inspiration for writing 'Going Mobile'. He intended the motor home to solve the accommodation logistics of the tour, but in the event it caused him problems of a different kind – like how to negotiate traffic jams in strange towns and where to park the thing! After arriving in Cardiff in the motor home, he was lucky enough to park near the Sophia Gardens and walk to the venue with his boilersuit under his arm "feeling like a local Welsh lad made good", as he wrote in *Melody Maker* (October 17). Pete enjoyed the concert: "The crowd were incredible. It was the first airing of the now shortened *Tommy* in Wales and we enjoyed the

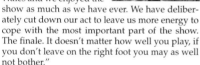

show as much as we have ever. We have deliberately cut down our act to leave us more energy to cope with the most important part of the show. The finale. It doesn't matter how well you play, if you don't leave on the right foot you may as well not bother."

Wednesday October 7
Free Trade Hall, Manchester

This concert was a sell-out attended by 2,500 fans. Pete commented in his *Melody Maker* column (October 17): "The show went so well at the Free Trade Hall that night. The James Gang played a superb set... We can tell how the band before us go down by the audience response to our own opening. At Manchester it was just as exhilarating as Cardiff to feel the wave of familiarity and warmth from the crowd as we began."

Thursday October 8
Orchid Ballroom, Purley, Surrey

A highly-rated gig, the band apparently opened with 'I Can't Explain', suggesting that 'Heaven And Hell' had been dropped by this time. Caroline Boucher reported in *Disc and Music Echo* (October 17) that on the new songs 'Water' and 'I Don't Even Know Myself' "Townshend's freeform guitar work did tend to go off rather too much at a tangent at times." But she concluded that The Who were indeed "the best live group in the world. They're exciting visually, exciting musically – and don't quit as soon as 45 minutes are up. The Who play for nearly an hour and a half".

Pete Townshend wrote in *Melody Maker* (October 17): "The Orchid, Purley just wiped me

out. Not just the physical exhaustion... but also the place and the people. The last time we played there was so long ago I can't remember, and as we walked through the audience to the stage, surrounded by bouncers, I heard elderly Mods asking for 'Can't Explain' and 'Substitute' with such zest that I began to believe they were new releases. From the stage, however, the feeling was not one of nostalgia. Things had clearly changed. The crowd was a mixture of neat mohair suits and long shaggy Swedish army coats. The hall from this new aspect (our roadie had a special ten foot high stage built over the existing one) took on the mood of somewhere like the Chicago Kinetic Theatre, or the Shrine Auditorium in LA. It really was amazing."

Saturday October 10
University of Sussex, Brighton

Set included 'I Can't Explain', 'Young Man Blues', 'I Don't Even Know Myself', *Tommy*, 'My Generation', and 'Magic Bus'.

Not officially part of the UK tour, but slotted in along the way, this show evoked mixed feelings from *Melody Maker*'s Michael Watts. The concert was opened by Roger Ruskin Spear and The

UOS & bcOe unions present at
THE UNIVERSITY OF SUSSEX, NR. BRIGHTON
ON SAT. 10th OCT., FROM 8 p.m.

THE WHO

THE JAMES GANG
ROGER SPEAR'S GIANT KINETIC WARDROBE

UOS £1. GUESTS 25/-. Send s.a.e. and cheque payable
to UOS Students' Union

Booked through Trigrad. 01-499 5364

James Gang. Pete Townshend found the stage surface too slippery for his leaps, and early in the set (through accident or intent) he stomped a hole in it which had to be patched up. Watts reported (October 17) that: "It would be fatuous to criticise unduly The Who. The band are indubitably the most professional live performers on the rock scene... There are no highs or lows in their current performances – just a general-level of all-round competence, which ultimately has a slightly unsatisfying feeling about it. They neither take you to the heights, or plunge you in the depths, of emotional strata... It was hot stuff, but they never got it on properly. Maybe it was because The Who was disappointed with the venue... I feel essentially, though, that their act needs reconstructing to an extent... *Tommy* really is getting a bit thin, by now."

John Sebastion of The Lovin' Spoonful joined the band on stage to help out on 'Magic Bus'.

Sunday October 11
Odeon Theatre, Birmingham
2,500 fans were on hand to see Pete Townshend bring his spaniel dog Towser onto the stage to introduce the audience to the co-writer of 'Dogs Part 2'.

Tuesday October 13
Locarno Ballroom, Leeds

Friday October 16
Trentham Gardens, Stoke-on-Trent
The band postponed this concert as well as the Norwich gig the following night because Roger came down with bronchitis. This show was reset for Monday, October 26.

Saturday October 17
University of East Anglia, Norwich
The second performance postponed due to Roger's bronchitis.

Sunday October 18
Odeon Cinema, Lewisham, South London; one performance at 7 pm

Thursday October 22
ABC Cinema, Stockton-on-Tees; one show at 7:30 pm

Friday October 23
Green's Playhouse, Glasgow, Scotland; one concert at 8 pm
3,300 attended this show.

Saturday October 24
Sheffield University

Sunday October 25
Empire Theatre, Liverpool; one concert at 6:30 pm
2,500 watched The Who.

Monday October 26
Trentham Gardens, Stoke-on-Trent
This show was to make up for the gig postponed on Friday October 16.

THE WHO IS SOLD OUT
No door admission. — sorry
BRYAN, SOCIAL SECRETARY

Thursday October 29
Hammersmith Palais, West London; one show at 8:30 pm
Supported by Roger Spears Giant Kinetic Wardrobe. This was the last scheduled date of the autumn tour.

Chris Charlesworth: "I had started work at *Melody Maker* that summer. The Who had been my favourite band for ages and I gave them a great write-up after the show I saw at Dunstable (July 25). That was the first time I ever wrote about them. Much to my surprise Keith rang me up a week later to thank me. I was amazed that someone of his stature would take the trouble to ring up a reviewer. It hadn't happened before and it never really happened since. Keith was a great PR for the band but he was also genuinely pleased to meet anyone who loved The Who. We met for a drink a few days later at La Chasse Club in Wardour Street, the first time I'd met any of The Who. Keith said the next time The Who played in London I could be his guest at the show, so we went to Hammersmith Palais together in his lilac Rolls-Royce. This was just arranged between us – no PRs involved at all. Keith even gave me his phone number so I could call him and confirm arrangements. No other rock stars behaved like that, giving out their numbers to journalists.

"The Palais was absolutely heaving and what today would be called a mosh pit had assembled on the ballroom floor at the front of the stage. It was another great show and at the end Pete threw his guitar high into the air, almost hitting the lighting rig. It broke into two parts and he threw them into the crowd. There was a fight over them... someone had hold of the body and someone the neck, but the strings held them together. It was very frightening."

*Guitar destroyed: Gibson SG.

Saturday November 21
Leeds University
Less than a month after they last appeared in this city on the UK tour, The Who returned to the site of their triumphant February concert.

As an experiment, and mindful of the criticisms that *Tommy* was getting a bit stale on-stage (see entry for Brighton, October 10) and the fact that the band were sick of playing it, The Who used this concert to rearrange their live act. The set was restructured and *Tommy* was much curtailed in length. Despite the changes and a much shorter set, the concert worked well, as Pete later mentioned in *Sounds* (January 2, 1971): "It worked because they asked us back on again and we did an hour and a quarter encore. Just a blurb of old songs like 'Daddy Rolling Stone' and riffs we made up on the spare of the moment – 'Cinnamon Girl' – things like that. It was spontaneous and exciting." Amongst the other spontaneous and impromptu material that The Who had begun to play on stage during this period was a version of Free's 'All Right Now'. After this concert, Pete had overheard two fans talking in the gents' toilet. They both agreed that The Who had been very good, but one said that Deep Purple – who had played in Leeds the month before – were

a lot better, which set Pete thinking!

No gigs were planned after the Hammersmith Palais show on October 29 but sporadic dates were eventually set through December.

Thursday November 26
Fillmore North, Newcastle
This concert was cancelled due to Roger Daltrey being unable to reach the venue. Heavy fog had left Roger stranded on the motorway, and Pete, Keith and John came onstage – where the band's equipment was set up and ready – to tell the disappointed crowd that The Who couldn't play the concert without their lead singer and front man. The date was rescheduled for December 15.

Saturday November 28
Lanchester Polytechnic, Coventry
Local police restricted the number of tickets to 900 instead of the normal 1,150 at this concert in the interest of public safety. Part of their decision was based on the band's requirements for a new, larger stage which reduced audience space in the venue. The Student Union paid the £100 cost of the stage in addition to The Who's fee of £1,200.

Like the Leeds concert the week before, the act here was considerably restructured. But unlike Leeds, Pete Townshend considered this show to be a disaster, saying that it was "just terrifying because we had altered round a few numbers. We had dropped out quite a considerable amount of *Tommy*, 'Summertime Blues', and 'Shakin' All Over'. We thought we'd leave them while we were on top rather than let them deteriorate so we went on to play and we had finished in 45 minutes. Normally we play about two and a quarter hours so it just felt like a pittance... At Coventry we never got an encore, it was pretty bad and when it was over we just sat in the dressing room. It was the first bad gig for at least a year. I mean it's the worst gig I think we've done since the Metropolitan New York and that was pretty dire". (*Sounds*, January 2, 1971)

Saturday December 5
The Lads' Club, Norwich
This was played to make up for the Norwich cancellation of October 17.

Tuesday December 15
Fillmore North, Mayfair Ballroom, Newcastle

Chris Jones attended this concert and recalled The Who playing 'Daddy Rolling Stone' and Free's 'All Right Now' among their usual set. Jones also remembered Pete Townshend playing his guitar in a crouching position, aiming it like a machine-gun at the audience in a manner of the MC5's Wayne Kramer.

After this concert, Pete felt so elated and emotionally heightened by the experience that he wandered among the audience, with unexpected results, as he recalled: "We've played at rock concerts and I know damn well that when I've walked off the stage, me and a few of the audience have had to piece themselves back together again, in order to reincarnate who they were. The last time it happened, it was an uncanny experience. We were playing at Newcastle... and we walked off and I couldn't remember who I was – I swear it. I wandered out into the audience. I didn't go back into the dressing room and I got into a fight. Somebody started making remarks and I didn't know what they were talking about and I got into a fight with this guy and he started to beat the living daylights out of me and I sort of came to and got up and I started to do lots of showy things, pieced myself together again, went back to the dressing room and got a drink. And then I drove all the way home at 120 miles per hour. And by the time I got home I was me again. It was an amazing thing." (*Zigzag* No. 44, August 1974, interviewed in October 1971).

Wednesday December 16
Futurist Theatre, Scarborough

Sunday December 20
The Roundhouse, Chalk Farm, North London

Produced by Implosion, The Who played a charity show to benefit a Christmas Party for underprivileged children and old-age pensioners of Camden, sponsored by The Salvation Army Band and Choir! A relatively new artist by the name of Reginald Dwight, better known as Elton John, was also on the bill and Pete dedicated the evening's performance of *Tommy* to Elton. It was not performed again in its entirety until the reunion tour of 1989.

There were no advance ticket sales and only 2,000 tickets were available. Running order for the show was: Patto (4:30 to 5 pm), The Salvation Army Band, 50 members strong joined by a 50–voice choir (5:45 to 6 pm), Elton John (7 to 8:30 pm) and The Who from 9:30 "for as long as things are permitted to carry on".

Caroline Boucher, writing in *Disc and Music Echo* (December 26), said that this concert offered "proof positive that they're the best band in the land – it was a sweaty implosion... we've reviewed them a million times before until the superlatives are running dry. Suffice it to say they're the guv'nors."

Who concert for the poor

160

ROSEMONT HORIZON
LUNT AVE. and MANNHEIM RD.
ROSEMONT, IL.
TUESDAY EVENING AT 8:00 P.M.
OCT. 5 SCHLITZ
PRESENTS
THE WHO
UPPER LEVEL — $15.00
NO REFUNDS OR EXCHANGES
A CONTEMPORARY PRESENTATION

Celebrating 25 Years of
The Who
The Kids Are Alright Tour
1964-1989

4 H 412
SEC. ROW SEAT

BALCONY

Arie Crown Theatre

GOOD ONLY 1975
THURSDAY
EVG. MCH. 20

THE ARGUS TICKET CO.
LAKE 1 St.
CHICAGO

H
50

Nürnberg
Open
The ★ Air '79
Who
and
more
1.Sept.

22   J   109
SECTION   ROW   SEAT

ORCHESTRA

AT THE
UNIVERSAL AMPHITHEATRE

THURSDAY, AUGUST 24, 1989 AT 7:30 P.M.

THE ROCK AND ROLL HALL OF FAME presents

The WHO

PERFORMING THEIR ROCK OPERA

"TOMMY"

with Special Guests

Non Deductible $25
Tax-Deductible Portion $125 $150
ADMISSION PRICE

The dilemma that faced The Who, and Pete Townshend in particular, was how to follow *Tommy* as the deaf, dumb and blind boy was laid to rest. The *Tommy* section had occupied a substantial part of The Who's concert set, and it was clear that a major new work, or plenty of new songs, was needed to replace it. *Live At Leeds*, of course, was merely a stopgap.

Townshend had wanted to move The Who in a new direction which would combine their music with film, as well as live performance. Negotiations had been undertaken with various companies to film *Tommy* since mid-1969, but nothing had emerged. By mid-1970, however, Universal Pictures were taking a keen interest in The Who, but by this time, the band – and Townshend in particular – were no longer committed to taking *Tommy* any further: they simply wanted something new that was envisaged as a film treatment from the start. *Lifehouse* was Townshend's solution to The Who's (and the rock world in general's) problems: a concept work that would be a double-album, song-cycle, theatrical workshop, concert performance piece and big-budget feature film. It had a futuristic plot involving computer technology, synthesisers, state oppression and youth rebellion with a revelatory Who concert performance at its core. Concerts at London's Young Vic Theatre near Waterloo Station were expected to lead directly to a "filmed as it actually happened" piece of rock'n'roll celluloid. In reality, things didn't work out quite as easily as Pete had hoped. But, when all else failed, The Who emerged with a brilliant set of new songs.

Pete had been deeply affected by the audience reaction during Who concerts over the past two years, and among the many ideals of *Lifehouse* was his ambition for The Who to somehow enter into a state of unity with their audience, to break down totally the barrier that exists between audience and performer, and to this end plans were

hatched to present a new type of rock concert early in 1971. The first of these experimental shows at the Young Vic took place on Monday January 4 before a small invited audience. The shows ran on Sundays and Mondays only all the way through to early May.

There was then a short break for recording sessions in New York as the group laid down tracks for what was to become the *Who's Next* album. Kit Lambert was producing but the recordings were scrapped in favour of new versions that would be recorded later in London with Glyn Johns as producer. As a result, The Who's relationship with Lambert began a terminal decline. Throughout May the band played a number of unpublicised shows previewing much of the forthcoming album in smaller venues around England, just prior to the first leg of a two-part American tour.

The tour opened in New York with two shows at the Forest Hills Tennis Stadium on July 29 and 31. A youth was stabbed outside the venue on the

Pete Townshend: "We are intending to produce a fiction, or a play, or an opera and create a completely different kind of performance in rock.   We are writing a story and we aim to perform it on the first day we start work in this theatre. Tied in with the whole idea is the use of   quadrophonic sound and pre-recorded tapes. About 400 people will be involved with us and we aim to play music which represents them."
(Press Conference at the Young Vic Theatre, January 13, 1971).

first night in a dispute over tickets, and in torrential rain the band played the show wearing rubber shoes on a rubber carpeted, canopy-covered stage. The show on the 29th had been added since the first scheduled concert on the 31st had quickly sold out. Two nights later the group broke the attendance record at The Saratoga Performing Arts Center, attracting around 30,000 people to the amphitheatre.

For most of the tour the band played in large arenas as venues accommodating 4,000 to 5,000 people could no longer meet ticket demand. In Boston and Chicago they played multiple nights in theatres. The Who had worked hard to achieve wide acceptance in America, and this tour was the first in which they would play the big sports arena facilities. They now travelled with mountains of equipment and an army of road crew under the command of Peter Rudge, a fast-talking Cambridge graduate who had taken over the immense logistical task of keeping the show on the road and collecting the cash.

It had been almost a year since the group had toured Britain. The unpublicised gigs in May were fairly low key, as were the Young Vic shows earlier in the year. They returned to the UK concert stage for 16 dates, starting with a preview gig at Reading University on October 2. Ticket demand for the single performance in Glasgow on October 21 prompted the group to put on an additional concert there on November 9, three days after the last scheduled date of the tour. They were due to open the second leg of their US tour on November 20 in Charlotte, North Carolina, so the road crew had their work cut out to get all the equipment shipped over in time.

The Who were at the top of their form in America, playing to arena sized audiences with the greatest rock'n'roll show on the road. The *Who's Next* material necessitated Keith's use of headphones on 'Baba O'Riley' and 'Won't Get Fooled Again' to keep time with pre-recorded backing tracks, but the rest of the set still allowed him free rein. The tour wound its way through to California and ended on December 15 in Seattle. It would be two years before The Who would play America again.

Monday January 4
The Young Vic Theatre, Waterloo, South London

The Young Vic was the smallest venue that The Who had played in for years, with a capacity of 450. Townshend had visited the theatre, which had opened only a few months earlier, and was very impressed, feeling that it had an ideal workshop atmosphere in which to develop and film *Lifehouse*. Theatre director Frank Dunlop was also enthusiastic. The theatre itself had a thrust stage in the centre of the auditorium surrounded by benches on all sides. Pete's enthusiasm for the venue was such that this impromptu trial concert was held. It began as a rehearsal with the group simply testing the acoustics and facilities of the place, but after they had begun playing they felt the need to relate to an audience rather than empty benches. "We threw the doors open and let anyone come who wanted to," said Frank Dunlop (*Record Mirror*, January 23). "Even the police came and wanted to dance to the music."

Sunday February 14
The Young Vic Theatre, Waterloo, South London

The Who's experimental concerts at The Young Vic were to be filmed and recorded. They were intended to bring the rock concert to a new level of performer/audience alliance. An invited audience of about 200 people was brought into The Young Vic for this preview performance.

Monday February 15
The Young Vic Theatre, Waterloo, South London

It was reported that this performance was to be filmed.

Monday February 22
The Young Vic Theatre, Waterloo, South London

Monday March 1
The Young Vic Theatre, Waterloo, South London

Monday April 26
The Young Vic Theatre, Waterloo, South London

The set: 'Love Ain't For Keeping', 'Pure And Easy', 'Time Is Passing', 'Behind Blue Eyes', 'Too Much Of Anything' (introduced as 'Too Much'), 'Gettin' In Tune', 'Bargain', 'Pinball Wizard', 'See Me, Feel Me', 'Baby Don't You Do It', 'Water', 'My Generation' (including 'Road Runner'), 'Naked Eye', 'Bony Moronie', 'Won't Get Fooled Again'.

A live recording was made of this show as part of the continuing effort to establish some way of presenting *Lifehouse* in a workable form. It also gave The Who a chance to try out the newly-completed Rolling Stones Mobile Studio. The concert was approached in a casual manner and certainly didn't fulfil any of Townshend's early hopes for his new project. The band played through a tentative running order of old and new songs, with a few recently revived cover versions. The resulting tape, although technically excellent, was not considered good enough to be of immediate use.

'Love Ain't For Keeping' started the show in strident form, with all of the band on form; Moon and Entwistle's interplay being particularly illuminating. A drum roll from Moon took the band straight into 'Pure And Easy'. Some good-humoured banter with the small audience took place between songs, as Pete smoked a cigar in celebration of the birth of his second daughter, Aminta two days earlier: "I'm smoking that cigar 'cause I'm a proud father for the second time on Saturday. And in a minute I'm gonna be extremely sick because the cigar doesn't quite go with the

feeling of elation what I've naturally got." Comments from the crowd then prompted Pete to add jokingly: "I've had more fucks than you've had, mate!" 'Too Much Of Anything', one of the lesser new songs, sounded somewhat tentative and plodding, and the key change halfway through was nearly missed. 'Getting In Tune', a far stronger song, was given a more robust performance, led by Daltrey's rough but committed vocal. This rendition, however, switched from delicate arpeggios to block chords from Pete with little of the finesse the song required. It picked up some pace with a lengthy guitar solo, and then the song was reduced to a stark passage of drums and voices for the repeated chant "getting in tune to the straight and narrow".

"Now we'd like to do another new song," said Pete. "The new ones are feeling a wee bit lame. They'll come together. A song called 'Barge In'...'Bargain'." Although one of the best of the new songs, 'Bargain' sounded very disoriented and imprecise – none of the band seemed very familiar with what they were playing, and Keith Moon, especially, seemed unsure of the beat. The song only briefly came alive towards the end during a heavy guitar solo. It wasn't just the new material that sounded untogether. 'Pinball Wizard' lacked its usual excitement, as did 'See Me, Feel Me', although this latter song finished with a burst of spontaneous guitar riffing from Townshend. Daltrey joined in with this jam and it led directly, via Moon's drum beat, into 'Baby Don't You Do It', which sounded more raw and spontaneous than the preceding material and attained a good feel. Even so, the bass and drums stopped altogether for the second verse before promptly resuming.

Throughout the set, the audience was constantly calling out for old hits between numbers, and the band finally conceded by playing 'My Generation', albeit in a mediocre fashion. 'Road Runner', however, was excellent, despite Daltrey missing his cue to begin singing after Pete's descending scrape down the guitar strings, which he had to repeat. The song was also affected by Roger being distracted by a disturbance in the crowd when a female friend was being molested by a leery faction of the unruly audience. The transition into 'Naked Eye' was a little awkward, although this performance of the song was impressively powerful. An unexpected 'Bony

Moronie' was, like 'Road Runner', superb, if a little ramshackle. It effortlessly generated The Who's essential vision of rock'n'roll: it also counterpointed the sophistication of the new synthesiser-based songs which were to be an important part of Townshend's plan for *Lifehouse*. The more complex and futuristic the new Who songs became, the more base and visceral were the cover versions. This was probably a deliberate effort to retain balance and continuity with what the band had done in the past.

The only synthesiser-based song performed was 'Won't Get Fooled Again'. The backing tape was mixed in seamlessly with the live on-stage sound. Some purists might have considered this approach to be cheating, and the band risked getting out of time with the backing tape, but it worked remarkably well. Keith Moon followed the tape closely through a pair of headphones and kept the band in time. Even on this early performance, no problems were encountered playing along to the tape despite a false start in which Pete had to tune up, necessitating the tape being rewound by Bob Pridden at the mixing desk. The use of the synthesiser backing tape was the most experimental aspect of the show, and was something that hadn't been done by a band before in quite the same way. Groups like Pink Floyd and the Grateful Dead had used tape effects at live performances, and many artists had played and sung along to backing tapes during television and cabaret appearances, but The Who's innovative move opened up possibilities for synthesisers to be programmed in advance.

For Townshend, the synthesiser tapes were a mere toehold into a future era where on-stage technology could be used to gain a much more powerful, flexible and controlled result. In all other respects, however, this concert is best considered a public rehearsal, and the resulting tape was not at the time thought sufficiently good to warrant release on record.

The undisciplined but still enormously exciting 'Bony Maronie' from this show was released in 1988 as the B-side of a reissue of 'Won't Get Fooled Again' and again on The Who's four-CD box set in 1993. The live 'Naked Eye' on the box set also came from this show, as did the live version of 'Water' found among the bonus tracks on the reissue of *Who's Next* in 1995. An edited version of the concert (sans 'Pinball Wizard', 'See Me,

Feel Me', 'Baby, Don't You Do It' and 'Bony Maronie') was issued on the second disc of the expanded *Who's Next* in 2003.

Wednesday May 5
The Young Vic Theatre, Waterloo, South London

This was probably the last show at The Young Vic.

Friday May 7
Top Rank Suite, Sunderland

This is the first known gig in a series of unpublicised shows. The Who played around Britain in the spring of 1971. The band now had an album's worth of new material to perform, and these dates previewed that material. Almost all of the new songs ended up on *Who's Next*.

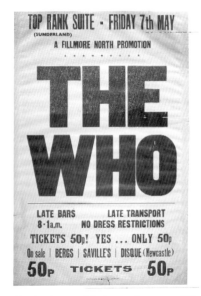

Despite the unsatisfactory performances at The Young Vic, The Who still felt a need to play their new material on stage in front of an audience. The stage was always their most natural environment and they yearned for the contact and immediate

audience response that concerts allowed. Unfortunately, the band were now so popular and conspicuous that every show they played became a massive event which created a frenzied clamour of media attention and enormous demand for tickets. After the disappointments at The Young Vic, they had become sensitive to possible adverse criticism of their as-yet-untested new material, and this prompted the most unusual tour of Britain they ever undertook. The tour took place intermittently during recording sessions at Olympic Studios for the new album.

The dates of this tour weren't announced or advertised and were all at provincial venues, although word soon spread that The Who were on the road. Leaflets and posters were distributed in each town a day in advance and the admission was 50p, less than half the average concert admission price at the time. Roger Daltrey even suggested that The Who would be accepting support slots, which were perhaps taking the "back-to-basics" maxim a little too far: "We're going to loon along to gigs and take second billing. It will be just a rehearsal to us. The people will be doing us a favour so we won't expect to get any money for it," he told *Record Mirror* (May 8). Even more surprisingly, he said that The Who were intending to play at the Oldfield Tavern in Greenford, London – perhaps the ultimate back-to-their-roots gesture. It remains unlikely that they did, however.

Despite the attempt at secrecy, the shows were packed out, and two of the first dates (in Birmingham and Liverpool) were even reviewed in *Disc and Music Echo* and *Melody Maker* respectively. Although fairly novel for a superstar act, these concerts were really very similar in practice to the weekend college gigs that the band had played throughout 1970. The venues were all well-known to the band and the new material was thoroughly worked into the set at these shows, although seven of the songs played on stage did not appear on the forthcoming LP, in spite of on-stage claims by the band that they would. Chris Jones (then studying at Newcastle University) reported that at this Sunderland gig, 'Shakin' All Over' was played as well as the new material. Jones commented that "'Behind Blue Eyes' was said to be a possible new single, the intro to 'Bargain' seemed much longer than on the recorded version, and 'Won't Get Fooled

Again' had the tape recorder with the backing track actually on the stage. It was a wonderful experience, and I felt high all the way back to Newcastle."

Thursday May 13
Kinetic Circus, Birmingham

"A strange show it was," recalled John Woffinden (*Generations*, No. 6, September 1991). "Much of the material was new. The opener was 'Love Ain't For Keeping' and the audience reaction was not the norm for a Who concert. The greatest memory though is 'Won't Get Fooled Again'. The second synthesiser passage when the lights went out was greeted with incredulity. No one knew what was going on, where were the lights? What was this 'one note organ' bit? Who was playing it? (It remains the only time I have heard this track live without a clapping audience.) Suddenly the drums, and then the scream. The lights came on (not on the audience) to show Roger's body arched back in mid-yell, Pete six feet in the air, arm windmilling, Keith flying over the drums and I'm sure John was smiling! It was a magic moment and the audience went crazy."

Nick Cavalier reviewed the show for *Disc and Music Echo* (May 22): "Over 3,000 delirious fans packed Birmingham's Kinetic Circus last Thursday to see The Who make a much awaited return to the city. It all added up to a wild night and The Who proved what a fine exciting band they really are. Roger Daltrey's vibrant vocals had everyone yelling for more. 'I Don't Even Know Myself' met with a tremendous reception, as did Bo Diddley's 'Road Runner' and another oldie, 'Water'. Roger Daltrey's microphone 'swinging' and Pete Townshend's on-stage perambulations and leaps made for complete all-round entertainment. After 90-minutes exhilarating guitar work by Pete on lead and John Entwistle on bass, plus the usual inimitable display on skins by Keith Moon, The Who called it a day, much to the disappointment of the fans, whose stomping and cries for more carried on for a full half hour after they had left the stage."

Friday May 14
Liverpool University

Set included: 'Love Ain't For Keeping', 'Pure And Easy', 'Time Is Passing', 'Behind Blue Eyes', 'Bargain', 'Getting In Tune', 'Too Much Of

THE WHO

OVER 2,000 tickets were sold within two days for a surprise concert by the Who — and with no publicity at all! The Who are frequent visitors to Liverpool and this time we were treated to an exclusive preview of their forthcoming album, which should be completed by mid-June.

The entire first half of their act was new material and each of the new ten songs was a gem. At last the Who have found something to replace "Tommy," though we did have "Pinball Wizard" and "See Me, Hear Me" to compensate. Also, they played the old Marvin Gaye song "Baby Don't You Do It" from their days at the Marquee. It was this song which got everyone going, led by Roger Daltrey.

No titles were given for the new songs but at a guess some were: "The Bargain," "Too Much Of Anything," "Time Is Passing," and their future single, which is a departure from the usual for the group, "Behind Blue Eyes."

which'll be out next year!" At this stage, of course, neither the band or the audience knew that out of the ten new songs played, only five would actually appear on the forthcoming Who's Next LP.

After 'Time Is Passing', Pete began to strum the opening chords to 'Bargain', and when the rest of the band did not join in, he abruptly stopped, wondering what had happened. The audience and the other members of the band burst out laughing. Realising he had started the wrong song by mistake, he went up to the mike and said: "We'd like to play an up-and-coming single, a bit untypical of The Who... It gets more typical later on. A new single, coming out in a couple of weeks and it's entitled 'Behind Blue Eyes'." Again, this beautiful song was played with a mastery that even The Who would not have been able to achieve a couple of years previously.

The introduction to 'Getting In Tune' was amusingly done by Keith, and the song sounded much stronger onstage than it eventually did on record. Regarding 'I Don't Even Know Myself', Daltrey commented: "It was supposed to be our last single, which never came out, and it's on the B-side of the new single which'll be out in two years!" As the band tore into Marvin Gaye's 'Baby Don't You Do It', Townshend encouraged handclaps, saying "it requires audience participation". This was a highlight of the show: a semi-funky Tamla beat (supercharged by Keith Moon) overlaid with Townshend's searing power-chord work, the full range of Daltrey's muscular voice, and the fluid agility of Entwistle's bass guitar. The Liverpool concert gained a favourable review by Peter Leay who noted that over 2,000 tickets had been sold in two days with no publicity at all: "The group's dynamics have matured and they have them off to a fine art... This has obviously evolved with them not having any personnel changes since the beginning... most of their new songs are more melodious than usual" (Melody Maker, May 22).

Anything', 'I Don't Even Know Myself', 'Baby Don't You Do It', 'Pinball Wizard', 'See Me, Feel Me', 'Water', 'My Generation', 'Won't Get Fooled Again'.

The Who were playing much better and seemed much more at ease with the new material, and turned in a classic concert. 'Bargain' was added to the set here, and was becoming a wonderful hard rocker. 'Love Ain't For Keeping' was much longer and much better played than previous shows. After a towering 'Pure And Easy', Daltrey said: "As you probably know, you'll probably only know a few of the numbers that we're doing early on in the act. We've only played them about twice to an audience before and so far they're going down very well. All written by Pete, every one of them. They're all on a new album we hope to complete around the middle of June,

Sunday May 23
Caird Hall, Dundee, Scotland

This was last known date in the series of May shows. Unlike the preceding concerts, this date was actually announced to the press as a one-off. Two and a half thousand fans attended. Maybe the band felt a Scottish venue would be beyond the reach of the London-based media and therefore the veil of secrecy could be lowered. As it turned out – unlike Birmingham and Liverpool – no reviewer was present at this show, and so no information has ever emerged. It should be noted that at this stage, The Who intended to continue with the *Lifehouse* film but had decided to release a double studio album of the work first. It was planned that filming should start later in the year when the stage act had matured. However, the series of concerts through April and May had proved that they could not play *Lifehouse* on stage as a solid central work like *Tommy*. Indeed, two of the most important songs, 'The Song Is Over' and 'Baba O'Riley', seemed technically impossible without a much-expanded line-up. The synthesiser backing tape was mastered on 'Won't Get Fooled Again' only, and it was some months before The Who actually attempted 'Baba O'Riley' on the stage.

Thursday July 1
Assembly Rooms, Worthing

Following a break in June during which The Who completed their recording work at Olympic Studios in preparation for the release of their new album, they returned to live concerts in readiness for a US tour. In the meantime, the band had made some decisions. The *Lifehouse* double concept album had been rejected in favour of a non-concept single album, *Who's Next*. 'Behind Blue Eyes' had been withdrawn as a single to be replaced by 'Won't Get Fooled Again'.

The second phase of The Who's 'secret' tour commenced here, with ticket prices still held at the ludicrously low 50p. In the 1990 BBC Radio programme *Classic Albums*, Pete Townshend recalled a concert around this time in Brighton. It is most likely that this date in nearby Worthing is the show he had in mind, as no trace of a Brighton concert can be found. This was The Who's final appearance in Worthing.

Saturday July 3
City Hall, Sheffield

The set: 'Love Ain't For Keeping', 'Pure And Easy', 'Time Is Passing', 'Behind Blue Eyes', 'Getting In Tune', 'Too Much Of Anything', 'Don't Even Know Myself', 'Baby Don't You Do It', 'Pinball Wizard', 'See Me, Feel Me', 'Water', 'My Generation', 'Naked Eye', 'Magic Bus', 'Won't Get Fooled Again'.

This show opened with the medium-paced rocker 'Love Ain't For Keeping', which was played a little awkwardly on this occasion and didn't flow quite as it should have done. 'Pure And Easy' which followed, however, was majestic and melodic, and built up powerfully over six minutes, including an extra verse which the recorded version lacked. It climaxed with a powerful guitar riff that was much extended under Daltrey's repeated line: "There once was a note – listen!" 'Time Is Passing' was a country-flavoured song that the band soon abandoned (both on stage and on record) and it came over as one of the lighter songs of the evening. 'Behind Blue Eyes', the stunning ballad, really made an impact with its impeccable backing vocals. Keith Moon introduced the next song, 'Getting In Tune', which stood out as one of the strongest of the new songs, played at about twice the length of the version released on record. In the middle of the song, the instrumentation dropped to just drums and three voices singing the catch line "Getting in tune to the straight and narrow". The song then built up again and finished with a tortured guitar solo from Pete Townshend.

In comparison, 'Too Much Of Anything' seemed weak. 'I Don't Even Know Myself' was familiar from the band's 1970 concerts and was here introduced as the B-side of the next Who single. Perhaps the biggest surprise to the audience was 'Baby Don't You Do It', introduced by Pete as a song revived from the Marquee Club circa 1964. Moon beat out the intro, to which the audience clapped along and the song built into a manic hard rocker. The crowd was then rewarded with the two songs from *Tommy*, followed by 'Water', which the band had previously played rather better than on this occasion. 'My Generation' developed into a jam based upon an unusual bluesy riff and featured great playing from Keith Moon and Pete Townshend. The epic 'Won't Get Fooled Again' was saved until last and sounded tight and hard as the band played along to the backing tape.

Sunday July 4
De Montfort Hall, Leicester

The Who played a 90 minute set for the 2,000 fans that packed the De Montfort Hall. The *Melody Maker* reviewer (July 10) of this Leicester concert, Howard Bennett, was obviously unaware of the concerts in May and assumed that this was the first Who gig since the Young Vic. It was noted that the best of the new songs was a "rip-roaring number with Townshend and Daltrey keying-up to provide vocals" entitled 'Barking' [sic]. Townshend introduced 'Behind Blue Eyes' by saying "this one is like we never have done before". Despite the wild applause and cheering for ten minutes, they didn't, of course, return for an encore. The audience was told the equipment had broken down, which sounds very much like an excuse. "They're back," Bennett wrote, "just as dynamic and exciting as ever... what a night it was... all at their very best."

It was on their way to this gig that the famous 'monolith' album cover photo for *Who's Next* was shot by Ethan Russell on a slag heap just outside of Sheffield. Keith and John had been discussing Stanley Kubrick's film *2001 – A Space Odyssey* in the car when the 'call of nature' prompted a roadside stop. Backstage, Russell photographed The Who larking around for the rear sleeve shot of *Who's Next*.

Thursday July 8
The Pavilion, Bath

A return to a venue last played in August 1969, this was the Who's final appearance here. Plans to stage an open air free festival in Bath in September were subsequently abandoned by promoter Fred Bannister.

Saturday July 10
Civic Hall, Dunstable

Set included: 'Substitute', 'I Can't Explain', 'Magic Bus', 'See Me, Feel Me', 'Pinball Wizard', 'My Generation'.

Chris Charlesworth resumed writing about The Who in *Melody Maker* with this show (July 17). (Charlesworth had seen the band earlier in the year at the Young Vic but Townshend had made it clear that he didn't want any publicity for the band's new project for fear of swamping The Young Vic with thousands of fans which it couldn't accommodate.) At the start of this show a "slight malfunction of Pete's amplifiers" caused him to knock them over in disgust, a feeling he obviously never lost, for at the end of the concert he smashed his guitar: "In a climax that only The Who can generate, Pete smashed one of his current three Gibsons into fragments to the obvious approval of the capacity crowd. While Keith knocked his drum kit off the platform, Pete hurled the remains of the guitar in the audience bent on rushing the stage for souvenirs. What a climax... and what a group." Charlesworth reported that the new material was in as good a shape as the old, but named only the classic material that was played (probably because *Who's Next* wasn't released in the UK until August 25). "Mountains may tumble and fall," he concluded, "and supergroups come and go, but The Who will always be with us. And while they are, they continue to wear the crown of the most exciting live band in existence."

*Guitar destroyed: Gibson SG Special

Monday July 12
Winter Garden, Eastbourne

As with the Worthing and Bath shows, Eastbourne was last visited by The Who in August 1969, and never again returned to as the band's touring policy increasingly eschewed smaller provincial towns.

Thursday July 15
Town Hall, Watford

A return to the scene of many past glories from their early days, the band here bade farewell to Watford, a town which the superstar touring schedules of the 1970s invariably passed by! Commenting on this series of concerts, Townshend told Chris Charlesworth in *Melody Maker* (July 17): "What we have to do now is rebuild ourselves because we were so heavily involved in the film idea. We have being doing gigs without any advance publicity here and there, not because we were testing out a new stage act and didn't want any publicity but because we always do gigs like that. They are not very big gigs and they will sell out instantly. If we advertise them in the press there will be lots of people turning up who can't get in. We like playing these small gigs. We did four shows before we started recording to try the new act out on stage. The audience knew that and so did the promoters. We are doing another three this weekend. We had to go back to gigging and find our feet again after the film business before we could start moving anywhere."

The Who Play First Program Of '71 Here Despite Downpour

Thursday July 29
Forest Hills Tennis Stadium, Flushing, New York

The band kicked off their 1971 US tour with two shows at this open-air venue.

Set: 'Love Ain't For Keeping', 'Pure And Easy', 'My Wife', 'I Can't Explain', 'Substitute', 'Bargain', 'Behind Blue Eyes', 'Won't Get Fooled Again', 'I Don't Even Know Myself', 'Baby Don't You Do It', 'Pinball Wizard', 'See Me, Feel Me', 'Water', 'My Generation', 'Magic Bus'.

Supported by Labelle (whose début album Kit Lambert had just produced), this show formed

The Who tied rubber blocks to their shoes to avoid electrocution and played a long concert in a steady rain Thursday at the Forest Hills Tennis Stadium in Queens.

part of the season of the "Forest Hills Music Festival", promoted by Ron Delsener. Despite the technical difficulties caused by the weather, the band reached its usual exciting peak on 'Bargain' – a song reliant upon the kind of precise musical dynamics of which The Who were capable – and sustained the frantic standard through the highlight of 'Baby Don't You Do It'. This song, with its loose, free-form structure, was emerging as the key number in which The Who as pure musicians triumphed. It functioned in the live set as 'Young Man Blues' had done during the previous few years: the semi-improvised heavy-metal blow-out of the set.

Mike Jahn, reviewing for the *New York Times* (July 31), wrote: "Most of the words were indecipherable, lost in the notorious volume that characterises The Who... Peter Townshend and Roger Daltrey maintained an insult match with their equipment handlers all evening." In his book *The Who* (1979), John Swenson described the finale of this concert: "At the end of 'Magic Bus', Townshend broke the neck off his guitar and flung it into the photographers' pit. When a jittery roadie scuttled out to retrieve the body, Townshend threatened him with menacing gestures to stand aside (Who roadies always turn out to be Townshend's straight men during a Who performance). Townshend then took a second guitar and, grabbing it like a paddle, picked up the body of the broken first guitar, tossed it into the air, and slammed it with the second guitar as it came down. Both guitars broke into pieces at Townshend's feet. He then picked up a microphone stand and beat the mangled guitar bodies into splinters..." John Entwistle even demolished one of his Gibson Thunderbird basses!

Chuck Pulin said in *Sounds* (August 7): "This concert re-affirmed in my mind that The Who are one of the most important rock bands working today, close on the heels of the Stones and perhaps passing them with their pure energy and skill."

The Who's original tour schedule proposed that the opening concert on this date be held at the 12,900-seat Civic Center in Baltimore, Maryland. This was scrapped when this second Forest Hills date was added.

*Guitars destroyed: Gibson SG Specials

Saturday July 31
Forest Hills Tennis Stadium, Flushing, New York

Set: 'Love Ain't For Keeping', 'Pure And Easy', 'My Wife', 'I Can't Explain', 'Substitute', 'Bargain', 'Behind Blue Eyes', 'Won't Get Fooled Again', 'I Don't Even Know Myself', 'Baby Don't You Do It', 'Pinball Wizard', 'See Me, Feel Me', 'Water', 'My Generation', 'Magic Bus', 'Naked Eye', improvisation, 'Road Runner'. The second of two sold out shows in New York where over 30,000 fans saw the two concerts.

In contrast to the first show, the weather was dry and hot for this concert, and the conditions had brought out a plague of cockroaches that intermittently crawled across the stage at the risk of being crushed underneath Pete Townshend's Doc Marten boots! A smoother and more stable concert than the first night, The Who emerged at their inspired best. 'Pure And Easy' suffered from a guitar cut-out midway through the solo, which disoriented the band until Daltrey intervened with the verse, promptly supported by a fine drum roll from Keith, guiding the band back into the rhythm of the song. "A few guitar problems which we'll sort out," explained Roger. "The first number was on our new album called 'Love Ain't For Keeping'. The second one isn't on an album at the moment, written by Pete, a number called 'Pure And Easy'. This one's by the Ox over here..." 'My Wife' which followed was a formidable performance, based upon John Entwistle's incessant bass riffing.

"Can we have some bloody monitors, thank you very much!" Roger snapped at Bob Pridden before 'I Can't Explain'. Daltrey later ribbed Pete a little about the guitar problems: "Big T... Gone very quiet tonight... Got a few problems with his guitars..." Pete then responded, sardonically: "No trouble... No trouble with the guitar... I don't like guitars, they don't like me!" Prior to 'Behind Blue Eyes', Pete yelled: "Another cockroach! When you find a cockroach in your cutlery drawer, this is what you do..." and he promptly jumped upon the offending insect. "Never mind the cutlery!" 'Baby Don't You Do It' prompted Townshend's account of the song: "We used to play it at a club in London and we were very chic because we played Tamla Motown songs. This is a song we play today, we still feel very chic. We still dig it." An exceptionally good version of 'Water' was also performed here and introduced by Pete with an allusion to the rain of two days previously: "It's a long way from Thursday, and any of you that were here on Thursday will remember how wet it was. Today it's dry, and it's hot and sticky... We would like to sing a song about hot and sticky weather... 'New York, New York'! And this one's called 'Water' and it's about a man trudging across the desert with footsteps like this... Killing cockroaches!"

A startling improvisation by Pete followed 'Naked Eye': a jagged profusion of guitar riffs which Moon managed miraculously to hold together with his imaginative beat. After a while, Townshend's reckless guitar figures stabilised into the boogie rhythm of 'Road Runner' – in all, a devastating conclusion.

Monday August 2
Saratoga Performing Arts Center, Saratoga Springs, New York

The Who set an attendance record with 27,753 paying customers at the Performing Arts Center. All told, about 30,000 were on hand, including gate-crashers. Set: as New York, July 29.

This concert was relayed to the audience on a closed-circuit video monitoring system, which was unusual at the time. Unfortunately, a video recording of the show seems not to have been made, or has languished unseen since this date. 'Pure And Easy' was a brilliant performance, and featured a very long guitar solo. The song was all-too-briefly included in The Who's live act, and this version at Saratoga must rate as the greatest live performance of the song they ever played. Pure inspiration, as John Swenson reported: "That night 'Pure And Easy' emerged as one of the keys to the magic Townshend had been reaching for, uniting audience and performers in the search for that one perfect note" (*The Who*, 1979).

'My Wife' started a little lamely but soon recovered its strident pace. Short and snappy versions of 'I Can't Explain' and 'Substitute' were followed by Pete telling the audience to sit down. Then, referring to the 2,000 gate-crashers when introducing 'Bargain', he said "it's what some of you are getting!" Amp problems prevented 'Bargain' being played for a short while, and when it did the guitar cut out towards the end of the first verse. 'Behind Blue Eyes' was very strong, and Roger discarded his mike before 'Won't Get Fooled Again', complaining it was faulty. "That one's no good" he quipped, throwing it onto the floor. "That one's a cockroach," retorted Pete – remembering Forest Hills – and threatening to stamp on the microphone! After 'Won't Get Fooled Again', its B-side 'I Don't Know Myself' was a bit of an anticlimax, although 'Pinball Wizard' was rapturously received. Some tuning problems were suffered at the beginning of 'Water', and at the end of 'Magic Bus', Pete solved the problem for good by viciously dismembering the cherry-red Gibson SG guitar!

*Guitar destroyed: Gibson SG Special

Tuesday August 3
The Spectrum, Philadelphia, Pennsylvania. 8 pm
Supported by Labelle (led by Patti LaBelle), this show was attended by 19,500 fans.

Wednesday August 4
Music Hall, Boston, Massachusetts
The group played to over 13,000 people during their four nights in Boston. Overwhelming popular demand necessitated a fourth show in

the 4,500-seat venue. On this opening night, The Who returned for a rare encore and the usual guitar-smashing finale.

*Guitar destroyed: Gibson SG Special.

Thursday August 5
Music Hall, Boston, Massachusetts
Set: 'Love Ain't For Keeping', 'Pure And Easy', 'My Wife', 'I Can't Explain', 'Substitute',

'Bargain', 'Behind Blue Eyes', 'Won't Get Fooled Again', 'I Don't Even Know Myself', 'Baby Don't You Do It', 'Pinball Wizard', 'My Generation', 'Magic Bus', 'See Me, Feel Me', 'Daddy Rolling Stone', improvisation, 'Road Runner', improvisation.

The Who ploughed through the beginning of the set at an ear-splitting volume, and it was soon apparent that the sound system was causing problems. Daltrey – perhaps unable to hear himself – mixed up the lyrics on the last chorus of 'Substitute'. Then prior to 'Bargain', Pete Townshend said: "I'm terribly sorry about you with your fingers in your ears. A very sad sight to see. We have slight problems adjusting from a 4,000-seat hall to a 30,000-seat hall. We're trying to bridge the gap. We're playing four nights. If we're a bit loud in Boston, it's because we're not loud enough in other places. Just don't put your fingers in your ears, otherwise I'll throw me guitar at you!"

A towering version of 'Bargain' then followed. Roger said to the audience: "I'd like to introduce you to a very unusual character and tonight he's playing the role of Mr Keith Moon!" Pete added: "And now all the little girls on the left, and all the little boys on the right – why don't you get together and make something happen in the middle?" Keith finally took the mike and delivered in

Tickets on sale·11am·July 10·Music Hall

a perfect American accent his "showbiz super-star" spiel: "I was born in Boston. I was born here. I met the rest of the guys in the band right here on this very stage. And we'd like to dedicate the next one to us..."

Later in the show, Pete introduced 'Pineball Blizzard', which put his guitar well and truly out of tune before 'My Generation'. A very long version of 'Magic Bus' featured some excellent harmonica playing from Roger. The end of the show adopted a looser and more improvised approach with a rare and jaunty reading of 'Daddy Rolling Stone' which moved into a spontaneous guitar riff before 'Road Runner'. Not being able to resist the feeling of the moment, after this hard rocking finale, Pete ploughed into yet another spur-of-the-moment guitar figure. These improvisations were becoming less frequent in 1971 than they had been over the previous two years, but they always added a welcome freshness and spontaneity to any performance.

Friday August 6
Music Hall, Boston, Massachusetts
The Music Hall shows had been plagued by sound problems and the third night brought everything to a climax. During 'My Generation' Roger yelled to Pete to turn down his amps but Pete refused. Roger then kicked two of Townshend's amps to the ground. As Who roadie Mick Bratby went to set up the fallen stack, Roger kicked a third amp and it came crashing down on Bratby's head causing a serious gash and knocking him unconscious. Roger ran off stage, pur-

sued by lighting engineer Tony Haslam, leaving The Who as a trio to finish a chaotic performance.

Saturday August 7
Music Hall, Boston, Massachusetts
The original itinerary called for the band to appear at the Yale Bowl in New Haven, Connecticut, on this date. Instead, the technical problems now resolved, they added a fourth and final night at the Music Hall. Set: 'Love Ain't For Keeping', 'Pure And Easy', 'My Wife', 'I Can't Explain', 'Substitute', 'Bargain', 'Behind Blue Eyes', 'Won't Get Fooled Again', 'I Don't Even Know Myself', 'Baby Don't You Do It', 'Pinball Wizard', 'My Generation', 'Magic Bus', 'Naked Eye', 'See Me, Feel Me', 'Daddy Rolling Stone'.

Conscious of the sound problems of the previous two nights, Daltrey mentioned The Who's new PA system: "We spent all day today trying to sort out the problems we had last night and we'll probably spend all day tonight sorting out for tomorrow evening. We're using a new sound system... it sounds all right up here. How's it sound out there, all right?"

Monday August 9
War Memorial Auditorium, Rochester, New York
A sell-out crowd of 9,000 people packed the War Memorial.

Guitar destroyed: Gibson SG Special

Tuesday August 10
Civic Arena, Pittsburgh, Pennsylvania
Attendance: 18,000

Thursday August 12
Public Hall, Cleveland, Ohio
The set: 'Love Ain't For Keeping', 'Pure And Easy', 'My Wife', 'I Can't Explain', 'Substitute', 'Bargain', 'Behind Blue Eyes', 'Won't Get Fooled Again', 'I Don't Even Know Myself', 'Baby, Don't You Do It', 'Pinball Wizard', 'See Me, Feel Me', 'My Generation', 'Magic Bus', 'Naked Eye'.

Prior to this concert, Pete was interviewed live in the radio studios of WMMS-FM, and during the conversation he uttered a prophetic sentence on the subject of his position as a rock figurehead: "One of the reasons The Who have been so long-lasting is because of the fact that we've been careful not to preach and careful not to teach..." This statement was later incorporated into the lyrics of 'The Punk And The Godfather' (from *Quadrophenia*).

Friday August 13
O'Hara Arena, Dayton, Ohio
Set included 'I Can't Explain', 'Substitute', 'My Wife', 'Bargain', 'Behind Blue Eyes', 'Won't Get Fooled Again', 'I Don't Even Know Myself', 'Baby Don't You Do It', 'Pinball Wizard', 'See Me, Feel Me', 'My Generation'.

Problems with the sound balance were encountered in Dayton, and the 7,500 strong audience witnessed a show which succeeded well despite the minor technical lapses which characterised The Who's performance. 'Bargain' almost fell apart from the beginning as Daltrey began to sing his first line and the instruments missed the beat, although they recovered quickly. Pete said of 'Behind Blue Eyes': "This is another one off the album... which might have been – could have been – a single, but we kinda figured it wasn't 'today', it was 'yesterday'. Listen to this... It's minus Keith Moon and then later on we find him. You listen to this." Following 'Behind Blue Eyes', Townshend delivered an interesting comment about Moon: "He's horrible but human! Here, listen. LISTEN! I'm getting complaints at the front at somebody who's standing up, believe it or not, to tell 'em to sit down. Which is about as fucked up as you usually are... Yes, here we go... I don't know what they mean but... rock'n'roll's all that

counts. It is, I'm telling you. In ten years you'll know, 'cause ten years has passed [and] we know. This song is about the last ten years. It's about you. It's about us. Mainly it's about rock'n'roll. A song called 'Won't Get Fooled Again'!"

The impact of the song was blighted by the accompanying backing tape being mixed slightly too high above the group. Keith Moon perpetuated an in-joke among the band that 'I Don't Even Know Myself' was the "A-side of a single that there were two A-sides to. So take your pick." The song was very well played and contrasted well with the more raucous material on offer. 'Baby Don't You Do It', claimed Pete, was "a chance for us to really get off on you. It's an old song we used to play a long time ago... It's turning out to be one of the best live numbers we do." This turned out to be a prescient comment: The Who delivered to the Dayton crowd what must have been the most exciting and inspired performance of 'Baby Don't You Do It' they ever played. It gelled with a musical explosiveness that showed just how untouchable they were. It lasted ten minutes and Daltrey and Moon took the honours during the first part of the song with the meaty, unstoppable drum beat and Roger's expressive vocal range. John's bass lines were all in place (as ever) and Pete's guitar just sang during the latter stages of the number, as he turned in a devastating guitar solo in which the rapturous notes followed each other in joyous and swift succession.

Saturday August 14
Cobo Arena, Detroit, Michigan, one show at 8:30 pm
Who's Next was released in the US on this date.

Sunday August 15
Metropolitan Sports Center, Minneapolis, Minnesota
The group gave a 95-minute performance for a capacity crowd of 18,000 fans, with LaBelle on the bill.

Monday August 16
Edwardsville Campus, Southern Illinois University, Edwardsville, Illinois
The Who attracted nearly as many people to one show as the St. Louis Symphony Orchestra did for their entire 1971 season. The annual Mississippi River Festival was assured a 1972 sea-

son with the success of this one concert. More than 34,000 people came to see The Who's performance with LaBelle and Wishbone Ash as the opening acts.

*Guitar destroyed: Gibson SG Special.

Tuesday August 17
The Auditorium Theater, Chicago, Illinois

The Who ended the first leg of a two-part American tour with three nights in this beautiful theatre in downtown Chicago. All shows were sold out well in advance. Set: 'Summertime Blues', 'My Wife', 'Love Ain't For Keeping', 'I Can't Explain', 'Substitute', 'Bargain', 'Behind Blue Eyes', 'Won't Get Fooled Again', 'Baby Don't You Do It', 'I Don't Even Know Myself', 'Pinball Wizard', 'See Me, Feel Me', 'My Generation', 'Naked Eye', 'Magic Bus'.

This show has a reputation as having been greatly marred by technical problems with the sound system, a similar situation to the earlier shows in Boston. However, The Who actually turned in a top-notch performance throughout, which the audience certainly greeted warmly. Prior to 'Bargain', Keith Moon had yelled at the audience: "Get your arses up, kick your legs in the air and listen to a song that Pete wrote!" Roger said that 'Behind Blue Eyes' was going to be released as a single "but unfortunately it was much too nice for what we really are." The performance here, however, was near-perfect, as was the epic performance of 'Won't Get Fooled Again', which went down very well. Daltrey reminisced with the crowd about previous Chicago concerts at the "Electric Circus" (meaning the Kinetic Circus, where the band last played in 1969). 'Baby Don't You Do It' was hard and heavy.

John Swenson commented in his book *The Who* that: "Throughout the tour, their sound people had gotten into the habit of turning everything up full blast. In the Auditorium Theater on the first

Mississippi River Festival
WALTER SUSSKIND, Music Director

TONIGHT AT 8:30
(Lawn Seating Only)

THE WHO
LABELLE

COME EARLY AND DINE

night, that produced disastrous results. The sound was so loud it was literally painful, and the extreme distortion made things very difficult to appreciate. Townshend's guitar was barely audible, washed under by a roar of deafening, undistinguished sound. Still, the audience contained more than a fair share of die-hard Who freaks who were happy with what they got. 'Won't Get Fooled Again' somehow had a chance to sink in, and the audience responded exultantly. But when the opening chords of 'Pinball Wizard' were cut off by a short in the overloaded power system, Townshend was at his wit's end. 'We'll take care of that later!' he snarled as they stood waiting for the power to be restored. Ten minutes later the show ended abruptly when Townshend, his face white with frustration and rage, nearly destroyed a bank of stage lights along with his guitar."

Wednesday August 18
The Auditorium Theater, Chicago, Illinois

Set: 'Summertime Blues', 'My Wife', 'Love Ain't For Keeping', 'I Can't Explain', 'Substitute', 'Bargain', 'Behind Blue Eyes', 'Won't Get Fooled Again', 'Baby Don't You Do It', 'Pinball Wizard', 'See Me, Feel Me', 'My Generation', 'Magic Bus'.

Bob Pridden was able to adjust the sound system to avoid the problems of Tuesday night, and this concert offered a much more stabilised sound quality: very loud, but clear and exact. The Who were always a band whose musicianship was adversely affected by technical hiccups, and Bob Pridden, John Wolff and the team of roadies knew all too well that they were employed by a group of notoriously temperamental perfectionists. If the equipment and sound engineering were up to scratch, then the band were more relaxed and able to deliver a brilliant show. If they weren't, then things started to break...

*Guitar destroyed: Gibson SG Special

Thursday August 19
The Auditorium Theater, Chicago, Illinois

The closing night of the summer tour and the last of three shows in Chicago. Set: 'Summertime Blues', 'My Wife', 'Love Ain't For Keeping', 'I Can't Explain', 'Substitute', 'Bargain', 'Behind Blue Eyes', 'Won't Get Fooled Again', 'Baby Don't You Do It', 'I Don't Even Know Myself', 'Pinball Wizard', 'See Me, Feel Me', 'My Generation', improvisations, 'Naked Eye', 'Magic Bus'.

The final show in Chicago was a classic Who performance combining musical brilliance with Townshend and Moon's between-numbers comic patter. 'I Can't Explain' was a particularly outstanding version, proving just how fresh the band managed to keep their oft-played older material. Pete announced: "This is our last show this tour. We're going home in a couple of days..." He then said that they would be returning to the States for another tour in a couple of months, but not to Chicago, which produced some disappointment from the audience. "Come to us, come to us!" Pete quipped. "There's nothing like an aeroplane... We'd like to dedicate this very sad song to those of you who'll never ever see The Who again because you got killed on the plane which crashes on the way to the gig..." After the song, Townshend introduced 'Won't Get Fooled Again' as Keith was putting on the headphones which he used to monitor the backing tape. "FM stations!" Pete said, as if Keith couldn't hear him. "He gets bored up there, you know, so he tunes into the local stations and grooves to Crosby, Stills, Nash & Young. He's a very funny guy. You should spend ten years of your life with Keith Moon. You'd know what funny means."

Roger Daltrey followed-up Moon's earlier joke by referring to 'I Don't Even Know Myself' as the A-side of The Who's new single. 'Pinball Wizard' was a little less charged than usual but 'See Me, Feel Me' proved to be the triumphant climax of the set. A lengthy guitar solo followed 'My Generation' and led into various spontaneous guitar phrases and riffs before concluding with a powerful reading of 'Naked Eye' which formed a seamless 20-minute medley. John Swenson wrote that "The last show in Chicago was appropriately climatic... The Who ended their *Who's Next* tour in a hailstorm of furious sound, leaving yet another American audience dazed in their wake."

The group had played for 215,000 people during the three week swing, their most successful tour to date. Another three week jaunt through the south and west was set for later in the year. The tour was originally planned to conclude with three large open air concerts. The Who attempted once more to play at the 9,000 capacity Red Rocks Amphitheatre in Denver for two nights on August 22 and 24. Again, the Denver authorities blocked the shows, as they had a year earlier. The band had also planned to hold a huge free concert in Central Park, New York City on August 29. "The Mayor wouldn't have us," commented Roger Daltrey in *Melody Maker* (August 28).

Who's Next would be released in the UK on August 27. It became the only Who album ever to top the UK album charts.

Saturday September 4
Hyde Park, London

What could have been The Who's biggest London concert to date was cancelled. The band had intended to stage a huge free concert on this date, with an anticipated audience of over 200,000. The Greater London Council authorities rejected this proposal on account of its size. Roger Daltrey angrily commentated in *Melody Maker* (August 28): "Sometimes I just don't understand England: they let an all-promotion-machine-band like Grand Funk do a free concert in Hyde Park but authorities won't let British bands do it... It's bloody tragic that free shows are being sabotaged by authority." Despite Daltrey's comments, a Hyde Park concert went ahead on this date albeit on a much smaller scale (and without The Who). Plans to hold the free concert in Bath later in September also foundered.

Who retain title at Oval

Saturday September 18
The Oval Cricket Ground, Kennington, South London

Set: 'Summertime Blues', 'My Wife', 'Love Ain't For Keeping', 'I Can't Explain', 'Substitute', 'Bargain', 'Behind Blue Eyes', 'Won't Get Fooled Again', 'Baby Don't You Do It', 'Pinball Wizard', 'See Me, Feel Me', 'My Generation', 'Naked Eye', 'Magic Bus'.

Well over 30,000 fans packed the Test Cricket and Surrey County Cricket Club ground for an event that ran from 11 am to 9:30 pm, making this the largest audience to date that The Who had attracted in their home town. George Harrison had staged the Concert For Bangladesh on August 1 in New York and this show was Britain's contribution to that cause. The Who donated their fee of £9,148 to the Bangla Desh Relief Fund and the day's total contribution came to £15,000, though there was some controversy over whether the money actually reached the victims it was intended to help.

Thwarted in their attempt to stage a concert in Hyde Park (see September 4), The Who considered alternative venues but finally opted to play at this event – billed as *Goodbye Summer* – instead. The bill featured (in order): Cochise, The Grease Band, Lindisfarne, Quintessence, Mott The Hoople, America, Atomic Rooster, The Faces, The Who.

The Who's set opened with the riff to 'My Size' from John Entwistle's recently-released solo album, *Smash Your Head Against The Wall*, which they had never played before (and never did again). It actually sounded like a parody of Led Zeppelin! This quickly abated, however, and the set proper began with 'Summertime Blues' and was swiftly followed by John Entwistle's steamroller riffing on 'My Wife'. The band were in high spirits and Townshend jokily introduced the new material: "what is currently riding high in the charts at number seven, on *Who's Next*, and it's a song called 'Love Ain't For Keeping'..." Pete then comically adopted a lecherous 'dirty old man' accent: "Specially not on a night like this, love, ho ho ho... See you round the gents... I'll see you round the silly mid-off after..."

The Who played a fine, tight show that was fired by the kind of nervous energy that pushed them to sublime limits. Townshend later asked the crowd: "You can't see my fancy outfit, then?

This song's for you that are blind, and can't see my fancy outfit. And you can have me guitar after an' all. Pick it clean... " 'Naked Eye' probably formed the high point of this superb concert and it segued into 'Magic Bus'. The show finished in noise and instrument destruction, and compere Jeff Dexter made his final address of the evening as The Who left the stage: "As you can see, an encore is impossible. We have drums everywhere. As they go to the dressing room, please say an incredible thank you to The Who." The Who's roadies wore cricket whites for the event, as did Dexter, while at one point Keith Moon played his drums with a cricket bat.

This concert was officially recorded on the Pye Mobile by a production company who were hoping to release a live album of the concert (as happened with the George Harrison event in New York), but this later proved too difficult to negotiate with the various acts. The eight-track tape of The Who's set subsequently proved to be of insufficient technical quality for release.

"The Who were amazing," wrote Bill McAllister in *Record Mirror* (September 25), "... they had all the punch and fire and professionalism that the Faces lacked."

The Oval concert was the only show The Who played in September, although they had originally proposed a concert at Bristol University on September 25, which was cancelled.

Guitar destroyed: Gibson SG Special

Tuesday September 28
Free Trade Hall, Manchester

Saturday October 2
Reading University

A low-key warm-up show, this was only publicised on campus the day before and attracted a capacity audience of 800. Charles Shaar Murray, future *New Musical Express* staff writer and long-standing Who fanatic, witnessed The Who for the first time at this show. He recalled a few years later: "That combination of power and humour, anger and compassion, gracefulness and clowning, all those incredible songs... the audience just sat on the floor and stared at them, open-mouthed and awe-struck."

After the show, Keith Moon quickly vacated his drum stool and ran round the outside of the hall. He burst in through the main entrance behind the

audience, and began to yell "rubbish" towards the stage! It is likely that this concert saw the first live performance of Pete's *Lifehouse* masterpiece 'Baba O'Riley', which after considerable rehearsal, the band had managed to master by playing along to a taped synthesiser part.

Saturday October 9
Surrey University Gymnasium, Guildford, Surrey

Chris Charlesworth: "Keith invited me along to this gig but I was sworn to secrecy. Entry was restricted to University students only and advertised only 24 hours in advance. Around 600 tickets were available, making this probably the smallest venue The Who ever played during the Seventies. The temporary stage in the gym was only a couple of feet off the ground. It didn't seem overcrowded but the crowd could almost touch the band. John Sebastian, who with his wife was Keith's house guest at the time, came along and jammed on harmonica during the set. It was also John's 27th birthday, so there was a merry mood on and off stage. It all contributed to a great set. They were on top form and because of the size of the venue it was one of the very best Who shows

I ever saw. A truly magic evening, but not without its downside for me…"

A report on the show by a staff writer in *New Musical Express* the following week puzzled the band and their entourage since the writer in question hadn't been there! Under Richard Green's by-line the following appeared (October 16): "'Oo's got the most exciting stage act in the world, then? The 'Oo, that's 'oo. And 'ow do I know? 'Cause I know all about a sneak preview of their tour that 'appened at Surrey University in Guildford on Saturday, that's 'ow. And what a show! It's a new Who in as much as the basic act has altered, most of the clothes have been changed and the sound and lighting equipment is new and improved, but it's still the good old Who we all know and love, presenting the ultimate in excitement and visual entertainment. Roger Daltrey has got rid of his fringed jacket in favour of a denim jacket and tattered old jeans, Pete's boiler suit has gone for a Burton to be replaced by a smart, tailored white linen outfit, John Entwistle still wears black trousers and shirt, but now topped by a coloured jacket. Mad Moon, of course, still sticks to his white T-shirt. The music is there, right there, all the time. 'See Me, Feel Me', 'Pinball Wizard', 'Substitute', 'My Generation', 'Magic Bus' for a closer, plus some numbers from *Who's Next*."

Charlesworth: "The Who had asked me not to review this show in *Melody Maker* because it was a trial run on certain new songs, and I kept my promise. When that report appeared in *NME*, I was very pissed off! What had happened was that a photographer who'd been there had sold his pictures to *NME* and told Richard Green about the show and he'd written a report as if he'd been there. That's why the report said more about what they were wearing than what they played – all he saw were the pictures. As *MM*'s unofficial 'Who correspondent' I was supposed to know everything about the band and certainly wasn't supposed to be scooped by *NME*. I explained what had happened but my editor was mad as hell that I'd put the band's wishes before the magazine. It was very embarrassing for me.

"About 25 years later, at a New Year's Eve dinner party with some friends of my wife in San Francisco, I actually found myself sitting next to someone who'd been in the audience at that show, one of the 600. She'd been a student there. An amazing coincidence!"

Sunday October 10
Eliot Masters House, Kent University, Canterbury

The third low-key college date prior to the start of the UK tour. These weekend concerts which The Who had played in unseated venues since 1968 ceased after 1971. This was the last unpublicised college show The Who ever played, although a return to Liverpool University had been scheduled as part of the official tour. From 1972, the band's UK policy of playing odd concerts in the far corners of the country drastically changed. For a while now the concerts had not been economically viable, but the band valued them because of the intimate contact they allowed with a keen and receptive (and mostly student) audience. Although it wasn't yet clear at the time, The Who lost a little of their accessibility and street-credibility when shows like this were abandoned exclusively in favour of the more conventional superstar package tours that followed in 1973 and 1975.

Monday October 18
Guildhall, Southampton

The Who began their first British for just over a year supported by Quiver. Amongst the 1,600 fans that attended this concert was Chris Charlesworth. Feedback marred 'I Can't Explain' and 'Substitute' but by 'Behind Blue Eyes' Charlesworth was noting the high quality of the band's new PA system. A combined 'Magic Bus' and 'Naked Eye' was followed by the 20-minute *Tommy* medley. Charlesworth wrote in *Melody Maker* (October 23): "They used the best combination of songs to whip up the excitement to an awe-inspiring climax as huge searchlights beamed down on delirious fans drunk with ecstasy at the group's new finale... There isn't a band in the land that couldn't take a lesson or two from The Who... Perhaps The Who are getting too good and that's why they are knocked for being predictable. Perhaps they are, but many an unpredictable band would be unable to generate like The Who. I hope to hell they never change."

Barry Dillon, of the *Southampton Evening Echo* (October 19), was equally impressed, though concerned about the extreme volume: "The Who must be regarded as the most exciting and LOUDEST rock group in the world after attempting to pulverise the sound barrier in Southampton Guildhall last night. So intense was the noise that many of the 1,600 fans who swarmed into the hall had splitting headaches and numb or aching ears. During the two-hour performance the volume was so great from elaborate equipment worth £20,000 and last used at the Oval Festival, that some fans were crying. Undoubtedly, The Who proved themselves as the finest exponents of live rock music around – so why this solid wall of sound which screamed at you? Obviously rock music has to be loud to really get across but frankly this was ridiculous. It hardly seems good for the health to endure such a supersonic level. Someone sitting next to me had to leave for fear of being sick... Despite the agony of the noise this was one of the best rock concerts I've ever attended."

Wednesday October 20
Odeon Cinema, Birmingham

Thursday October 21
Green's Playhouse, Glasgow, Scotland

Willie Wilson of Quiver: "The dressing rooms at Green's Playhouse were underneath the stage and our dressing room was right underneath the bit where Pete stood. We knew when he came onstage because he took this flying leap from the wings in his Doc Martens and came crashing down right over our heads. We all thought the stage was going to cave in!"

Tim Renwick of Quiver: "After the soundcheck at five o'clock everyone stood around waiting for the show to begin. Townshend was leaning against a wall getting more bored by the minute. There were crates of miniature bottles of mixers and he stood there lobbing bottle after bottle of ginger ale against the wall. I was so impressed by this that a couple of weeks later when Quiver were playing the Manchester College of Catering we took great delight in smashing dinner plates on the dressing room floor just for the sheer hell of it."

Willie Wilson: "Moonie had got hold of a loud-hailer from the Glasgow police and was having great fun ordering people about and crying stuff like 'Come in Number Nine! You're time is up' and so forth. The police found it very funny but it drove us all mad. Townshend grabbed him and threw him to the floor and proceeded to pour a bottle of vodka down the inside of the megaphone into Keith's waiting mouth."

*Guitar destroyed: Gibson SG Special.

Friday October 22
Opera House, Blackpool

This was the same theatre where The Who, then known as The High Numbers, had played support to The Beatles in August 1964.

"Exciting music from The Who," headlined the *West Lancashire Evening Gazette* (October 23). Reviewer "F.C." went on to say: "In one and-a-quarter hours last night The Who proved what a musically exciting group they are. Their one night stand at Blackpool's Opera House left the capacity audience pleading for more. It was an incredible spectacle, with Daltrey and Townshend playing softer than before. But the group's aggression still came through – especially in part of Townshend's brilliant opera. The Who surround themselves with electronic machines – about five men set up the sound equipment which still malfunctioned slightly. Using tapes with a lot of synthesiser in pieces like 'Won't Get Fooled Again', The Who proved that complicated equipment can help create beautiful sounds. Tickets for the show were sold out weeks in advance, which shows that there is a rich potential here for groups like The Who. Coach loads of fans came to Blackpool for the concert from other Lancashire towns. Fears of rowdy scenes, which may have deterred promoters from bringing groups to Blackpool in the past are simply not justified now. Today's audiences come to hear the music."

Saturday October 23
Liverpool University

Set included: 'I Can't Explain', 'Substitute', 'Summertime Blues', 'My Wife', 'Baba O'Riley', 'Bargain', 'Behind Blue Eyes', 'Won't Get Fooled Again', 'Baby Don't You Do It', 'Magic Bus', *Tommy* medley: ('Overture', 'Amazing Journey', 'Sparks', 'Pinball Wizard', 'See Me, Feel Me').

After a fine version of 'I Can't Explain', Roger Daltrey told the audience: "Needless to say, this is one of our favourite places." He went on to describe how the band's act had been changing. The newly installed live version of 'Baba O'Riley' tended to dampen the pace of The Who's live act but the band effortlessly achieved the precision playing that the number required, and Daltrey added some wild harmonica fills during the final build-up, in place of the violin which was featured on the recording. 'Overture' featured some fine guitar work from Townshend and 'Sparks' was equally exciting and frenzied. As previously mentioned, this was The Who's final UK college concert.

Sunday October 24
Trentham Gardens, Stoke-on-Trent

"Who just get better", headlined *Disc and Music Echo* (October 30). Mark Humphreys wrote: "The Who just get better and better and their incredible music just gets stronger and stronger... I liked the group's treatment of 'Behind Blue Eyes'. It afforded just the right break before the group were back on the heavy sounds again – rocking through some of the best *Tommy* numbers... This was The Who at their incredible best, a vocal and musical combination of sheer brilliance and a triumph for the group. Personally, I could watch this group seven nights a week given the chance – and providing my hearing stood up to it."

John Woffinden in *Generations* (No. 11, January

1994) also recalled "Roger getting the words wrong in 'Summertime Blues' and John doing his bit by saying 'I'd like to help you son, but you're on the wrong verse'... The other incident I always remember is Pete winding up the audience when he broke a string on his guitar. He apologised and someone shouted 'Smash it, Pete.' 'Shall I?' responded Pete. 'Yes' came the chorus. 'Shall I?' Pete asked again. 'Yes' shouted the audience louder. 'What will you do then?... Fuck off home because I haven't got a guitar to play, you stupid cunts!' Nothing like a rapport with the audience, is there?"

Thursday October 28
Odeon Cinema, Manchester

Set: 'I Can't Explain', 'Substitute', 'Summertime Blues', 'My Wife', 'Baba O'Riley', 'Bargain', 'Behind Blue Eyes', 'Won't Get Fooled Again', 'Baby Don't You Do It', 'Magic Bus', *Tommy* medley: (five songs, as October 23), 'My Generation', 'Naked Eye'.

After the usual enthusiastic versions of 'I Can't Explain' and 'Substitute', Daltrey told the crowd: "That's a bit of our history. We'd like to carry on with a bit of someone else's, about the only number we play in our act which is actually written by someone else – Eddie Cochran's 'Summertime Blues'." The following song, 'My Wife', had by this time developed into an insistent and thunderous blockbuster with Daltrey on backing vocals from the rear of the stage and Townshend playing a jagged and rhythmic guitar solo. Keith Moon gave an amusing introduction to 'Baba O'Riley', and when putting his huge Koss headphones on said that "they aren't as painful as they look!"

A letter had recently appeared in *Melody Maker* from a correspondent in Manchester, comparing 'Let's See Action' with its B-side 'When I Was A Boy', suggesting that John Entwistle's song should have been the A-side! This was alluded to by Pete during his lengthy introduction to

'Bargain'. Townshend asked: "Who wrote that letter? The one about John Entwistle should write The Who's next single?... This is one that I wrote on the *Who's Next* album, one of the fill-in tracks..." He then referred to Keith Moon's holiday arrangements: "He always goes on cheap holidays, package holidays, so I wrote this in memory of Keith who went on a package holiday and when he came back he wasn't the same... It's called 'Bargain'." In between each song, large numbers of the crowd called for the perennial favourite 'Magic Bus'. After they had played it, Townshend took some time tuning his guitar to notes played by Entwistle. The delay caused Pete to comment: "There once was a time when he used to have to get in tune with me. Now I'm not trusted so I have to get in tune with him!" *Tommy* received rapturous applause and was probably the highlight of the show with 'Overture' in particular featuring some wonderfully inventive guitar soloing.

Friday October 29
ABC Cinema, Hull

The much-anticipated return to Hull caused a headlong rush for tickets. The ABC seated a restricted 1,400 – 400 fewer than they had played to in February 1970! The *Hull Times* previewed the concert as follows: "Eight years of rock – and still pulling them in. The Who – louder than ever. Three five-ton trucks, a pink Rolls Royce and an assortment of other vehicles will roll into Hull on Friday, bearing the personnel and electrical accoutrements of the most exciting act in the history of rock and roll music – The Who. They hit the road 12 days ago, with an entourage resembling that of a travelling circus: a brand new £20,000 PA system, thousands of pounds' worth of lighting equipment, and a complete team of drivers, stage hands and technicians... On stage, under a battery of constantly changing multi-coloured light beams, the group pour forth the kind of super-aggressive rock music which put them at the top and has kept them there for more than eight years."

Tim Joseph wrote (*Generations*, No. 7, April 1992) that: "The review of the concert the following week was less than ecstatic, however. Headed 'The Who are still looking over their shoulders', it accused the band of relying on too many old songs. [The reviewer] noted that the band had come on stage late (causing slow handclaps from the audience) following a backstage row between Pete Townshend and Keith Moon, which he felt had ruined their inspiration somewhat. Additionally, Roger Daltrey 'had a bit of a cold', which rather restrained his performance. The review lists the following songs: 'I Can't Explain', 'Substitute', 'Summertime Blues', 'My Wife', 'Baba O'Riley', 'Won't Get Fooled Again', 'Magic Bus', a *Tommy* medley (including 'Pinball Wizard' and 'See Me, Feel Me') and a long version of 'My Generation'.

After the show the *Hull Times* spoke to Pete Townshend. He found the Hull audience 'quite pleasant', comparing well with earlier audiences on the tour. He was a little disappointed when the lights were turned on the audience during 'See Me, Feel Me', as other audiences had 'been thrown into a frenzy, leaping around and chanting. But they were pleasant enough,' said Pete. 'You don't split hairs over audiences, you only split hairs over performances.' He had split a fingernail midway through the gig while windmilling his arm at the guitar which caused him some pain. He hadn't smashed his guitar as he only did that after a very good or very bad gig. From this it would appear that Hull was just another date on the tour."

Willie Wilson: "There certainly had been a row backstage between Pete and Keith! We heard this huge argument break out and it transpired that Sandie Shaw had turned up at the gig and Keith had said something to offend her. Townshend, defending Sandie Shaw's honour, had him up against the wall ready to punch him. In the end he stuffed Keith into a wardrobe and nailed him up in it!"

Saturday October 30
Odeon Cinema, Newcastle
Set: as Manchester (October 28).

The last show of the tour prior to London was an absolute triumph of inspired and exciting rock'n'roll. The Who were very comfortable with their live act now that a tight segment of *Tommy*

had been reinstated, and five *Who's Next* songs had become well-established live favourites. The Who could enjoy themselves playing the songs and this enthusiasm rubbed off on the audience. Few groups could inject songs as old as 'My Generation' or 'I Can't Explain' with as much enthusiasm and fire night after night like The Who could. In Newcastle, 'Summertime Blues' hit an energetic early peak which was sustained through 'My Wife'. Townshend told the appreciative north-east audience: "We miss very much the crowds from up here when we go to the States... This is probably one of the last gigs we do before we go back to the States again... So to commemorate the event we're sending Keith off the stage..."

Moon duly vacated the stage until halfway through 'Behind Blue Eyes' which followed. 'Won't Get Fooled Again' was marred by the guitar going out of tune and Townshend seemed to lose his concentration thereafter. Keith, who turned in a superb drum solo before the finale, redeemed the song, however. The crowd clapped through 'Baby Don't You Do It' despite the usual shouts for 'Magic Bus'. John's fluid bass runs carried through the entire song and Townshend also contributed a breakneck solo before the intensity dropped and Pete alone played a flourish of quick rhythm guitar before the beat picked up again. Pete even added some vocal backups of "I just can't live without you..." This version of the song almost rivalled that which was played in Dayton (August 13), and certainly far surpassed the version recorded in San Francisco (December 13) and released on the B-side of the 'Join Together' single in June 1972.

Thursday November 4
Rainbow Theatre, Finsbury Park, North London

The Rainbow Theatre, the old Astoria Cinema in Finsbury Park, was opened as a regular rock venue by John Morris, an American entrepreneur/promoter who'd been the stage manager at the Woodstock Festival and whom The Who had befriended along the way. As a favour to Morris, the band agreed to open the Rainbow by playing the first three nights, with Quiver as support act.

To mark the occasion Pete wore a jump suit made from silver lamé material with the red Rainbow logo emblazoned across the back. A chorus line of dancing girls preceded The Who on to

the stage after an opening address by Morris. The light show had apparently been imported for the occasion from the Fillmore East, a venue from which the Rainbow took much of its approach. "Thanks for coming," Pete told the audience. "I suppose you had to come really, 'cause there's nowhere else to go, is there?"

Chris Charlesworth noted in *Melody Maker* (November 13): "Certainly Thursday night was an occasion in the history of British rock. They couldn't have chosen a better group than The Who to take the first steps on the Rainbow stage." After the show there was a party in the theatre's foyer at which Keith entertained the invitation-only guests with sketches from *Monty Python's Flying Circus*.

Willie Wilson of Quiver: "We turned up for the soundcheck around five o'clock and Moonie cornered me in the dressing room. 'Willie, dear boy! Brandy and Coke all right?' he cried, pressing a pint glass into my hand. It was hard to find much Coke in the pint. He then proceeded to get me rat-

arsed drunk. We'd rented a brand-new Ford Escort to get us to and from the gig and on the way home I was so out of it I turned the car over on Ealing Broadway, spilling me and the rest of the band out onto the street. Tim Renwick, our guitarist was carrying the band's bag of Mandies (Mandrax) and in a moment of panic hid it in a pelican-crossing sign, coming back the following day to pick it up!"

Unfortunately, the renaissance in London rock venues was short-lived; the Rainbow closed after about six months due to financial difficulties, although it did subsequently reopen for spells later in the Seventies.

Friday November 5
Rainbow Theatre, Finsbury Park, North London

Saturday November 6
Rainbow Theatre, Finsbury Park, North London
The British tour was originally scheduled to include concerts in Cardiff on October 21, and Dundee on October 30, while the London shows were to have been held at the Lyceum on November 2 and 3.

Tuesday November 9
Green's Playhouse, Glasgow, Scotland
The Who agreed to play an extra concert in Glasgow after riots by disappointed fans when the October 21 show had sold out. The extra show put added pressure on The Who's technical crew to get all the equipment shipped to America in time for their November 20 opening date in Charlotte, North Carolina.

Saturday November 20
Charlotte Coliseum, Charlotte, North Carolina
First night of a 19-date tour, taking the band through six southern states and out to the west coast. The Coliseum was packed with 13,000 fans for the band's début in North Carolina. Graham Bell and his band Arc supported.

Set: 'I Can't Explain', 'Summertime Blues', 'My Wife', 'Baba O'Riley', 'Bargain', 'Behind Blue Eyes', 'Won't Get Fooled Again', 'Baby Don't You Do It', 'Magic Bus', *Tommy* medley (five songs, as October 23), 'My Generation', 'Naked Eye'.

On plugging in his guitar at the start of this

concert, Pete thrashed out a few heavy riffs to which Moon joined in, fooling the audience into thinking this was the (new) opening song. However, this soon ran into deafening feedback, out of which Townshend then fashioned the classic chord sequence of 'I Can't Explain'. 'Summertime Blues' featured some exceptional guitar soloing and Daltrey said: "That was a bit of our history in 'I Can't Explain' and a bit of rock-'n'roll history in 'Summertime Blues'." Keith Moon introduced a powerful version of 'Bargain', and then introducing 'Behind Blue Eyes', Townshend said: "This next one is a song from *Who's Next*; it's a very quiet song. You have to remember there are certain points even in rock-'n'roll concerts where one has to be incredibly discreet and quiet. And we have a person in our midst who isn't capable of that discretion and isn't capable of that quietness..." At this point Keith shouted loudly and made an indiscriminate racket on his drums. "We have to ask him to leave the stage," Pete continued.

Pete later referred to 'Won't Get Fooled Again' as an "old-fashioned rock'n'roll song". 'Baby Don't You Do It' was a lengthy jam. 'My Generation' concluded with a brilliant guitar solo which jolted into feedback before Pete went into an improvised riff to which Moon and Entwistle joined in, finally concluding with 'Naked Eye'.

Chris Charlesworth reported in *Melody Maker* (November 27): "The Tommy medley was the highlight and the vast sea of faces illuminated when the arc lights shone down on the crowd was an indescribable sight... Townshend knocked his speakers over at the end as the group rushed from the stage."

Charlesworth: "While The Who were waiting to go on stage Keith and I went for a stroll along the backstage corridors of the Coliseum where, in a storeroom, we discovered a hollow wooden egg large enough to conceal a man and a four wheeled cart on which it could be mounted and transported. Keith concealed himself inside the egg and I towed him towards The Who's dressing room where he intended to leap out and surprise everyone. Indeed, he was hatching a plot to be wheeled on stage in this contraption. Unfortunately, en route to the dressing room there was a steeply sloping downhill curve, and I lost control of the vehicle, causing it to crash, the egg to topple over and break and the world's

greatest rock drummer to come tumbling out head first amid the wreckage. Keith and I narrowly avoided being ejected from the premises by a security guard who heard the crash and thought we were a couple of vandals... which I suppose we were. Of course, he failed to recognise The Who's drummer. I think only our English accents saved us from being chucked out into the car park."

Monday November 22
University of Alabama Memorial Coliseum, Tuscaloosa, Alabama
This performance was witnessed by 16,500.

Tuesday November 23
Municipal Auditorium, Atlanta, Georgia
Supported by Bell & Arc.
*Guitar destroyed: Gibson SG Special

Thursday November 25
Miami Beach Convention Hall, Miami, Florida
Two nights in Miami with shows at 8 pm each night.

Friday November 26
Miami Beach Convention Hall, Miami, Florida
The two concerts attracted over 30,000 fans.

Sunday November 28
*Mid-South Coliseum,
Memphis, Tennessee*
Supported by Bell & Arc for an 8 pm show. Set: 'I Can't Explain', 'Substitute', 'Summertime Blues', 'My Wife', 'Baba O'Riley', 'Bargain', 'Behind Blue Eyes', 'Won't Get Fooled Again', 'Baby Don't You Do It', 'Magic Bus', *Tommy* medley (five songs, as October 23), 'My Generation', 'Naked Eye'.

Charging on stage, Pete Townshend did a somersault and Keith yelled: "Oy, Memphis! Can't Explain'!" and thus started another classic Who performance. Pete later commented to the 12,000-strong audience that coming straight from sunny Florida, The Who arrived in Memphis to find that it was "pissing down... You made us feel at home already! Tears in my eyes here!" Sound problems persisted on stage and Daltrey spoke to Bob Pridden after 'Behind Blue Eyes', but the concert was largely faultless.

During the band's stay in Memphis, Keith "got bored" and "renovated" his hotel room to the tune of $1,400.

Monday November 29
The Warehouse, New Orleans, Louisiana
Set included: 'I Can't Explain', 'Substitute', 'Summertime Blues', 'My Wife', 'Baba O'Riley', 'Bargain', 'Behind Blue Eyes', 'Won't Get Fooled Again', 'Baby Don't You Do It', *Tommy* medley: (five songs, as October 23), 'My Generation', improvisations.

The intimate venue of 3,500 capacity witnessed a tight

show that concluded with a medley of 'My Generation' with improvised riffs.

Tuesday November 30
The Warehouse, New Orleans, Louisiana

Wednesday December 1
Sam Houston Coliseum, Houston, Texas
Set included: 'I Can't Explain', 'Substitute', 'Summertime Blues', 'My Wife', 'Baba O'Riley', 'Bargain', 'Behind Blue Eyes', 'Won't Get Fooled Again', 'Baby Don't You Do It', 'Magic Bus', Tommy medley (five songs, as October 23), 'My Generation'.

This concert was attended by 11,500 fans.

Thursday December 2
Memorial Auditorium, Dallas, Texas

Saturday December 4
Denver Coliseum, Denver, Colorado
Concert promoter Barry Fey had deliberately withheld advance information about the two Who shows so as not to jeopardise ticket sales for a Ten Years After concert on November 16. At that show he announced that Who tickets would go on sale the following day. In spite of a winter storm that dumped six inches of snow in the area, fans began lining up the same night. Eleven thousand tickets were sold between 10 am and 6 pm. Fey personally delivered pasteboards to outlets, and when his own vehicle got stuck in the snow, he forged ahead in taxicabs.

Sunday December 5
Denver Coliseum, Denver, Colorado

Tuesday December 7
Arizona Veterans Memorial Coliseum, Phoenix, Arizona
Set included: 'I Can't Explain', 'Substitute', 'Summertime Blues', 'Baba O'Riley', 'Behind Blue Eyes', 'Won't Get Fooled Again', 'Baby Don't You Do It', 'Magic Bus', Tommy medley (5 songs as October 23).

It was over three years since The Who had last played Phoenix (August 17, 1968). The set started with a strong 'Can't Explain', but 'Substitute' and much of the set was marred by microphone feedback. While this was traditionally an excuse for tantrums, the band, particularly Pete, were in good humour with much hilarious ad libbing between songs, resulting in one of the tour's best shows. Roger told the 13,000 audience, "Those two songs were from our past history, a number called 'Can't Explain', another one 'Substitute', both written by Pete Townshend in about '65 and '66. Here's one which is a song which is a lot older by somebody else who didn't have the chance to live as long as we did in the rock scene (!) Eddie Cochran's 'Summertime Blues'." Daltrey introduced 'My Wife': "We'd like to do, at this time, somebody's else's song, John Entwistle, our bass player, we call him the Ox and quite a few other things sometimes!"

Pete remarked, "Watch this foot", a reference to his six foot stomps start cue. "Who said cockroach? There was a cockroach… there IS a cockroach. Don't keep telling me, I hate cockroaches! They're all over the place!" Moon moaned in sympathetic terror. "There's cockroaches everywhere! I've never seen so many cockroaches in my life. Look at the size of that one. Moon: "Hideous!" Townshend: "Fourteen inches across and full of chilli!" After stomping on the offending insect, he said, "So much for that cockroach. And now I will count in John's number. Thank you."

An out-of-breath Moon announced 'Baba O' Riley'. "Thanks… we'd like to do another number off of *Who's Next* and I'd like to say that we haven't played Pheonix for some time but … it sure is … f-f-f-funny to be back but the way you've looked after us … Thank you … This is a song written by Pete and on this one we use a tape because it saves paying for an organist and also we use a synthesiser. Only we know how to play with it so if we got any other guys in here they'd probably make a right f-f-f-fool of themselves."

Moon was deliberately toying with using the 'f' word as Arizona laws banned swearing on stage, and The Who had been warned. Pete joined in using a Goons-type voice: "They'd probably f-f-f … completely fool it up. They'd probably completely f-f-f… forget all the parts. They'd probably completely p-p-p- … pathetically make mistakes."

'Bargain' was played as tight and powerful as ever but the mike feedback returned. 'Behind Blue Eyes' was prefaced by another extended Townshend and Moon double act. Townshend: "We're doing all our swear words backwards tonight. Have you worked it out yet? It's very

hard." Moon: "And very expensive". Townshend: "And very expensive. If we're naughty up here on the stage, it costs us $5,000. That's two and a half hovercrafts, three and a quarter snowmobiles! That's three 47 Les Paul guitars. That's three hotel rooms. It's just unjust. If I were you I'd move out … out there somewhere … This is one which doesn't include … and for you all out there that are listening to the tape which is going to cost us all that money… Keith Moon in the group is always swearing so for this number we decided to exclude him entirely because he's always swearing!" Moon: "Blimey, guv'nor, Blimey!" Townshend: "You get off the stage!" Moon: "Blimey, guv'nor, Blimey!" Townshend: "How dare he say 'Blimey' on the stage!" Moon: "You mother… mother …" Townshend: "I've never heard anything like it in my life. My auntie Min would have a heart attack if she heard language like that."

For his next comic interlude, Pete paid tongue-in-cheek tribute to The Who's road crew and promised the audience a surprise later. "If you can keep your eyes open after all you've been doing, you'll be in very good shape! This one's for you that think it's all happening up here on stage. WON'T … GET … FOOLED AGAIN!" Roger mentioned the group's Marquee past to introduce 'Baby Don't You Do it' while Pete pushed it further: "What we need 'ere is some intercourse between the audience and the group! We want you all to clap your hands … in the key of A … which stands for …" This ten minute version was absolutely mesmerising with some incredible Townshend soloing and improvisations jousting with Moon's fills and Entwistle's florid bass lines.

After a marathon 13-minute 'Magic Bus' Moon announced "And now, ladies and gentlemen, as you paid your money to see four of the biggest scum on the face of this earth, four of the filthiest, most perverted ratbags under the sun, I'd like to introduce our lead guitar player and songwriter extraordinaire, Peter Townshend!" Pete stopped tuning. "I would like to introduce, in return, a famous conductor, someone that has thrown more batons, pierced more eyebrows, than Leonard Bernstein, Otto what's-is-name, or any of those geezers… He conducts with two batons, one of the worst, most unkempt orchestras on the road, the Who Philharmonia, professor Keith Moon …"

While Moon did his usual trick of tapping his snare rim, demanding silence, Townshend started a funny discourse: "Inferior imitations. *Tommy* is only available at Walgreen's Drugstores. Take any freeway and get off anywhere and you'll come to *Tommy* … Used Cars." He and Moon then slipped into stoned Cheech and Chong accents. "Hey man, I've been saving up so long for this record, man!" Moon: "What for, Chuck? What for, Chuck?" Townshend: "A far out record … Hey man, handle it by the edges, for Christ sake, man, handle it by the edges!" Moon: "Far friggin' out, man!" Townshend: "OK man. I'm gonna be cool with this record but you wait till you hear this record, man. Now put it on the turntable real easy… whatever you do put it on the turntable real easy, right? It's a real good record, man. I've been saving for over three weeks for this. OK Track 1…" He and Moon then simulated a record being scratched.

The 'Overture' was rather ragged with some awry chords but a brilliant series of guitar improvisations led into 'Amazing Journey'. The available tape cuts after the *Tommy* segment but the set presumably finished with 'My Generation' and more improvisations with Pete's earlier promise being a broken guitar.

* Guitar Destroyed: Gibson SG Special.

Wednesday December 8
San Diego Sports Arena, San Diego, California

A sell-out for a gross of over $77,000 from 15,000 fans. Mylon, a gospel-flavoured band led by Mylon LeFevre, was the opening act.

Noted by the *Los Angeles Times* (December 10) as the "greatest show on earth". Robert Hilburn wrote: "See rock'n'roll at its most powerful. See young minds twisted before your very eyes by the evil powers of this music. See four musicians in this group from across the seas manipulate their audience in an irresistible combination of showmanship and music. Believe what I say. See The Who... There is a majestic splendour to The Who's instrumentation and an attitude expressed in its lyrics that speaks directly to the rock generation in a way few other groups do... there hasn't been too much excitement in the big rock'n'roll tent lately. So when the greatest show on earth comes to town, I've got to get a little excited."

Thursday December 9
The Forum, Los Angeles, California

The Who sold out all 18,000 tickets in 80 minutes, the fastest rock concert sell-out in the LA area, including The Beatles and Rolling Stones. The band also insisted that the first ten rows of seats went on sale to the general public instead of being reserved for the record company or media. The Who were the only band to have such a clause in their contract. Gate receipts came to $110,000 with Mylon and Holy Smoke as opening acts.

Set: 'I Can't Explain', 'Substitute', 'Summertime Blues', 'My Wife', 'Baba O'Riley', 'Bargain', 'Behind Blue Eyes', 'Won't Get Fooled Again', 'Magic Bus', *Tommy* medley (five songs, as October 23), 'My Generation', 'Goin' Down', 'Naked Eye'.

This was generally a flawless performance, with the sound system behaving and the band very comfortable with the large venue. At one point Pete wore a crown on his head, which eventually went flying into the crowd. To cap the performance, the band played a new variation on their improvisations: a jam based on Freddie King's 'Goin' Down', with vocals by Pete Townshend (a rudimentary chant "I'm goin' down, goin' down, down..." over a descending riff). Writing in *Melody Maker* (December 25), Jacoba Atlas said: "The Who belong to that small group of rock and roll bands that inhabit Mount Olympus... They introduced 'Summertime Blues' saying 'we never get tired of singing this'. Daltrey told us that Pete Townshend had bought boots guaranteed to last two years which fell apart after six months... They gave you what makes them one of the best rock'n'roll band's in the world. Just around midnight I found myself making that statement without any qualifications whatsoever."

Nat Feedland, however, in *Billboard* (January 1, 1972) was less than impressed: "I have never had very strong feelings about The Who one way or another... I enjoyed Peter Townshend's spectacular, standing-split leaps and Roger Daltrey's twirling his handmike... I still find the bulk of their music rather monotonous and the lyrics hard to hear..."

Following the concert, The Who adjourned to the Continental Hyatt House on Sunset Strip for a party, during which they received gold and platinum discs for *Who's Next* and *Live At Leeds*. A total of 32 award discs were lined up on the small stage as MCA/Decca Records president Mike Maitland made a short presentation speech before the invitation-only audience. Record company representatives, press and assorted guests including Mick and Bianca Jagger, John and Catherine Sebastian and Cass Elliot were on hand. Shortly after midnight, Pete, Roger, Keith and John made their way past the gleaming discs and chromium stands to accept the prestigious awards. Grabbing as many discs as he could, Pete began yelling "They're all mine, they're all mine!" The other three jumped on top of him and the entire display went flying around the stage with Jagger shouting encouragement from the front of the audience.

Friday December 10
Long Beach Arena, Long Beach, California

13,000 people packed the Arena for a gross of $78,000. The show had sold out the same day as The Forum for a combined total of 31,000 seats sold in eighty minutes.

Set: 'I Can't Explain', 'Substitute', 'Summertime Blues', 'My Wife', 'Baba O'Riley', 'Bargain', 'Behind Blue Eyes', 'Won't Get Fooled Again', 'Baby Don't You Do It', 'Magic Bus', *Tommy* medley (5 songs, as October 23), 'My Generation', 'Naked Eye'.

Disturbed at the audience activity, Pete yelled after 'Summertime Blues': "This one's 'My Wife'. I'll tell you fuckers somethin' – all right – now listen! Just fucking listen and shut up! Right? Either sit down or stand up or lay down or do something but shut up! All right! This is a fucking rock 'n'roll concert, not a fucking tea party! Dig it! You at the back don't like it, do what these motherfuckers did... come down here and all kill one another." An edited version of this rant became the opening to the *Thirty Years Of Maximum R&B* box set.

Sunday December 12
Civic Auditorium, San Francisco, California

Monday December 13
Civic Auditorium, San Francisco, California

Set: 'I Can't Explain', 'Substitute', 'Summertime Blues', 'My Wife', 'Baba O'Riley', 'Behind Blue Eyes', 'Bargain', 'Won't Get Fooled Again', 'Baby Don't You Do It', Tommy medley (five songs, as October 23), 'My Generation', improvisations, 'Naked Eye' improvisations, 'Goin' Down', 'Magic Bus'.

An exceptionally good performance, which yielded a recording of dynamic quality, this represented the band's 1971 set at its best. A definitive 'My Wife' featured some breathtaking guitar work, and introducing 'Baba', Roger said: "We use a tape to put a synthesiser sound on stage because it was a lot easier than getting someone to play it. We'd get all that hang up we couldn't handle really if we got someone else. Anyway, Pete plays the synthesiser on the tape so it's just like having two Pete's!" At this point Moon interjected with "bloody hell, one's enough!" After 'Baba O'Riley', Townshend introduced the next song: "No sooner than we've taken you up, we're gonna bring you back down again very slowly. This is a number which is a cameo, if you like, of The Who performance. It starts off nice and easy and it ends up sort of bouncing all over the stage... We start off without Keith Moon and we end up with him." Keith then disputed that the next song in the set should be 'Behind Blue Eyes', but Townshend said "I've announced it now!" Moon said: "All right then, I'll piss off." Pete replied: "It wasn't that I was trying to get rid of you or anything, Keith... You're actually getting a different list... Special, special, we've changed two numbers round... I leap on the off beat instead of the on beat, it's all rehearsed you know. We go in the studios and we work out these dance steps me and Roger for hours..."

'Behind Blue Eyes' featured some fine singing from Daltrey, with Townshend and Entwistle's tight harmonies making this one of the best versions played of the song. Explaining the meaning of 'Bargain', Pete told the 7,500 San Francisco audience: "A song about what you get from being here. If you're alive... whether you're rich or you're poor, whether you're up or you're down – if you're alive you're getting a bargain." During the opening chords Pete gleefully shouts something off mike which sounded like an urgent call to arms and midway through yells 'Take it up' as he hurtles into a solo. A new coda was tagged on to the end, lengthening the song in a manner which suggested the band simply never wanted it to end.

Before the next song, Pete said: "If you were here last night you'll have noticed my knees trick. If you're wondering why I've got such funny shaped knees... that's 'cause I'm wearing knee pads, so I don't agitate the fractured knee cap that I'm wearing unwittingly, unhappily." "Have it off, have if off, amputate!" yelled Keith. "I'll just skid around the stage on one of those boards on casters," continued Pete. "Talking about boards on casters, we're gonna start moving this stage out in your direction any minute... The stage comes and it mashes the lot of you. Back! Back! And it's in this song that's about groups and the revolution and we're gonna play you a song all about that as soon as I get in tune!" The band then launched into 'Won't Get Fooled Again', cued in by Moon's three bass drum thuds. The highlight of the set was 'My Generation' – a 20-minute medley featuring some fine hard rock riffs before moving through 'Naked Eye' and then 'Goin' Down'. The show closed with an 18-minute version of "Magic Bus", probably the longest The Who ever played.

Guitar destroyed: Gibson SG Special

Several songs from this show have appeared on record over the years, although until recently it was thought that they came from the December 12 performance, largely because of an inaccurate date on the tape box! They include what is widely regarded as the best ever live version of 'Bargain' (on *Who's Missing* in 1987 and the *30 Years...* box-set). Also available from this show is 'Goin' Down', credited to Freddie King (on *Two's Missing* in 1988), and 'Baby, Don't You Do It', the Holland-Dozier-Holland song recorded by Marvin Gaye, released as the B-side of 'Join Together' in June 1972.

Wednesday December 15
Seattle Center Coliseum, Seattle, Washington

The final show of 1971 was seen by 14,000 fans as The Who wrapped up their last American concert tour for two years. Some 700,000 people had seen the group on the two-part US tour.

Set: 'I Can't Explain', 'Substitute', 'Summertime Blues', 'My Wife', 'Baba O'Riley', 'Behind Blue Eyes', 'Bargain', 'Won't Get Fooled Again', 'Baby Don't You Do It', 'Magic Bus', *Tommy* medley (five songs, as October 23), 'My Generation', 'Naked Eye'.

Disaster threatened to strike on this date, as one of the band's equipment trucks crashed en-route from San Francisco and couldn't reach the venue on time. The Who had to borrow some equipment from the supporting act. Oddly enough, The Who hadn't played in Seattle since the Herman's Hermits tour of 1967. By way of reintroducing themselves to each other, The Who and the 14,000 fans combined to make this concert probably the best of an already phenomenal tour. 'Substitute' was a particularly good version, and 'Summertime Blues' maintained a manic pace. Keith introduced 'My Wife' by saying that the band liked playing it very much, written by "*Let's Make A Deal* (a well-known US gameshow) John Entwistle". Following 'Magic Bus', Townshend said: "You can have the good news now. We've played four weeks on the road in America and we've done some heavy gigs man! And you're the best audience. And I totally mean it, no bullshit. And this one we dedicate the past, the present and the future of what we're about to play to you. This is *Tommy*!" The powerful 'Naked Eye' concluded a superlative performance that lived on in Seattle folklore for decades.

Three of the band returned to England for a lengthy hiatus but Keith flew to New York to emcee Sha Na Na's Carnegie Hall concert and even sat in with them for an instrumental version of 'Caravan'. According to publicist Nancy Lewis, the number was "pure dynamite".

I t was impossible, and also unnecessary, for The Who to sustain the momentum of previous years. Success had brought them the opportunity to relax. The coffers were full. They could buy big houses and flash cars. They could spend time with their families, do things that the hectic tour itineraries of the past had always prevented. Most of all, they could get away from each other.

So The Who, the hardest working band of them all, finally did what every other successful band had ever done or would ever do. They took things easy. The six-month break during the first half of 1972 was the longest they had ever had from group activities, and the individual members enjoyed their leisure in different ways. Pete devoted time to his family and the Meher Baba network, and worked on his first, Baba-influenced, solo album. Roger took pleasure in working on his country estate, enjoying a healthy outdoor life. John bought suits of armour and guitars galore and continued to work on solo material. Keith maintained a high profile as 'Moon the Loon', took on some small film roles and missed the camaraderie of the group more than anyone will ever know.

The Who hadn't intended 1972 to be quite so bereft of activity as it turned out to be. The European tour was initially planned to follow an album release. The band had arranged to record at Olympic Studios during May and June with Glyn Johns, and this album was provisionally to include 'Join Together', 'Too Much Of Anything', 'Relay', 'Long Live Rock', 'Put The Money Down', 'Love Reign O'er Me', 'Is It In My Head?', 'Can't You See I'm Easy', 'Ladies In The Female Jail', 'Time Is Passing' and 'Pure And Easy' among others. However, the group were dissatisfied with the result and Townshend began to work on a new concept based upon 'Long Live Rock' – a musical analysis of the group's origins ten years earlier. This idea initially expanded to a "mini-opera", then Pete finally realised that a whole new canvas was needed, and that all but two of the recently recorded songs wouldn't fit. 'Join Together' and 'Relay' were released as singles to keep the band's fortunes bubbling over while Pete worked on his new material. Throughout 1972 and the first few months of 1973, Pete composed *Quadrophenia*.

The Who regrouped in the late summer of 1972 to play continental Europe, sixteen dates in nine countries in a month-long campaign which included a show in Paris that attracted 400,000 fans, their biggest ever audience, anywhere. It was the last time the group would ever appear in so many countries in so short a time, and they would never play Europe on such a large scale again. The trek ended in Rome on September 14.

Their only other appearance in 1972 was in the Lou Reizner production of *Tommy* at the Rainbow Theatre in London. As well as the four members of The Who, the production included an all-star cast with Rod Stewart, Steve Winwood, Ringo Starr and Maggie Bell taking on various roles.

Friday August 11
Festhalle, Frankfurt, Germany

It had been seven months since the American tour had concluded in Seattle the previous December, the longest break to date from live appearances. The Who had not played in Europe for two years so 1972's only live appearances were scheduled for a lengthy tour that began in West Germany.

The Who broke all previous attendance records at the Festhalle on the opening date of the tour, drawing a crowd of 16,500 people.

Set: 'I Can't Explain', 'Summertime Blues', 'My Wife', 'Baba O'Riley', 'Behind Blue Eyes', 'Bargain', 'Won't Get Fooled Again', 'Baby Don't You Do It', 'Magic Bus', 'The Relay', 'Pinball Wizard', 'See Me, Feel Me', 'My Generation', 'Long Live Rock'.

Following 'Behind Blue Eyes', Roger said: "See what we think we've had after playing for the first time in six months, playing for you a number called 'Bargain'." Pete then said: "I just wasn't ready! You can't come up and say... 'Bargain'. I wasn't... You got to do 1, 2, 3, go. Go on! Go on!" Roger, rather annoyed at Pete's japes, duly complied by saying: "1, 2, 3, Go." Pete then said sarcastically: "Thank you."

Saturday August 12
Ernst Merck Halle, Hamburg, Germany

Set: 'I Can't Explain', 'Shakin' All Over', 'My Wife', 'Summertime Blues', 'Baba O'Riley', 'Behind Blue Eyes', 'Bargain', 'Won't Get Fooled Again', 'Relay', 'Pinball Wizard', 'See Me, Feel Me', 'My Generation', 'Naked Eye', 'Long Live

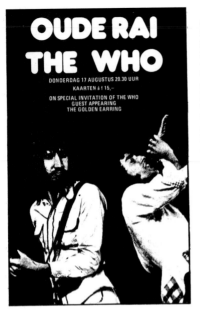

OUDE RAI THE WHO

DONDERDAG 17 AUGUSTUS 20.30 UUR

KAARTEN à f 15,–

ON SPECIAL INVITATION OF THE WHO
GUEST APPEARING
THE GOLDEN EARRING

'Relay' was the first new song of the evening and wouldn't be released for another couple of months. A messy 'Pinball Wizard' was linked by some improvised guitar arpeggios to 'See Me, Feel Me', which also suffered a few mistakes. A very strong 'My Generation' was followed by 'Naked Eye', then the second new song of the night, 'Long Live Rock', which was good fun. Roger sang all the vocals on this song (for the whole tour) unlike the recording (not released until 1974) where Pete sang the verses. The guitar cut out during the rare encore number, 'Daddy Rolling Stone'. 'Sparks' was then begun and abandoned as Pete went into some guitar soloing to conclude the show.

Wednesday August 16
Forest Nationale, Brussels, Belgium

A capacity crowd of 15,000 filled the Forest Nationale. Set: 'I Can't Explain', 'Shakin' All Over', 'My Wife', 'Summertime Blues', 'Baba O'Riley', 'Behind Blue Eyes', 'Bargain', 'Won't Get Fooled Again', 'Magic Bus', 'Relay', 'Pinball Wizard', 'See Me, Feel Me', 'My Generation', 'Sparks', 'Naked Eye'.

"Hello Brussels Sprouts!" Pete greeted the audience. An early highlight was 'My Wife', which featured some excellent guitar soloing, and 'Summertime Blues' sounded as strong as ever. Pete mentioned that the last time the band had played in Brussels had been in 1966 (actually '67) in a tent, and that the place was still as boring as it was then! 'Bargain' extended into a frenzied epic length while 'Won't Get Fooled Again' was tight and hard. After a lengthy 'Magic Bus', Keith Moon introduced 'Relay' as "a number written by Pete and featuring a synthesiser played by the cheapest member of the group". Pete then added "the tape recorder is never drunk!" As the synthesiser tape began playing over the PA system, Pete shouted over it: "What's that peculiar funny noise? Get it off!"

Thursday August 17
Oude Rai Auditorium, Amsterdam, Holland

Ten thousand people saw the first of two Dutch concerts of the '72 tour. The Dutch group Golden Earring was the opening act for the 8:30 pm concert. Set included: 'I Can't Explain', 'Summertime Blues', 'My Wife', 'Baba O'Riley', 'Behind Blue Eyes', 'Bargain', 'Won't Get Fooled Again', 'Magic

Rock', 'Daddy Rolling Stone', 'Sparks' (intro only).

The second German concert mixed some great performances with a number of flaws which made for a memorable evening. A strident version of 'Shakin' All Over' was followed by a very strong 'My Wife'. 'Summertime Blues', oddly, featured no guitar solo. During 'Behind Blue Eyes', Roger's mike failed and he missed a few lines. Townshend told the crowd: "Yesterday in Frankfurt they were an incredible crowd but because they couldn't understand what we were saying, there was no point in cracking any jokes! Have you heard the one about....?" 'Bargain' concluded with a new boogie riff from Pete that led directly into a flawless and epic 'Won't Get Fooled Again'. 'Relay' was lumpy and disjointed – a key change was missed but the performance retained an appealing spontaneity, even when the synthesiser backing tape stopped sooner than scheduled. Pete simply played a riff and the band continued.

WHO'S RECORD

THE WHO, currently on their first tour of Europe, drew 16,500 to their Hamburg concert on Saturday breaking a previous house record held by the Rolling Stones.

The group's next album, as yet untitled, is set for release in October. Pete Townshend's solo album " Who Came First " is released next week and John Entwistle's second solo set " Wistle Rhymes " is set for release in October.

Bus', 'Pinball Wizard', 'See Me, Feel Me', 'My Generation', 'Naked Eye'.

Monday August 21
KB Hallen, Copenhagen, Denmark

Golden Earring play support. The set: 'I Can't Explain', 'Summertime Blues', 'My Wife', 'Baba O'Riley', 'Behind Blue Eyes', 'Bargain', 'Won't Get Fooled Again', 'Magic Bus', 'The Relay', 'Pinball Wizard', 'See Me, Feel Me', 'My Generation'/'Naked Eye'/'Sparks' medley-jam

Once again, 'Behind Blue Eyes' provided an early high point to this set, and 'Won't Get Fooled Again' was introduced by Townshend in a zany high-pitched voice of the *Monty Python/Goon Show* ilk. After 'Magic Bus', Townshend said: "I'd like to educate you chaps, now. It's a long time since we've been over here... Eighteen months or something... I've forgotten what I was going to say. Have a jolly good time, do come again. This one is a number... On 'Baba O'Riley' and 'Won't Get Fooled Again' you probably noticed we were using a tape of synthesiser and on this one we've got another synthesiser track... And it's an album off our forthcoming track... A track off our forthcoming album which is coming out in 1974... You're hearing a preview of it now. It's called..." Moon then shouted "'Can't Explain'". "We started off with 'Can't Explain'", continued Pete. "Time is passing and this one is called 'The Relay'." The song began rather badly with the band playing out of time with the backing tape,

although it soon developed into a fierce rocker. A manic version of 'My Generation' was another outstanding performance and it led into a new improvised riff to which Daltrey sang "Do you feel all right..." This then led into another riff and eventually 'Naked Eye' took shape, followed by the 'Sparks' instrumental.

Lasse Ellegaard wrote: "The professionalism of the group's performance makes the concert a memorable experience with its extravagant stage act. The Who performs some of the most well structured rock music that can be heard at the moment... the powerful music places The Who not only as history's largest rock group but as an illustration of Modern reality."

Wednesday August 23
Kunglinga Tennishallen, Stockholm, Sweden

The Who played their last concerts in Sweden with this show and the following night in Gothenberg, with Golden Earring as the opening act. They would not play Sweden for the next 25 years!

"The concert started in the usual manner," wrote Björn Lanner, "very loud and in a very fast tempo, which seemed to increase from the very beginning. Tennishallen is, of course, built for tennis and not for rock, so they had a temporary stage just for this occasion. Halfway through the show, the stage started moving and swinging. A concert is usually stopped on these occasions. But to stop The Who was impossible, now they were getting warmed up. THEN, a little man appeared at the edge of the stage. He crawled up on stage and started to hit with a hammer. The show continued with Pete Townshend and Roger Daltrey looking notably thrilled by this little happening. It all ended with smoke and thunder, the way it should. We left Tennishallen with a memory for life."

Swedish director Urban Lasson obtained rare permission to film The Who at this concert. Subsequently an impressive version of 'Won't Get Fooled Again' appeared in his television documentary *Roadies*, which was shown between 9:15 and 9:55 pm on April 22, 1973. The film also included footage of The Who arriving at Stockholm's Arlanda Airport, and interviews with Bob Pridden and Alan Smith.

Thursday August 24
Scandanavium, Gothenburg, Sweden

An eyewitness recalled that "Golden Earring from Holland left the stage after a boring performance. The well-behaved Swedish audience was quietly watching as The Who appeared on stage with their gear. Pete Townshend approached the microphone and asked the audience not to panic. The Who was obviously used to a different reaction. Anyway, Pete backed up a few steps and made an enormous standing jump straight up into the air and landed on his knees on the stage floor with a great crash. The music started, extremely loud. After the song, Townshend grinned and pulled up his trouser legs revealing a pair of enormous knee-pads. After the hour-long show, it was time to go home, accompanied by the ringing in one's ears. So what, considering we had seen Pete, Roger, Keith and John, it was all worth it."

Friday August 25
KB Hallen, Copenhagen, Denmark

The initial tour itinerary kept this date open for a possible tour second show in Copenhagen. A second concert was added to the tour for Tuesday August 22 but switched to this night instead to allow for

the transfer of the group's equipment to and from Sweden. One show at 8 pm with a new song, 'Long Live Rock', as a rare encore.

Set: 'I Can't Explain', 'Summertime Blues', 'My Wife', 'Baba O'Riley', 'Behind Blue Eyes', 'Bargain', 'Won't Get Fooled Again', 'Magic Bus', 'Relay', 'Pinball Wizard', 'See Me, Feel Me', 'My Generation', improvisation, 'Naked Eye', 'Long Live Rock'.

One of the most notable inclusions of this concert was the improvisation following 'My Generation'. Over a familiar repeated three-chord riff Pete sang an embryonic version of what would later become 'However Much I Booze', with the vocal line: "I don't care what you say boy, there ain't no way out".

Lasse Ellegaard reviewed the second Copenhagen concert in the Copenhagen press thus (August 28): "The experience was more uplifting this time. The group's timing, choreography, light and sound was however this time less precise. But contrary to the last concert, the audience had an active role in the performance... That is why it was a better performance and to me it was a splendid example of how one, with the right elements and effects, can illustrate the Modern reality."

Pete leaps. The crowd roars. And the Who crash out their unique brand of rock

Wednesday August 30
Deutschlandhalle, Berlin, Germany

Set: 'I Can't Explain', 'Summertime Blues', 'My Wife', 'Baba O'Riley', 'Behind Blue Eyes', 'Bargain', 'Won't Get Fooled Again', 'Magic Bus', 'Relay', 'Pinball Wizard', 'See Me, Feel Me', 'My Generation', 'Naked Eye', 'Long Live Rock'.

The show attracted 10,000 fans although

reviewer Peter Radszuhn complained The Who were "far too loud" and the best songs were 'Magic Bus' and the *Tommy* selections. Golden Earring was support act.

Townshend turned in some fine – if unorthodox – soloing on 'My Wife'. "Give us a chance to get properly drunk," said Pete. "Where are we again? Ludwigshaven? Great to be back in Ludwigshaven!... Berlin?" Daltrey then introduced Keith Moon, who said: "Ladies and gentlemen... For your edification and delight I bring you a number from *Who's Next* on which I play the violin. A number called 'BABA O'RILEY'!!!!"

Later in the show, 'Magic Bus' featured some exceptional rhythm guitar as it stretched out over ten minutes.

Thursday August 31
Grugahalle, Essen, Germany
Set: 'I Can't Explain', 'Summertime Blues', 'My Wife', 'Baba O'Riley', 'Behind Blue Eyes', 'Won't Get Fooled Again', 'Magic Bus', 'Relay', 'Pinball Wizard', 'See Me, Feel Me', 'My Generation', 'Naked Eye', 'Long Live Rock'.

Pete announced 'Behind Blue Eyes' as "a song of subtle harmonies... It appears Keith Moon has gone to the lavatory. He's got a very weak bladder. This one's a song we'll have to play without Keith Moon. It's called 'Behind Blue Eyes'." Keith excelled during the stark synthesiser passage before the finale of 'Won't Get Fooled Again', where his dazzling drums rolls were particularly good. As the show progressed, the audience became unruly and finally downright violent during 'See Me, Feel Me', which affected the performance. As soon as the song finished, Daltrey lost his temper with some of the crowd, shouting: "Stop fucking hitting people, right! Just stop it!"

Pete then attempted to sort the problem out: "All right, well let's keep it cool, then eh? Don't stick two fingers up at me, you, I saw what you were fucking doing. Just keep it cool, otherwise we'll just fuck off out. They're playing at Hell's Angels down the front here. Little fourteen-year-old nippers." Someone in the crowd then threatened Pete, who responded saying: "You'll take on all of us, will you? All of us? Come on... You stupid git... You, yeah, I saw you. Trying to play some fucking music. Go home, go fucking home!" The band then launched into an aggressive and inspired version of 'My Generation'.

Saturday September 2
Viennerstadthalle, Vienna, Austria
Roger called this concert "the highlight of the tour" as The Who put on a two-hour, twenty minute performance for 9,000 fans. Set: 'I Can't Explain', 'Summertime Blues', 'My Wife', 'Baba O'Riley', 'Behind Blue Eyes', 'Bargain', 'Won't Get Fooled Again', 'Magic Bus', 'Relay', 'Pinball Wizard', 'See Me, Feel Me', 'My Generation', 'Naked Eye', 'Long Live Rock'.

Another problem with crowd control and faults with the backing tapes rendered this concert somewhat uneven. After 'Summertime Blues', Townshend told the audience not to push and to remain seated. The security staff had become heavy-handed with the fans. 'Bargain' was much extended, and after it had concluded Pete said: "Can everyone... sit back down again. No, don't bother to cheer, somebody just got their teeth knocked out down here. Just fucking sit down. Just sit down, will you! It's a bit tricky 'cause it's the people down the front that suffer. Those are the ones that come up against these geezers in the white overalls. I usually wear overalls like this and I'm fucking glad I didn't today... This one's for all you people that claim you've got a ticket with a seat number on it. 'WON'T GET FOOLED AGAIN'!!!"

The backing tape came in slightly behind the band on this version. Similar problems occurred on 'Relay', which Pete introduced as "a song which is on our forthcoming album, coming out in 1976, written by yours truly and featuring a synthesiser and a cardboard cut-out for a lead guitarist." Unfortunately, the pitch of the backing tape was unstable, playing faster and slower, but the band valiantly attempted to keep the song together. However, at various points Townshend, Moon and Entwistle periodically stopped playing to hear what the other two (and the errant tape player) were doing! Roger Daltrey literally carried the song with his superb singing which never flagged. 'See Me, Feel Me' received rapturous applause and 'My Generation' was dedicated to "you in the Union Jack jacket". A fine version of 'Long Live Rock' concluded the concert.

LIVE!

Who

FRANCE'S Communist Party has been holding its annual fund-raising rallies for 40 years now. Last year, they included pop music among the multimedia of the 'Fete de l'Humanite' (l'Humanite is the main organ of the Communist press) and had Joan Baez to top the bill.

This year, they really went to town, and got The Who, led by that well-known M. Townshend from the boiler-makers union.

Monday September 4
Deutsches Muzeum, Munich, Germany

Set: 'I Can't Explain', 'Summertime Blues', 'My Wife', 'Baba O'Riley', 'Behind Blue Eyes', 'Bargain', 'Won't Get Fooled Again', 'Magic Bus', 'Relay', 'Pinball Wizard', 'See Me, Feel Me', 'My Generation', 'Naked Eye'.

After some exemplary guitar work on 'My Wife' – the song where the band really warm-up on this tour – Townshend said: "The next one we're gonna play is a number where we use a synthesiser on the record... one of the first ones we used on *Who's Next* with a synthesiser, and on the stage we put the synthesiser on a tape and the brilliant Keith Moon with arms like metronomes plays along with it. For your edification and delight... 'Baba O'Riley'." After the song, some Moon-inspired lunacy took place and Keith was eventually ordered off the stage. Daltrey commented: "That is the only way we'll get this song done at all." They then played a fine version of 'Behind Blue Eyes'. "Magic Bus' was very lengthy and built to a pitch where Moon, Entwistle and Townshend were maniacally thrashing away with Daltrey wailing on harmonica. Daltrey introduced 'Relay': "Here's a very new song which we recorded before we came away. We started a new album. They may be on it. It's a good number written by Pete. One called 'Relay'."

One reviewer complained of the high ticket prices (DM27) and that The Who were too loud, but praised the show as being as good as their previous Munich appearance in April 1967.

Tuesday September 5
Mehrzeckhalle, Wetzikon, Zurich, Switzerland

Set: 'I Can't Explain', 'Summertime Blues', 'My Wife', 'Baba O'Riley', 'Behind Blue Eyes', 'Bargain', 'Magic Bus', 'Won't Get Fooled Again', 'Pinball Wizard', 'See Me, Feel Me', 'My Generation', 'Naked Eye', 'Baby Don't You Do It', 'Long Live Rock', 'Goin' Down'.

The slightly rearranged set made for an energetic and powerful performance. 'My Wife' was shorter than usual and 'Bargain' worked in some interesting quieter moments before it finished. Daltrey then announced 'Won't Get Fooled Again' but after some delay the band launched instead into 'Magic Bus'. 'Naked Eye' expanded into a long solo before reducing to just Townshend's guitar and erupting into a crashing barrage of noise. A welcome revival of 'Baby Don't You Do It' followed, and then Pete introduced 'Long Live Rock' as "a tribute to rock-'n'roll... in the style of Chuck Berry". The rare interpretation of 'Goin' Down' was played in a more loose manner than in December 1971 and featured some fine bursts of guitar soloing over Entwistle's throbbing bass line, before stretching out into a minimal riff and a climax of total noise.

Saturday September 9
Fete De L'Humanité, Paris, France

This was a huge open-air event sponsored by the French Communist Party! (L'Humanite was the main Communist newspaper in Paris.) The massive crowd was estimated at upwards of 400,000 people, the biggest audience that The Who would ever face. The set included 'I Can't Explain', 'Summertime Blues', 'My Wife', 'Baba O'Riley', 'Behind Blue Eyes', 'Bargain', 'Won't Get Fooled Again', 'Magic Bus', 'Relay', 'Pinball Wizard', 'See Me, Feel Me', 'My Generation', 'Naked Eye'.

The Who took to the stage at 6 pm after a set from Country Joe McDonald. Behind the band was the large logo of the promotion company RTL, and a number of red flowers were thrown onto the stage as The Who played. One faction of the huge crowd were to be heard chanting for *Tommy* during the early stages of the set. Pete described 'Baba O'Riley' as "a number about all sorts of things... Synthesiser in the background, Roger Daltrey in the foreground, Keith Moon asleep – but a deadly aim". Daltrey commented that "we'd like to speak in French. Unfortunately, we didn't go to school, so we can't," and Townshend mentioned the rain. A searing guitar solo characterised 'Bargain' and a new riff was added to conclude the song to which Roger sang the lines "It's gonna be all right. I call that a bargain." 'Magic Bus' began sounding rather sparse and ragged with little guitar work, but built up more strongly with Roger's excellent mouth-harp playing. Roger went on to describe 'Relay' as a song "recorded before we came away, hopefully on an album much later on. All Who albums seem to take a long, long time. Anyway, this one's Françoise Pete called 'Relay'." The structure of 'Relay' broke down until only the drums and vocals remained then built up again with Townshend and Entwistle producing simultaneous solos from their instruments.

Jerry Gilbert wrote in *Sounds* (September 16): "Mid-set, The Who reached their peak with 'Won't Get Fooled Again' and 'Magic Bus', Townshend vacillating hideously between a resigned poker face and an evil grimace. 'Get on board... Come on,' he urged, and then lurched to the front of the stage, dripping with perspiration, and went through the motions of taking the stalk between his teeth and hurling a grenade into the crowd gesticulating a mighty explosion. It was a positive allusion to the large Vietnam banner that hung over the fete and a clear mnemonic of Pete Townshend, revolutionary."

Pete had invited along a reclusive Eric Clapton to see this show, but during The Who's set he was mistaken for an intrusive fan and escorted from the wings by one of the stage crew!

Sunday September 10
Sportpalace, Lyons, France

Thursday September 14
The Palaeur, Rome, Italy

10,000 fans saw the last show and the only smashed guitar of the entire European tour. Set included: 'I Can't Explain', 'Summertime Blues', 'My Wife', 'Baba O'Riley', 'Behind Blue Eyes', 'Bargain', 'Won't Get Fooled Again', 'Magic Bus', 'Relay', 'Pinball Wizard', 'See Me, Feel Me', 'My Generation', 'Naked Eye', 'All Right Now'.

The Who had not played Rome since February 1967, but according to Chris Charlesworth, who was with the group at this date, "despite the long absence the audience sat impassively throughout the kind of set that most groups would swap their PA's for." This was a fitting conclusion to the tour and a great show. As ever, 'My Wife' was the song on which the band warmed up. "Watch this foot... When I say go..." said Pete before his foot-stamping introduction to the song. His long solo was spellbinding, even if he did eventually play the Gibson out of tune. The pace hardly let up from there and the spirit of the evening was compounded by a rare revival of Free's 'All Right Now' for a few bars at the end!

The local promoter convinced the band that the 10,000 people present simply wanted to listen hard to the music which was why they appeared subdued. "It's as good as it always is," wrote Charlesworth in *Melody Maker* (September 23) "a combination of violent excitement, near perfect

Tommy tickets sold out

TICKETS FOR the Tommy rock opera on December 9 are completely sold out.

Some 6,000 tickets were sold in two days, for the concert at London's Rainbow, with queues forming early on Friday night in readiness for the box office opening on Saturday morning.

Says Rosemary James of the Rainbow, " Demand for tickets has been tremendous. We thought the ticket rush for the Osmonds was chaotic, but this beats all."

sound and those power-packed Who songs... Townshend smashed his guitar into fragments – the first break of the tour – at the end and the Italian fans didn't know what had hit them. He swung it wildly at Moon's kit, and took three heavy blows against the stage floor before the instrument succumbed... The Who are so good they could probably put their shows over with their eyes shut. The inevitable problem arises – what next for The Who?"

Surprisingly, *Who's Next* had sold only 7,000 copies in Italy! The Who never returned there.

*Guitar destroyed: Gibson Les Paul Deluxe.

Saturday December 9
Rainbow Theatre, Finsbury Park, North London

The stage performance of Lou Reizner's production of *Tommy*. The recorded concert was broadcast on December 26. John was Cousin Kevin, Keith was Uncle Ernie and Roger, of course, was Tommy. Pete took on the role of narrator and played acoustic guitar.

The all-star cast included Rod Stewart singing 'Pinball Wizard', Steve Winwood as the Father, Peter Sellers as the Doctor, Maggie Bell as the Mother, Merry Clayton as the Acid Queen, Richie Havens as the Hawker, Ringo Starr and Sandy Denny as the Nurse, all with the London Symphony Orchestra and Chambre Choir. Originally intended for the Royal Albert Hall, the performance was banned by that venue's general manager because *Tommy*, in his estimation, "was not an opera" and he considered the programme "unsavoury".

The quiet period following the *Who's Next* tours continued well into 1973. Solo activities now took up more and more time between group projects. John had released two solo albums by early 1973 and had a third effort in the works. Roger also recorded away from the band – albeit only in order to promote singer-songwriter Leo Sayer, who was managed by his friend Adam Faith – and released his own album – titled simply *Daltrey* in the spring. Pete had issued a Meher Baba influenced record the previous year called *Who Came First*, recorded largely at his home studio with the assistance of fellow Baba followers Ronnie Lane (of The Faces) and Billy Nicholls. Keith had pursued his own projects, maintaining a high profile through looning about and landing acting roles in *That'll Be The Day*, with David Essex and Ringo Starr, and *200 Motels* with Frank Zappa.

The Who did appear for one show at the Pop Gala in Voorburg, The Netherlands, on March 10. The concert was taped for broadcast on Dutch television by the VARA network. There would not be another concert performance by The Who for seven months.

The band reconvened in late spring and recorded a new album all through the summer, a thematic piece developed by Pete over the past 18 months. As autumn approached, The Who emerged from their collective hiatus with the *Quadrophenia* double album. With plenty of new material to perform, The Who took to the road in the autumn, first in Britain and then America.

A significant incident that occurred just prior to the *Quadrophenia* tour served to illustrate the inner tensions that were always simmering beneath the surface of The Who's public facade. During rehearsals for the new stage act at Shepperton Studios in September, Pete Townshend – who was apparently very drunk – picked an argument with Roger Daltrey and finally knocked Daltrey across the shoulder with the neck of his guitar. Roger then punched Pete and knocked him out. Townshend was taken to hospital where an anxious Daltrey was waiting for him to come round. Daltrey and Townshend later laughed off the incident, but it indicated the level of frustration Pete was feeling with the difficulties *Quadrophenia* was presenting in terms of live presentation.

The tour opened at Stoke-on-Trent on October 28 with nine more UK dates to follow. Unfortunately, the backing tapes of pre-recorded synthesiser music that enabled them to reproduce *Quadrophenia* as it sounded on record were the cause of a major breakdown in Newcastle on November 5. Playing out of sync infuriated Pete and he lost his temper, dragging the band's long-suffering soundman Bob Pridden out from his mixing desk in front of the audience. After wrecking some gear and storming offstage, Pete reappeared after a short break to finish the show with a set of more familiar material. He went on local television the next day to apologise for his outburst and even helped out with equipment repairs.

The rest of the English dates were less eventful apart from unruly crowd behaviour over ticket demand, particularly at London's Lyceum. The last time The Who played in their home town, back in 1971, they'd attracted a vast crowd to the Oval cricket ground, then played three nights in the large Rainbow Theatre six weeks later, so the relatively small Lyceum ballroom seemed an unwise choice of venue, even though three nights were booked.

Exactly one week later, the group flew to America for the opening show of their US tour in San Francisco. It was a jet-lagged Who that arrived to begin the tour, and Keith had been drinking as usual, but he was unaware that his liquor had been spiked with PCP, a powerful tranquilliser used to calm wild horses. This potentially lethal combination might have killed lesser men but Moon survived, albeit after collapsing twice during the show. In what was seen

Roger Daltrey: "A lot of The Who has been lost in volume since we left *Tommy* out of the live show; it's lost some of the light and shade, and I've found it a lot less rewarding without the character of Tommy. There will definately be another *Tommy*. We said we never would, but we will, and it will be about one person with quadrophenia, and will form one-half of a double album." (*Record Mirror, December 23, 1972*).

as an extraordinary gesture for a group of The Who's status, a substitute drummer was recruited from the audience.

Quadrophenia was somewhat esoteric to most American fans since for them Mod never meant much more than a passing fashion of Carnaby Street-styled clothes on the racks of major department stores. With this in mind, the group decided to offer brief introductions to sections of the new material so that audiences might better understand the plot. As a result, many of the concerts suffered from a lack of continuity. The spontaneous headlong rush that was a feature of previous Who concerts, the wild abandon that fans loved, was often lacking.

The next stop was Los Angeles for two nights at the Forum. Keith was in fine form on the opening show as the band again performed *Quadrophenia* and even rewarded the audience for their 15-minute ovation with a rare encore. Pete smashed his Gibson Les Paul Deluxe, a gesture seldom seen during the tour.

The tour moved on to Dallas, Atlanta and St. Louis. They played a triumphant show at the International Amphitheatre in Chicago on November 29, "one of the two solidest performances of the tour" according to Pete in a *Rolling Stone* magazine article. After a stop in Detroit on December 2, the band arrived for a sell-out show at the Forum in Montreal where, after a hotel room party got out of hand, the entire entourage wound up in jail. The tour ended three nights later at the Capital Centre in Largo, Maryland just outside Washington, DC with all 17,500 seats sold out a week in advance.

The group finished the year by playing four well-received Xmas shows at the Edmonton Sundown, in North London, due to heavy ticket demand during the UK tour in October.

Saturday January 13
The Rainbow Theatre, Finsbury Park, London

Pete helped to organise the concert that brought a reclusive Eric Clapton out of self-imposed exile and back to the stage. An all-star band was assembled with Pete, Eric and Ron Wood on guitars and vocals, Jim Capaldi and Jimmy Karstein on drums, Rich Grech on bass, Steve Winwood on keyboards and vocals and Rebop on percussion.

Both performances, 6:30 and 8:30 pm, were

> **Pete Townshend:** "I've got to get a new act together for The Who. And I don't care if it takes me two years before you see The Who again. We've got to get something fresh... We've tried going through all the old hits, basing our show on that, but that doesn't work. It's all in the past now. People don't want to sit and listen to all our past."
> *(Melody Maker, February 10, 1973).*

recorded and a selection of tracks were released in September 1973 on the RSO album, *Eric Clapton's Rainbow Concert*.

Songs performed: 'Layla', 'Badge', 'Blues Power', 'Nobody Loves You When You're Down And Out', 'Roll It Over', 'Why Does Love Got To Be So Sad', 'Little Wing', 'Bottle Of Red Wine', 'After Midnight', 'Bell Bottom Blues' (first show), 'Presence Of The Lord', 'Tell The Truth', 'Pearly Queen', 'Key To The Highway' (second show), 'Let It Rain', 'Crossroads'.

Saturday March 10
Sporthall De Vliegermolen, Voorburg, The Netherlands
Set: 'Pinball Wizard', 'Baba O'Riley', 'Summertime Blues', 'Won't Get Fooled Again', 'My Generation', 'See Me, Feel Me', 'Magic Bus', 'Naked Eye'.

The policy of long lay-offs from live performance from 1972 onwards meant that when the band regrouped for one-off engagements such as this, they rarely regained their form straight away. This performance was notably under par: the sound was poor, the live setting in an outdoor amphitheatre somewhat artificial, and the band very untogether. Pete's Gibson SG guitar wouldn't stay in tune and Pete himself may well have overindulged in some backstage hospitality! The show had some decent moments, but was generally a huge disappointment to those who had seen The Who before. "I keep thinking it's Thursday!" said Pete before yelling drunkenly into the mike, "I'm pretending to be a member of the audience." An average version of 'Pinball Wizard' was played without the slow intro, and the audience reaction was understandably cool. 'Baba O'Riley' was decent enough but 'Summertime Blues' sounded like a disaster, with Pete's guitar well out of tune. 'Won't Get Fooled

Sunday October 28
Trentham Gardens, Stoke-on-Trent

Quadrophenia got off to a bad start at this concert. It had not been exhaustively rehearsed beforehand and The Who thought, with extensive use of backing tapes, that the complete piece could be played live. This show unfortunately proved them wrong. After only one performance, three songs, 'The Dirty Jobs', 'Is It In My Head?' and 'I've Had Enough', were dropped from the set (not to re-appear until the *Quadrophenia* revival shows in 1996). Other difficulties were encountered with guitars: because many of the songs required capos, Townshend found he had to change guitars over 20 times. No reviewers had been invited to this concert and the only documentary evidence that remains is Robert Ellis's photographs. The fans, however, weren't as disappointed as the band themselves were, and had been treated to several novelties such as a quadrophonic PA system delivering storm and sea sound effects and John Entwistle playing a large trumpet on 'Helpless Dancer'.

During the concert, Entwistle had a white leather jacket and the flying lady emblem on his Cadillac stolen! This prompted him to comment that he had, in effect, played the concert for free!

Monday October 29
Civic Hall, Wolverhampton

Set: 'I Can't Explain', 'Summertime Blues', 'My Generation', *Quadrophenia* ('I Am The Sea', 'The Real Me', 'Punk And The Godfather', 'I'm One', 'Helpless Dancer', '5.15', 'Sea And Sand', 'Drowned', 'Bell Boy', 'Dr. Jimmy', 'The Rock', 'Love Reign O'er Me'), 'My Generation', 'Pinball Wizard', 'See Me, Feel Me', 'Won't Get Fooled Again', 'Magic Bus'.

This was a much better show than Stoke but still rife with problems. The synthesiser backing tapes used on 'Helpless Dancer', 'Bell Boy', 'Dr. Jimmy', 'The Rock' and 'Love Reign O'er Me' proved difficult to play along to and didn't mix too well with the band's stage sound. The instrumental piece 'The Rock' was a courageous inclusion at best, and Townshend, Moon and Entwistle were tested to their limits to keep it in shape. Other frustrations weighed heavily on Pete. A new lighting rig in the small (1700 capacity) hall produced a level of heat on the stage that bent the strings of Pete's white Gibson SG out of tune. To

Again' had a bit of energy about it but Townshend looked unhappy throughout and gesticulated to Bob Pridden that the sound was poor. 'My Generation' managed to retain some of its usual punch, and stood out well in the set. 'See Me, Feel Me', however, failed to work its usual magic on the audience, and Pete didn't even bother to sing his backing vocals during the first part of the song. Daltrey yelled "get off your arses!" to the Dutch crowd, whose lack of enthusiasm was overwhelming, even when the powerful white lights were shone onto them. Pete's solo towards the end of this number went badly wrong, by which time he was past caring and The Who left the stage.

Surprisingly, they returned for an encore and redeemed themselves by launching into a 16-minute version of 'Magic Bus', which was by far the best song of the performance. Pete changed his guitar midway through the song from a white SG to a Les Paul, and the sound improved dramatically as a result. 'Naked Eye' followed, although this was omitted from the TV broadcast. A stereo sound recording of the show was also aired on Dutch radio. A small segment of 'Magic Bus' was released on the *Who's Better Who's Best* video and 'My Generation' was included on *Thirty Years Of Maximum R&B Live*. This show stands out, infamously, as one of the few black holes in The Who's live career. It is doubly regrettable that the only Who concert officially filmed in its entirety during the whole 1971–1973 period should be the very worst!

This show was part of the Grand Gala du Pop, organised over two nights by the Dutch Broadcasting Association (VARA), and The Who's performance was supposed to have been the highlight of the festival.

of Slade audience manipulation right in their own backyard. 'Arms up, down', he ordered. Of course, he was obeyed... Three hours of The Who is well worth a foggy journey down the M1 any day." *Disc* carried a review by Ray Fox-Cumming (November 10): "Despite PA problems which swallowed up much of the lyrics, it was a triumphantly successful evening with the fans going bananas and the band enjoying themselves just as much." Roy Carr praised the performance *in New Musical Express* (November 3): "Townshend is 101 per cent pure raw nervous energy; his licks are as fresh and aggressive as in his old auto-destruct days." *Melody Maker*'s Chris Welch said (November 3): "Roger Daltrey, stripped of his famous fringes and now in more Spartan attire, sang with demonic power. Screams of 'Roger!' from the milling throng crushed in the front rows show how The Who have gone full circle and become a teenage band again, at least in some respects... "

Thursday November 1
King's Hall, Belle Vue, Manchester

Set: 'I Can't Explain', 'Summertime Blues', 'My Generation', *Quadrophenia* (12 songs as October 29), 'My Generation', improvisation, 'Pinball Wizard', 'See Me, Feel Me', 'Won't Get Fooled Again', 'Magic Bus', 'All Right Now'.

The Who got into their stride with the third song, a good fierce version of 'My Generation' which had an extended solo. Townshend then said: "We'd like to do something from the forthcoming album now... We were expecting the album to be out and in your possession by now, but of course it isn't. The Japanese have bought up all the plastic and this album doesn't need too much explanation 'cause it's about everybody here, I'm sure. Though the way you're behaving, it's outrageous! A young, screwed-up, frustrated, idiotic teenager. Like us! I feel like a teenager. Watch this..." Pete then did a cartwheel across the stage. "This is an album called *Quadrophenia*," he continued, "and it's the story about a kid who goes down to the rock in the middle of the sea and looks back on a couple of weeks when he leaves home and a few backwardly nostalgic glimpses... Anyway, it starts off with the sound of the mighty sea. In quadrophonic. So open up your three left ears and experience quadrophonic for the first time…"

cap it all, each time he leapt across the stage, the lead fell out of his guitar.

Quadrophenia was symbolically sandwiched between versions of 'My Generation'. Daltrey mentioned that the band had played *Quadrophenia* for the first time the previous evening, to which Pete added: "Yes, and it was bloody horrible!" Townshend then went on to say that "It should have been in the bleeding shops by now." He explained the reasons for not playing the full work: "If we played it all, you'd fucking fall asleep!"

It was perhaps equally courageous of the band to invite London-based journalists to this concert as a press launch for the new work. Rob Mackie wrote in *Sounds* (November 10): "Like *Tommy*, *Quadrophenia* builds to a fine climax... In case that wasn't enough, the audience got a lot more for their money... Pete even found time for a jokey bit

The atmospheric 'I Am The Sea' was relayed entirely from tapes. After an energetic 'The Real Me', Townshend attempted to tune his guitar to the impatience of the audience, which had begun to chant. Over the riff of 'The Punk And The Godfather' Pete yelled "shut up!" Daltrey and Townshend sang alternate verses on 'I'm One' and Daltrey explained the plot a little before introducing 'Helpless Dancer' as *Quadrophenia*'s political song. This unusual number – unlike any other the band had done on stage – was sung as a round with Roger, Pete and John taking a line each over the backing tape of piano. '5.15' was a powerful performance and 'Sea And Sand' incorporated lines from The High Numbers' 'I'm The Face' along with various seagull cries on tape. Although the album had yet to be released, the audience keenly anticipated 'Bell Boy' and called out for this song. Some joking and insane banter preceded 'Drowned', which featured a lengthy guitar solo.

Daltrey then said: "If you had the bloody record you'd all know the story. That's the trouble. He doesn't drown himself, the water's too cold. So he goes to a hotel... and he sees this geezer who used to be the gang leader... and now he's a bloody bell boy in a hotel. Of course is another huge shock to his system. He cannot really get that one together at all, especially as the bell boy is played by Mr Keith Moon." This provoked great applause, prompting Pete to say: "Wait till after he's sung. You wait till you hear his singing voice, and you'll regret that ovation! He is fucking great actually..." 'Bell Boy' commenced with Pete shouting "go!" and the band managed to play very tightly with the backing tape, likewise with the following 'Dr. Jimmy' which was linked to 'The Rock' with another quadrophonic effects tape of the sea, much longer than the link on the album. 'Love Reign O'er Me' was notable for Daltrey's impassioned vocals.

The second version of 'My Generation' served to frame *Quadrophenia* in a perspective of The Who's history. The song broke down into a sparse jam and concluded with a new hard rock riff played by Townshend and Entwistle. This lasted only a few bars and worked into the introduction to 'Pinball Wizard'. During 'See Me, Feel Me', Daltrey stopped singing entirely for a while to allow the audience to join in, a rare practice at Who concerts, prompted here by the guitar

momentarily cutting out. A strong version of 'Won't Get Fooled Again' was followed by Townshend saying: "We're gonna play now for you, something you've wanted us to play... I'll tell you what, let's do a test... The first person to break the silence with a number you want to play – we'll play it!" The crowd then collectively roared a plethora of titles towards the stage, after which Townshend announced that the winner was 'Magic Bus'. A 15-minute version of the song followed, one of the best they ever played: very loose, hypnotic and insistent but with much vocal and guitar improvisation. The riff finally worked itself into an impromptu version of 'All Right Now', the Free song which the band had favoured in 1970. Overall, this show was most successful.

Friday November 2
King's Hall, Belle Vue, Manchester

Set: 'I Can't Explain', 'Summertime Blues', 'My Generation', Quadrophenia (12 songs as October 29), 'My Generation', 'Pinball Wizard', 'See Me, Feel Me', 'Won't Get Fooled Again', 'Magic Bus'.

The two nights in Manchester saw The Who playing for the first time at the 5,000-seat King's Hall within the Belle Vue amusement park. This was the largest capacity venue on the whole tour, and a demand for tickets throughout meant that many fans were left disappointed. That day, *Quadrophenia* finally reached the shops. A conceptual storyline album told in song-cycle, *Quadrophenia* is the tale of Jimmy Cooper the Mod, partly based on 'Irish' Jack Lyons, an old Mod-friend from Shepherd's Bush, Goldhawk Club regular and the co-author of this book. Within The Who only Pete was a true Mod. He believed in the style and sometimes led that style to the letter. What he may not have realised was that he was regarded by most West London Mods as a leading face.

Having received rave reviews in the music press, *Quadrophenia* became The Who's third biggest selling album, reaching the number 2 spot both in the US and the UK.

Monday November 5
Odeon Cinema, Newcastle

This was the night of the infamous 'tape disaster'. At some point in the show, the *Quadrophenia* backing tapes malfunctioned and Pete exploded

THE WHO

A ridiculous display of unwarrented violence

into a furious rage. He screamed at soundman Bob Pridden, smashed his guitar onto the stage and began tearing down the backing tapes and equipment. Roger, Keith and John stared on in disbelief.

The curtain was dropped and the audience sat in the darkness for about ten minutes until the band reappeared. The rest of the show was devoted to a set of "oldies", concluding with 'My Generation' and a vicious display of Gibson guitar demolition by Pete. He smashed his second guitar of the night and threw one of his Hi-watt amps to the ground as Keith ploughed through his drums, spilling them across the stage. They received "thunderous applause" as they left the stage.

"The Who - A Ridiculous Display Of Unwarranted Violence" wrote Steve Hughes in the *Newcastle Evening Chronicle* (November 6): "The Who rock band lived up to its reputation for violence on stage with an expensive display of guitar and amplifier-smashing at the Odeon Cinema last night. The concert was stopped in chaos when guitarist Pete Townshend bawled out sound engineers, destroyed pre-recorded backing tapes and smashed up £100 worth of equipment during the group's presentation of its latest rock opera. It was a ridiculous display of unwarranted violence witnessed by thousands of easily-influenced teenage pop fans.

"Townshend, a temperamental but brilliant guitarist, is quite notorious for sudden fits of violence on stage which have almost become accepted as part of the act by his many followers. But this time stage hands rushed to disconnect electric amplifiers and Townshend's electric guitar after he swiped it into the stage floor. Tempers flared after drummer Keith Moon had trouble with headphones. He let the drumsticks fly as the sound engineers battled to fix them. Then Townshend intervened, yelling at the engineers behind control panels on the side of the stage. He ripped out backing tapes and heaved over equipment into the side curtains. The three other members of the band – lead singer Roger Daltrey, guitarist John Entwistle and drummer Keith Moon – just stared. The safety net was lowered to the stage but the lights stayed out. Fans sat, quietly at first in total darkness and usherettes – obviously quite frightened – frantically flashed torch lights across the audience. After 10 minutes, with absolutely no trouble from the audience, the curtain was raised and Daltrey launched the band into a medley of 'oldies'. Then he yelled four-letter words at the audience, calling them – among many other derogatory terms – bastards and tried to explain everything by singing 'My Generation', a song about the generation gap and how no one understands the younger generation.

"Then Townshend hurled his guitar against the upstanding microphone and smashed it into a score of pieces by banging it against the stage floor. He then turned on a row of piled amplifiers at the back of the stage and hurled a top one to the floor. Moon waded through his range of drums, spilling them across the stage and Daltrey took a last kick at his microphone. They all left to thunderous applause. It was, in my opinion, an extremely childish publicity stunt with potentially damaging effect on the thousands of youngsters who invariably follow their idols in all they do. Otherwise, they were musically immaculate, as always. Concerts tonight and tomorrow will go ahead as planned.

The local TV show *Look North* on November 6 had picked up on the story and invited Keith Moon and Pete Townshend into the studio for a live interview. It was confirmed that the two following concerts would commence as planned and Moon and Townshend attempted to explain the problems that had occurred and laugh the incident off. Indeed, Townshend said very little and Moon carried most of the conversation. When asked about how disappointed the fans were, Moon jokingly replied: "Well, nobody asked for their money back, did they?" Moon was wrong, however, to assume that some fans weren't disappointed.

"The Who's Antics An Insult To Fans", ran a headline in the *Newcastle Evening Chronicle*, (November 8): "We are four girls who attended The Who concert on November 5, paying a total of £7 for tickets. Although we found the music and general conduct of the group exemplary, we feel justified in complaining about the antics of

Pete Townshend. Halfway through the performance he, because of a fit of temper over a technical difficulty, saw fit to throw his guitar to the stage and walk off, followed by the rest of the group. There then followed a complete stoppage of about 25 minutes. On the group's return no apology was given for this delay and [Townshend] abused the audience by saying (using bad language) that the group was too good to play to an 'audience of no goodies' and that there was no appreciation for the music. This was followed by another session of guitar and amplifier breaking. While we appreciate that Mr. Townshend's guitar breaking is a recognised part of the act, his use of bad language and immature attitude was completely unnecessary and completely spoilt our enjoyment of an otherwise praiseworthy performance..."

A retrospective account of this incident was given by Dave Marsh in *Before I Get Old*. Marsh believes that 'Irish' Jack's presence backstage at Newcastle, and his revelation that he had turned 30 (older than Townshend) had disturbed Pete unduly. Marsh wrote that: "Fifty minutes into the Newcastle gig, during '5.15', Townshend flipped out completely when the tape sync came in fifteen seconds too slow. He stepped to the side of the stage, grabbed Bobby Pridden by the scruff of his neck and pulled the poor road manager bodily over the mixing desk, then tossed him toward centre stage. As Pridden sprawled in front of the crowd, Townshend began pulling at the sound board, yanking out wires, demolishing many of the pre-recorded tapes it had taken so many weeks work to piece together." Pridden walked straight out of the Odeon and was pursued by John Wolff and Bill Curbishley, who persuaded him to return."

Townshend later apologised and Pridden set about repairing the damage. Cashflow problems also necessitated Pridden buying a replacement guitar out of his own pocket the following day!

Guitars destroyed – two Gibson Les Pauls

Tuesday November 6
Odeon Cinema, Newcastle
The second and third shows in Newcastle went on without incident after the opening night disaster.

Wednesday November 7
Odeon Cinema, Newcastle. 7:30 pm

LYCEUM, STRAND

THE WHO

It is regretted that all tickets for the concerts on 11th, 12th, 13th November are sold out.

There will be no tickets available at the door

Sunday November 11
The Lyceum, The Strand, Central London
Set included: 'I Can't Explain', 'Summertime Blues', 'My Generation', *Quadrophenia* (12 songs as October 29), 'My Generation', 'Pinball Wizard', 'See Me, Feel Me', 'Won't Get Fooled Again', 'Magic Bus'. Chaotic scenes at the box office prompted The Who to add four London shows in late December.

In *Melody Maker* (November 17), Michael Watts wrote of this performance of *Quadrophenia*: "The Who haven't yet worked out their sound logistics on it; a huge fist of sound crashes about one's ears but it's often hard to divine the thread of the story... what saved a sagging storyline at several points was the pure ferocity of their playing and singing and Townshend's startlingly visual sense (one leap onto the stage from the wings was eye-boggling)... the real high moments of the evening came not during *Quadrophenia* but towards the end... For the first time on Sunday there was real heat and love in the audience for a band that has remained true to its working class roots, and is striving to find a balance between its aggression and its intellect. Whatever the underlying conflicts, The Who's musicianship only increases in stature."

Monday November 12
The Lyceum, The Strand, Central London
Set: 'I Can't Explain', 'Summertime Blues', 'My Generation', *Quadrophenia* (12 songs as October 29), 'My Generation', improvisation, 'Won't Get Fooled Again', 'See Me, Feel Me', 'Magic Bus', 'Spoonful/Smokestack Lightning', improvisation.

When Pete came to introduce *Quadrophenia*, he was interrupted by a vociferous heckler, whom he promptly told to "fucking shut up, will you!" 'The Real Me' was looser and more improvised than the recorded version and it tended to vary each show in terms of length and feel. Following 'The Punk And The Godfather', Townshend told the audience: "That song was all about when the hero goes to a rock concert. He queues up, pays his money and he decides he's gonna go and see the stars backstage as they come out the stage door. And one of 'em comes up and says 'fuck off'. And he suddenly realises that there's nothing really happening in rock'n'roll... It's just another cross on his list. But he thinks a lot about the other side... He's not such a snappy dresser." Again, shouting from the audience interrupted Townshend. "Why don't you fucking shut up?" he continued. "Go and fucking see someone else, man... Or come up here and rock yourself. I'm talking, aren't I?" Ironically, Townshend sounded here not unlike the Godfather figure of his song, although he was clearly annoyed.

After 'I'm One', Daltrey explained why 'The Dirty Jobs' had been omitted from the performance: "It doesn't really work on stage, so we've left it out. Anyway, he gets a job as a dustman like most kids have to do when they leave school at 15. There's nothing much else. He gets pissed off with that... Of course, when you do something that stinks there's always a lot of other stinky things around. And he gets mixed up with the most stinky thing of all – politics!" The three lengthy central songs in *Quadrophenia* - '5.15', 'Sea And Sand', and 'Drowned' – all featured prolonged instrumental solos and occupied nearly half an hour of the concert.

Prior to 'Bell Boy', Keith Moon received rapturous applause and this song had begun to establish itself as the highlight of the *Quadrophenia* suite, although this version was a little sloppy due to the guitar not sounding too well integrated with the backing tape. The second version of 'My Generation' worked into a lengthy jam,

which developed into a new riff to which Daltrey sang, and Pete played some fine solos. Once more, as in Manchester, 'See Me, Feel Me' stopped dead halfway through and Roger encouraged the audience to continue singing. Again, 'Magic Bus' emerged as the highlight of the set – a loose, pulsating rhythm which finally developed into a bluesy jam based on 'Spoonful' and 'Smokestack Lightning'. This improvisation finally concluded the concert with a tighter hard rock riff that resembled Richard Berry's rock-'n'roll perennial 'Louie Louie'.

Tuesday November 13
The Lyceum, The Strand, Central London

By the third show it had become painfully clear that the old Lyceum theatre – home of British actor Sir Henry Irving a century earlier – was grossly inadequate for The Who's latest show. Pete particularly liked the theatre, but the band hadn't played there since 1968. With the new quadrophonic PA system and lighting gear, the venue didn't allow many people anything like a decent view. *Melody Maker* (November 24) was inundated with letters from fans who, having paid the top price of £2.20 for tickets, found they couldn't see the stage at this final London show.

As disgruntled fans tried to move elsewhere to gain a better view, a good deal of jostling and pushing occurred. Most fans blamed the layout of the theatre rather than the band, and one correspondent – Miss D. Nunn – gave "all credit to The Who, especially Roger Daltrey, who tried his utmost to organise us, admitting that the Lyceum was not their ideal venue either". As usual, not wishing to evade responsibility, Pete wrote to *Melody Maker* himself: "To all the people who inevitably will complain about the organisation at the Lyceum, The Who say, please, please hang on. Next year we will be playing larger, more suitable places, with cheaper seats. And to those who were hurt, or even just disgusted at not being able to see. Nobody feels as bad about it as ourselves." One direct result of this problem was the scheduling of four concerts in late December at Edmonton Sundown. It is perhaps worth mentioning, however, that The Who played all the London venues of all sizes through their career and they never really found a place that they liked... Nor did The Who ever offer "cheaper seats"!

In general, the British tour had been grossly inadequate in terms of regional coverage, and many fans – especially in Scotland and Wales – had little chance of seeing the band.

Tuesday November 20
The Cow Palace, San Francisco, California, USA

Set: 'I Can't Explain', 'Summertime Blues', 'My Generation', *Quadrophenia* ('I Am The Sea', 'The Real Me', 'Punk And The Godfather', 'I'm One', 'Helpless Dancer', '5.15', 'Sea And Sand', 'Drowned', 'Bell Boy', 'Dr. Jimmy', 'Love Reign O'er Me'), 'Won't Get Fooled Again', 'Magic Bus', improvisation, 'See Me, Feel Me', 'Smokestack Lightning/Spoonful', 'Naked Eye'.

The 1973 North American tour got off to an inauspicious start when Keith collapsed on stage during 'Won't Get Fooled Again'. He was carried off, revived in a shower backstage and given a short break before he rejoined the rest of the group. Then he collapsed again, not to return. The Who had sold out all 13,500 seats in four hours, three weeks prior to the concert. Lynyrd Skynyrd was the opening act for the entire tour.

Although, like Newcastle 15 days earlier, this concert is infamous in Who folklore, much of the music played during the early stages of the show was very good. Particularly notable was 'The Real Me' where John Entwistle's careering bass lines gave the song a manic energy. *Quadrophenia* progressed well until 'Drowned', which got into the middle solo section before Moon started to flag. The song was completed, however, and Keith then managed to give 'Bell Boy' his usual panache, amending the chorus lyric to "get the fucking baggage out!" Moon's drumming ceased entirely during 'Won't Get Fooled Again' where he failed to complete the solo passage towards the end. With Moon being revived backstage, Pete tried to explain to the audience that there was a problem, concluding by saying: "The 'orrible truth is that without him we're not a group!"

The band left the stage while the audience waited. After about 15 minutes, the band reappeared. Townshend and Moon grappled for a few moments until Pete – holding Keith in a mock wrestling hold – pulled the ailing drummer over towards his mike and shouted a few jokey comments about Moon trying to bottle out of finishing the gig. Soon afterwards, Daltrey also grabbed Moon and he and Townshend dragged him backwards towards his drums. Keith took all this in good part despite the fact that he obviously must have been feeling lousy.

With Moon seemingly ready to complete the performance, Pete picked up his Les Paul and began to tune it up. Soon after this The Who began playing 'Magic Bus', with Keith tapping together his two wood blocks. When he came to play the actual drums, however, he faltered once more, finally slumping forwards onto the kit amid a noisy climax in which Daltrey threw his mouth organ into the crowd. Roadies lifted Keith from the kit while Townshend started to play an improvised riff, Daltrey ad-libbing some singing. Then, without any interruptions, they moved directly into a drumless 'See Me, Feel Me', which was tightly paced, Daltrey using a tambourine to add some percussion. After the song had gained an o v e r w h e l m i n g response, Townshend applauded the audience for putting up with a 75 per cent complete band.

Instead of leaving the stage, however, Pete – tentatively and jokingly – said: "Can anybody play the drums?" Then he repeated the question more forcefully, adding "I mean somebody good!" Soon afterwards, Scott Halpin of Muscatine, Iowa, appeared on stage. After a roadie showed him to the kit, Townshend shook his hand and went straight into the riff of 'S m o k e s t a c k Lightning'. This was a very loose arrangement, and Halpin's drum work fitted in well enough, and it

anything out. I didn't want to stop playing. It was also a shame for all the people who'd waited in line for eight hours" (*Rolling Stone*, January 4, 1974).

Halpin had bought a scalper's ticket to get into the show and suddenly found himself as a temporary member of The Who! Afterwards he enjoyed the post-show backstage hospitality with the group and then slipped back into obscurity. In 1989, Halpin recalled to *Drums and Drumming* magazine, "The size of the drums was ridiculous. The tom-toms were as big as my bass drum. Everything was locked into place; any place you could hit there would be something there. All the cymbals overlapped." The whole concert was recorded on a crude 2-camera video system in B&W which was part of Bill Graham's personal archive, and the Moon collapsing incident can be seen in *Thirty Years Of Maximum R&B Live*.

Thursday November 22
The Forum, Los Angeles, California

Set: 'I Can't Explain', 'Summertime Blues', 'My Wife', 'My Generation', *Quadrophenia* (11 songs, as November 20), 'Won't Get Fooled Again', 'Pinball Wizard', 'See Me, Feel Me', 'My Generation', 'Let's See Action', 'Magic Bus', 'Naked Eye', 'Baby Don't You Do It'.

Keith was in better form for the LA shows and the group treated the first-night crowd to a rare event at a Who concert when they came back for an encore of 'Baby Don't You Do It'. Pete also smashed one of his numbered Gibson Les Paul Deluxe guitars.

Chris Charlesworth reported in *Melody Maker* (December 8): "19,500 fans had stomped and cheered for over 15 minutes in the Forum, refusing to leave even though the house lights had been raised and probably well aware that The Who rarely do encores. But tonight their enthusiasm was rewarded with just that. The group came back and did an encore – actually 'Baby Don't You Do It' – only the second time I've seen this happen in watching The Who around 20 times... they blasted through the song, climaxing with Townshend unstrapping the Gibson and, gripping the fretboard as if it were an axe, bringing it

shortly became 'Spoonful'. Less successful, however, was his contribution to the more complex 'Naked Eye', and he failed to provide the contrasting tempi despite Pete attempting to give him instructions. Halpin didn't look at all flustered and established a steady beat during the guitar solo. The second verse was missed entirely and Pete and Roger took turns to sing the final verse. Towards the end, Pete indulged in a mad spate of windmilled power-chords before the drawn-out "it don't really happen that way at all..." passage. Thus ended one of the most bizarre occurrences in the band's career.

Pete later explained why they didn't leave the stage after 'Magic Bus': "When Keith collapsed, it was a shame. I had just been getting warmed up at that point. I'd felt closed up, like I couldn't let

The Who's first show on the road falls apart

down on to the stage with a resounding crash time and time again until it cracked around the 12th fret."

Friday November 23
The Forum, Los Angeles, California
Set: 'I Can't Explain', 'Summertime Blues', 'My Wife', 'My Generation', *Quadrophenia* (11 songs, as November 20), 'Won't Get Fooled Again', 'Pinball Wizard', 'See Me, Feel Me', 'Magic Bus', 'Naked Eye'.

A second house of 19,000 witnessed *Quadrophenia* getting off at a cracking pace with 'The Real Me' and 'The Punk And The Godfather'. Even the unusual structure of 'Helpless Dancer' retained an impact. Townshend introduced 'I'm One' by saying: "I don't know if you ever get the feeling that maybe there's always somebody else that's a little bit better looking than you, a little bit better dressed than you, a little bit smarter than you, a little bit more up to the minute than you, a little bit tougher... Well, this song's about the feeling that it doesn't matter what shape you are, or small you are, or out of date you are, of how significant one is – only royalty ever say 'one'... You're still... All right." He then gave up on the explanation and began the song.

After 'Helpless Dancer', Daltrey said: "That song was basically about the frustrations that happen when you get mixed up with dirty things like politics... You needn't say that in the US of A. Anyway, from there the kid is very disillusioned and like a lot of kids still today, and when we were Mods – which we never really were – he runs away from home and he runs down to the seaside. He goes to Victoria Station – there was only trains in them days... '5.15'." There followed a powerful and energetic version of this song

(which had not been released as a single in America), with some fine guitar work. Towards the end of the song, Moon's drums established a beat uncannily like that of a train slowing down and the clatter of the wheels on the tracks. Daltrey introduced 'Sea And Sand' but Pete found his guitar needed tuning, and he changed it for another.

Robert Hilburn had reservations in the *Los Angeles Times* (November 27): "The Who showed much of the power, precision and desire that made it one of rock's most rewarding and influential bands. But even the improved performance Friday didn't erase the troubling impression that the group's momentum – and therefore, importance – is waning..."

Sunday November 25
Memorial Auditorium, Dallas, Texas
Set included: 'I Can't Explain', 'Summertime Blues', 'My Wife', 'My Generation', *Quadrophenia* (11 songs, as November 20), 'Won't Get Fooled Again', 'Pinball Wizard', 'See Me, Feel Me'.

The *Dallas Morning News* writer, Terry Kliewer, gave the show a one-word review of "WOW" before elaborating on a superb performance, but Roger thought differently. In an interview with the *Washington Post* (December 7) regarding the tour, Daltrey commented that The Who "only had one weak concert. Dallas". He didn't elaborate as to why this was the case but his judgement stands. Charles Perry and Andrew Bailey wrote in *Rolling Stone* (January 3, 1974): "'Rock & roll!' cried one lone voice, as Peter Townshend continued to explain where the upcoming song fit in his latest rock opera. The Dallas Convention Center Arena is like the inside of a UFO, perfectly circular with concentric rings of lights in the ceiling. Down on the stage beneath 144 coloured spotlights The Who were walking the tightrope of their first tour in two years, trying to put across songs from their first album in as long.

"After the US début in San Francisco they'd decided the selections from *Quadrophenia* needed a bit of synopsis. The surprising thing is that only one cry of 'Rock & Roll!' split the air, to say nothing of the possible 'Boogie!', 'Party!' or 'Get it on!' Because the story of *Quadrophenia* is not the fairy tale triumph of a trebly-handicapped teenage guru... And only one voice shouted 'Rock & Roll!'

10,000 college and high-school age Texans crowded the sold-out Arena November 25th to watch four men in their late twenties, including a singer and guitarist who are bywords for athleticism, perform powerful crashing music about... events in 1965, and their possibly misspent youth."

Tuesday November 27
The Omni, Atlanta, Georgia

The gate receipts totalled $107,000 from a near capacity house of over 15,000. By this concert, the difficulties of *Quadrophenia* were becoming apparent. It wasn't just the technical problems involved in playing it, but the added difficulty of putting across the concept, story and characters. And to audiences unfamiliar with Mod, this was an uphill struggle at best. Both Roger and Pete's long explanations of the plot between the songs certainly seemed to divert the flow and intensity of the live act.

Additionally, the backing tapes – especially on 'Bell Boy' and 'Dr. Jimmy' – never achieved the precision dovetailing that had been notable on 'Baba O'Riley' and 'Won't Get Fooled Again'. It must have somewhat disheartened Pete Townshend that the audiences invariably responded most warmly to the *Tommy* songs.

Wednesday November 28
St. Louis Arena, St. Louis, Missouri

Set included: 'I Can't Explain', 'Summertime Blues', 'My Generation', *Quadrophenia* (11 songs, as November 20), 'My Generation', 'See Me, Feel Me', 'Magic Bus' 'Pinball Wizard', 'Let's See Action', 'Naked Eye'

'Let's See Action', the British-only single from 1971, was being played live for the first time on a handful of dates on this tour. It took the form of a semi-improvised jam and the vocals were added in an equally casual way. The bridge section sung by Pete was always completely omitted. Also, this was one of the few US concerts where 'My Generation' was played twice.

The St. Louis concert was reviewed by Ken Barnes in *Phonograph Record* (January 1974): "For the most part The Who again proved peerless hard-rockers... Abetted by a much clearer sound than on the last tour... *Quadrophenia*... was, in a word, stunning. The concert rendition supplied all the raucous power seemingly latent in the storyline, and the added dimension invested the

monolithic *Quad* with the true rock & roll excitement missing in large part from the album. The Who, especially Townshend, seemed genuinely enthusiastic playing the new material... and it showed in a galvanising performance. Inevitably the remainder of the concert was a trifle anticlimactic ... It was definitely reassuring to witness a 1973 Who triumph... The group's brand of hyperkinetic excitement hasn't faded away; and at their best, The Who are still, simply, the best."

Thursday November 29
International Amphitheater, Chicago, Illinois

The Who sold out the Amphitheater over three weeks prior to the gig, grossing $87,000 in the

process. Tickets were available through mail order only to avoid trouble at the box office. Later, Pete said he thought that this show and Montreal "were the two solidest performances" of the tour.

The *Chicago Tribune* (November 30) carried a review of this concert by Lynn Van Matre, who was among 12,000 fans who attended. She wrote: "Well, the highest energy rock band has come and gone. The Who arrived on stage at the Amphitheater last night in the usual way, lead singer Roger Daltrey's legs chugging like pistons, microphone twirling, Peter Townshend's guitar arm windmilling, Keith Moon manic on drums and John Entwistle minding his business on the bass. The din from the stage was incredible; the din from the audience matching that and then some... When it comes to rock theater, The Who must be the masters. No Alice Cooper theatrics needed, no props other than voices and the charge the group self-generates. With them it's all energy, transcending the music, transcending the scene. Harness 'em up, and they could probably transcend the energy crisis as well..."

According to Van Matre, Pete sardonically referred to *Quadrophenia* as "a pot-boiler album we put together to please the industry and a long drawn-out piece of shit". She concluded: "They are, in the final analysis, pure, raw energy – which is, after all, what rock'n'roll's always been about."

Friday November 30
Cobo Hall, Detroit, Michigan

Set: 'I Can't Explain', 'Summertime Blues', 'My Wife', 'My Generation', *Quadrophenia* (11 songs, as November 20), 'Won't Get Fooled Again', 'Pinball Wizard', 'Magic Bus', 'Naked Eye', 'Let's See Action'.

This concert saw one of the stronger *Quadrophenia* performances, with the band feeling very comfortable with the Detroit audience. Daltrey acknowledged the city by referring to it as "our home from home in the USA" and went on to introduce 'My Wife' as The Who's favourite John Entwistle song. This performance careered along with the three instrumentalists playing flat out. Daltrey mentioned prior to 'My Generation' that Who fans in Detroit were the only Americans who bought the single when it was first released. 'Won't Get Fooled Again' was dedicated to those who had seen The Who play *Tommy* at Detroit's

Grande Ballroom in May 1969 at the beginning of the first ground-breaking *Tommy* tour. The Who returned for an encore that began with 'Magic Bus' – received with great applause – which segued into 'Naked Eye'. The set closed with a loose version of 'Let's See Action', with the second verse being sung by Pete, and at the end of the chorus, Daltrey amended the lyric to "let's see who fucking cares".

Sunday December 2
The Forum, Montreal, Canada

Set: 'I Can't Explain', 'Summertime Blues', 'My Wife', 'My Generation', *Quadrophenia* (11 songs, as November 20), 'Won't Get Fooled Again', 'Pinball Wizard', 'See Me, Feel Me', 'Magic Bus'.

A fine concert, which loosened up at an early stage when 'My Generation' developed into a formless jam. Townshend's introduction to 'I'm One' was met with some impatience: "It's all about – shut up for a minute and I'll tell you what it's all about – the song is all about a kid when he gets to that part of life when he feels he's just not worth a dime... It's like the fucking French

"ABRI ATOMIQUE"
THE WHO
TOURNEE NORD-AMERICAINE
1973
Dimanche 2 decembre 8 h p.m.
FORUM de MONTREAL

Revolution. That's what they said in Chicago. They were crazier than you in Chicago. And after the show somebody said to me 'That was like the French Revolution.' And the promoter said 'You wait till you get to Montreal!'" This concert featured the last live performance of 'Helpless Dancer' which was subsequently dropped for the remainder of the tour. Again, the concert was dominated by the three epic length songs, '5.15', 'Sea And Sand' and 'Drowned', all explained by Daltrey. Keith Moon sang some of his 'Bell Boy' lines in French!

The Who celebrated their sell-out performance in Montreal with post show renovations to a suite at the Bonaventure Hotel which had been booked not to accommodate anyone in particular but simply to use for hospitality purposes. Unfortunately, the last person to leave left the lights on and the door ajar. This was spotted by a night porter who glanced inside and was horrified by the damage.

The police were summoned and The Who and 14 members of their entourage (plus transitory female guests) were arrested and jailed. Roger, who as usual had retired early to protect his throat and who'd played no part in the hotel destruction, was not best pleased. The following afternoon local promoter Donald K. Donald delivered $5,995.34 in cash to the police station and everyone was released at 1:15 pm. (John gave an amusing account of the incarceration in his song 'Cell Number 7' on The Ox's *Mad Dog* album in 1975.)

The episode caused the group to miss their scheduled flight to Boston but they eventually left at 4 pm in time for the show that night at Boston Garden.

Monday December 3
Boston Garden, Boston, Massachusetts

Set: 'I Can't Explain', 'Summertime Blues', 'My Wife', 'My Generation', Quadrophenia ('I Am The Sea', 'The Real Me', 'Punk And The Godfather', 'I'm One', '5.15', 'Sea And Sand', 'Drowned', 'Bell Boy', 'Dr. Jimmy', 'Love Reign O'er Me'), 'Won't Get Fooled Again', 'Pinball Wizard', 'See Me, Feel Me', 'Magic Bus', 'Naked Eye'.

A crowd of 15,500 fans witnessed The Who venting their spleen against the Canadian police! Introducing 'My Wife', Pete Townshend mentioned that the band had spent all day in prison

When The Who tour the U. S. and Canada later this month, it is estimated the 11-city, 13-date trek will make them available to 61 per cent of the nation's concert-going and record-buying public.

Two years in the planning stage, the tour will take The Who to all major cities. They hope to make it the most audience and media-oriented concert tour in history.

and that he had come to the conclusion that John Entwistle is a "rotten dirty criminal, and I don't like him!" An amazing level of energy was reached on 'The Real Me' and was maintained with 'The Punk And The Godfather', although there was a brief pause between the two for Pete to retune his guitar. Talking of the Montreal police, he said "fuck their fucking arseholes" and added that he wished they were up on stage after seven hours in a police cell. However, prior to 'Drowned', Pete said – perhaps sarcastically – "I feel fucking incredible!" Townshend played an unaccompanied solo during 'Drowned' for a short while before the band picked up the song again. Daltrey later said: "About ten hours ago this gig was absolutely fucking impossible. So this one's for the filth – or whatever you like to call 'em – the police in Montreal. We're 'ere and it's good to be 'ere and this is for them: 'Won't Get Fooled Again'!"

Tuesday December 4
The Spectrum, Philadelphia, Pennsylvania

Set included: 'I Can't Explain', 'Summertime Blues', 'My Wife', 'My Generation', Quadrophenia (ten songs, as December 3), 'Won't Get Fooled Again', 'Pinball Wizard', 'See Me, Feel Me'.

A sell-out crowd of 19,500 packed the Spectrum for a gross of $135,000. The show was recorded for broadcast on the *King Biscuit Flower Hour*, as was the following night in Largo, Maryland. It was an edited version of this night's concert that was aired on Sunday March 31, 1974.

After a lengthy version of 'My Wife' followed by a superbly fast and hard performance of 'My Generation', which maintained its energy through seven minutes and some brilliant guitar soloing from Townshend, the *Quadrophenia* section of the show was less impressive. Pete said "The better part of an album what we wrote about ourselves being Mods, when we were little. The story about the Mod kid and we call it *Quadrophenia*... Being Mod meant a lot more in England I think than it ever did in America. I think you think of it being a Carnaby Street thing... And it's not just a looking back, it's a kind of bringing up to date. *Quadrophenia*'s about where we all are today, maybe you too. The story is set on a rock in the middle of a stormy sea. In quadrophonic, as well!"

Pete started playing a little too soon before the tape of 'I Am The Sea' had finished. Explaining 'I'm One', Pete said: "The next song is called 'I'm One', what I sing and it's all about the way I felt, 'cause I wrote it. When I was a nipper I always used to feel that the guitar was all I had... I wasn't tough enough to be in a gang, I wasn't good looking enough to be in with the birds, not clever enough to make it at school, not good enough on my feet to be a good football player, I was a fucking loser. I think everyone feels that way at some point. And somehow being a Mod – even though I was too old to be a Mod really – I wrote this song with that in mind. Jimmy, the hero of the story, is kinda thinking he hasn't got much going for himself but at least he's one."

'Sea And Sand' slowed down into a single guitar riff and built up again as Daltrey sang 'I'm The Face', and 'Drowned' featured some fine ensemble playing. 'Bell Boy' sounded rather clumsy but Keith Moon enlivened the song with his funny amendment of the lyric to "remember the place in Canada that we smashed". The average quality of the *Quadrophenia* performances was more than compensated for by 'Won't Get Fooled Again', a fine 'See Me, Feel Me' and 'Pinball Wizard'. Townshend introduced the latter as 'Pineball Blizzard!'. The radio broadcast omitted 'My Wife', 'The Punk And The Godfather', '5.15', and 'Love Reign O'er Me'. The remaining show had the four-letter words in the announcements edited out, as well as from 'Dr. Jimmy', although Daltrey had slipped a "fucking" into the last verse of 'My Generation' which seemingly was broadcast unnoticed!

The 16-track mastertapes of this show (and Largo, below) have been carefully preserved by King Biscuit Flower Hour for future use, but The Who have always considered them unsuitable for release.

Guitar destroyed: Gibson Les Paul Deluxe – cherry sunburst.

Thursday December 6
The Capital Centre, Largo, Maryland

Set included: 'I Can't Explain', 'Summertime Blues', 'My Wife', 'My Generation', *Quadrophenia* (ten songs, as December 3), 'Won't Get Fooled Again', 'Pinball Wizard', 'See Me, Feel Me'.

This sell-out show before 17,500 fans was reviewed by Tom Zito of the *Washington Post* (December 7): "Perhaps because it was their last night on a long tour schedule, or because of a PA system that steadily distorted Roger Daltrey's rustic, raw vocals, or because the mammoth hall echoed the vocals and Pete Townshend's screaming guitar surges, The Who just didn't have the snap, crackle and pop and the sheer energy exuded in a 1970 summer concert at Columbia's Merriweather Post Pavilion that attracted a gate-trampling 20,000. The spirit seemed present in showmanship form, but not in musical content... musically this wasn't the old wild-but-precise Who... the band sounded tired and sloppy, almost like a second rate rock outfit trying to imitate The Who... There were occasional flashes of former glory: Townshend leaping across the entire stage, sounding the bridge chord to 'Won't Get Fooled Again' just as he touched down... But these were exceptions. And the audience, bathed in huge klieg lights aimed out from the stage during the final overture from *Tommy*, clapped wildly, especially as Moon demolished his drum kit in old Who fashion – at least one Who fan last night felt the group to be only an echo of an old tidal wave."

The show was supposedly recorded by DIR Radio for broadcast on the *King Biscuit Flower Hour* but it was the previous night's concert that was broadcast on March 31, 1974. (That show was rebroadcast on the *KBFH* - December 29, 1974.)

Thursday December 13
Rainbow Theatre, Finsbury Park, London

Tommy was once again presented at the Rainbow as it had been the year before. The all-star line-up was completely different with Roger being the only Who member to participate in the

WHO HIT LONDON

two performances. Pete was not able to take part due to work commitments (probably pre-production on the film version of *Tommy*).

Tuesday December 18
Sundown Theatre, Edmonton, North London
Set included: 'I Can't Explain', 'Summertime Blues', 'My Generation', 'My Wife', *Quadrophenia* (ten songs, as December 3), 'Won't Get Fooled Again', 'Pinball Wizard', 'See Me, Feel Me'.

The band agreed to play four shows in London due to overwhelming demand for tickets during the UK tour in the autumn. The chaotic crowd scenes at the London Lyceum in particular had influenced this decision, and tickets for Edmonton were available by mail order only. Pete Townshend later expressed the opinion that this series of four concerts were the best the band had ever played, and certainly the best *Quadrophenia* concerts. "I felt like one of The 'Oo an' all that," he commented in *Melody Maker* (February 16 1974). "But I also felt like one of the crowd."

Wednesday December 19
Sundown Theatre, Edmonton, North London
Set included: 'I Can't Explain', 'Summertime Blues', 'My Wife', 'My Generation', *Quadrophenia* (ten songs, as December 3), 'Won't Get Fooled Again', 'Pinball Wizard', 'See Me, Feel Me'.

Saturday December 22
Sundown Theatre, Edmonton, North London
Set: 'I Can't Explain', 'Summertime Blues', 'My Wife', 'My Generation', *Quadrophenia* (ten songs, as December 3), 'Won't Get Fooled Again', 'Pinball Wizard', 'See Me, Feel Me', 'Substitute', 'Magic Bus', 'Naked Eye', 'Spoonful'.

Pete Townshend's introduction to *Quadrophenia* at this fine concert was as follows: "I tell you we're gonna play *Quadrophenia* next and I'm gonna try and tell you the story of Jimmy. You probably know it by now. When we came to

America a lot of people really didn't understand what the Mods were all about. They thought they were Carnaby Street types, I don't know, it's hard to explain. They didn't quite understand what the Mods meant to us or what we meant to our audience at the time. It's just about being an adolescent, really: out of touch with what's up. It's what made me pick up a guitar in the first place. I was fucked up in the eyes of everybody in this particular group, I can assure you. The story starts off with the kid already in a fucked up condition and he's thinking about the events in a week that led up to him contemplating, I suppose, suicide. So, we start off by the sea... You've never done it? Contemplate. The scene is a rock in Brighton... Offshore." During *Quadrophenia*, various visual backdrops were lowered and raised, and at the end of the set prior to the encore – after 'Substitute' – a giant animated Santa Claus figure descended, complete with "yo ho ho" sound effects!

Townshend also mentioned that The Who had now found themselves unexpectedly excited once more about *Tommy*, and he dedicated 'Pinball Wizard' and 'See Me, Feel Me' to Ken Russell, who was due to start directing the feature film in the new year. Jeff Ward reviewed the concert for

Melody Maker (January 5, 1974): "The Who, to be honest, seemed to tire rapidly as their two and a half hour set progressed. Roger Daltrey, believed to be suffering from some throat trouble, was consequently not in best voice... Pete Townshend was in good humour and carried on a repartee with the audience while narrating the story of *Quadrophenia* in between numbers. 'Too many in tonight,' he mused at one point. 'Send them round after the show and I'll pummel 'em into the ground with me brain – and me nose, yeah!' Several sections of *Quadrophenia* sounded grand... it generally seemed more melodic and more integrated and on a more epic scale... The band came back for 'Magic Bus', which was played very low key and laid back, charged with hardly any excitement at all. But, shortcomings ignored, the crowd cheered on, throwing streamers, waving hats and scarves, and stamping till the house-lights went up. It was a set that had blown hot and cold."

Sunday December 23
Sundown Theatre, Edmonton, North London

Set: 'I Can't Explain', 'Summertime Blues', 'My Wife', 'My Generation', *Quadrophenia* (10 songs, as December 3), 'Won't Get Fooled Again', 'Pinball Wizard', 'See Me, Feel Me', 'Substitute', 'Naked Eye', 'Let's See Action', 'Magic Bus'.

On this final night The Who sounded happy, inspired and relaxed. As mentioned in the billing, the Christmas Party atmosphere really did pervade the whole show. They played a blinding set which must rate as the very best of the whole year. Luckily, the show was recorded from the mixing desk, although it hasn't been retained in The Who's sound archives. The announcements were funny and good-humoured, the PA sound crystal clear and the audience simply in the palm

of the group's hands from the first high-energy chord of 'I Can't Explain'. "Old rock'n'roll," yelled Roger, "will be the same as ever. And here to prove it: 'Summertime Blues'!" By the time of *Quadrophenia*, the band were going full pelt, and 'The Punk And The Godfather' was charged with the kind of excitement that seemed somehow to have been missing on the US tour.

Pete then said: "The story goes like this. He's a young man, once upon a time, there was a young man in the world these days..." The audience had sang along so Pete played a quick jazzy variant on the 'Young Man Blues' riff. "The last song was all about the kid, he goes to this rock'n'roll concert and there's a group playing called The 'Oo. At the Hammersmith Odeon to be exact and he lived on the same street as one of the geezers in the band and when he goes around backstage and says 'Hello, do you remember me?' they say 'Fuck off!'. It does happen! Actually, my own mother, only tonight my own mother was up and I wouldn't let her in. I told her to 'Fuck off...' No, I didn't tell her to... And so he got a bit pissed off at his Mum and Dad, he got a bit pissed off with rock'n'roll, he got a bit pissed off at everything. This song is about how pissed off he was with everything except himself. If everything else was no good he was still all right. Called 'I'm One'. And I sing it and I would like a little bit of quiet please! Otherwise, I'll stick me bouncers on you."

Pete later jibed at Roger's alleged financial parsimony ("Roger Daltrey bought me a drink – water!"), at Slade's then-current No. 1 hit (and the curse of every Christmas party since!) 'Merry Xmas Everybody' saying in a dumb voice "the future... It's only just begun!" Meanwhile, Roger dedicated a song to all the members of the audience who lived in council flats without chimneys with which Father Christmas couldn't enter.

Against all odds, this show concluded 1973 with the band again reaching the peak they had sustained between 1969 and 1971. Unfortunately, it was simply a good season of shows where *Quadrophenia* worked, the venue was most hospitable and the fans – who this time were familiar with the new album – were responsive. It did not convince The Who that *Quadrophenia* was finally assuming *Tommy*-like proportions on the stage, although they didn't give up on it just yet.

Guitar destroyed: Gibson Les Paul Deluxe – cherry sunburst.

Seasoned Who watchers couldn't help but notice that one-off gigs and very short tours never really brought out the best in the band. The Who were like a high-performance sports car which needed to be kept in tune in order to obtain optimum results. When they took on a lengthy tour the first few shows might have been slightly under par but when they hit their stride, Olympic fitness as it were, they were still supreme. When they played the odd show here and there they suffered through being out of condition – and sometimes it showed. They didn't play much in 1974, and when things weren't gelling, the disparate personalities in the band clashed to detrimental effect. It's unlikely that The Who looked back on 1974 with any great fondness.

Behind the scenes, Kit Lambert and Chris Stamp had been negotiating to bring *Tommy* to the big screen, and a film version of Pete's rock opera went into production in April. Before filming began, the group conducted a leisurely tour of France in February. They were still playing *Quadrophenia* but when the French tour was over, *Quad* was put aside until its revival in 1996. The filming of *Tommy* and solo projects would dominate the year, leading to persistent rumours of The Who's demise. In addition, Pete was tied up producing the soundtrack for the movie, a burdensome task which involved re-recording the entire song cycle with different musicians and singers, some of whom couldn't sing.

The group did play a few shows in the midst of their filming schedule: one at the New Theatre, Oxford, another at a huge outdoor concert on May 18 at Charlton Football Stadium in South London, and a special 'closed concert' for the extras of the *Tommy* film (many of whom were students from a local college) in Portsmouth on May 22. The American tour the previous November had bypassed New York, so the band set up four shows at Madison Square Garden in mid-June. Amazingly, all four dates sold out on the strength of a single 60-second radio spot. As a testament to The Who's popularity in the New York area, the venue received 50,000 additional requests for tickets after the 80,000 had already been sold. Gate receipts exceeded $500,000.

The shows were acclaimed as a triumph in the New York press but Pete would later express dissatisfaction. The band had abandoned *Quadrophenia* as a stage act and at the Garden they performed a "greatest hits" style show. The reaction of the crowd was ecstatic since The Who had not appeared in New York for almost three years, but for Pete it was all too predictable. For him the excitement had gone out of performing, and the fans' blind adulation – regardless of the quality of the show they saw – depressed him still further. Many fans, especially those at the front, had bought tickets for all four nights and it might have seemed to him as if the nightmare he'd described at the Fillmore East in October 1969 – playing to the same audience every night – was really happening. Pete made no secret of the fact that his condition at the time was made worse by excessive drinking and an overall feeling of having to "force" a performance. It would be over a year before Pete thought differently and The Who took the stage again.

LE GROUPE BRITANNIQUE ‹WHO›

John, the ultimate professional to whom playing music was the staff of life, couldn't stomach the long lay-offs. In the past he had talked about forming his own touring band, and in the second half of 1974 he finally assembled an outfit called Ox, his nickname within The Who. Although it was an expensive exercise, he played three English gigs in December with more dates planned in the New Year including a US tour.

Saturday 9 February
Palais des Grottes, Cambrai, Lille.

The tour was promoted by RTL (Radio Tele-Luxemberg), the leading European promotion agency which had previously presented The Who at the Fete De L'Humanité in Paris in September 1972. For the French tour, the quadrophonic PA system was curtailed. This had only been used for the tape effects and had necessitated two additional speaker columns at the back of the hall. This had provoked many complaints from the audience about their vision being blocked. Consequently, 'I Am The Sea' and a tape link of storm sounds that was used between 'Dr. Jimmy' and 'Love Reign O'er Me' were dropped. The support act for the French dates was John Keene (previously known as 'Speedy') of Thunderclap Newman fame.

Set included: 'I Can't Explain', 'Summertime Blues', 'My Wife', 'My Generation', *Quadrophenia* ('The Real Me', 'Punk And The Godfather', 'I'm One', '5.15', 'Sea And Sand', 'Drowned', 'Bell Boy', 'Dr. Jimmy', 'Love Reign O'er Me'), 'Won't Get Fooled Again', 'Pinball Wizard', 'See Me, Feel Me'.

Roger introduced *Quadrophenia* as being "all about kids. And how we remember our own childhood. And childhood today, and, I suppose, childhood ever more". After the *Quad* section, Pete delighted the audience by playing a chugging blues variation of the 'My Generation' riff as he introduced some "old melodies from yester-year!"

A crowd of about 10,000 attended the concert which started at 5 pm.

Sunday February 10
Palais Des Expositions, Paris

Set: 'I Can't Explain', 'Summertime Blues', 'My Wife', 'My Generation', *Quadrophenia* (nine songs, as February 9), 'Won't Get Fooled Again', 'Pinball Wizard', 'See Me, Feel Me', 'Substitute', 'Magic Bus', 'Naked Eye', improvisation, 'Let's See Action', 'My Generation'.

This was the biggest show of the tour with 26,000 fans, and the band were on good form. The venue did not initially inspire the band much, and 10,000 fans rioted on the morning of the show, breaking into the arena while the roadies were erecting the gear. After three songs, a cloud of blue smoke drifted from behind the stage, and the band stopped playing while an electrical fault was rectified. As Roger introduced the "selection from our latest album *Quadrophenia*", Pete played a funky version of the four-chord sequence of the chorus of 'The Real Me'. This was very effective and unusual for The Who, after which Pete went into the louder, full-blown riff that started the song proper. In fact, Townshend was in very lyrical mood on guitar, playing melodic phrases and riffs between numbers. Roger Daltrey described 'Summertime Blues' as "one of the first records we ever copied from another artist", while Pete dedicated 'My Generation' to "every one of you that feels you can identify with our age group". The band returned for an encore which started with 'Substitute'. Following 'Naked Eye' came a fast improvisation to which Daltrey added some vocals before moving into 'Let's See Action' and the second performance of 'My Generation'.

Steve Lake witnessed the show for *Melody Maker* (February 16): "'Drowned' from *Quadrophenia* was the absolute killer, reaching a crescendo with Townshend demolishing another £350 guitar, bouncing it twice off the stage, and finally snapping it at the base of the neck with a sledgehammer swipe at his speaker stack. Sparks flew from the jack-plug socket. Moon, looking as crazed as ever, offered out-of-tune vocals on 'Bell Boy', despite the fact that he was wearing headphones. He redeemed himself a little later by revealing a surprisingly delicate touch on the quieter passages of 'Sea And Sand'. Elsewhere he threshed like a combine harvester on amphetamines... [on 'Naked Eye'] Townshend played the best guitar of the night. He stumbled around in circles, eyes closed, alternately resembling a Modigliani portrait and an Irish navvy, scrubbing across the strings, working from scratchy, scrappy rhythms to weaving and ducking lead lines of thunderous power. Double bass drums kicked pneumatically, and it was all over. The Who huddled stage centre, arms entwined, sweating pro-

LES WHO

Ce qui frappe d'abord chez les Who, dix ans après leur formation, c'est la cohésion du groupe, un évident plaisir à jouer, une complicité entre quatre musiciens qui sont avant tout des « showmen ». Mais Pete Townshend, Roger Daltry, Keith Moon et John Allison n'ont pas seulement su maintenir leur punch, leur jeu rageur, ni parfaire l'exécution de morceaux rock. Ils ont développé leur travail harmonique et, sous la conduite de Pete Townshend, se sont dirigés vers la création d'œuvres plus ambitieuses : ce fut *Tommy*, le premier opéra rock de la musique pop' ; c'est aujourd'hui *Quadrophonia* qui, sous forme d'une chronique sociale, raconte l'histoire d'un jeune « mod ».

fusely. They grinned their appreciation and staggered off, carrying the triumphant Moon aloft. Paris won't forget for a long time."

*Guitar destroyed: Gibson Les Paul Deluxe.

Friday February 15
Les Arenas, Poitiers, France
Nine thousand fans turned out for this concert.

Sunday February 17
Foire De Toulouse, Toulouse, France

Friday February 22
Palais Des Expositions, Nancy, France

Sunday February 24
Sports Palais, Lyons, France
Set: 'I Can't Explain', 'Summertime Blues', 'My Wife', 'My Generation', *Quadrophenia* (nine songs, as February 9), 'Won't Get Fooled Again', 'Pinball Wizard', 'See Me, Feel Me', 'Magic Bus', 'Substitute'.

A rioting crowd of 1,000 threw fireworks and injured police as they fought to gain entrance to the venue. The Who ended the French tour at Lyons and put away the troublesome backing tapes for *Quadrophenia* until its June 1996 presentation at London's Hyde Park and the subsequent tours that followed.

Sunday April 14
The Roundhouse, Chalk Farm, North London
In this, the first solo concert by any member of The Who, Pete performed in a benefit show for the Camden Square Community Play Centre to help them buy a coach.

The set included 'The Seeker', 'Big Boss Man', 'Substitute', 'My Generation' (two taped demo versions and a live version), 'Pinball Wizard', 'If I Were A Carpenter', 'New York City Blues', 'Behind Blue Eyes', 'Join My Gang' (an early song of Pete's recorded in 1966 by Oscar), 'Corrina Corrina', 'Girl From The North Country' (trad), 'No Face, No Name, No Number' (Traffic), 'If I Were A Carpenter' (Tim Hardin) and 'Let's See Action'.

At one point in the show, Pete got so angry with a heckler in the audience that he climbed off the stage and threatened him! Other artists appearing were Coast Road Drive and Byzantium.

Monday May 6
New Theatre, Oxford
Low-key, unannounced warm-up show.

Saturday May 18
Charlton Athletic Football Club, South London
Set: 'I Can't Explain', 'Summertime Blues', 'Young Man Blues', 'Baba O'Riley', 'Behind Blue Eyes', 'Substitute', 'I'm A Boy', 'Tattoo', 'Boris The Spider', 'Drowned', 'Bell Boy', 'Dr. Jimmy', 'Won't Get Fooled Again', 'Pinball Wizard', 'See Me, Feel Me', '5.15', 'Magic Bus', 'My Generation', 'Naked Eye', 'Let's See Action', 'My Generation Blues'.

Starting at noon, the supporting acts were Montrose, Lindisfarne, Bad Company, Lou Reed, Humble Pie, and Maggie Bell. The Who took the stage at 8:45 for an hour and 45 minute set in front of 50,000 fans. Amid uncomfortable conditions, the band worked their way through a patchwork of old and more recent material. The PA sound was less than perfect and many fights erupted in the audience. The Who played well, but Pete later revealed that he was extremely drunk and the show never got into a 'classic Who' groove. Some songs sounded messy – especially the *Quadrophenia* material – and '5.15' was a near disaster. But towards the end of the set, the 'My Generation' medley really struck home with a

SUMMER OF '74

the Who

20p

LOU REED
HUMBLE PIE
BAD COMPANY
LINDISFARNE
MAGGIE BELL

SATURDAY 18TH MAY
CHARLTON ATHLETIC
FOOTBALL CLUB

brilliant 'Naked Eye' and 'Let's See Action', and the fans didn't leave disappointed. All the songs apart from 'I Can't Explain' and '5.15' were broadcast in FM stereo in the London region on Nicky Horne's *Rock Pile* programme on Capital Radio later in the year.

The concert concluded with the first ever performance of the slower 12-bar blues arrangement of 'My Generation', known within the group initially as 'Slow Generation Blues'. Despite the shortcomings, Charles Shaar Murray found little to complain about in his review in *New Musical Express* (May 25): "They performed with a freshness and enthusiasm that they haven't had for quite some time, and generally acted like the epitome of what a rock and roll band should be...The Who are it; as good as it ever gets, and good as we can expect from anybody."

Pete Townshend: "At Charlton I got completely pissed... I was so happy to get out of it. For Madison Square Garden we had to fight and snatch the time off from the film and consequently when we got there it wasn't really all that wonderful from our point of view... I felt really guilty I couldn't explode into the exuberant and happy energy our fans did. I screwed up every inch of energy doing it then would be brought down by a monitor whistling or something and I'd have to work myself up again..." (*New Musical Express*, 20 July 1974).

The show was taped by BBC Television and broadcast on the BBC 2 programme, *Second House* on October 5, 1974. Songs featured were 'My Generation' (part),'Young Man Blues', 'Baba O'Riley', 'Substitute', 'Drowned', 'Bell Boy', 'See Me, Feel Me', 'Naked Eye', 'Let's See Action' and 'My Generation Blues'.

Pete was also interviewed by Melvyn Bragg during the programme, part of which may be seen in *The Kids Are Alright*. Four songs from this show, 'Substitute', 'Drowned, 'Bell Boy' and the 'My Generation' jam can be seen in the video, *Thirty Years Of Maximum R&B Live*.

Tentative plans had been made for The Who to play at Shawfield Stadium in Glasgow on Saturday May 25 but the local authorities barred such a show following the death of a fan at a Glasgow concert by David Cassidy.

Wednesday May 22
Guildhall, Portsmouth

Set: 'I Can't Explain', 'Young Man Blues', 'Baba O' Riley', 'Behind Blue Eyes', 'Substitute', 'I'm A Boy', 'Tattoo', 'Boris The Spider', 'Drowned' 'Bell Boy' (false start), 'Bell Boy', 'Dr. Jimmy', 'Won't Get Fooled Again', 'Pinball Wizard', 'See Me, Feel Me'. Encore: '5:15', 'Magic Bus', 'My Generation Blues', 'My Generation', 'Naked Eye', 'Feelin'' (an obscure Johnny Kidd & The Pirates song from 1959), 'My Generation Blues' (reprise) and 'Let's See Action'.

The Who played a special "thank you" concert for the extras who worked in the *Tommy* movie. It was a "closed concert" and by all accounts the relaxed atmosphere inspired the band to play as well as they ever had. The general public weren't admitted, though a 'sold out' notice appeared in *Melody Maker* on May 11, 1974.

During 'Bell Boy', the band got so out of time with the synthesiser backing that Pete ordered everyone to stop, had Bob Pridden rewind the tape, and the song was begun again. This was probably the worst experience the band had with the difficult *Quadrophenia* backing tapes but, since the show wasn't before a paying audience, it didn't seem to matter so much. The band started again in good humour, and Bob Pridden probably breathed a sigh of relief!

Monday June 10
Madison Square Garden, New York

Set: 'I Can't Explain', 'Summertime Blues', 'Young Man Blues', 'Baba O'Riley', 'Behind Blue Eyes', 'Substitute', 'I'm A Boy', 'Tattoo', 'Boris The Spider', 'Drowned', 'Bell Boy', 'Dr. Jimmy',

'Won't Get Fooled Again', 'Pinball Wizard', 'See Me, Feel Me', 'Magic Bus', 'My Generation', 'Waspman', 'Naked Eye', 'My Generation Blues', (drum solo), '5.15'.

The Who sold out all four nights in New York on the strength of a single 60-second radio spot! It was their first appearance in New York in three years and all 80,000 seats sold out in record time. Maggie Bell was the support act on the opening night, and outside the Garden one enterprising marketer was selling High Numbers T-shirts. This show featured the only known performance of Keith Moon's crazy instrumental 'Waspman', the B-side of the 'Relay' single. At one point Keith unwittingly found himself playing a drum solo which earned an ovation. Moon promptly took a mike and shouted "Drum solos are exceedingly boring!"

The crowd of 20,000 stamped and cheered for 15 minutes but the band did not return for an encore, largely because they were arguing with each other backstage about the concert's shortcomings. Unjustly, the ever loyal Bob Pridden was the focus of their anger.

Chris Charlesworth: "It turned out that much of the problem could be attributed to those fans in the front few rows who began shouting 'Jump, Pete, Jump' to Townshend, which shocked him enormously. For the first time, he said later, he felt he was parodying himself, even resembling a circus act, and he was having to force his unique stage mannerisms which were so much a part of The Who and which had previously come naturally to him. He drank like a fish during these shows, brandy straight from the bottle. In the long term, the behaviour of these fans had a profound effect on his attitude towards his work and, in fact, contributed to what shrewd observers felt was an unsatisfactory season of concerts in New York, at least by the amazing standards The Who had set themselves in the past. Most fans loved the band no matter what, of course, and their blind faith depressed Pete yet further.

"From where I was sat I couldn't see the fans up front but I could tell something wasn't right. I put it down to sound problems, as was so often the case with The Who, especially when they hadn't played for a while and were in a new place for the first time. This was the first time they'd played the Garden, which Pete hated. I thought they'd sort out the problems after the first gig but

they didn't... not really. It was only later that I realised that the real problem ran far deeper, and I suspect that the band used the sound problems as a scapegoat when they, or at least Pete, knew the problems lay deeper too. They hadn't recorded any new material since *Quadrophenia*, so the set they played was a run-through of their past, a kind of greatest hits selection. The only real surprise was that they re-introduced 'Tattoo' into the set which the fans loved but which somehow contributed to a slightly unsettling feeling of nostalgia. Pete always wanted to progress but the others were content with the way things were, and I think this was also part of the problem. It was a problem that would never go away.

"There was a terrible atmosphere backstage after the opening concert. The Who were screaming at each other behind a locked dressing room door. Kit Lambert, who wasn't often seen at Who concerts by 1974, had turned up unexpectedly, drunk as a lord and demanding to mix the on-stage PA in future, a ludicrous suggestion, and that didn't help matters at all. Bobby Pridden ran out of the dressing room shouting that he was through with The Who, and I took him aside into another room and spent ages telling him not to quit, and of course he didn't. He would never quit because he loved them so much. Poor Bob really caught it in the neck so many times. He was the real fifth member of The Who. They couldn't do without him. Eventually everyone calmed down and Pete Rudge, who was managing them in the US at the time, asked me to quietly steer Lambert away from the scene which I somehow managed to do. On our way back uptown to the Navarro I asked Kit if he could ask his limousine driver to stop so I could buy a packet of cigarettes. We stopped and Kit rushed into a liquor store and came back with two cartons for me – 20 packets!"

Unfortunately, these shows were widely reviewed across the States. A typical response was that of John Rockwell, who wrote in the *New York Times* (June 12): "On the standard of past performances, the first of the band's four New York dates at Madison Square Garden Monday night was a little disappointing. There was no new material. The ensemble wasn't as tight as it should have been. The sound system was poorly balanced and prone to feedback. And the pace and tension of the group's 100-minute set tended to wander a bit towards the end. But all of that is said in the service of reportorial objectivity. For some of us, The Who remains the best rock band in the world." Jim Melanson, in *Billboard* (June 22) was even more willing to overlook The Who's shortcomings when he described the show as "one of the finest concerts ever in the Garden."

Tuesday June 11
Madison Square Garden, New York

Set: 'I Can't Explain', 'Summertime Blues', 'Young Man Blues', 'Baba O'Riley', 'Substitute', '5.15', 'Behind Blue Eyes', 'Tattoo', 'Boris The Spider', 'Bell Boy', 'Dr. Jimmy', 'Won't Get Fooled Again', 'Pinball Wizard', 'My Generation', 'My Generation Blues', 'The Punk And The Godfather', 'Drowned'.

Golden Earring, the Dutch band newly signed to Track Records, was the opening act for the rest of the New York shows.

The towering 'The Punk And The Godfather' was reintroduced into the set at this show.

Charlesworth: "The concerts improved as the week went by but the band were never really firing on all four cylinders throughout the run. Tuesday was much better than Monday, though. I did an interview with Pete the day after this show and he seemed in a bad way, stressed out with working on the *Tommy* soundtrack, drinking too much and torn between the wishes of the fans, the band and what he wanted to do himself. Although the Who hadn't been working as a band, he'd certainly been working for the benefit of The Who, and I think he felt a great responsibility to everyone: the other three, the fans, the film producers and, of course, his family. Everybody wanted him. He needed a break from everything.

"I remember that during their stay in New York, Pete stayed at the luxurious Pierre Hotel on Fifth Avenue while the rest of the band took suites at the Navarro on Central Park South which over the years had become the band's regular New York hotel. It was the first time that the whole group hadn't stayed together in the same hotel, but Pete stayed in touch with developments at the Navarro by using a rudimentary cordless mobile phone, probably one of the earliest of its type, that had been assembled by the group's sound crew."

Thursday June 13
Madison Square Garden, New York

Set: 'I Can't Explain', 'Summertime Blues', 'Young Man Blues', 'Baba O'Riley', 'Behind Blue Eyes', 'Substitute', '5.15', 'Tattoo', 'Boris The Spider', 'Bell Boy', 'Dr. Jimmy', 'Won't Get Fooled Again', 'Pinball Wizard', 'See Me, Feel Me', 'Drowned' 'My Generation', 'Gloria', 'You Really Got Me', 'Big Boss Man', 'Punk And The Godfather'.

'My Generation' developed into a loose jam during which Pete sang a version of Them's 'Gloria'. This then moved through 'You Really Got Me', to which John added some vocals, although the band came unstuck at the upward key-change! These performances were both unique to the mature Who set. The medley was finished with 'Big Boss Man', a more familiar Who staple.

During the stay in New York, Pete was interviewed by John Rockwell of the *New York Times* (June 13), to whom he made the amusing comment: "The Who is a bloody wild animal, and it has to be fed chunks of raw meat and Southern Comfort. It can't feed on anything less."

Friday June 14
Madison Square Garden, New York

Set: 'I Can't Explain', 'Summertime Blues', 'Young Man Blues', 'Baba O'Riley', 'Behind Blue Eyes', 'My Wife', 'Magic Bus', 'Tattoo', 'Bell Boy', 'Dr. Jimmy', 'Won't Get Fooled Again', 'Pinball Wizard', 'See Me, Feel Me', 'My Generation', 'Drowned', 'Boris The Spider', 'Substitute', 'Punk And The Godfather', 'I'm One', 'Naked Eye'.

'I'm One' was played towards the end of this

engineer, was operating the board. Chris Charlesworth: "I was covering this tour for *MM* and met up with Bobby in Pittsburgh. He told me that doing the sound for Clapton was like a holiday compared with working for The Who!"

On August 1 at Atlanta's Omni, Pete and Keith sat in on 'Layla', 'Baby Don't You Do It' and 'Little Queenie'; the next night in the Greensboro Coliseum, Pete played on 'Willie And The Hand Jive' and 'Get Ready', and was joined by Keith for 'Layla' and 'Badge'. The third and final guest appearance was at Palm Beach International Raceway on August 4 with Pete and Keith sitting in at various points in the show.

set, but was then unheard in The Who's live act until 1982. Pete smashed three of his Gibson Les Paul Deluxes on the final night. Keith joined in and smashed the fourth and only remaining instrument!

After this final New York concert most of the band attended a party at a roller skating rink thrown by MCA Records. Four nights at the Garden grossed $530,000, the second-best gross of the year at the venue for promoter Ron Delsener.

Guitars smashed: Les Paul Deluxe x 4!

late-July

Pete and Keith flew to America to appear as guests at three gigs on Eric Clapton's 'comeback' tour for which Bob Pridden, The Who's sound

Sunday December 8
City Hall, Newcastle upon Tyne

While The Who were on sabbatical John took his band Ox on a British tour in December 1974 and January 1975. It was the one and only time during the career of the original group that any member undertook a full tour away from The Who. Unfortunately, John's début show with Ox was attended by a sparse crowd of only 300 fans in a hall that held 2,168 people. Other UK dates were at the Odeon Theatre, Southport (December 13) and City Hall, Sheffield (December 17).

Chris Charlesworth: "I went to the show in Newcastle and John's bass actually made his band sound a lot like The Who. It brought it home to me, and probably other Who fans who were there, how much John actually contributed to the noise The Who made."

After two years of relative inactivity by The Who's normal standards, the group bounced back in the second half of 1975, firing on all cylinders. Individual pursuits in 1974 had led some to believe The Who were finished, and there was plenty of evidence to support this assumption. John had begun touring with his own band Ox in December 1974, and he took the group to America in early 1975 with the release of his *Mad Dog* album. Roger was busy taking on the lead role in Ken Russell's *Lisztomania* and recording his second solo album, *Ride A Rock Horse*. Even Keith, now roaming Los Angeles like a loose cannon, released his own album *Two Sides Of The Moon* in the spring of 1975.

By the summer Pete was lamenting in the music press the disintegration of the band's ties to managers Kit Lambert and Chris Stamp, as well as voicing his personal doubts about being able to carry on with the group past the age of 30. Around the same time the UK music press also carried interviews with both Pete and Roger in which they openly sniped at one another. No wonder some thought The Who's days were numbered.

All this was forgotten when the group reconvened in the autumn to begin the year-long *Who By Numbers* tour. Opening with 11 dates in Britain, they played with renewed energy, easily reclaiming their crown as the world's greatest live rock'n'roll band. Pete rediscovered his mastery of the electric guitar, playing searing solos and slashing rhythm, jumping and windmilling in his inimitable style, all with new-found vigour. Overjoyed at his enthusiasm, Roger, John and Keith performed as if their lives depended on it. Many fans still consider that The Who's rebirth in 1975/76 represented some of their finest moments.

The tour moved on to Europe for eight concerts before setting off to America for a month's work, starting on November 20 in Houston, Texas. The Who were the first group to play at the gigantic Silverdome in Pontiac, Michigan, performing for more than 75,000 fans. The tour wound up in Philadelphia on December 15 before they headed home to play three concerts at the Hammersmith Odeon just before Christmas. In a year of superstar tours, The Who had outshone them all for power and energy without the need for special effects and props. As always, the band itself was the show.

The consistent high level of performances throughout this era of Who live history is partly due to the fact that the band more or less played the same set each night. Unlike many acts, who by the end of a particular tour sounded bored with over-familiar material, The Who suffered no such ennui. Whenever they launched into 'Substitute', 'I Can't Explain' or 'My Generation' they sounded as if they meant it – as sharp and relevant as ever. They had an enthusiasm and freshness that few other acts could muster after playing a song maybe 300 times over a ten-year period. However, it always infuriated Pete that the band ended up relying upon established classics, although this feeling never blighted his inspiration or musical commitment (at least not yet – by the Eighties, Townshend did fall foul of his doubts). In the face of so many superb concerts it is difficult to proffer criticism, but one fact cannot be overlooked: *Quadrophenia* and *The Who By Numbers* contained 27 tracks between them – the total output of all The Who's creative work since 1972. During these concerts, no more than four songs from both albums were ever played at any one show. More often than not *Quadrophenia* was completely neglected, and *The Who By Numbers* represented only with 'However Much I Booze', 'Dreaming From The Waist' and the unWho-like 'Squeeze Box'.

The reintroduction of a *Tommy* medley might well have been considered a retrograde step, but it was prompted by the success of the feature film, which was on general release throughout this period. Real Who fans, however, might well have appreciated more material from *By Numbers* or something unexpected, such as a reworking of 'Heatwave' or 'Leaving Here' in the manner of 'Baby Don't You Do It' or 'Young Man Blues'. Also lamentable was the absence of any new material being introduced through 1976 (apart from a brief taster of 'Who Are You'). The act included a few standard features through 1975 and 1976: Keith Moon's comic introductions to 'Behind Blue Eyes' and the *Tommy* segment (as witty and unpredictable as ever); John Entwistle's two drinking bottles affixed to his mike stand (brandy and white wine!); laser beam effects during 'Sparks' and at the end of 'Won't Get Fooled Again'; Pete Townshend's Les Paul guitars adorned with large white Letraset numbers.

The European dates initially took a few more chances with the material, and these set lists have been given in full. However, early in the American tour, The Who established a successful formula and barely deviated from it. From the beginning of the US tour on November 20, through to the Toronto date of October 21 of the following year, the band essentially played exactly the same set, drawing from the following songs: 'I Can't Explain', 'Substitute', 'My Wife', 'Baba O'Riley', 'Squeeze Box', 'Behind Blue Eyes', 'Dreaming From The Waist', 'Boris The Spider', 'Magic Bus', *Tommy* medley ('Amazing Journey', 'Sparks', 'Acid Queen', 'Fiddle About', 'Pinball Wizard', 'I'm Free', 'Tommy's Holiday Camp', 'We're Not Gonna Take It', 'See Me, Feel Me'), 'Summertime Blues', 'My Generation' medley ('My Generation', 'Join Together', 'My Generation Blues', 'Road Runner'), 'Won't Get Fooled Again'. The Who's equipment for the 1975-76 era was as follows:

Keith Moon: 2 Premier 22" bass drums, 3 Premier 14"x10" tom toms, 2 Premier 16"x18" floor toms, 1 Premier 10" tom tom, 1 Premier 12" tom tom, 1 Premier 13" tom tom, 1 Premier 14" tom tom, 1 Premier 15" tom tom, 1 Premier 16" tom tom, 2 Premier Timbales, 2 Premier 22 1/2" timpani, 1 Premier 14" snare drum, 2 Paiste gongs (1x30" & 1x36"), various Paiste cymbals, Premier C drum sticks;

Roger Daltrey: Shure microphones, Premier tambourines, Hohner harmonicas;

Pete Townshend: 4 or 6 Hi-watt 4x12" speaker cabinets, 3 Hi-watt 100 watt amplifiers, 1 Superfuzz fuzz box, Gibson Les Paul guitars, Gibson guitar strings, Mannys guitar picks;

John Entwistle: 2 Sunn 1x18" bass speakers, 2 Sunn 4x12" bass speakers, 2 Sunn 3x12" bass speakers, 2 Crown DC 300 power amplifiers, 2 Alembic pre-amplifiers, custom built Alembic bass guitars, Rotosound guitar strings, Herco guitar picks;

PA System: JBL bass, mid-range & high-range speaker & horn units, Crown power amplifiers, 3 Mavis mixing desks, 1 Alice mixing desk, 1 Scully 4-track tape machine, 2 Verispeed Revox tape machines, 2 WEM copycat echo units, 1 Digital Delay unit, 1 Phasing unit, Shure and Neauman microphones.

The size of the PA, designed by Showco, was varied to suit the venue, and the average arena-sized hall would use a system giving an output of 56,000 watts. For the large outdoor shows at Charlton, Glasgow, Swansea and Oakland in 1976, The Who used a Showco/Tasco 76,000 watt PA system driven by 80 x 800-watt Crown DL300 amplifiers and 20 x 600-watt Phase Linear 200s. Lighting System: 30 x Par 64 1000 watt lamps, 32 x Leko 1000 watt lamps, Hydraulic "Genie" towers, Electrosonic control desks, Electrosonic Dimmer packs, Strand Patt 765 follow spots, 38 "00" three section Truss, Vermet towers, Ramport Lasers.

The Who's permanent road crew at this time were: Bob Pridden (Sound Engineer), John 'Wiggy' Wolff (Lasers/Production Manager), Tony Haslam (Lights Tech), Jim Hubbard (Lights Tech), Roger Searle (Lights Tech), Mick Double (Drum Tech), Alan Smith (Sound Engineer/Guitar Tech), Alan Rogan (Guitar Tech), Bill Harrison (Bass Tech), and Dick Hayes (Sound Tech). Although the crew were often on the receiving end of the band's bad tempers when something went wrong, the members of The Who – with ample justification – considered their road crew to be the best in the business, and Pete Townshend even went as far as calling Bob Pridden "untouchable" on UK television.

Friday January 10
Edinburgh University, Scotland

John's band Ox continued their UK tour through January, appearing at Leeds University (11), Plymouth Guildhall (14), Exeter University (15), Brunel University Students Union, Uxbridge

(17), Liverpool University (22), University of East Anglia, Norwich (24) and Leicester University (25).

Friday February 21
Civic Auditorium, Sacramento, California

John's début US Ox concert had them slated as the opening act for the J. Geils Band, attracting 3,980 people. Other Ox dates in the US included Winterland Auditorium, San Francisco, California (22 and 23), Long Beach Arena, California (26), Massey Hall, Toronto, Ontario, Canada (March 1), Masonic Auditorium, Detroit, Michigan (2), Orpheum Theatre, Boston, Massachusetts (7), Academy of Music, New York (8), Buffalo, New York (9), Constitution Hall, Washington, DC, (10), The Spectrum, Philadelphia, Pennsylvania (15), Calderone Concert Hall, Hempstead, New York (16), Aire Crown Theatre, Chicago, Illinois (20), Indiana Fairgrounds Coliseum, Indianapolis, Indiana (21), Eastern Illinois University, Charleston, Illinois (22), St. Louis, Missouri (23).

Ox's set generally consisted of 'Heaven and Hell', 'Whiskey Man', 'My Size', 'Boris The Spider', 'Do The Dangle', 'Cell Number 7', 'Not

Fade Away', 'Who Cares', 'Gimme That Rock'n'Roll', 'My Wife' and 'Somethin' Else'.

Friday October 3
New Bingley Hall, County Showground, Stafford

Set: 'Substitute', 'I Can't Explain', 'Squeeze Box', 'Heaven And Hell', 'Tattoo', 'Baba O'Riley', 'Behind Blue Eyes', *Tommy* medley ('Amazing Journey', 'Sparks', 'Eyesight To The Blind', 'Fiddle About', 'Acid Queen', 'Pinball Wizard', 'I'm Free', 'Tommy's Holiday Camp', 'We're Not Gonna Take It', 'See Me, Feel Me'), 'Drowned', 'Bell Boy', 'Punk And The Godfather', 'My Generation', 'Join Together', 'Won't Get Fooled Again', '5.15'.

Although far better than the shows at Madison Square Garden 16 months earlier, this concert in a new 8,000–seater venue showed all the signs of a band sounding rusty and stiff after a long lay-off. It had enough redeeming qualities, however, to provide help all round. The worst problem occurred when 'The Punk And The Godfather' fell apart during Pete's solo verse. Pete stopped singing, shouted at Moon and then angrily carried on. Apparently, Keith Moon couldn't hear his monitors properly due to his drum kit being placed on a riser for the first time, and he had drummed out of place. By the next concert, both the riser and 'The Punk And The Godfather' had been ditched. Unfortunately – much to Moon's chagrin – so had 'Bell Boy'. Daltrey also managed to forget the second verse of 'Won't Get Fooled Again'.

On the plus side, 'Squeeze Box' and 'Join Together' were played live for the first time, and 'Heaven And Hell' was John Entwistle's vocal showcase after a five year lay-off. 'Eyesight To The Blind' featured a new arrangement based upon the version recorded for the *Tommy* film soundtrack, and was notable for a funkier bassline than the earlier version. Also influenced by the soundtrack re-recording was 'I'm Free', which now had a slightly re-arranged harder riff. A highlight of all these shows was Keith Moon's vocal duties as Uncle Ernie on 'Fiddle About' and 'Tommy's Holiday Camp' (again reflecting the film version). Finally, another change for *Tommy* was that Roger rather than Pete now sang 'Acid Queen'.

Chris Charlesworth noted in *Melody Maker* (October 11) that "The band made a few mistakes but laughed them off with uncanny good humour. Few other bands could stop a number halfway through, have a hurried exchange of comments, and begin the tune again without arousing discord in the audience."

The Steve Gibbons Band played support on all the UK dates. *The Who By Numbers*, released on this day, contained much lighter material than usual. Its songs reflected the difficulties that Pete Townshend and The Who were experiencing as they grew older. The mood was darker and The Who's main writer incorporated his fears and personal doubts into an album that, despite its laboured depth, still managed to gain a creditable number 7 in the UK album charts and number 8 in the US.

Saturday October 4
New Bingley Hall, County Showground, Stafford

Set: 'Substitute', 'I Can't Explain', 'Squeeze Box', 'Heaven And Hell', 'Tattoo', 'Baba O'Riley', 'Behind Blue Eyes', Tommy medley (Ten songs, as October 3), 'Summertime Blues', 'Drowned', '5.15', 'My Generation', 'Join Together', 'Magic Bus', 'Naked Eye', 'Won't Get Fooled Again'.

A rearranged set provided a far better performance and The Who really regained their old form at this show. Chris Charlesworth said (*Melody Maker*, October 11): "From the opening notes of the first song... it was apparent that the band were on better form." However, it was perhaps sad that songs such as 'The Punk And The Godfather' and 'Bell Boy' had been replaced by the safer, less-demanding 'Summertime Blues' and 'Magic Bus' – a fact that hadn't escaped Pete's notice.

Monday October 6
Belle Vue, Manchester

Set: 'Substitute', 'I Can't Explain', 'Squeeze Box', 'Heaven And Hell', 'Tattoo', 'Baba O'Riley', 'Behind Blue Eyes', *Tommy* medley: (ten songs, as October 3), 'Summertime Blues', 'Drowned', '5.15', 'My Generation', (drum solo), 'Naked Eye', 'Won't Get Fooled Again'.

An unusual contribution from Keith in the form of an impromptu drum solo after 'My Generation'. This seems to be only the second occasion when Keith played a drum solo at a Who concert (see earlier entry for Madison Square Garden, New York, June 10 1974).

Tuesday October 7
Belle Vue, Manchester

Set: 'Substitute', 'I Can't Explain', 'Squeeze Box', 'Heaven And Hell', 'Tattoo', 'Baba O'Riley', 'Behind Blue Eyes', *Tommy* medley: (10 songs, as October 3), 'Summertime Blues', 'Drowned', '5.15', 'My Generation', 'Join Together', 'Let's See Action', 'Magic Bus', 'Won't Get Fooled Again'.

Calls from the audience for 'Bell Boy' angered Pete: "I'm sick of all this shit about 'Bell Boy'," he snapped.

Wednesday October 15
Apollo Centre, Glasgow, Scotland

Set: 'Substitute', 'I Can't Explain', 'Squeeze Box', 'Heaven And Hell', 'Tattoo', 'Baba O'Riley', 'Behind Blue Eyes', 'However Much I Booze', *Tommy* medley: (ten songs, as October 3), 'Summertime Blues', 'Bargain', '5.15', 'My Generation', 'Join Together', 'Naked Eye', 'Magic Bus', 'Won't Get Fooled Again'.

The first of two sell-out shows of 3,300 fans witnessed the first ever stage performance of 'However Much I Booze' and the revival of 'Bargain' for the first time since 1972.

Thursday October 16
Apollo Centre, Glasgow, Scotland

The following day, Keith got into a fracas at Prestwick Airport, outside Ayr, where the Who's London-bound plane was diverted from Glasgow because of fog. Keith was held overnight on charges of breach of the peace and maliciously damaging a British Airways computer. A special plane was chartered to fly him to Leicester.

SECTION

A P 1

KING'S HALL, BELLE VUE

HARVEY GOLDSMITH for John Smith Entertainments
by arrangement with TRINIFOLD LTD. presents

THE WHO

plus Guest STEVE GIBBONS BAND

MONDAY
OCTOBER **6**

at 7-30 p.m.

STALLS
£2·50
incl. VAT
NO TICKET EXCHANGED NOR MONEY REFUNDED
THIS PORTION TO BE RETAINED

Saturday October 18
Granby Halls, Leicester

Set: 'I Can't Explain', 'Substitute', 'Squeeze Box', 'Baba O'Riley', 'Behind Blue Eyes', 'However Much I Booze', 'Dreaming From The Waist', *Tommy* medley ('Amazing Journey', 'Sparks', 'Fiddle About', 'Acid Queen', 'Pinball Wizard', 'I'm Free', 'Tommy's Holiday Camp', 'We're Not Gonna Take It', 'See Me, Feel Me'), 'Summertime Blues', 'Bargain', 'My Generation', 'Join Together', 'Won't Get Fooled Again'.

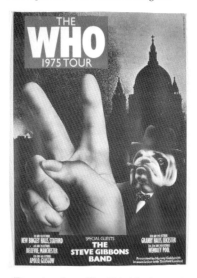

'Dreaming From The Waist' had now been added to the set and was to become the most enduring song in the live act from *The Who By Numbers* album. Besides being a fine song in itself, it provided a superb opportunity for John Entwistle to display his awesome skills on a bass solo. 'Eyesight To The Blind' was permanently dropped from the *Tommy* section.

Sunday October 19
Granby Halls, Leicester

Tuesday October 21
Wembley Empire Pool, London

Set: 'I Can't Explain', 'Substitute', 'Squeeze Box', 'Boris The Spider', 'Baba O'Riley', 'Behind Blue Eyes', 'However Much I Booze', 'Dreaming From The Waist', *Tommy* medley (nine songs, as October 19), 'Summertime Blues', 'Bargain', 'My Generation', 'Join Together', 'My Generation Blues', 'Maybelline', 'Won't Get Fooled Again'.

Each show attracted a sell-out audience of 7,000. This concert featured the Who's only known performance of Chuck Berry's 'Maybelline', although this was worked into the medley and was best described as a loose interpretation.

Thursday October 23
Wembley Empire Pool, London

Set: 'I Can't Explain', 'Substitute', 'Squeeze Box', 'Boris The Spider', 'Baba O'Riley', 'Behind Blue Eyes', 'However Much I Booze', 'Dreaming From The Waist', *Tommy* medley (nine songs, as October 19), 'Summertime Blues', 'Bargain', 'My Generation', 'Johnny B. Goode', 'Join Together', 'Won't Get Fooled Again'.

Chuck Berry's 'Johnny B. Goode' here replaced 'Maybelline', and featured an enthusiastic but somewhat imprecise lead vocal from Keith Moon! In his review of this show in *New Musical Express* (November 1), Charles Shaar Murray contributed perhaps the most ecstatically over-the-top review The Who ever received: "The most powerful and majestic heavy-metal roar available... The Who make you take pride in them, yourself and rock-'n'roll. They just fill you up with it until you're lighter than air and you can walk down the street standing straight and moving fast. They're the greatest band that rock'n'roll has ever spawned, and there ain't another band living can make me feel as good."

Friday October 24
Wembley Empire Pool, London
   John Woffinden wrote in *Generations* No 6 (September 1991): "The last night of the '75 UK tour was at Wembley and I think that this has to be my favourite Who show. They were faultless and without parallel. 'Won't Get Fooled Again' never sounded better. At the end of the night the man in front of me fell to his knees in prayer. It was that sort of night..."

Monday October 27
Sportpalais Ahoy Halle, Rotterdam, the Netherlands
   Set: 'Substitute', 'I Can't Explain', 'Squeeze Box', 'Baba O'Riley', 'Behind Blue Eyes', 'However Much I Booze', 'Dreaming From The Waist', *Tommy* medley (nine songs, as October 19), 'Summertime Blues', 'Bargain', 'My Generation', 'Join Together', 'Won't Get Fooled Again'.
   The group travelled to the Netherlands to open the European leg of the tour with The Steve Gibbons Band as support act.

MAANDAGAVOND 27 OKTOBER 8 UUR IN SPORTPALEIS AHOY' - ROTTERDAM

THE WHO

Supporting Act: **STEVE GIBBON'S BAND**
Prijzen: f 10,— f 15,—, f 20,—, f 25,—. Kaartverkoop vanaf zaterdag 4 oktober bij de voor-verkoopadressen en aan de zaal. Per brief of giro te bestellen: rangen f 20,— en f 25,—.

Tuesday October 28
Stadthalle, Vienna, Austria

Wednesday October 29
Stadthalle, Bremen, Germany
   The Who were seen by 6,000 fans.

Thursday October 30
Phillipshalle, Düsseldorf, Germany
   Set: 'Substitute', 'I Can't Explain', 'Squeeze Box', 'Baba O'Riley', 'Behind Blue Eyes', 'However Much I Booze', 'Dreaming From The Waist', 'Boris The Spider', *Tommy* medley (nine songs, as October 19), 'Summertime Blues', 'My Generation', 'Join Together', 'Won't Get Fooled Again'.

Friday October 31
Phillipshalle, Düsseldorf, Germany
   Set: 'Substitute', 'I Can't Explain', 'Squeeze Box', 'Boris The Spider', 'Baba O'Riley', 'Behind Blue Eyes', 'Dreaming From The Waist', *Tommy* medley (nine songs, as October 19), 'Summertime Blues', 'Bargain', 'My Generation', 'Join Together', 'Won't Get Fooled Again'.

WHO STIJGT OP!

Sunday November 2
Messehalle, Sindelfingen, Germany
   Set: 'Substitute', 'I Can't Explain', 'Squeeze Box', 'Baba O'Riley', 'Dreaming From The Waist', 'Boris The Spider', 'Behind Blue Eyes', *Tommy* medley (nine songs, as October 19), 'Summertime Blues', 'Bargain', 'My Generation', 'Join Together', 'Won't Get Fooled Again'.

Monday November 3
Messehalle, Sindelfingen, Germany
   Set: 'Substitute', 'I Can't Explain', 'Squeeze Box', 'Baba O'Riley', 'Behind Blue Eyes', 'Dreaming From The Waist', 'Boris The Spider', Tommy medley (nine songs, as October 19), 'Summertime Blues', 'Bargain', 'My Generation', 'Naked Eye', 'Join Together', 'Won't Get Fooled Again', '5.15'.
   A rare encore was played in the shape of '5.15'.

Thursday November 6
Friedrich Ebert Halle, Ludwigshafen, Germany

Friday November 7
Friedrich Ebert Halle, Ludwigshafen, Germany
   The European tour concluded here and the group had a two–week break before flying to America for the opening gig in Houston.

Thursday November 20
The Summit, Houston, Texas

The first band to play in this new basketball arena, The Who gave it a high–decibel benediction on the opening date of the American tour. The show grossed $134,676 from 18,000 fans.

Gerry Wood wrote in *Billboard* (December 6): "Just about the best showman band in rock history... the Gibraltar of the rock groups has done it again." The Performance was relayed onto a back projection screen by a closed-circuit video system. The opening act on all dates was Toots & The Maytals, a noted reggae band from Kingston, Jamaica.

After the Houston gig John Entwistle and John 'Wiggy' Wolff managed to get themselves arrested by the local police when the after-show party got out of hand.

Friday November 21
Louisiana State University Assembly Center, Baton Rouge, Louisiana

'Drowned' and 'However Much I Booze' were played at this show. Reviewer Chuck Swanson, writing in *Vieux Carre Courier*, claimed that they played 'Imagine A Man' at this concert but this may be a mistake, as the band didn't play it live at any other show. "From the opening crash of 'I Can't Explain'," wrote Swanson, "it was apparent that The Who had lost little of their earlier exhilaration while acquiring a more acute sense of timing than ever before."

The group earned $112,630 from a near sell-out crowd.

Sunday November 23
Mid-South Coliseum, Memphis, Tennessee

Walter Dawson in *Commercial Appeal* (November 24): "The only bad part of the show was the volume. It was extremely loud as is fitting for The Who's intensity, but at times, as when Townshend took a guitar solo, it was bearable only to those whose eardrums have been bored out by many rock shows." This concert featured the final performance of 'However Much I Booze'.

Attendance was 10,882 for a $90,355 gross.

Monday November 24
The Omni, Atlanta, Georgia

In the *Atlanta Journal* (November 25), Scott Cain wrote: "For intensity, the concert would be difficult to duplicate. The Who didn't let up for a minute, leaping from one powerful arrangement to another..."

Gross was $129,297 from 18,376 people.

Tuesday November 25
M.T.S.U. Murphy Center, Murfreesboro, Tennessee

Eve Zibart, *Tennessean Living* (November 27): "The Who in concert radiate a terrifying energy... The very forcefulness of their music is nearly blinding... The Who played without respite for nearly two hours... The volume was deafening..."

The attendance was 11, 000, the takings $92,000.

Thursday November 27
Hampton Coliseum, Hampton Roads, Virginia

A rare US reading of 'Tattoo' was played here, followed by 'Drowned'. Sean Brickell reviewed the show for the *Virginian Pilot* (November 29): "Townshend is among the best guitarists in the business, and his awesome playing and attack, musically, was the best of the 20-song show. His playing guided the rest of the band in tempo..."

Gate receipts were $106,855 from 11,906 fans.

Friday November 28
Memorial Coliseum, Greensboro, North Carolina

Mack Hofmann in the *Winston-Salem Journal* (November 30): "Never in the performance did the band falter... If their Greensboro concert was a typical performance, it would seem that they, rather than the Rolling Stones, are now the world's greatest rock group."

Attendance was 17, 437, and receipts totalled $127, 241.

Sunday November 30
Indiana University Assembly Hall, Bloomington, Indiana

The band grossed $108,357 from 14,841 fans.

Monday December 1
Kemper Arena, Kansas City, Missouri

Marshall Fine (*Kansas Journal-World*, December 2): "If this was the last time The Who will play together, the group left its followers with the memory of a truly superior performance."

The band's first Kansas City gig in more than

five years was seen by 13,414 people. Gross was $96,284.

Tuesday December 2
Veterans Memorial Auditorium, Des Moines, Iowa

An equipment failure occurred early in the show, blowing out John Entwistle's amps and the band retreated to the dressing room for twenty minutes while repairs were undertaken. "The granddaddy of full-bore, wild rhino, thunder rock bands left a full house stunned..." wrote Jim Healey in *Des Moines Register* (December 3). "It will be recalled, no doubt, as THE rock event for some time to come."

For the rare appearance in Des Moines 13,534 fans paid $97,747.

Thursday December 4
Chicago Stadium, Chicago, Illinois

The set: ' I Can't Explain', 'Substitute', 'Squeeze Box', 'Baba O'Riley', 'My Wife', 'Behind Blue Eyes', 'Dreaming From The Waist', 'Magic Bus', 'Amazing Journey', 'The Acid Queen', 'Fiddle About', 'Pinball Wizard', 'I'm Free', 'We're Not Gonna Take It', 'Summertime Blues', 'My Generation' (with segues into 'Join Together', 'My Generation Blues', and 'Roadrunner'), 'Won't Get Fooled Again', 'Drowned'.

The Who gave a magnificent performance on the opening night of two dates in Chicago. They answered the crowd's ten–minute standing ovation with a rare encore, a blistering version of 'Drowned'.

"That wonderful energy, so real you could almost reach out and touch it, transcended everything... the spirit of rock and roll at its finest..." commented Lynn Van Matre in the *Chicago Tribune* (December 5).

Friday December 5
Chicago Stadium, Chicago, Illinois

Two sell-outs here tallied $330,739 from 37,479 fans.

While in Chicago, Keith bought a policeman's uniform for 300 dollars from an officer who'd been detailed to protect the band, leaving the cop standing outside the Who's dressing room clad only in underpants, socks and gun-belt! Keith delighted in patrolling the queues outside venues where the group were appearing, confiscating contraband alcohol and certain substances from likely looking suspects!

Saturday December 6
Metropolitan Stadium (The Silver Dome), Pontiac, Michigan

Bill Gray, writing for *Detroit News* (December 8), said: "There was none of the phoney we-are-all-one feeling coming from the stage. Gone are the days when The Who and their counterparts hide their irritation with overzealous fans. When the crowd pushed too close for Townshend's comfort he didn't rely on a manager or promoter to tell the crowd to refrain and back away. Townshend himself openly scolded the crowd's yearning to get a little closer. He sternly put it this way: 'Everybody's got to take a step backwards. There's too much blood and guts going on up here. Do something the fuck about it!'"

Recorded on videotape from the closed-circuit back-projection with stereo sound, concert footage of the 'Road Runner' jam at the end of 'My Generation' from this show was used by Jeff Stein for *The Kids Are Alright* but the concert now appears to be missing from The Who's archives. A terrific performance by The Who, but the colossal size of the venue dissipated all the atmosphere. The band swore never to play here again, but they returned in 1979, 1982 and 1989!

Union Board Concerts Presents'
THE WHO
IN CONCERT

SUNDAY NOV. 30 8 PM IU ASSEMBLY HALL TICKETS $8, $7, $6.

ON SALE: KARMA RECORDS IN INDIANAPOLIS and ASSEMBLY HALL TICKET OFFICE INDIANA UNIV.

PRODUCED BY SUNSHINE PROMOTIONS

BAMBOO PRODUCTIONS & BELKIN PRODUCTIONS

Presents THE WHO & TOOTS & THE MAYTALS

SATURDAY DECEMBER 6-8 P.M. PONTIAC STADIUM

ALL SEATS $8.50 ADVANCE
Tickets Available At
All J. L. Hudson's in Mich.

The concert grossed $614,992 from a sell-out crowd of more than 75,000 fans.

Monday December 8
Riverfront Coliseum, Cincinnati, Ohio

"The quartet totally mesmerized the audience..." wrote Cliff Radel in the Enquirer (December 10).

Gate receipts were $138,500 from 18,000 fans.

Wednesday December 10
Memorial Auditorium, Buffalo, New York

Total attendance was 11,700 with a take of $140,000.

Thursday December 11
Maple Leaf Gardens, Toronto, Ontario, Canada

This was a stunning show on every level and one of the peaks of a generally excellent tour. The Who grossed $157,879 from 17,600 fans during an hour and forty minute set.

Saturday December 13
Civic Center, Providence, Rhode Island

The *Providence Sunday Journal* (December 14) had a review by Tony Lioce: "The phenomenal Who... all but blowing the roof off the joint with the sheer pure power of rock'n'roll music at its very, very finest. Yeah, it was that good. It was glorious, in fact."

The group's first Providence gig in seven years attracted 14,000 people and grossed $112,324 to see.

Sunday December 14
Civic Center, Springfield, Massachusetts

The *Greenfield Recorder* (December 16) had a review by Dave Kowal: "They're explosive, they're energetic, they're talented, they're creative, they're dynamic, they're the best rock band in the world – they're The Who... The audience left the Civic Center stunned, euphoric and

The Who is the world's finest rock 'n' roll band

Tuesday December 9
Richfield Coliseum, Cleveland, Ohio

A compelling performance which was filmed on a semi-professional two-camera video system. 'Dreaming From The Waist' was included on the *Thirty Years Of Maximum R&B Live* video. 'Spoonful' was worked into the 'My Generation' medley. "The Who is the finest rock 'n' roll band in the world," wrote Bruno Bornino in the *Cleveland Press* (December 19) "... one of the greatest – if not the greatest – rock concert ever performed in Cleveland... the most exciting and moving rock presentation I've ever witnessed."

Gross was $160,148 from a sell-out crowd of 19,000.

impressed with a musical act which has been imitated by many, equalled by few."

The attendance was 10,000, the takings $84,000.

Monday December 15
The Spectrum, Philadelphia, Pennsylvania

The band ended the 1975 tour with a devastating display in the Spectrum, cited as the best concert in Philadelphia all year. The gig grossed $146,000 from a sell-out house of 19,000 people.

John David Kalodner wrote in the *Philadelphia Inquirer* (December 16): "With awesome power and vitality, British superstar rockers The Who pounded the Spectrum... their show was a spectacle on the grandest scale, showing rock'n'roll to

"The Who's live performances have become almost like a ritual. You don't watch their show, you experience it."

be an art form on the highest level of contemporary culture. Let it be said that The Who gave Philadelphia its best pop concert of the year."

Chris Charlesworth: "I remember they played an outstanding version of 'Sparks' from *Tommy* and when it finished I and everyone around me just rose from our seats to applaud. At that moment I caught the eye of John Rockwell, the *New York Times* rock critic who was sitting nearby, and we shook our heads together in shared appreciation of what we'd just heard. It was just phenomenal."

Guitar destroyed: Gibson Les Paul Deluxe gold top

Sunday December 21
Hammersmith Odeon, Hammersmith, West London

The Who agreed to play three London concerts just before Christmas due to the overwhelming ticket demand during the UK tour in the autumn.

Monday December 22
Hammersmith Odeon, Hammersmith, West London

Tuesday December 23
Hammersmith Odeon, Hammersmith, West London

The Who finished the last of the three shows at the Odeon, closing a phenomenal year which proved they were still the best rock'n'roll band in the world.

Steve Clark wrote in *Melody Maker* (January 3, 1976): "If you thought rock was dead at that moment in time, you must have been born in the wrong age. Easily the year's best display of rock-'n'roll."

During this season of shows, Keith had arranged to be hoisted aloft on a cable, and Roger wore a 'George Davis Is Innocent' T-shirt in support of a campaign to free a taxi driver supposedly wrongly-convicted of murder.

This was the last year of The Who's reign as the best live rock act in the world. It was the last year in which the original group – Townshend, Daltrey, Moon and Entwistle – worked together as a regular live band, the last time audiences could see and hear for themselves the curious chemistry that kept those disparate tangents together, the last time The Who roared like no band before or since. Most of the time they were on top form, too, although there were occasions when Moon seemed past his best, the result of his alcohol and substance abuse. Pete's motivation might have been compromised by the lack of new material and need to keep creating, but he never allowed this to affect his attitude on stage. The fraternity seemed strong: most shows ended with the band stepping to the front, bowing low together and hugging each other, their union apparently as solid as ever.

Most of the year was spent touring the same countries as the previous autumn but playing different cities on each leg. A short jaunt through Switzerland, Germany and France began in late February in preparation for their US trip, due to kick off in Boston on March 9. Keith was said to have had a severe case of the flu as the band arrived in the States but his condition was probably due to his lifestyle. Whatever the reason, he passed out at the opening gig in Boston Garden in front of 13,000 fans. Efforts to revive him were unsuccessful and the group had to abandon the concert. A show was added on at the end of the tour to make up for the cancellation. It was the second time in a little over two years that Keith had been unable to perform. It was the beginning of the end for the greatest rock drummer of them all.

Two shows in France preceded three huge stadium gigs in the UK in the early summer. Billed as The Who Put The Boot In tour, the band were at their zenith in Britain. Strong support bills were set, but once again the band was out to show everyone how it should be done. Unfortunately, apart from two hastily arranged concerts for filming purposes, they would not play Britain again for almost three years.

They returned to America in August for a mini-tour of four concerts, two shows in Largo, Maryland and stadium dates in Jacksonville and

Miami, Florida. *The Who By Numbers* tour wrapped up a year after it had begun with a three–week junket through the west coast of the US and Canada in October 1976.

This last segment found the band in fine form, devastating audiences with the trademark energy that defined The Who. Pete destroyed a Gibson Les Paul Deluxe at the last show in Toronto where, on October 21, Keith took his final bow before a paying audience.

Friday February 27
Hallenstadion, Zürich, Switzerland

The Who began their 1976 campaign with a four–date tour of Europe. The show started at 7:30 pm.

At this concert, The Who played 'Slip Kid' for

the first time, with the piano and percussion on backing tape. This made the arrangement more complicated than it need have been and the band never really did the song justice in this form. Eight shows later 'Slip Kid' had been permanently dropped.

Good News present exclusively IN CONCERT:

THE WHO

A SUPPORTING ACT

Freitag, 27. Febr. 76, 19.30 h
Kasse und Türöffnung: 18.30 h

Hallenstadion Zürich

Vorverkauf:
Zürich: Hallenstadion, Tel. 01 463030,
Jelmoli-City, Jecklin Pfauen,
Grammo- Studio Shop-Ville / Aarau:
Coop City / Luzern: Grammo-
Studio / Winterthur
Pick-Up

Die neusten LP's der WHO
TOMMY (Film Soundtrack)
Best. LP 2625 026
Best. Nr. MC 3502 102
The Who By Numbers
Best. LP 2480 309
Best. MC 3194 283

...natürlich von Polydor
erhältlich in Ihrem Fachgeschäft

Saturday February 28
Olympiahalle, Munich, West Germany; 8 pm

With the Steve Gibbons Band as opening act.

Monday March 1
Pavilion de Paris, Paris, France

The Who played two nights in this converted slaughterhouse with the Steve Gibbons Band as special guests on both nights. It was also Roger's 32nd birthday.

Writing in *Sounds* (March 20), Barbara Charone was mightily impressed: "The Who... rolled through ninety minutes of gut wrenching rock that made 12,000 euphoric Parisian kids forget they were cramped into what one astute observer described as a cross between Victoria Station and the Roundhouse... Although the venue was ice cold, the band erupted like a ravaging volcano spewing forth electric heat. It felt great... Loudspeaker cabinet MB22 shook with an extended version of 'My Wife' that allowed Pete Townshend and John Entwistle to connect on the solidest groove imaginable. Keith Moon played great throughout the whole show. Roger Daltrey destroyed several tambourines. It

was his birthday... Smack in the middle of the *Tommy* finale the electricity and power in this Victoria Station venue blew out. A near riot was carefully averted..."

A girl was injured when the lighting tower she had climbed toppled over and she fell 30 feet to the ground.

Tuesday March 2
Pavilion de Paris, Paris, France

Barbara Charone continued: "The first show was good but the second show was exceptional... Clenched fists greeted unbelievably aggressive versions of 'Baba O'Riley' and 'We're Not Gonna Take It'. Right in the middle of 'Behind Blue Eyes' I got one of those infrequent chills brought on by rock'n'roll magic. It is possibly the greatest Who song ever written and this particular showing was exquisite. Daltrey almost hit Townshend several times with his whirling microphone cord. The whole of the *Tommy* sequence was the best I'd heard since they quit playing the piece on stage. 'Summertime Blues' and 'My Generation' with its lovely 'Join Together' interlude was sensational. Townshend duck walked during 'Road Runner'. Daltrey spat. Townshend pouted. Entwistle tapped his foot. Moon played flawlessly. When it was over, loudspeaker cabinet MB22 was still shaking."

Tuesday March 9
Boston Garden, Boston, Massachusetts

Like the *Quadrophenia* tour two years before, this leg of the 1976 tour got off to a bad start. Keith Moon, who was reportedly suffering from the flu, collapsed at the opening gig and left the stage after only two songs.

A correspondent to *Generations* magazine, John McCabe, recalled that the atmosphere had been fairly unsettled even before The Who came onstage, and that a fire had been started by fireworks thrown from an upper tier: "The Who came onstage shortly thereafter, launching immediately into 'I Can't Explain'. My first impression of the group was one of incredible power and energy as the first chords rang out. But as the song progressed I sensed that something was wrong. The drumming was sluggish, almost as if Keith Moon was being left behind by the rest of the band. They finished that song and went right into 'Substitute'. I was using binoculars to get

234

Flu wipes out The Who before 15,000 at Garden

close-up views of the band and when I focused on the drum set, there was no one behind it. The song stopped immediately after that and the house lights came on. Townshend and Daltrey talked to the crowd, trying to buy some time while they assessed the situation.

"The situation was not good. The audience was worked into a frenzy by this point. They expected to see The Who and were not about to settle for anything less. Once the decision was made that Moon could not continue and the concert would have to be cancelled, Townshend and Daltrey did their best to soothe the audience with promises of a make-up concert [on Thursday March 11, although this proved impractical].

Unfortunately, this was not very effective. Their announcements were met with screams of protest. When Townshend and Daltrey left the stage, the crowd went wild. After about 15 minutes of shouting, people realised that there would be no further show and slowly began to leave the Garden with lots of pushing and shoving and general mayhem... On our way out we noticed that several large glass windows in the lobby were smashed. Radio news reports the next day mentioned that in addition to extensive damage to the Boston Garden itself, several subway trains were damaged too. What a night!"

A replacement show was scheduled for Thursday April 1 and ticket stubs from the cancelled gig were honoured on the new date. The Steve Gibbons Band, making their début in America, were the opening act for the entire tour.

Thursday March 11
Madison Square Garden, New York

Moon's illness caused postponement of the New York gig from Wednesday March 10 to the following night. In spite of the date change, 19,500 fans filled the Garden for a gross of $162,000. 1,500 fans milled around outside the Garden in the hope of buying tickets from ticket scalpers who were selling a pair of $8.50 seats for as much as $80.

Supported by the Steve Gibbons Band, The Who blasted through a 100–minute set, treating the Big Apple audience to encores of 'Naked Eye' and 'Let's See Action'. The *New York Times* (March 13) carried a review by long-term Who fan John Rockwell: "What remains incontrovertible is the sheer excitement of the playing. In concert even more than on records, The Who sticks to the rock-and-roll basics, and executes them with an angry passion that nobody has matched. Even at less than its very best, it works for this listener every time, and it clearly worked for the screaming, cheering crowd on Thursday."

Chris Charlesworth: "I went back to the Navarro after this show to have a drink with the band and I was told that Keith was locked in his room with a security guard outside to stop him from getting out. They didn't want him going out and getting drunk and staying up all night and collapsing at any more shows!"

Saturday March 13
Dane County Coliseum, Madison, Wisconsin

The Who played Madison for the first time since August 1967 and easily sold out the 11,000–seat Coliseum.

Sunday March 14
The Civic Center Arena, St. Paul, Minnesota

THE WHO

Concert has been rescheduled for today at 3:00 P.M. If you have purchased tickets for Friday, March 12, by mail order or in person, and are unable to attend today's performance, return your tickets as soon as possible to

Schon, 1645 Hennepin, Mpls. 55403

Please help us save time by including a stamped, self-addressed envelope.

The show was originally scheduled for Friday March 12, but rescheduled for 3 pm, Sunday, March 14. Postponement of the Madison Square Garden show from Wednesday, March 10 to the next night was the reason for the date change in St. Paul.

Monday March 15
The Myriad, Oklahoma City, Oklahoma

A sell-out crowd of 14,801 saw the band's return to Oklahoma City after a nine–year absence. This show saw the last performance of 'Slip Kid' on the tour. Gate receipts totalled $101,028.

Tuesday March 16
Tarrant County Convention Center, Fort Worth, Texas

The attendance was 13,737, the receipts totalled $100,583.

Thursday March 18
The Salt Palace, Salt Lake City, Utah

Surprisingly, the show did not sell out with about 3,000 seats left empty. Nevertheless, gate receipts came to $87,127.

Friday March 19
McNichols Arena, Denver, Colorado

This show was postponed because The Who's equipment trucks could not reach Denver in time for the show due to roads blocked by snow-storms. The concert was rescheduled for Tuesday, March 30.

Sunday March 21
Anaheim Stadium, Anaheim, California

The only outdoor show of the tour took place, not surprisingly, in southern California at the home stadium of the California Angels baseball team. A crowd of 55,000 fans saw a 90–minute set, and it was at this show that Pete suffered immediate and noticeable hearing loss right from the opening guitar chord and Roger's first vocal.

"The Who's set on Sunday was designed to celebrate its own history and tradition..." commented Robert Hilburn in the *LA Times* (March 23). "The Who put on a firmer, more convincing performance than in its somewhat stale, mechanical effort in 1973."

Wednesday March 24
Memorial Coliseum, Portland, Oregon

The Who returned to the site of their first gig on the 1967 Herman's Hermits tour.

Thursday March 25
Seattle Center Coliseum, Seattle, Washington

The entire band was suffering from the flu but, according to the *Seattle Times*, "you couldn't tell from their performance". Moon was still the only member "who looked under the weather".

Saturday March 27
Winterland Auditorium, San Francisco, California

The Who easily sold out the 5,400–seat venue,

chosen as a sort of apology to the Bay Area for the 1973 fiasco at the Cow Palace when Keith passed out on stage. Apparently all was forgiven as there were ten requests for every available ticket. The Saturday night audience gave a 20-minute standing ovation calling, to no avail, for an encore.

Robert Hilburn reported in the *LA Times* (March 29) that The Who "bristled with the kind of tension, grandeur and celebration that audiences once associated with the band... Townshend was once again a captivating figure on stage".

The box lid photo of the *Thirty Years Of Maximum R&B* was taken at this gig by Neal Preston.

Sunday March 28
Winterland Auditorium, San Francisco, California

Tuesday March 30
McNichols Arena, Denver, Colorado

More than 19,000 fans filled the arena for the show, rescheduled from Friday March 19. The band then flew east to play the replacement show in Boston for the postponement on March 9.

Who plus lasers — wow!

Thursday April 1
Boston Garden, Boston, Massachusetts

The Who paid in full any debt owed from the cancelled March 9 show, giving a brilliant performance. This date ended the first segment of a three–part American tour that ran, on and off, all the way into late October.

John McCabe: "The concert on April 1 was almost an anti-climax. The crowd was noticeably smaller. Keith Moon made his entrance on stage ahead of the others, did a somersault, then jumped up and ran around the stage waving to the crowd. Pete Townshend directed a couple of playful verbal jabs at Keith, which Keith took good-naturedly. This seemed to break the ice with the crowd and put The Who back in favour. The crowd gave the band an enthusiastic welcome and the band picked up where they had left off on March 9. I would have to rate the April 1 concert as one of the best I've ever seen – certainly the most memorable. The Who's stage presence was almost overwhelming to someone seeing them

for the first time. It was quite an experience." After the opening two numbers, Daltrey said to the audience: "Thanks for waiting for the encore!"

Saturday May 22
Parc Des Expositions, Colmar, France

The group played two warm-up shows in France just prior to The Who Put The Boot In stadium concerts in the UK. The 'My Generation' medley here included 'The Punk And The Godfather' and the 'Is it me, for a moment?' refrain from 'Dr. Jimmy'.

Tuesday May 25
Palais Des Sports, Lyons, France

As with the Colmar show, this concert featured 'The Punk And The Godfather' and 'Is It Me, For A Moment?'

Monday May 31
Charlton Football Ground, Charlton, South London

The Who played a three-date stadium tour in the UK to satisfy overwhelming demand, and 65,000 (including 5,000 gatecrashers) attended this lead-off show. All three concerts started at 2 pm and featured The Sensational Alex Harvey Band, Little Feat, The Outlaws, and Streetwalkers.

The day was blighted by heavy downpours and sporadic fighting in the huge crowd, although the concert itself was run with surprising efficiency. Pete ran on at full tilt, skidding across the stage, landing flat on his back. Roger solved the slippery stage problem by singing in

Saturday June 5
Celtic Football Ground, Glasgow, Scotland

The Who's biggest Scottish concert with an audience of 35,000, grossing £140,000. All of The Who's cut of this income was donated to charity. Proving the magic of Charlton was by no means a one-off, the band once more turned in a classic performance. Barbara Charone wrote in *Sounds* (June 12): "The Who have never been better... No other rock'n'roll band supplies good entertainment plus that extra special something... The Who are electric... non-stop excitement. Look out Swansea!"

Saturday June 12
Vetch Field, Swansea, Wales

Recorded by Glyn Johns on the Ronnie Lane Mobile Studio and later broadcast in 1976 on Capital Radio's *Your Mother Wouldn't Like It*. Although the band stuck to their usual set they played an improvisation prior to 'Won't Get Fooled Again' which mixed some tortured guitar soloing with a heavy riff. It was generally accepted that Swansea lacked some of the intensity and electric atmosphere of Charlton and Glasgow, although the music itself was immaculate. Attendance was 25,000, and the concert grossed £100,000.

Melody Maker's reviewer, Allan Jones (June 19), drew the somewhat exaggerated comparison between Charlton, at which he called The Who "magnificent", and this concert, which he considered "overbearingly contrived and mechanical"!

After this mini-tour, apart from two private shows, the band would not appear in Britain again until 1979. Two songs from this Swansea

bare feet. The Who played a powerful 90-minute set but failed to return for a much demanded encore.

Barbara Charone reviewed the show for *Sounds* (June 12): "Charlton was magic because it pulled the very best out of The Who... the lasers were just decoration, The Who were the real magicians... absolutely brilliant." The concert grossed around £200,000. This gig is officially logged in the *Guinness Book Of Records* as the loudest concert ever played. The sound measured 120 decibels.

Richard Evans: "Bellboy, the programme for *The Who Put The Boot In* gigs, was a spoof of *Playboy* and featured Keith as the nude centrefold 'Baggage Of The Month.' The shots were done in Keith's suite at the Royal Garden Hotel in Kensington. Keith thoroughly enjoyed himself prancing around in the bellboy outfit we'd brought for him to wear on the front cover - albeit it four sizes too small!"

show, 'Dreaming From The Waist' and 'My Wife', were released on the *Thirty Years Of Maximum R&B* box set plus 'Squeeze Box' and 'Behind Blue Eyes' from Swansea were included on the 1996 reissue of *The Who By Numbers*.

Fans who held tickets for the Charlton show but who could not enter the stadium because of overcrowding were allowed to claim a refund or take a special coach to Wales to the Swansea concert. The Who paid for onboard light refreshment for those fans opting to go to Swansea.

Tuesday August 3
Capital Centre, Largo, Maryland
The summer mini-tour of the US kicked off with two shows in Largo. The group was set to play markets that had been bypassed on the first two segments of *The Who By Numbers* tour. This first night drew a less than capacity crowd of 15,024 in the 18,787-seat arena.

Wednesday August 4
Capital Centre, Largo, Maryland
The second night in Largo also failed to sell-out with 15,177 people in attendance. Even though ticket sales had fallen short, The Who grossed $259,655 for the two dates.

Saturday August 7

The Gator Bowl, Jacksonville, Florida
The Who had never appeared in Jacksonville before but muggy weather kept attendance short of capacity. Fewer than 40,000 people came to the show, far short of the 60,000 capacity.

Chris Charlesworth: "This was the last Who concert I saw with Keith on drums. They were closing an open air all-dayer in a big stadium in muggy, unpleasant weather after an ill-judged, weak supporting cast had limped on and off stage to little purpose. A greedy promoter had overcharged and Florida was never Who territory, so the crowd numbered 35,000 instead of a potential 60,000. This hurt their pride and they were angry at what had happened, furious in fact, and having watched The Who at close quarters scores of times by then I knew all too well that anger could bring out the best or the worst in them. Sharp words were exchanged backstage and I kept my distance; only Keith, fuelled as ever by Remy Martin brandy, seemed sociable. But come show-time there was an extraordinary transformation and all their fury, all the frustration and pent-up rage that spilled out of Pete and Roger, was channelled into the music, and they played an absolute blinder, as powerful as any show in the classic '69-'71 era.

"The Who at their almighty best came flooding over everyone in that stadium that night. At the end they smashed their equipment in an orgy of gleeful destruction and the crowd exploded with endless ovations because they'd never seen or heard anything like it before, nor would they ever again. Afterwards, backstage, in the calm of the caravan that served as a dressing room, I clearly remember sitting down next to Pete and remarking to him on how good this show had been. Exhausted, slumped in a corner, his fingers shredded and covered in blood, his skinny, loose-limbed body wrapped in a towel, he knocked back a huge plastic beaker of brandy in one gulp. There was a strange, faraway look in those deep blue eyes of his as he looked up at me. He thought for a minute, fingered the Meher Baba badge that hung from his neck, then managed a wry smile. 'We were playing for the people who weren't there,' he said."

Monday August 9
Miami Baseball Stadium, Miami, Florida
"Without question they are the finest live band

in the world... Everything was superb," wrote Pam Brown in *Creem* (November 1976).

The mini-tour ended with the second of two stadium shows in Florida and their first Miami appearance in almost five years. Only 200 shy of a complete sell-out, gate receipts came to $204,000. The Who would make one more swing across America in October and there were tentative plans to tour Australia, Japan and possibly even South America in November. These plans, of course, never came to fruition.

Wednesday October 6
Arizona Veterans Memorial Coliseum, Phoenix, Arizona

The beginning of the last leg of the year-long *The Who By Numbers* tour.

Thursday October 7
Sports Arena, San Diego, California

"No one..." wrote Robert Hilburn of the *LA Times* (October 9) "plays with as much ferocity and splendour on a good night as The Who, and The Who had a good night Thursday... The Who's repertoire continues to reflect the youthful

urgency and passion that has long been at the heart of rock'n'roll..."

"Pure rock'n'roll, distilled to its essence and served full strength, with no artificial ingredients" is how the band's performance was described in the *San Diego Union*.

Saturday October 9
Alameda County Stadium, Oakland, California

The Who teamed up with The Grateful Dead for two shows in the massive Oakland stadium for Bill Graham's *Day On The Green # 9*. The Dead graciously accepted the supporting slot on the bill, and despite both group's fervent followings and immense drawing power, attendance was a little short of a sell-out with 50,809 spectators in the 55,000 capacity venue. The Who played a 90 minute set at the first show, John's 32nd birthday.

"The Who gave their best... Really fine," wrote Harvey Kubernik in *Melody Maker* (October 23).

Sunday October 10
Alameda County Stadium, Oakland, California

The Who performed for 110 minutes but were coaxed back onstage to do an encore by Bill Graham. Pete dedicated 'Shakin' All Over' to The Grateful Dead and their fans. Keith took over lead vocals on 'Spoonful' and 'Johnny B. Goode' as

THE WHO TOUR
USA & CANADA

October 6—Phoenix, AZ
October 7—San Diego, CA
October 9 & 10—Oakland, CA
October 13—Portland, OR
October 14—Seattle, WA
October 16—Edmonton, Alberta
October 18—Winnipeg, Manitoba
October 21 & 22—Toronto, Ontario

MCA RECORDS

they finished their set at 5:30 pm.

This second date attracted fewer people than the first show, 43,923.

Wednesday October 13
Memorial Coliseum, Portland, Oregon

The Who returned to Portland for the second time in seven months and again sold out all 11,000 seats.

Thursday October 14
Seattle Center Coliseum, Seattle, Washington

As they had done only seven months before in the same venue, The Who played to a capacity crowd of 15,000 fans. This was Keith's last concert in the United States.

Saturday October 16
Northlands Coliseum, Edmonton, Alberta, Canada

The show got off to a late start due to a power supply problem with the band's laser lighting system, and the group didn't take the stage until 10:30 pm. They proceeded to awe the assembled 16,000 spectators, the biggest concert draw to date in Edmonton's history.

Monday October 18
Winnipeg Arena, Winnipeg, Manitoba, Canada

The Who devastated the capacity crowd with a highly charged set, the same venue where they had played as opening act to Herman's Hermits in August 1967.

Thursday October 21
Maple Leaf Gardens, Toronto, Ontario, Canada

The tour had initially set two dates in Toronto, the second gig booked for Friday October 22, but The Who played one night only. Also scrapped was a concert set for Montreal on the 23rd and a provisional date for a third concert back in Toronto on the 24th.

The group wrapped up their 1976 tour with a tremendous show, giving the 20,000 fans who packed the Gardens a performance "of such nerve shattering power that not even The Rolling Stones four years ago did for the crowd what The Who did last night," according to one local reviewer. During the 'My Generation' jam Townshend went into a very unusual riff and he sang "I want to know, I want to know, who are you?" which presaged the song 'Who Are You', although it bore only a passing resemblance to the final version.

Pete smashed one of his Les Paul Deluxes at the end and the tour was over. It was Keith's farewell to North America. "The whole band was fucking amazing," said John of The Who's last tour with Keith. "Usually someone would like it and someone would hate it, but we could have gone on playing forever. That, to me, was the peak of the Who's career."

241

As far as The Who were concerned, 1977 didn't really exist. Not since 1963 had a whole year elapsed with no Who records released at all. In May, Roger's third solo LP, *One Of The Boys* was released and in September, Pete released *Rough Mix*, his album with fellow Meher Baba follower and former Faces and Small Faces bass player, Ronnie Lane. John kept a low profile and Keith wasted away in California, vainly hoping that his film career might take off. It didn't. In June, Pete demoed 'Who Are You' at his Goring studio and recorded it with The Who in October with other tracks that would materialise on *Who Are You* the following year.

In December the band regrouped to play one unsatisfactory private show in London, filmed for their biopic *The Kids Are Alright*.

Thursday December 15
Gaumont State Theatre, Kilburn, North London
Set: 'I Can't Explain', 'Substitute', 'Baba O'Riley', 'My Wife', 'Behind Blue Eyes', 'Dreaming From The Waist', 'Pinball Wizard', 'I'm Free', 'Tommy's Holiday Camp', 'Summertime Blues', 'Shakin' All Over', 'My Generation', 'Join Together', 'Who Are You', 'Won't Get Fooled Again'.

The band's on-stage comments indicated their utter lack of cohesion. Pete commented on the show being a waste of film and at one point mockingly sneered at the audience: "There's a guitar up here if any big mouth little git wants to come up and fucking take it off me!" John Entwistle was fairly drunk, Pete likewise, and at one point before 'Won't Get Fooled Again' either Keith or John yelled at Pete: "Play the fucking song, Townshend!" The only new song was 'Who Are You' – an embryonic version without a synthesiser backing tape. The band played the first verse only and the repeated: "Who are you, who-who-who-who" section, although Pete added some good guitar figures.

Tony Stewart writing in *New Musical Express* (December 24) was oddly impressed: "Townshend looks thinner and meaner, wasted even, as he glares angrily at the young pups playfully woofing and yelping at the grand old master and his band, The Who... The energy, the music and the atmosphere have the makings of a classic Who gig."

This was one of two shows specifically filmed by Jeff Stein for inclusion in *The Kids Are Alright* but, understandably, the footage wasn't deemed worthy.

The main event of 1978 was the release of *Who Are You* in August but this was overshadowed by Keith Moon's accidental, but tragically predictable, death the following month. Ironically, he was photographed on the cover sitting on a chair with the words 'Not To Be Taken Away' on its back. The other irony was that on one song, 'Music Must Change', Keith didn't play drums because he couldn't handle its unusual tempo. "But I'm the best Keith Moon style drummer in the world," he is reported to have told Pete when he couldn't play it.

Moon, more than any of his three colleagues, represented the thundering recklessness of the old-style – and younger – Who. But although his death freed them from the grip of the past, the

Dave Lewis: "I got a ticket through a guy called Steve Margo who later put on the ICA Who exhibition. We were all taken into Shepperton Studio canteen and fed and given large amounts of wine. This obviously got us in the mood. After shooting various numbers they seemed so enthusiastic that the show began to turn into a standard Who gig. Even though it was a bit ragged, Pete in particular seemed to enjoy himself. Afterwards we all went into the garden to be photographed for what was originally intended as the sleeve of the new Who album. We stood in four lines, and at the front of each was a member of The Who.

"We went back the next day when they filmed the laser show used in the middle of 'Won't Get Fooled Again.' This took about three hours and Keith played his drums all the time... he never

Who: Out of sight, but fans haven't forgotten

future, as the final two albums demonstrated, turned out to be a barren land all the same, creatively at least.

The only concert the group performed in 1978 was specifically for *The Kids Are Alright*.

Thursday May 25
Shepperton Studios, Shepperton, Middlesex
Set included: 'Baba O'Riley', 'My Wife', 'Won't Get Fooled Again', 'Substitute', 'I Can't Explain', 'Magic Bus', 'Summertime Blues', 'My Generation', 'My Wife' (2nd version), 'Won't Get Fooled Again' (2nd version).

This was the last show Keith Moon ever played with The Who. Jeff Stein filmed this gig, like the previous Kilburn show (December 15 '77), in an effort to bring up to date *The Kids Are Alright* by capturing definitive versions of key songs, most notably 'Baba O'Riley' and 'Won't Get Fooled Again', both of which appear in the film. The actual performance is ragged, especially from Keith's quarter, but it does give one last glimpse of the fierce and frantic style the group had maintained for almost exactly 14 years with Keith behind the drums.

At the close, Keith stumbled somewhat unsteadily over his drums to embrace Pete and acknowledge the applause of a crowd for the final time.

flagged. He was just like a big boy with a huge grin."

Richard Evans: "I got a call from Chris Chappel at Trinifold. 'Stop what you're doing and get down to Shepperton as quick as you can.' After being plied with lunch and as much booze as we needed we all assembled in the sound stage where Jeff Stein was to film The Who playing 'Won't Get Fooled Again' on account of how they (or he) had cocked it up when he'd filmed them in Kilburn. Me and my friend Sonnie were right in the front between John and Roger. Behind us was

the camera on a dolly tracking back and forth. After various takes of 'Won't Get Fooled Again' the band decided they'd just carry on and do a regular gig for the two hundred or so people who had turned up. It was a nice sunny afternoon and none of us had anything better to do! We got talking to a couple standing next to us. The bloke was a bit of a Ted and the girl was an American called Chrissie who kept screaming "Keith!... Keith!... Keith For President!" They told us they'd got a band together and they'd just got a record deal with Warner Bros. 'Oh, yeah? What's your band called?' I asked. 'The Pretenders' she said."

Friday August 18

After a three year gap The Who released their tenth album, *Who Are You*. The group has barely seen each other for two years and when they finally got together in the studio there was so much tension that a frustrated Glyn Johns had to pass the production duties over to Pete's brother-in-law, Jon Astley half way through the sessions.

It was to be last album on which Keith played the drums. His drinking and harmful lifestyle had begun to take its toll on his skills to the point where his three colleagues had to seriously consider his future as a band member. But they soldiered on and after a lot of spilt blood, shed tears and frazzled nerves, and despite the growing climate of punk hysteria, *Who Are You* did surprisingly well and managed a healthy number 6 in the UK album charts and even made number 2 in the US.

Many fans continue think that this is when The Who should have called it a day. In two years of Who inactivity, the band members had become virtual strangers to each other and Keith's death on September 7 signalled an end to a collective career that would remain unrivalled in rock-'n'roll. The real Who was no more.

244

Keith Moon's death threw The Who into confusion, but it wasn't long before Pete, Roger and John announced the group would continue. Drummers from all over the world offered their services. Replace Keith? At first it seemed absurd. No other group, ever, had relied so heavily on the skill of its drummer to sustain its musical dynamics. More than that, Keith had been a character in his own right whose contribution to The Who went way beyond sitting at the back. He had been their comedian, the wisecracking member of the gang, a crucial cog in the wheel. Also, in the eyes of their fans, there was the tradition of The Who to uphold. At a time when many top groups were fragmenting, breaking up or diluting their identity through employing back-up musicians on stage, The Who had retained their integrity by sticking together. They might not always have been the best of friends but their solidarity was a key factor of their collective personality. Until now, Who tradition had demanded that the group consist solely of Pete, Roger, John and Keith – no changing personnel, no additional musicians, just the four members, the original Who.

But when the dust had settled all that would change. One idea was to have various drummers sit in on group projects without any actually joining the band. Then, in December 1978, it was announced that Kenney Jones, formerly with The Faces and before that The Small Faces, would become The Who's permanent drummer.

The 'new Who' rehearsed together at Shepperton and made their stage début on May 2, 1979 at the Rainbow Theatre in London. They were augmented by John 'Rabbit' Bundrick on keyboards and, later in the year, by a four-man horn section. The passing of the 'old Who' had freed the group from the traditions of the past, enabling them to use additional musicians on stage. Unfortunately, within a year, the group settled into a familiar pattern of shows which differed only slightly from the tours in 1975 and 1976. Only three songs from *Who Are You*, the title track, 'Music Must Change', and 'Sister Disco', found their way into the regular set, along with song fragments that Pete would throw in as they came to him. Most ended up on his subsequent solo album, *Empty Glass*, released in April 1980.

After London, the group headed to France for two nights at an ancient Roman amphitheatre in Frejus, near Cannes, and two concerts at the Pavilion des Paris. The first of these shows coincided with the release of the band's biopic *The Kids Are Alright* which, along with the film of *Quadrophenia*, was premiered at Cannes.

Ten thousand people turned out for the first night at Frejus as The Who demonstrated a rediscovered enthusiasm for stage work. A strong contingent of British music press journalists was present for the French gigs and turned in glowing reports of the performances. Less than a year after Keith's death, The Who were back.

The group returned to Britain for two Scottish dates in early June followed by a ten week break from live gigs. Pete played two shows away from The Who during this respite, appearing on one night of the 1979 Amnesty International Comedy Gala's four-night run at Her Majesty's Theatre in London and playing at the Rainbow in a Rock Against Racism benefit on July 13 with a backing band that included Kenney Jones and Rabbit.

The Who resumed live shows on a grand scale with an open air gig at Wembley Stadium on August 18, supported by Nils Lofgren, AC/DC and The Stranglers.

The group moved on to Nuremburg, Germany, for another stadium date on September 1 with Cheap Trick, Scorpions, Nils Lofgren, AC/DC, Miriam Makeba, Steve Gibbons and Zanki & Band rounding out the bill.

Even though Pete was reluctant to go on tour around this time, five nights in New York were set for September. Two more nights were added at the 3,250-seat Capitol Theater in Passaic, New Jersey on September 10 and 11. A three-man horn section joined the group onstage to expand the range of the material which now included 'Music Must Change'.

The crowds in New York, which had always been a 'Who town', gave the band a hero's welcome. Radio station WNEW had announced the shows on June 6, and by 10 am on June 7 the Garden had received 10,081 requests for 40,000 tickets. Over the seven nights, the band played for 110,000 people. The Who replied in kind with most shows running two hours plus. Besides the material from *Who Are You* that was new to the stage, Pete was throwing in everything, from excerpts of songs in the works to bits of covers like 'Pretty Vacant' by The Sex Pistols and 'Big Boss Man' by Jimmy Reed. There was even a big pie fight onstage at the end of the show on September 16 in honour of Kenney's birthday. The only setback to the gigs was on September 17 when Pete slashed the palm of his hand on the controls of his guitar during 'Who Are You'. Not only did he return to the stage after receiving three stitches backstage, the band also gave the longest performance of the five shows at the Garden. All in all, The Who's return to America was a resounding success in a year of triumphs and overwhelming acclaim. A short tour of the east coast and Midwest was set for late November, a result of the New York stand and the demand for concerts in other parts of the country.

In preparation for the American tour that was due to begin on December 2, the band set up three dates in England at the Brighton Conference Centre on November 10 and 11 and Bingley Hall, Stafford on the 16th. Ticket demand necessitated the addition of another date in Stafford on the 17th.

The US tour had been scheduled to open in Pontiac, Michigan but an extra date was added when all 40,000 tickets were sold more than three weeks in advance. (It had been decided to play the 'mini-Dome', half the normal capacity of the 75,000-seat Metropolitan Stadium.) The Who pencilled in the second show at the 4,647-seat Masonic Auditorium as a gesture to play a 'personal' gig for the fans. Detroit had always been a special town for the group since 'I Can't Explain', 'My Generation' and 'Happy Jack' had all garnered airplay in the area, and their first gigs in America outside New York had been in Ann Arbor, just west of the city, back in June 1967.

All the jubilation of the year came to a sudden and tragic end on Monday December 3 when 11 fans were trampled to death outside the Riverfront Coliseum in Cincinnati. There had been the expected crowds gathering all day in the Coliseum's west plaza level, enduring freezing temperatures and blustery winds. According to a city police officer, only two doors were opened out of more than a dozen available and fans had surged forward when they heard the band completing their soundcheck. Thinking the show had already begun, the crowd pushed those in the front into the doors and people started falling down. Six thousand of the 18,000 tickets to the

show were 'festival seating', meaning first come first served; those who could muscle their way to the front would get the best view. This arrangement was not uncommon at rock concerts, even though the Coliseum had previously experienced problems with unruly crowds at shows by other acts. The Who weren't told of the tragedy until after the show. The tour moved on to Buffalo but irreparable damage had already been done.

They carried on with the tour. The city of Providence, Rhode Island, cancelled the December 17 concert there because of the Cincinnati tragedy but a second show in Largo, Maryland, was added for the same date. It was the last night of the tour and The Who then went back to England to play one night of the Concerts For Kampuchea at the Hammersmith Odeon on December 28.

In general, the concerts were more well-paced and longer than pre-1979 Who gigs, and offered a wider variety of material, including more demanding songs that they would not previously have attempted. Overall, these concerts were a rock spectacle where the music could still produce a very real charge of emotional thrill. The band's dynamics were altered slightly by Keith's absence but the theatrical pull of Townshend, Daltrey and Entwistle out front was still as dramatic and compelling as any other contemporary group. Technical improvements in the band's equipment could be felt as well, not to mention the addition of keyboards and a brass section. In general, the band's efforts were vindicated by the warm response of the audience. People didn't leave these shows disappointed and many younger fans were able to see the band for the first time during the 1979-82 era: not the definitive Who, to be sure, but a reasonable substitute (if you'll pardon the pun!). *Rolling Stone* Readers and Critics Poll also voted The Who 'Best Band Of 1979'.

The basic set for the 1979 concerts was as follows: 'Substitute', 'I Can't Explain', 'Baba O'Riley', 'The Punk And The Godfather', 'Boris The Spider', 'Sister Disco', 'Behind Blue Eyes', 'Music Must Change', 'Dreaming From The Waist', 'Bargain', 'Drowned', 'Who Are You', '5.15', 'Pinball Wizard', 'See Me, Feel Me', 'Long Live Rock', 'My Generation', 'My Generation Blues', 'Magic Bus', 'Won't Get Fooled Again', 'Summertime Blues' and 'The Real Me'.

Occasional performances through the tour – including jams, improvisations, encores and medleys – were: 'Dancing In The Street', 'Dance It Away', 'Country Line Special', 'My Wife', 'Pretty Vacant', 'Young Man Blues', 'I Am An Animal', 'How Can You Do It Alone', 'Blue Blue Blue', 'Trick Of The Light', 'Sweets For My Sweet', 'Spoonful', 'Big Boss Man', 'Let's See Action', 'I'm London', 'Sparks', 'Cat's In The Cupboard', 'Road Runner', 'All Right Now', 'Naked Eye', 'I Can See For Miles', 'I'm A Man', 'How Can You Do It Alone', 'That's Rock'n'Roll', 'Fuck All Blues', 'Pictures Of Lily', 'Relay', 'Shakin' All Over'.

Wednesday May 2
The Rainbow Theatre, Finsbury Park, North London

The set: 'Substitute', 'I Can't Explain', 'Baba O'Riley', 'The Punk And The Godfather', 'Boris The Spider', 'Sister Disco', 'Music Must Change', 'Behind Blue Eyes', 'Dreaming From The Waist', 'Pinball Wizard', 'See Me, Feel Me', 'Long Live Rock', 'Bargain', 'Who Are You', 'My Generation', 'Join Together', 'My Generation Blues', 'Won't Get Fooled Again', encore: 'The Real Me'.

SUMMER OF '79

The Who began the second phase of their career with a one-off show in London which inspired Mark Williams to pen a rave review in *Melody Maker* (May 12): "Townshend was simply a gas, joking with the audience and the rest of the band, chaperoning Jones with an occasional nod or a smile, and delivering an exceptionally impressive display of what is expected of him. If anyone doubted his will to continue strutting the boards in the face of the punk onslaught, they'd have to reconsider after Wednesday night.

"Sometimes Townshend would simply strum furiously into a middle-eight or an instrumental break, pushing the band into a relentless, pile-driving beat that got you in the gut, 'Who Are You?' and 'Bargain' being two prime examples… How long and hard Townshend had been rehearsing the new Who will remain a mystery, but it was surprising how effectively they accomplished a *Tommy* medley and, to an even greater extent, an amalgam of 'My Generation', 'Join Together In The Band' and 'Magic Bus', which involved some cute segues and nice harp playing from Daltrey - even if he got stuck into Bo Diddley's 'Mona' for about an hour-and-a-half.

"Very rarely did anyone screw up, although it should be said that Jones didn't take any chances and wore headphones linked direct to the onstage mixer during several numbers. On the other hand, when Townshend and Bundrick started running a bit too fast during the diminuendo passage on 'Who Are You?' they were conducted back to the correct tempo by Jones' assertive right hand.

"In the main, though, it was Daltrey who directed the pace, throwing himself and, of course, his microphone around the stage in a manner that might easily have been construed as complacent or haughty if this had been a heavy metal exposition, but in the event was the measure of a man who likes to face up to an audience.

Hair clipped short and wearing a black leather bomber during the early numbers, he looked and sang tougher than he's done for ages, giving new hope to any other 35-year-olds in the hall who might've been wondering if they could make it to 40 in some sort of style.

"Incongruities and reservations flew quietly down the toilet as we got sucked into the whole joyous experience of rock'n' roll excellence. Confirming this, the audience declared their unanimous adulation for the whole band as they came together one by one, linked arms and took the Big Bow after the uplifting 'Won't Get Fooled Again'. There followed but one encore, 'Doctor Doctor', after which Townshend demolished half the group's amplification with more than perfunctory gusto.

"Relatively adventurous arrangements of material both obscure and well-worn, irresistibly urgent treatments of their simpler stuff, and a new-found enthusiasm for performance suggest that the new Who might prove to be even better than the old Who. The incipient sleekness of an AOR mega-group would've been an easy option at this point in their career, but the Who have not let finesse get the better of them. They've retained the sense of mischief that some feared would die with Keith Moon, and that was possibly the best news of Wednesday evening."

APOLLO THEATRE, GLASGOW

HARVEY GOLDSMITH ENTERTAINMENTS
presents

THE WHO

Friday, 8th June, 1979
at 7.30 p.m.

CIRCLE

Nº 30 C

TICKET £5.00
TO BE RETAINED
TICKETS CANNOT BE EXCHANGED

Saturday May 12
Arenes Des Frejus, Frejus, France

The Who performed for 8,000 ecstatic fans in an ancient Roman amphitheatre just outside Nice. *The Kids Are Alright* and *Quadrophenia* films were premièred in nearby Cannes the following Monday night.

Sunday May 13
Arenes Des Frejus, Frejus, France

A second night option in Frejus was taken up by the group after the overwhelming response to the previous night's show. The band hit the stage at 8:56, indicative of their newfound enthusiasm for live work, and steamed through a 19 song, two-hour performance. Kit Lambert arrived in Frejus and Pete told reporters "Kit Lambert has just spent fifteen minutes telling me what's wrong with The Who - and he was right."

Wednesday May 16
Pavilion De Paris, Paris, France

Broadcast live on French radio.

Thursday May 17
Pavilion De Paris, Paris, France

Kit Lambert was present at this Paris gig.

Richard Evans: "The two nights at this former slaughterhouse were sell-outs for The Who. Both shows were great - very tight. The French audiences really went wild for The Who."

Friday June 8
Apollo Centre, Glasgow, Scotland

The Who set two 'off the cuff' gigs in Scotland for this weekend.

Saturday June 9
Green's Playhouse, Edinburgh, Scotland

Wednesday June 27
Her Majesty's Theatre, London

Pete took part in *The Secret Policeman's Ball*, Amnesty International's Comedy Gala held over four nights, June 27-30.

Performing acoustically, he played solo on 'Pinball Wizard' and 'Drowned' and was joined by classical guitarist John Williams on 'Won't Get Fooled Again'. Townshend later claimed he was so drunk he fell asleep during Williams' solo!

Friday July 13
The Rainbow Theatre, Finsbury Park, London

Pete appeared with his own group at a benefit concert for Rock Against Racism. The group consisted of Kenney Jones, Rabbit Bundrick, Tony Butler on bass and Peter Hope-Evans on harmonica. The set: 'Won't Get Fooled Again', 'The Real Me', 'Tattoo', 'Drowned', 'Bargain', 'Let's See Action' and an encore of 'My Generation'. Steve Gibbons also joined in for two songs.

Guitar Smashed: Black Les Paul Standard

lows: 'Substitute', 'I Can't Explain', 'Baba O'Riley', 'The Punk And The Godfather', 'Boris The Spider', 'Sister Disco', 'Behind Blue Eyes', 'Music Must Change', 'Drowned', 'Who Are You',' '5:15', 'Pinball Wizard', 'See Me, Feel Me', 'Trick Of The Light' (featuring John on eight-string bass and Pete on one of John's Alembic basses), 'Long Live Rock', 'My Generation' and 'Magic Bus'. ('Trick Of The Light' was dropped by the end of the week.)

At this point in the show the band usually started to stretch out a bit and improvise new, as yet unrecorded, material, throwing in cover songs as the mood took them. Pete sang fragments of songs known only as 'Blue, Black, White' and 'I'm London' during 'My Generation' and 'Magic Bus'.

Encores on this night were 'Young Man Blues' and 'The Real Me'.

Saturday August 18
Wembley Stadium, Wembley, London

The band's official London relaunch, supported by Nils Lofgren, AC/DC and The Stranglers, attended by 77,000 fans. The Who played as consistently as they had done earlier in the year but the huge stadium didn't seem so sympathetic to the band as Charlton had been a few years earlier. The main problem was that the Greater London Council had put a restriction on the volume level and the PA system failed to carry an adequate quality of sound at the lower level. Consequently, the band sounded muted and dulled, lacking their customary sharpness and fire. In addition to the restricted sound system, John Wolff's plans to present The Who performing under a breath-taking pyramid of laser lights was ruined when the GLC safety inspectors instructed him to switch them off.

AC/DC were delighted to have been invited to play on the bill by The Who, as their guitarist Angus Young once rated Pete Townshend as the only guitarist he was ever influenced by.

Saturday September 1
Olympic Stadium, Nuremburg, Germany

This open air stadium was filled by 65,000 fans.

Monday September 10
Capitol Theatre, Passaic, New Jersey

A little over a year after Keith's death, The Who returned to America to play seven shows in the New York area. The first two gigs were at this small theatre in Passaic, just across the Hudson River from New York City.

The basic set for these seven shows was as fol-

Tuesday September 11
Capitol Theatre, Passaic, New Jersey

Pete continued improvising at this show, tossing in lines from a song called 'That's Rock'n'Roll' during the 'My Generation' medley. The band also ran through parts of 'Pictures Of Lily', Free's 'All Right Now', 'Road Runner' and 'Big Boss Man'.

Thursday September 13
Madison Square Garden, New York

The band segued 'Summertime Blues' into another new song called 'Cats In The Cupboard' (later recorded by Pete for his 1980 solo album, *Empty Glass*) before ending the show with 'Naked Eye'.

Friday September 14
Madison Square Garden, New York City

The post-'My Generation' medley included a fairly complete version of 'Let's See Action' followed by 'Blue, Black, White' and 'Join Together' before closing with 'Magic Bus' and 'My Generation'.

Encores for this second night in the Garden were 'Young Man Blues' and an extended 'The Real Me'.

Sunday September 16
Madison Square Garden, New York

The group included 'My Generation Blues' just before the standard reading of the song. 'Dreaming From The Waist' found its way into the set followed by yet another new number, 'Dance It Away'.

Monday September 17
Madison Square Garden, New York

The band played their longest show in New York. Unfortunately, Pete cut his hand on the controls of his guitar during 'Who Are You' and had to leave the stage to receive stitches. Roger, on harmonica, led the group through a jam which developed into a drum solo from Kenney. Still directing the band, Roger strapped on one of Pete's guitars, something he hadn't done since the days of The Detours, and a rare sight until the 'Farewell Tour' three years later. The trio eventually worked their way into 'Magic Bus' when Pete rejoined them onstage.

The Who return for twelve shows in December

The first song of the 'My Generation' medley was 'Shakin' All Over' which included snippets of 'Please Don't Touch' (Johnny Kidd & The Pirates), 'Sweets For My Sweet' (The Searchers) and 'Pretty Vacant' (The Sex Pistols). 'Cats In The Cupboard' made another brief appearance before 'Won't Get Fooled Again'.

The encore started with 'The Real Me', working 'Sparks' and 'Big Boss Man' into the medley. 'Dance It Away' ended the show.

Tuesday September 18
Madison Square Garden, New York

The Who replaced 'Boris The Spider' with 'My Wife' for this show but the song was interrupted about halfway through by a fight in front of the stage. Roger even jumped down into the crowd to sort it out.

After 'Magic Bus' Pete sang a couple of verses from 'I Am An Animal' (also recorded for his solo album, *Empty Glass*) before the closer, 'Won't Get Fooled Again'. The first encore was 'The Real Me' after which Pete said a few words: "If any of you were here last night you would have seen a very special sight... Roger Daltrey was playing the guitar while I was getting my hand fixed. So, after that I thought I'd buy him a little present. Wheel it out, please." A roadie wheeled out a cheap guitar and small amp and placed the guitar on Roger. Roger played a chord to which Pete responded "too loud!" so Roger took off the guitar and the band launched into 'Shakin' All Over' and 'Road Runner' which ended the music but not the show. Pies were wheeled out on to the stage and a pie fight ensued, a perfect ending to five nights of The Who at the Garden.

10th-11th NOVEMBER, 1979

Saturday November 10
Conference Centre, Brighton

The band kept this date low key to prevent "outsiders from causing chaos". While fans waited in line at the ticket window, they were treated to refreshments and live entertainment provided by promoters. People had started lining up 40 hours before the box office opened!

Sunday November 11
Conference Centre, Brighton

The hall was packed with 9,000 fans for the second of two shows.

Friday November 16
New Bingley Hall, Stafford

This was initially the only Stafford gig booked.

Saturday November 17
New Bingley Hall, Stafford

The group added a second night at Stafford due to overwhelming ticket demand.

Friday November 30
Masonic Auditorium, Detroit, Michigan

The Who returned to America for a full tour to introduce Kenney Jones as a member of the group and to promote *The Kids Are Alright*. This show was added to the itinerary as a gesture of apology to Detroit fans since the only area concert that had been initially announced was at the cavernous Metropolitan Stadium (The Silver Dome) on December 7.

The shows were structured like the New York gigs in September with a fairly standard set for the first half and a looser selection of material towards the end.

Tonight's performance included a surprise 'I Can See For Miles' leading off the post-'My Generation' medley. The encore started off with 'Dancing In the Street' and segued into 'Dance It Away' before the band kicked into 'The Real Me' and 'Young Man Blues'.

Sunday December 2
Civic Arena, Pittsburgh, Pennsylvania

A rousing show complete with Pete's 'machine gunning' of the audience during 'My Wife' and his 'birdman' stance during 'Sparks'. The 'Dancing In The Street'/'Dance It Away' medley ended the show.

Rock Concert Crush Kills 11

Monday December 3
Riverfront Coliseum, Cincinnati, Ohio

Tragedy struck when 11 fans were trampled to death in the crush to enter the venue. General seating (first come, first served) was partly to blame as well as the cold weather fans had endured while waiting for the doors to open.

Questions were raised as to just how many of those doors were actually available to the crowd at the time of the incident and whether they had been opened on time. The Who weren't told of the tragedy until after their performance, one that even they felt had been a great show.

Tuesday December 4
Memorial Auditorium, Buffalo, New York

It was a shattered Who that travelled to Buffalo for the next stop of the tour. Despite the sense of loss and sorrow, they gave Buffalo "one of the best rock shows this city has ever seen". It seemed that band and audience were determined to get lost in the music.

The show, which started at 9:30, was moved back to allow the 17,400 fans leisurely entry to the arena. The Who also did without their customary soundcheck.

Thursday December 6
Richfield Coliseum, Cleveland, Ohio

All 19,647 seats had been sold since October 18 and officials took extra precautions in admitting ticket holders to the venue. No one was allowed into the Coliseum parking lots unless they had a ticket. The gates opened at 6:30 pm, an hour and a half before showtime, allowing the crowds ample time to enter the arena.

Friday December 7
The Silverdome, Pontiac, Michigan

An estimated 41,000 people converged on the Silverdome for the 8 pm concert but were admitted into the venue at 3:30 because of afternoon rains, unseasonable for Michigan where snow is common at that time of year. There were no incidents as fans entered the cavernous arena.

Saturday December 8
International Amphitheatre, Chicago, Illinois

Set: 'Substitute', 'I Can't Explain', 'Baba

O'Riley', 'The Punk And The Godfather', 'My Wife', 'Sister Disco', 'Behind Blue Eyes', 'Music Must Change', 'Drowned', 'Who Are You', '5.15', 'Pinball Wizard', 'See Me, Feel Me', 'Long Live Rock', 'My Generation', 'I Can See For Miles', 'Sparks', 'Won't Get Fooled Again', 'The Real Me', 'Dancing In The Street/Dance It Away', 'Young Man Blues', 'Road Runner', 'Big Boss Man/I'm A Man', 'How Can You Do It Alone'.

This concert was "simulcast" live to nine Chicago-area cinemas. The Who received no revenues from the movie theatre ticket sales which totalled $168,385. Attendance at the actual concert in the Amphitheatre was 12,000 for a gross of $152,000. The nine theatres were the Granada, Gateway, Nortown and Uptown in Chicago, the Pickwick in Park Ridge, Illinois, the Varsity in Evanston, Illinois, the Rialto in Joliet, Illinois, the Genessee in Waukegan, Illinois, and the Parthenon in Hammond, Indiana. All theatres were sold out.

Following the broadcast, the video mastertape and 24-track sound recording were retained in The Who's archives. '5.15', 'My Wife', 'Music Must Change' and 'Pinball Wizard' were included in the video *Thirty Years Of Maximum R&B Live* (1994) with remixed sound and a minor edit of less than a minute in 'My Wife' where the videotape reel had to be changed over during the live recording. Shots from one of the cameras suffers interference throughout.

Without any painful dwelling upon the Cincinnati incident, The Who charged straight into the usual set with an unusual display of camaraderie between Daltrey and Townshend.

Roger leant his head back onto Pete's shoulder, while the latter blasted out the chords to 'Substitute', probably thinking "you fucking wanker" (as we later learned). This song and 'I Can't Explain' were short and tight and full of the customary sparkle. 'Baba O'Riley' suffered (on the original video mix) from the synth backing tape being too loud and the guitar and lead vocal too low. Pete had switched his guitar here for a gold Les Paul. "There's another band playing at the end of the hall," Daltrey commented in response to the echoey sound on-stage – "And they're better than we are!" quipped John in response. Townshend gave a phony greeting to the cinema audiences prior to 'The Punk And The Godfather', which was agreeably powerful. A last minute substitution of 'My Wife' was then announced by John in place of 'Boris The Spider', and this song gave John and Pete their first chance to stretch out on some solos, with Pete particularly on form and Daltrey wearing a cap given to him by a member of the audience.

'Sister Disco' was given an enthusiastic performance by the band – rather odd for what clearly isn't an obvious classic, and for the first time the Pete/Roger 'Everly Brothers' duet at the end was captured on film, although the pair weren't sitting down on the drum platform. Pete played the loose, jazzy arpeggios with his right foot on his monitor. 'Behind Blue Eyes' featured a very prominent organ accompaniment from Rabbit from the second verse, and even on the faster riff section, the organ almost dominated with heavy chord work. Townshend then asked for a new guitar for 'Music Must Change', and played a natural wood Telecaster-shaped instrument that was rarely seen. The performance was confident and strong, with the brass section adding much to the jazzy feel of the organ break.

More sardonic comments from Pete followed: "I'd like to say hello to everybody in Acton..." he quips, and Daltrey added "and my mum." To which Pete responded with "And my mum back in Ealing Common." After a guitar change to a sunburst Les Paul, there followed 'Drowned' – the great, sprawling, ramshackle leviathan of a song, with Pete, John and Rabbit flying away merrily in the middle. 'Who Are You' which followed, however, went badly wrong towards the end and Pete took the blame. '5.15' saw Pete's fifth guitar of the evening being strapped on. The delicate introduction to 'Pinball Wizard' on Pete's guitar was a beautiful improvisation that led up to some ferocious strumming, while behind him Daltrey ran his mike around the underside of a cymbal.

'See Me Feel Me' was the only part of the tape where any kind of optical effects were used, and the screen was reduced to a circle fixed on Daltrey's head as he sang the opening part. Pete adopted a very casual, monotonous punk-like delivery for the verses of 'Long Live Rock' and even threw in a Chuck Berry duck-walk for good measure. 'My Generation' lost some pace because Kenney Jones stopped drumming before each of Roger's vocal lines – Keith used to continue drumming throughout, which maintained the drive of the song. The jamming towards the end incorporated snatches of 'Join Together' and 'Relay' in the ad-libbed vocals. It was great to hear The Who play 'I Can See For Miles' after all those years of utter neglect. The vocal harmonies didn't quite hit the immaculate feel of the record and for that reason it sounded a little strained. 'Sparks' was less tight than it might have been, with Pete playing fairly loosely, but breaking his string on the massive bottom E chord in the middle didn't help things. And so – after much doodling about by Pete (and a guitar change of course) – they reached 'Won't Get Fooled Again'. A decent version – powerful but agreeably messy. However, Rabbit's additional organ work was superfluous and at times annoying. During the quiet synthesiser section, Rabbit laid another organ solo over the top, which spoiled things a little.

Undoubtedly, the encore was the very best part of the whole show. Less structured than the main set, it consisted of a more spontaneous selection of favourites, perhaps unrehearsed, and certainly less polished than the set proper. A sparkling 'The Real Me' was cut rather short to make way for the lumbering but loveable 'Dancing In The Street'. This was the song where the brass section really proved its worth and justified its inclusion. Daltrey and Townshend seemed to be enjoying themselves mightily, and Pete contributed his impromptu 'Dance It Away' rap. From here, the encore became even more spontaneous – while the slower 'Dance It Away' beat was still pounding, Daltrey started to sing 'Young Man Blues', which didn't flow through very smoothly, but after a readjustment the band went full tilt for it one more time, albeit without any of the precision that characterised the *Leeds* version. "The old man's got all the oil," sang Daltrey in a neat variation, "all the gold. But we've got all the energy!" An equally uneasy transition followed into 'Road Runner', again rather abbreviated before Pete led into a more relaxed blues riff and intoned the line 'Big Boss Man'. This became, with Daltrey's singing, a mixture of 'I'm A Man' and 'Hoochie Coochie Man' – a kind of composite, all-purpose melange of cynical blues: not The Who's strong point but an interesting diversion nonetheless.

Finally, in the spirit of true improvisation there was seven minutes of high-energy thrash with 'How Can You Do It Alone', with entirely improvised lyrics by Pete, proving that an old dog like The Who can still feed on the adrenalin and excitement that will forever encapsulate the rock-'n'roll spirit. Pete barked out the lines between staccato riffs and brought off an epic climax after which Kenney Jones slumped forward over his kit. Ten years later, it would be called "Grunge". ('How Can You Do It Alone' was not the song that appeared on *Face Dances* under the same title, although some of the lyrical themes were similar.)

"It was most enjoyable, as we say in England," said Pete gormlessly, and after some larking about they left the stage after playing probably the best show of the whole tour. Marc Cohen, in *Who's News* No 8, 1980: "The Chicago Amphitheatre is a piss-hole of a different sort. Located next to what were the old Chicago stockyards, in a downright lousy part of town, and with terrible acoustics, it became transformed into a palace once The Who 'hit the stage'. The show was being aired live on closed circuit TV at several theatres across the city and the band played not only to their concert audience, but the theatre crowds as well. In other words, they hammed it up. The show was visually stunning. Many times Pete or Roger would move to the front of the stage and direct the cameramen to focus in close, then unleash a mike twirl or scissor kick for the hungry crowd... Backstage, Roger tells us the show might find its way out to the general public in videodisc form. He asks us if we liked the show with a devious smile, knowing full well how great it was for the band and crowd alike..."

Monday December 10
The Spectrum, Philadelphia, Pennsylvania

Again, authorities opened the doors at 6:30 pm in order to maintain control of the crowds as they entered the venue and made their way to their seats. This first night's show saw 'Trick Of The Light' reincorporated into the set but then immediately dropped again.

Tuesday December 11
The Spectrum, Philadelphia, Pennsylvania

Two nights here grossed $361,045 from a total of 39,134 fans. The two Philadelphia shows were professionally recorded.

Thursday December 13
Capital Centre, Largo, Maryland

The encore included a speeded up version of 'How Can You Do It Alone', followed by 'The Real Me'.

Saturday December 15
Memorial Coliseum, New Haven, Connecticut

The Who's first appearance in New Haven easily sold out all 10,670 seats. The 'Dancing In The Street/Dance It Away' medley and 'How Can You Do It Alone' were the encores. This show was professionally recorded.

Sunday December 16
Boston Garden, Boston, Massachusetts

The show was seen by a capacity crowd of 15,509. The encore consisted of 'Shakin' All Over', 'Big Boss Man' then into the 'Dancing In The Street'/'Dance It Away' medley which included a verse of 'Baby Don't You Do It'.

Monday December 17
Capital Centre, Largo, Maryland

Cancellation of the Providence, Rhode Island gig brought The Who back to the DC area for an added show. The Providence cancellation was the result of a city council vote denying the group use of the Civic Centre because of the Cincinnati tragedy.

Friday December 28
Hammersmith Odeon, Hammersmith, West London

Set: 'Substitute', 'I Can't Explain', 'Baba O'Riley', 'Punk And The Godfather', 'My Wife', 'Sister Disco', 'Behind Blue Eyes', 'Music Must Change', 'Drowned', 'Who Are You', '5.15', 'Pinball Wizard', 'See Me Feel Me', 'Long Live Rock', 'My Generation', 'I'm A Man'/ 'Hoochie Coochie Man', 'Sparks', 'I Can See For Miles', 'Fuck All Blues*', 'Won't Get Fooled Again', 'Summertime Blues', 'Dancing In The Street/Dance It Away', 'The Real Me'. (* 'Fuck All Blues' is what seems to be the most appropriate title of the blues jam played here, based upon Daltrey's words!)

Closing out the year, the band played as part of a series of Concerts For Kampuchea benefits with The Pretenders and The Specials on the bill. Professionally filmed and recorded, a four-song segment from The Who's set was heard on the Concerts For The People of Kampuchea album, released in March 1981.

The concert was shot on videotape and the resulting highlights surfaced on UK television as Rock For Kampuchea (ITV) on January 4, 1981. The programme featured 'Sister Disco', 'Behind Blue Eyes' and 'See Me, Feel Me'. 'Behind Blue Eyes' was later included on Thirty Years Of Maximum R&B Live (1994) in a slightly different version to the TV broadcast (having had various optical effects removed). When first contacted about this footage while researching the Thirty Years video, Nick Ryle was told that all the footage not included in the TV broadcast had been dumped, and it was therefore assumed that the complete performance had been irretrievably lost. However, Ryle discovered the video master tapes in Pete's film archive, although the accompanying 24-track sound tape was not located at that time, the videotape having only a rough "instant" sound mix dubbed on.

It's a great pity that The Who didn't play more UK shows in 1979, as this stands as probably the best concert they did in this country with Kenney Jones. The shows which the band played in 1981 and 1982 seemed to lack the epic forcefulness that was in evidence here. The atmosphere at the Hammersmith Odeon was clearly electric. The band were giving their services free and enjoyed a freedom and sense of fun missing from Chicago. For some reason, the band were set up right at the back of the stage at the small venue. Between the audience and the band was a gap of what looked like ten feet. When they came onstage, Daltrey immediately said he didn't like such a distance – "Bleedin' miles away".

From the outset, Pete was clearly out to have a good time. His face looked free from the weary burden of the US tour, replaced by a sardonic buoyancy. Yes, Pete knew that there were younger and sharper bands on the Kampuchea bill (The Clash, The Specials) and he knew The Who weren't offering any new material or burning ahead with a radical new vision. Their last London concert at Wembley Stadium four months previously wasn't entirely satisfactory. The Who could have been an embarrassment. (Indeed, by all accounts, Paul McCartney and Wings, on the following night, *were* an embarrassment.) But it seemed that The Who had a value and purpose (not making money) and Pete seemed intent on proving that (certain seniorities accepted) The Who could still bash it out with the best of them.

Immediately on plugging in, John and Pete hammered out a few random shards of noise

before settling into 'Substitute'. Noticeable from the very start, and positively annoying as the show went on, was Pete Townshend's black jacket. He had it unbuttoned and the right-hand front bottom edge of the jacket kept flapping down over the guitar strings, causing him to quickly tuck it back in behind his guitar. Every time he jumped or windmilled, the same thing happened. He missed chords and fluffed solos because of it. The jacket and playing on stage were obviously incompatible – yet he waited until after 'Drowned' before taking it off for good! 'I Can't Explain' was fine apart from a brief moment when the guitar cut out completely.

Daltrey then had another moan about the stage lay-out: "What is this here... Bloody awful isn't it? They're gonna build a moat round the next stage with barbed wire, machine guns..." "Piranhas," added John. Daltrey then told the audience they could sit up on the front of the stage if they wanted. In the wake of the Cincinnati tragedy, his heedless

words led to a frenzied audience charge to the front of the stage. Minutes later he had to tell them to sit back in their seats again, having been prompted by security staff. As at Chicago, Pete changed his black Scheckter for his No 3 gold Les Paul with capo. Rabbit was introduced and Townshend playfully bashed him over the head with a tambourine before indicating for 'Baba O'Riley' to start. Then Pete had cause to bend down near his amps, and the neck of his guitar accidentally struck the amp with a discordant thud. Pete viciously punched the tambourine in front of his mike, and in a reckless moment banged down onto the neck of the guitar hard with his left fist, which emitted another tuneless noise. When he came to play the first chord, the guitar was well out of tune, and although he tried to adjust it, it never recovered, effectively ruining the whole performance – witness the *Kampuchea* soundtrack album, which perversely included this song! Pete seemed to give up on the guitar towards the end and indulged instead in some idiot dancing.

"Listen," Pete told the audience after 'Baba' and a change of guitar, "we'd like to thank you all, really, and all the bands that are playing this week... I'll do my sermon a bit later on when I'm drunker. Aren't you glad you were born in London and not in poxy Kampuchea? This one's about London called 'The Punk And The Godfather'..." The performance of this classic song was rough but explosive, and Pete amended his verse to "... And yet I lived your future out, by pounding stages like a lout", rather than "clown". The final verse produced a mass of frenzied pogo-ing and fists flying upwards. Daltrey struggled at the top of his range on the stuttered "M-m-m-my G-g-generation" lines, but the overall effect of this neglected song was very positive.

Starting with Pete's high jumps as a count-in in front of the monitors, 'My Wife' turned into something special, and stretched out a few minutes longer than normal simply because it felt so good that the band obviously didn't want to stop. It wasn't musically perfect, however. During the first verse the band briefly got out of time, and John's vocals seemed miked a little too loud, resulting in him straying slightly off-key. But the solos were great, with Pete really going wild, playing half the time with his foot up on the monitor and the remainder with some manic dancing. Unusual for this song, the solo broke down into a much softer, sparse sound before Pete built it up again with a repeated power-chord riff. Pete's and Roger's dancing was incessant, hopping from one foot to the other with the driving rhythm. Rabbit, who started the song merely bashing a tambourine, joined in during the solo with some great piano work, which added considerably to the formidable beat. Townshend went through a spate of thrashing chords with his fingernails before a second quieter passage. Rabbit then switched from piano to a wah-wah organ sound, which was slightly less effective than the piano. The jam that had developed gave such an obvious buzz to the band that they all seemed to be enjoying themselves.

'Sister Disco' was serviceable but not spectacular, somewhat lightweight after 'My Wife'. "Getting on with it," said Pete, prior to 'Behind Blue Eyes', "is something we know all about." Kenney Jones was introduced next by Pete: "Great drummer, good friend, we call him our blood transfusion. He's done us a power of good.

Except I'm not into philosophy..." Pete also jokingly sang a line from The Small Faces' 'Lazy Sunday' before going on to introduce the brass section for 'Music Must Change'. A song which he said has "portentous lyrics. You toerags don't know what that means, do you? It means full of, like, potent meaning. I wasn't the only one who went to grammar school". He pointed to Daltrey. "He went to fucking grammar school as well! We're all intelligent... Well, we were. That's what went wrong!"

A different kind of mood was struck with 'Music Must Change' - Townshend approached the song with a casual air, cigarette in mouth, playing a few cool jazzy flourishes, before discarding the cigarette prior to his four lines of singing. An extended "music's an open door" passage ended with Daltrey's yell of "Change!" which was the jumping-off point for the improvisation. Townshend seemed musically fulfilled because The Who were simply doing something different. The fierce solo commenced with Rabbit taking the lead on the organ, and for a long while Pete was happy just to echo the basic riff. When Pete joined in, a real jazzy feel was achieved, much like the original.

A little-seen Les Paul (No.8) appeared for 'Drowned', which was performed in a very loose and at times sparse manner. Indeed, many passages had no guitar at all, and Pete danced to the interplay of Roger's mouth organ and the ever-inventive Entwistle bass lines. Pete ad-libbed a Cockney rap about Ian Dury (an old friend of The Who and fellow Kampuchea performer), before launching into a full-blast finale. Finally, after 'Drowned', Pete took off his jacket – no more fluffed chords or missed cues. A relief!

Some of the fluidity of feel that the band enjoyed during the previous two songs caught them out during 'Who Are You' where a greater degree of musical discipline was required: before the final verse there was some confusion as to where they should be, and they lost synchronisation with the backing tape for the remainder of the song. It isn't very noticeable but for whatever reason, John and Pete's "Who are, who are, who are..." harmonies were slightly off-key.

Pete then announced another *Quadrophenia* track and was met with a plethora of requests from the audience. He listened to the suggestions and said: "'Dr. Jimmy'? – that one we're acting. This one's one where – dare I say it – we'd never be able to play this without 'the big band'! We've got the big band now like The Specials. I mean there's less of us than them but we've got a few, you know, we've got a few. And we're gonna get more. Have hundreds of people all over us. Gonna replace the audience with string players and cellists and masochists and sadists." "Oh, no. I'm definitely leaving," responded Daltrey. '5.15' which followed had real drive and dynamics, with Pete dashing from one side of the stage to the other, thrashing hell out of his Les Paul No.9. This was a faultless display of power and control and featured probably the longest version of the song ever played: eight glorious minutes with no indulgent chaff. '5.15' was one of the highlights of the concert and far exceeded the Chicago version.

A few tantalising (and deceptive) snatches of 'I Am The Sea' could be heard before 'Pinball Wizard'. Daltrey sang, off-mike, "Is it me, for a moment?" and Pete followed this with 'Love Reign O'er Me' and finally 'Can You See The Real Me?' 'Pinball Wizard', like Chicago, featured an extended but less inspired guitar intro and a similarly improvised tailpiece, during which it became clear that Pete's guitar was slightly out of tune. Maybe because of this guitar defect (Pete didn't change it), 'See Me Feel Me' wasn't quite up to normal standards: John's vocal harmonies were pitched slightly flat, and Pete's between-verse solos were a mess. Whatever, the audience reacted wildly when the white spotlights were ignited.

A more casual approach was also in evidence with 'Long Live Rock'. Pete began casually with a few stop-start chords before the rhythm was established, and Rabbit joined in before Pete commenced his cynical, Cockney-styled vocals. The piano was fairly high in the mix but the song overall was not quite as focused as it might be. One main deviation was that instead of singing the last verse, Pete unexpectedly broke into a wild spate of windmilling for a few bars, before returning to sing his verse. In contrast, 'My Generation' started with real power and drive, as sharp as ever, until Pete's guitar lead fell out. John's solo bursts were twice as fast and even more breath-taking than usual (and that's saying something!). Finally, the song was driven by Kenney's staccato machine-gun snare drum riffs into a wild and reckless solo from Pete, playing with his right leg up on the drum platform. This eventually developed into a passage of very unusual chord blasts from the guitar, played high up on the fretboard, before moving into 'I'm A Man'. Daltrey sang the first verse correctly, then repeated the "I'm a man, now" refrain, and finally added a few lines of 'Hoochie Coochie Man'.

'Sparks' lacked its customary intensity. Pete was intent on a few tangents and variations, and threw in some different chord work, which somehow seemed to rob this great instrumental of some of its vigour. Indeed, at one point Pete repeated an unscheduled guitar phrase over and over, and John and Roger just stood watching him, wondering where the song was going to go next. A guitar string broke (see Chicago!) and 'Sparks' was closed with a quick guitar change for 'I Can See For Miles'. This song was being given a rare UK performance and was serviceable enough, with Pete hamming up his one note guitar solo. Too much of 'I Can See For Miles' relied

257

'Won't Get Fooled Again' with his bass drum beats.

A diffuse performance, 'Won't Get Fooled Again' was merely party-time for Pete. He just danced wildly during the first verse, hardly touching the guitar at all. The whole song sounded erratic and chaotic, with only odd passages of inspiration and excitement. Pete completely missed the cue for the third verse, still playing a solo which jarred horribly as the key changed from under him. Daltrey indulged in plenty of running and walking on the spot, as Pete mercilessly thrashed and banged uncoordinated noise from his guitar. The explosive final passage erupted with a sheet of white light that took the audience aback. Unfortunately, the band had lost the song completely: guitar, bass, synth were all out of sync with each other and Daltrey's "Meet the new boss" was greatly misplaced. So the song ended in chaos with no one really bothering anyway.

Minutes later the band were all standing at the front of the stage, Rabbit and Pete shaking hands and Roger dispensing drinks to the front row of the audience. The band lined up to formally acknowledge applause and Roger said: "Well, we had a good time anyway. We'll have some new stuff next year. We'll see you then." This seemed like a pretty definite end to the concert, but of course, the band returned. The Who playing encores was still a novelty but younger fans present wouldn't have known that they didn't ever play them.

After a long gap, the band did reappear, and Pete started a sparse rockabilly riff that eventually took shape as 'Summertime Blues'. It seemed only by chance that the bass and drums came in on time, so loose was Townshend's riff. The guitar solo was similarly idiosyncratic and as the song closed, the drums led straight into the epic 'Dancing In The Street' while Townshend changed his guitar. In addition to his guitar duties, Pete demonstrated various dances as the song progressed, before his long-promised 'sermon' is delivered:

upon vocal harmonies that demand just a little too much from the three vocalists in the band.

Listeners more familiar with blues would perhaps have been more able to appreciate 'Fuck All Blues'. It was not a familiar Who blues jam, being quite slow and featuring input from Rabbit. It began with some nice bluesy guitar doodles from Pete which the piano joined, and, shortly afterwards, pulled into shape a song which Daltrey could sing. Roger's vocals were inaudible to begin with, and he paced around in circles, repeating the lines "I don't wanna be an old man, cos' there ain't fuck all that's good about that." After one full verse, Townshend accelerated his chord work – perhaps signalling his boredom with the song – and used his mike stand to run up the fretboard while frantically strumming pure noise from all six strings of the guitar. After expunging his last stray impulses towards improvisation, he allowed Jones to cue in

"They say we've got nothing left,
They say we've used it all up.
You've got to scrap your car,
And turn your telly off.
You've gotta save it!

What you gonna do?
Turn off your electric guitar,
Turn off your electric guitar...
Now I come from a small neighbourhood,
I ain't used to dealing with no fucking Arabs,
I know what I need when I turn my television on:
Coronation Street, *Crossroads*, *Dallas*, *Top Of The Pops*,
That's about it really – *Mastermind*!"

And later Pete alluded more closely to the situation of Kampuchea: "You put your money down tonight and we appreciate it. Kids in boats out on the ocean, and no one'll take them in. I've felt like that all my life. I'm sure you have. They're our people. But don't worry about it. You can only do what you can do. Go out and have your fish and chips, have your pint, be happy. It's what you owe. You owe it to them. Come on, dance it away..."

The final performance, signalled by Pete's slashing guitar figure, was a tight, hard 'The Real Me'. This was the full length (unlike Chicago) version and Daltrey was in fine voice, despite being at the end of a gruelling performance. The song finished with a gloriously over-extended staccato climax, with Pete and Roger matching each other jump for jump. Eventually, after a cataclysmic crash of noise, the music cut out and the concert was truly over. Congratulations were offered all round and a fan ran onstage and stole one of Roger's tambourines.

The Who maintained their fairly heavy touring schedule throughout 1980, taking in a quick jaunt to Europe in late February followed by 18 dates in America. They returned to the States in June for 18 more gigs, adding an extra date in Toronto, Canada, which ended the tour on July 16.

Some of the adventurousness of the concerts of the year before had gone, and the band's set took on a fairly rigid shape, as follows: 'Substitute', 'I Can't Explain', 'Baba O'Riley', 'My Wife', 'Sister Disco', 'Behind Blue Eyes', 'Music Must Change', 'Dreaming From The Waist', 'Drowned', 'Who Are You', '5.15', 'Pinball Wizard', 'See Me, Feel Me', 'Long Live Rock', 'My Generation', 'I Can See For Miles', 'Sparks', 'Won't Get Fooled Again' and 'The Real Me'. Occasional performances during the tour – including jams, improvisations, encores and medleys – were: 'Dancing In The Street', 'Dance It Away', 'Pretty Vacant', 'Young Man Blues', 'You Belong To Us', 'Big Boss Man', 'Let's See Action', 'Magic Bus', 'Summertime Blues', 'Going Down', 'How Can You Do It Alone', 'Another Tricky Day', 'Twist And Shout', 'It's The End Of The Night', 'Punk And The Godfather', 'Relay', 'Shakin' All Over'.

Thursday March 27
Grugahalle, Essen, Germany

The Who began the new decade with a minitour of five European cities.

Friday March 28
Zurcher Hallenstadion, Zürich, Switzerland

Sunday March 30
Stadthalle, Vienna, Austria

Monday March 31
Festhalle, Munich, Germany

Tuesday April 1
Festhalle, Frankfurt, Germany

Police fought a running battle with fans at this, the last gig of the European tour. The brawl erupted when authorities arrested two American servicemen for allegedly selling drugs in the audience. Some of the injured received karate kicks to the head in the fracas and had to be taken to hospital. According to fans, security had been unusually tight at this show.

Monday April 14
PNE Coliseum, Vancouver, British Columbia, Canada

In response to one small ad in *The Vancouver Sun*, fans mailed in 800,000 requests for 3,200,000 tickets, even though there were only 16,000 seats available.

Concert box offices sent an affidavit to the *Guinness Book of Records* in London in recognition of the largest mail-order response in history for a single musical event.

And to really squeeze the hype, Switlo has asked His Worship Jack Volrich to declare Monday "Who Day" in Vancouver. That'll be the day.

Tuesday April 15
Seattle Center Coliseum, Seattle, Washington

The first-night crowd heard encores of 'Young Man Blues' and 'Dancing In The Street'.

Wednesday April 16
Seattle Center Coliseum, Seattle, Washington

Two sell-outs in Seattle grossed $319,100.

Friday April 18
Alameda County Coliseum, Oakland, California

The opening night in Oakland saw 'Summertime Blues' and 'Dancing In The Street' as the encore.

Saturday April 19
Alameda County Coliseum, Oakland, California

Sunday April 20
Alameda County Coliseum, Oakland, California

Three nights in Oakland grossed $459,293 from 41,199 fans.

Tuesday April 22
The Salt Palace, Salt Lake City, Utah

The Who played to a capacity crowd of 13,000 fans with an encore of 'Young Man Blues' and 'Dancing In The Street'. Surprisingly, they had not

An incredible display of physical stamina from lead singer Roger Daltrey (left) and guitar-playing nothing short of spectacular from Peter Townshend

sold out the arena on their last visit here in March 1976.

Wednesday April 23
McNichols Arena, Denver, Colorado
Two nights in Denver took in $422,943 from 35,461 fans.

Thursday April 24
McNichols Arena, Denver, Colorado

Saturday April 26
Kemper Arena, Kansas City, Missouri
A crowd of 16,782 paid $184,202 to see the band's first gig in Kansas City in five years.

Monday April 28
The Checkerdome, St. Louis, Missouri
Gross was $202,070 from 18,370 fans with The Pretenders as support act.

Tuesday April 29
Iowa State University Hilton Coliseum, Ames, Iowa
An estimated crowd of 14,000 fans watched a 110-minute performance.

Wednesday April 30
The Civic Center, St. Paul, Minnesota
The first of two shows in St. Paul was seen by 16,836 people.

Friday May 2
The Civic Center, St. Paul, Minnesota

Saturday May 3
International Amphitheatre, Chicago, Illinois
The Who returned to Chicago after only five months and easily sold out the 13,000-seat Amphitheatre.

Monday May 5
Maple Leaf Gardens, Toronto, Ontario, Canada
A total of 35,458 fans saw two shows in Toronto.

The Who
IN CONCERT
THE WHO
THE Gurus of Mod return to restore the faith, Monday and Tuesday, May 5 and 6 at Maple Leaf Gardens, 8 p.m.,

Tuesday May 6
Maple Leaf Gardens, Toronto, Ontario, Canada
Blackfoot were the opening act for both shows in Toronto and the following night in Montreal as well.

Wednesday May 7
The Forum, Montreal, Quebec, Canada
The closing night of the first half of the two-part 1980 American tour.

261

Wednesday June 18
San Diego Sports Arena, San Diego, California

The Who began their summer tour before a sell-out crowd of 14,217 fans. In a moment of exhilaration (or stupidity!), Pete punched a wall backstage after the show and broke several bones in his right hand. He wore a cast and large bandage for the rest of the tour but continued to thrill audiences with his inimitable windmill strum.

Friday June 20
The Forum, Los Angeles, California

The group sold out all seven shows in LA, performing for 112,200 people in nine days. The two Forum gigs were added to the schedule due to overwhelming ticket demand and the non-availability of the LA Sports Arena. (An off-road vehicle race and a dog show had been booked into the hall on the two nights required.)

Saturday June 21
The Forum, Los Angeles, California

Monday June 23
Sports Arena, Los Angeles, California

Tuesday June 24
Sports Arena, Los Angeles, California

Pete briefly left the stage for attention to his bandaged right hand but returned to play the rest of the show without interruption.

Thursday June 26
Sports Arena, Los Angeles, California

English group The Only Ones were the opening act in LA but were off the tour by the time it reached Tempe, Arizona.

Friday June 27
Sports Arena, Los Angeles, California

Saturday June 28
Sports Arena, Los Angeles, California

The Who closed their seven-night stand in Los Angeles.

Monday June 30
Arizona State University Activity Center, Tempe, Arizona

The show was interrupted at 10 pm by a power cut which was probably caused by the demand on electrical power to combat the extreme heat in the US during the summer of 1980. This was compounded by the fact the band were in Arizona in June!

Roger signed autographs and Pete mimed guitar playing on a broom for the crowd of 13,709 fans while power was being restored. The Who had promised that they would wait up to an hour and a half for the electricity to come back on, and come back on it did, exactly 90 minutes after the blackout. Willie Nile was the opening act on all subsequent dates of the tour except where noted.

Wednesday July 2
Reunion Arena, Dallas, Texas

The band delivered a dazzling display "of pure power rock" for the 19,012 fans who packed the Reunion Arena despite 100+ degree temperatures in Dallas that day.

Thursday July 3
University of Texas Frank C. Erwin Special Events Center, Austin, Texas
The band's sole Austin appearance was seen by 15,918 fans.

Saturday July 5
The Summit, Houston, Texas
A sell-out crowd of 16,505 paid $209,672 to see the first Who concert in Houston since November 1975.

Monday July 7
Louisiana State University Assembly Center, Baton Rouge, Louisiana
Surprisingly, this gig was not a complete sell-out, although only 1,000 seats were left unoccupied.

Wednesday July 9
The Omni, Atlanta, Georgia
The crowd gave a ten-minute standing ovation and were rewarded with an encore, appropriate in the sultry heat, of 'Summertime Blues'.

Thursday July 10
Mid-South Coliseum, Memphis, Tennessee
The Who performed for 11,999 paying customers at the Coliseum, one of the smallest venues on the 1980 tour.

Friday July 11
University of Kentucky Rupp Arena, Lexington, Kentucky
The group attracted 20,713 spectators to the cavernous Rupp Arena.

Sunday July 13
Greensboro Coliseum, Greensboro, North Carolina
A crowd of 13,761 jammed the Coliseum.

Monday July 14
Hampton Coliseum, Hampton Roads, Virginia
The summer tour was supposed to conclude in Hampton Roads but the group headed to Toronto for an added date on the 16th. The Hampton Coliseum was filled to capacity with 10,628 fans for a take of $124,777 at the gate.

Wednesday July 16
CNE Stadium, Toronto, Ontario, Canada
The Who added an extra date in Toronto at the end of the tour despite Pete's broken hand. A crowd of 70,003 fans turned out, and hundreds suffered heat exhaustion as the hottest summer in 50 years made even Ontario sizzle. Heart, The J. Geils Band and Nash The Slash were also on the bill.

A drastic restructuring of the act meant that the set on the 1981 British tour contained more new material from the *Face Dances* LP, released March 6. The album reached the number two spot in the UK album charts and a highly creditable number four in the States. Unfortunately, this tour coincided with a bleak period in Pete Townshend's life when alcohol and heroin addiction began to blight his performances. Amazingly enough, Pete always played well, even on a bad night, but he seemed to try the patience of his fellow band members with tangential diversions and solos inserted in unexpected places! His contempt for The Who and what it had become seemed barely disguised.

The basic set was 'Substitute', 'I Can't Explain', 'Baba O'Riley', 'The Quiet One', 'Don't Let Go The Coat', 'Sister Disco', 'Music Must Change', 'You Better You Bet', 'Drowned', 'Another Tricky Day', 'Behind Blue Eyes', 'Pinball Wizard', 'Punk And The Godfather', 'Who Are You', '5.15', 'Long Live Rock', 'My Generation', 'Won't Get Fooled Again', 'Twist And Shout'. More occasional performances, jams, medleys and encores included 'Dreaming From The Waist', 'Did You Steal My Money', 'The Real Me', 'Dancing In The Street', 'Dance It Away', 'Let's See Action', 'Naked Eye', 'How Can You Do It Alone', 'Bargain', 'You Stand Naked', 'See Me, Feel Me', 'Young Man Blues', 'My Wife', 'Magic Bus', 'Summertime Blues'.

THE WHO 1981

playing two nights in most cities on the tour due to the small capacity of the halls.

Sunday January 25
Granby Halls, Leicester

The Who began their most extensive tour of Britain ever. While they had played arenas of 10,000 seats or more in America, they chose to play in theatres for this tour of their homeland, much to the chagrin of volume-loving John Entwistle. According to *Melody Maker* reviewer Lynden Barber, the group performed a new song called 'Just Another Chicken'! Support act was Paul Young's band, The Q-Tips.

Monday January 26
City Hall, Sheffield

Friday January 30
Cornwall Coliseum, St. Austell

The Who were the first band to play this venue;

Saturday January 31
Cornwall Coliseum, St. Austell

Tuesday February 3
Rainbow Theatre, Finsbury Park, London

The Who added this date to their UK tour, a charity concert for Erin Pizzey's Chiswick Family Rescue Organisation. The Who donated their services free, tickets were priced at five pounds and special arrangements were made with the Rainbow to keep expenses to a minimum.

Richard Evans: "This was a great Who gig! They announced it at the last minute on Capitol Radio the afternoon before. Mod kids were camped out all night on the pavement outside the Rainbow in the pissing rain waiting for the tickets to go on sale at 10 o'clock the following morning. Me and (Who employee) Chris Chappel picked up a pile of Who albums from Trinifold (The Who's office) and went down and handed them out to the fans. We were like The Who's meals-on-wheels!"

Wednesday February 4
Rainbow Theatre, Finsbury Park, London

Saturday February 7
Conference Centre, Brighton

Sunday February 8
Odeon Theatre, Lewisham, London
   The Who literally 'brought the house down' as the following week, the cinema was demolished!

Monday February 9
Odeon Theatre, Lewisham, London

Saturday February 14
Apollo Centre, Glasgow, Scotland

Sunday February 15
Apollo Centre, Glasgow, Scotland

Thursday February 19
Playhouse Theatre, Edinburgh, Scotland

Friday February 20
Playhouse Theatre, Edinburgh, Scotland

PLAYHOUSE THEATRE
Greenside Place
Edinburgh
Friday
20 Feb. 1981
at 7.30 pm
Doors Open 6.30 pm
HARVEY GOLDSMITH by arrangement with TRINIFOLD LTD. presents
THE WHO
IN CONCERT
PLUS SUPPORT
STALLS **£5.00**
INC. VAT
No Ticket Exchanged or Money Refunded—Retain this portion
R 16

Tuesday February 24
City Hall, Newcastle
   The Who were supported by The Ruts for the first of two shows in the 2,385-seat City Hall.

Wednesday February 25
City Hall, Newcastle
   Supported by The Ruts.

Saturday February 28
Deeside Leisure Centre, Deeside
   One of the larger venues of the tour with an audience of 6,400. Nine Below Zero were on the bill as opening act.
   John Atkins: "A very rough capacity audience had gathered in the Deeside ice rink (covered in mats for the evening) and included a fair number of teenage Mods from Liverpool, who were clustered in small gangs at the front in anticipation of witnessing their gods for the first time. As soon as the band came on, Pete Townshend was noticeably drunk but for the whole evening his guitar playing was flawless. From the moment 'Substitute' started, the young Mods were pogoing in a reckless frenzy that resulted in a few minor injuries. Pete played up to them by saying that he'd heard the area was a bit of a Mod stronghold. The pace and quality of the show dropped briefly because no one really wanted to hear 'Don't Let Go The Coat' or 'Another Tricky Day' but the final hour offered classic after classic. Even on possibly their worst tour The Who were strong and memorable. The sound, lighting and laser effects, I was told by another member of the audience, required special permission from the National Grid to supply extra power for the evening!"

Sunday March 1
The Apollo Theatre, Manchester
   The Who celebrated Roger's 37th birthday with the first night of two shows in Manchester's 2,645-seat Apollo. Support act was The Ruts.

Monday March 2
The Apollo Theatre, Manchester

Thursday March 5
National Exhibition Centre (NEC), Birmingham

Friday March 6
NEC, Birmingham

Monday March 9
Wembley Arena, Wembley, North London

Tuesday March 10
Wembley Arena, Wembley, North London

Richard Evans

THE WHO
INVITE YOU TO A LUNCHEON PARTY
at
SEARCY'S
30 Pavilion Road London SW3
at 12-30 pm, on Wednesday 11th March

TO CELEBRATE THE RELEASE OF

Face Dances.

Featuring
A special viewing of the original portrait.

Wednesday March 11
Wembley Arena, Wembley, North London

During the day The Who held a 'luncheon party' for the press to launch *Face Dances* at Searcy's in Pavilion Road, Knightsbridge. The album cover artwork was on display prior to it's showing at the Tate Gallery. Many of the various artists who contributed to the album cover attended the party which was a strange mix of music biz people and the fine art world.

Saturday March 14
Gaumont Cinema, Southampton

Sunday March 15
Gaumont Cinema, Southampton

Monday March 16
Arts Centre, Poole, Dorset

Last show of the UK tour.

Saturday March 28
Grugahalle, Essen, Germany

The Who and The Grateful Dead appeared on *Rockpalast*, the popular Eurovision programme broadcast on WDR, starting at 10:30 pm. After The Who's set, Pete joined the Dead onstage for a lengthy jam as the programme ended at 5:30 in the morning. The show also went out live on BBC Radio 1 and on BBC 2's *The Old Grey Whistle Test*.

The Who had planned a European tour in May but all subsequent dates were cancelled.

Saturday May 30
Brockwell Park, Brixton, South London

Pete played a solo show in support of a march against unemployment in Britain. The set: 'A Little Is Enough' (performed twice due to sound problems), 'Cats In The Cupboard', 'Big Boss Man', 'Substitute', 'Corrine Corrina', 'Body Language', 'Join Together', 'Let My Love Open The Door'.

The band comprised: Neil Abbot (guitar), Mark Brzezicki (drums), Tony Butler (bass), Peter Hope-Evans (harmonica), and making a surprise appearance on vocals on 'Substitute', former Traffic drummer Jim Capaldi.

The final year in continuous Who history, 1982 was a curious mixture for fans. Recording began in June at Glyn Johns' Turn Up-Turn Down Studios for what was to become The Who's final studio album. With Pete now weaned off the drink and drugs that almost killed him, The Who were able to sustain a series of very tight, smooth and musically stable concerts that, again, incorporated a high percentage of songs from their current *It's Hard* LP, released on September 4, which made number 11 in the U.K and number eight in the US. While the concerts suggested no obvious single point of criticism, they sounded sterile and bland for a band whose live reputation was built upon unpredictability and spontaneous musical combustion. The biggest surprise was not what they played, but what they didn't play: the first 23 shows of the year managed well without 'My Generation'!

The basic set was as follows: 'Substitute', 'I Can't Explain', 'Dangerous', 'Sister Disco', 'The Quiet One', 'It's Hard', 'Eminence Front', 'Behind Blue Eyes', 'Drowned', 'Cry If You Want', 'Who Are You', 'Pinball Wizard', 'See Me, Feel Me', '5.15', 'Love Reign O'er Me', 'Long Live Rock', 'Won't Get Fooled Again', 'Twist And Shout'. More occasional inclusions were: 'My Generation', 'I'm One'/'The Punk And The Godfather', 'A Man Is A Man', 'Tattoo', 'I Can See For Miles', 'Dr. Jimmy', 'Boris The Spider', 'Love Ain't For Keeping', 'Naked Eye', 'Squeeze Box', 'Magic Bus', 'Young Man Blues', 'I Saw Her Standing There', 'Athena', 'Cooks County', 'Summertime Blues', 'Join Together' and a brief snatch of 'Happy Jack'. (During stage performances of 'Eminence Front', Roger played guitar for the first time since the early days of The Detours.)

A lengthy American tour was to begin in September playing the biggest indoor arenas and outdoor stadiums. Tim Gorman, who played piano and synthesiser on *It's Hard* played keyboards on the whole tour. Part one ended in Tempe, Arizona on October 31 with the second leg scheduled to open on November 26 in Atlanta but switched to the next day in Orlando, Florida. The trek ended in Toronto, Canada on December 17 with a major pay-per-view event on cable television broadcast all over America.

The Who had called it a day but this wasn't made official until a year later when Pete Townshend issued a press statement to formally announce his departure from the group.

Tuesday July 21
Dominion Theatre, London
Pete played another gig away from The Who when he joined Robert Plant, Kate Bush, Gary Brooker, Phil Collins and others for the Prince's Trust Gala Benefit at the Dominion Theatre. Townshend took centre stage for three songs, 'Let My Love Open The Door', 'Amoreuse' and 'Slit Skirts', playing piano on the last number.

Friday September 10
NEC, Birmingham
It had been more than 17 months since The Who played a live concert, the longest break from stage work they had ever taken. These two shows were scheduled as a warm-up for the forthcoming American "farewell" tour.

On both Birmingham shows, The Who were

supported by Midnight Oil. John Atkins: "Who fans of all ages gathered for this show, including several parents and children. At least one member of the audience proudly displayed a 1973 tour T-shirt! The atmosphere of the show was terrific and I think many people sensed that this would be the last time they might see the band. Pete told the audience that The Who would be doing a "proper British tour next year", but of course they never did. They sounded immaculate and powerful, and gave great hope for the future, displaying none of the apathy that seemed to set in mid-way through the subsequent US tour. It was really a last gasp for the band, of course. It just happened to be a good night from an era when they had stopped having good or bad nights and performances now merged into a highly regulated uninspired stability.

"Once again, Pete was on top form, playing stupendous solos. This was the first show where Roger played guitar – unfortunately it was hardly noticeable! I thought the flash bombs that exploded at the start of 'Won't Get Fooled Again' were wholly unnecessary; this band never needed such things in the past. Some fans, I know, just couldn't believe they'd witnessed a Who show without hearing 'My Generation'. Post-concert entertainment was provided immediately afterwards in the grounds of the National Exhibition Centre. Several exuberant (male) fans stripped naked and swam towards the centre of a huge ornamental lake and succeeded in stopping a giant water fountain. The Who makes people do some odd things!"

Saturday September 11
NEC, Birmingham
This show was originally scheduled for Thursday September 9, but switched due to date availability.

Wednesday September 22
Capital Centre, Largo, Maryland
The Who began their Farewell tour of America with two dates just outside Washington, DC. David Johansen, formerly of The New York Dolls, opened the shows.

The basic set for the tour was: 'Substitute', 'I Can't Explain', 'Dangerous', 'Sister Disco', 'The Quiet One', 'It's Hard', 'Eminence Front', 'Behind Blue Eyes', 'Baba O'Riley', 'I'm One/Punk and

The Godfather', 'Drowned', 'A Man Is A Man', 'Cry If You Want', 'Who Are You', 'Pinball Wizard', 'See Me, Feel Me', '5:15', 'Love Reign O'er Me', 'Long Live Rock', 'Won't Get Fooled Again'. Encores included 'Naked Eye', 'Athena', 'Squeeze Box', 'Magic Bus', 'Young Man Blues', 'Summertime Blues' and 'Twist And Shout'.

Thursday September 23
Capital Centre, Largo, Maryland
A total of 37,600 fans saw the two Largo shows, grossing $564,000.

Saturday September 25
JFK Stadium, Philadelphia, Pennsylvania
Two shows had been booked into the massive football stadium but the first, set for Friday September 24, was cancelled due to lack of sales. In spite of this, the group performed for 91,451 people when they took the stage at 3:55 pm for the one and only concert on Saturday afternoon. Opening acts were Santana and The Clash.
This show grossed $1,440,353.

Sunday September 26
Rich Stadium, Orchard Park, New York
A crowd of 85,000 fans attended for a gross of $1,200,000 breaking all previous house records. A 1:30 pm start with opening acts The Clash and David Johansen. Rain fell during '5:15' and highlighted an inspired version of 'Love Reign O'er Me'. When the song was over, Roger looked up to the skies and shouted "Him! The greatest effect in the world! Even The Stones couldn't afford that one!"

Who shows no signs of f-f-f-fading away

Tuesday September 28
Civic Arena, Pittsburgh, Pennsylvania
The attendance of 17,200 grossed $257,000. The band gave a two-hour and 15-minute performance here for a sell-out crowd, "playing like there was no tomorrow". They had dropped 'A Man Is A Man' in favour of 'Naked Eye' and moved 'Athena' back to the encore. Pete was in fine form, playing blazing solos and slashing his guitar with particular fury. Again, the opening act was David Johansen.

to catch it as it fell back to the stage.

The two shows grossed $541,035 from a total of 36,496 people. T. Bone Burnett took on the opening slot for the two Horizon dates as well as the following concert in Louisville.

Wednesday September 29
Market Square Arena, Indianapolis, Indiana

Another sell-out with 15,500 in attendance, grossing $231,630, with David Johansen as the opening act.

Thursday September 30
The Silverdome, Pontiac, Michigan

A capacity crowd of 75,000 people attended this show for a gross of $1,119,000. The Clash and Eddie Money were the support acts.

Saturday October 2
The Civic Center, St. Paul, Minnesota

More than 17,000 people saw the first of two shows in the Twin Cities.

Sunday October 3
The Civic Center, St. Paul, Minnesota

Surprisingly, the band had scheduled two dates in the Twin Cities even though it had never really been one of their strongest markets. Not surprisingly, the second show did not sell out.

Tuesday October 5
The Horizon, Rosemont, Illinois

'Athena' was back in the set after a two-gig absence. Pete broke a string on one of his guitars during '5:15' so he sang the guitar riff at the end of the song and sent the instrument hurling upwards towards the lights, making no attempt

Wednesday October 6
The Horizon, Rosemont, Illinois

The band played 'Cooks County' instead of 'It's Hard' as the sixth song in the show, the only time it was played on the entire tour. Pete had written the song after seeing a television special about Cook County Hospital. (Chicago is in Cook County.)

Thursday October 7
Freedom Hall, Louisville, Kentucky

A crowd of 18,337 fans packed Freedom Hall. Gate receipts were $271,755. By all accounts, this was one of the most unruly audiences of the whole tour. The show opened with 'My Generation' then followed with 'Substitute' and 'I Can't Explain'.

Saturday October 9
CNE Stadium, Toronto, Ontario, Canada

John Entwistle celebrated his 38th birthday with 68,000 fans at a show that was only added to the itinerary after the date near Buffalo on September 26. Gross was $1,280,000. Joe Jackson was the opening act.

Sunday October 10
The Meadowlands, Brendan Byrne Arena, East Rutherford, New Jersey

Another date added to the tour. The band continued to experiment with the set list with 'My Generation' as the opener and 'Substitute' placed between 'Long Live Rock' and 'Won't Get Fooled Again'. Dropped from the set were 'I'm One' and 'The Punk And The Godfather'. The show attracted 20,062 fans, grossing $315,453. David Johansen appeared as the opening act on all three New York area concerts.

Tuesday October 12
Shea Stadium, New York City, New York

The Who were the first rock band to play Shea Stadium since Jethro Tull in 1976. All 72,000 seats sold out in under two hours! The fastest selling show in the history of the Ticketron agency. Promoter Ron Delsener had to put in an additional 24,000 tickets on general admission giving people access onto the grass playing field.

'A Man Is A Man' was back in the set with 'My Generation' replacing 'I'm One/ Punk And The Godfather'. The Clash opened both shows and Roger wore silver and gold lamé suits on consecutive nights.

Wednesday October 13
Shea Stadium, New York City, New York

The band dropped 'A Man Is A Man' in favour of the surprise selection 'Tattoo'. The encore was comprised of 'Young Man Blues', 'Naked Eye', 'I Saw Her Standing There' with John on lead vocal, 'Summertime Blues' and 'Twist And Shout'. During the show, Roger pointed to his silver suit and remarked "The Beatles wore suits when they played here so now I'm wearing mine!" Total gate receipts were $2,200,000 for the two Shea Stadium dates.

On Friday October 22, *Newsnight* (BBC 2) broadcast a report on The Who's concerts at Shea Stadium, featuring live footage and Robin Denselow's interview with the band.

Friday October 15
University of Northern Iowa Uni-Dome, Cedar Falls, Iowa

Attendance totalled 23,729, grossing $352,170, with Novo Combo as the support act.

Sunday October 17
Colorado University Folsom Field, Boulder, Colorado

Boulder had already seen snowfall earlier in the month but the weather was agreeable on the day of the show as The Who attracted 60,000 fans for a gross of $960,000. 'A Man Is A Man' was back in the set in place of 'Tattoo', and 'Substitute' came after 'See Me, Feel Me' with 'My Generation' still in the opening spot. Opening acts were Jethro Tull and John Cougar.

Wednesday October 20
The Kingdome, Seattle, Washington

The city of Seattle had a municipal ordinance that performances could not begin before 7 pm, hence the odd starting time of 7:01 pm. Fans did get to hear 'I Can See For Miles' in the set.

Thursday October 21
Memorial Coliseum, Portland, Oregon

This was one of the smallest venues The Who played on the whole two-part tour, and they easily sold out all 11,000 seats. Roger seemed to be bothered by throat trouble and walked off stage when Pete began his solo during 'Cry If You Want'. Unaware that Roger had left, Pete sung the last line himself and announced "a short intermission". He returned to the stage to say that "Roger had a lot of pain in his throat" and they were going to take a short break. After about 15 minutes, they returned with Roger and finished the show.

Saturday October 23
Alameda County Stadium, Oakland, California

The Who played two shows in the Bay Area, an outdoor stadium date in front of 60,300 fans and a show in a smaller indoor arena for a crowd of 14,372. Total gross for the two dates was $1,269,424. The first-night crowd heard 'Let's See Action', played only this one time during the whole tour, right after 'Magic Bus'. T. Bone Burnett and The Clash opened the show.

Monday October 25
Alameda County Coliseum, Oakland, California

The second Bay Area gig saw the longest show of the tour as well as the last performances of 'Athena' and 'A Man Is A Man'. During the encore, at the beginning of 'Young Man Blues' a sign was brought out and placed in front of Bob Pridden's mixing desk. It read: "This space is reserved for the Employee Of The Month." Roger then announced that the prize was a one-way ticket back to England.

Wednesday October 27
Jack Murphy Stadium, San Diego, California

The group continued their west coast swing with a near sell-out in San Diego, attracting a crowd of 51,771. Gross was $776,565. The gig was professionally videotaped but never aired on television or made available for home video purchase. Supporting acts were John Cougar (Mellencamp) and Loverboy.

Friday October 29
Los Angeles Memorial Coliseum, Los Angeles, California

The group attracted 93,000 fans to this gigantic football stadium. Gross was $1,365,415. The show

included 'Tattoo' and 'I Can See For Miles', the first time that two songs from *The Who Sell Out* had been played onstage since 1968. Supporting acts were T. Bone Burnett and The Clash.

Sunday October 31
Arizona State University Sun Devil Stadium, Tempe, Arizona

The band closed the first half of the Farewell Tour with a stadium show in the Phoenix area at 6pm. Unlike all but two other dates on the tour, this concert did not sell out. Capacity was 65,000 but only 44,132 seats were sold. A total of $754,657 was grossed. Supporting again were John Cougar and Loverboy.

Saturday November 27
The Tangerine Bowl, Orlando, Florida

The band kicked off part two of the Farewell Tour with a show before a sell-out crowd of 65,000 people for a gross of $1,018,946. The B-52's opened the show but were booed off after only 25 minutes, followed by Joan Jett and The Blackhearts. 'Substitute' was dropped entirely in favour of 'My Generation', and 'Squeeze Box' made a surprise appearance as an encore.

Monday November 29
Rupp Arena, Lexington, Kentucky
A crowd of 23,000 people packed the Arena and heard encores of 'Naked Eye/Squeeze Box'.

Tuesday November 30
Jefferson Civic Center Coliseum, Birmingham, Alabama
Some 13,000 people paid $254,000 on this date, the first time The Who had played Birmingham since July 1967. Roger jokingly remembered that "only about 100 people turned up" for that first performance.

Wednesday December 1
Mississippi Gulf Coast Coliseum, Biloxi, Mississippi
Total gate receipts were $223,320 from an audience of 13,000 who heard a 75-second snippet of 'Love Ain't For Keeping', the first (however brief) rendition since 1971.

Friday December 3
The Astrodome, Houston, Texas
The stadium was not sold out, although the crowd numbered about 60,000 fans for a gross of $1,050,000. Radio stations in Dallas and Houston bought up all the remaining tickets ensuring no loss of gross revenues. Supporting acts were Billy Squier and Steel Breeze.

Saturday December 4
The Cotton Bowl, Dallas, Texas
Pete smashed his guitar at this show, the only occasion on which he did so on the whole Farewell Tour. By all accounts, this was the most problematic gig of the trek because of the cold wind playing havoc with guitar tunings. The weather may also have accounted for the 13,389 empty seats but 66,661 fans were still present for a gross of $1,165,698.
Opening acts for the 2 pm performance were Billy Squier and Steel Breeze.

Monday December 6
The Checkerdome, St. Louis, Missouri
The band earned $274,440 from 12,564 paying customers.
'Dr. Jimmy' was added to the set after 'Baba O'Riley' but 'Cry If You Want' was dropped, the only time this occurred on the tour.

Tuesday December 7
Milwaukee Arena, Milwaukee, Wisconsin
The Who added this gig to the itinerary after WQFM DJ Tim 'The Rock'n'Roll Animal' spent 14 days, 15 hours and 57 minutes on a tenth floor window ledge until the group agreed to play in Milwaukee. He had collected 75,000 signatures petitioning the band to come to the city and it was Roger who called the DJ to announce that The Who would play. The band arrived in the city at

around 7 pm and left for Chicago at 1 am, immediately after the show.

Wednesday December 8
The Horizon, Rosemont, Illinois

A crowd of 18,195 jammed the Horizon for this return date to the Chicago area for a gross of $267,750. 'Love Ain't For Keeping' made a 95 second appearance (with Roger on guitar) and Pete tagged on a rockabilly ending to 'Long Live Rock' which, until this gig, had been played in a slowed-down blues style.

Friday December 10
The Carrier Dome, Syracuse, New York

The Who set house attendance and house gross records at the Carrier Dome as 47,716 turned out for the show. Earnings tallied $711,374 with David Johansen as the opening act.

Saturday December 11
The Centrum, Worcester, Massachusetts

A sell-out crowd of 12,907 paid out $202,112 for the band's only New England date of the entire 1982 tour. About 3,500 people milled around outside the venue trying in vain to buy tickets.

Monday December 13
Richfield Coliseum, Cleveland, Ohio

A crowd of 18,500 fans saw the first of two nights in Cleveland with Little Steven & The Disciples of Soul as opening act for both nights.

Tuesday December 14
Richfield Coliseum, Cleveland, Ohio

Thursday December 16
Maple Leaf Gardens, Toronto, Ontario, Canada

The last two nights of the Farewell Tour. Both shows were taped in case there were problems with the second night's live broadcast. There was no opening act for these dates and both concerts started at 10 pm.

'Love Ain't For Keeping' finally went over the two-minute mark on the second night. Previously unreleased recordings of 'It's Hard', 'Eminence

Front', Dangerous' and 'Cry If You Want' from these shows appeared on the 1997 CD reissue of *It's Hard*.

Friday December 17
Maple Leaf Gardens, Toronto, Ontario, Canada

The final appearance of the Farewell Tour was broadcast over pay-per-view systems in the US

Roger Daltrey leads The Who into a two-night farewell in Toronto's Maple Leaf Gardens. Group says it won't tour again. Story, Page E7.

and Canada. Two shows in Toronto grossed $C 571,520 from a combined audience of 28,576 – a house gross record.

The live album *Who's Last* was recorded at this concert, as was the home video release *The Who Rocks America*.

Saturday July 13
"Live Aid", Wembley Stadium, London

The Who reunited to take part alongside dozens of other big acts in the greatest live televised rock event in history; performing 'My Generation', 'Pinball Wizard', 'Love Reign O'er Me', and 'Won't Get Fooled Again' for 75,000 people at Wembley Stadium and a world-wide TV audience of over 100,000,000.

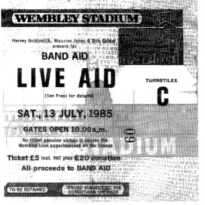

Unfortunately, the band were under-rehearsed and played a less than inspired set, despite the fact that they were given a prestigious time slot in the early evening. The live transmission broke down during the first song (the only time it did so during the day) and John's Alembic bass went on the blink, further contributing to the sub-standard performance. During 'Won't Get Fooled Again' Pete lost his balance after aiming a kick over his microphone stand (something he had always been able to execute with faultless precision in the past) and Roger also fell over, heightening the emotion and to a certain extent covering Pete's slip-up. As if to make matters even worse, the band appeared to lose their way during the song, and ran over the strict time limit.

At the end of the show, while Paul McCartney sang 'Let It Be' at the piano, Pete reappeared on stage with David Bowie and Alison Moyet. Townshend and McCartney then hoisted Bob Geldof, the inspiration behind the affair, onto their shoulders.

Later in the year Pete played two shows at London's Brixton Academy, both of which were recorded and videotaped for home video release as well as a show in Cannes and a benefit show at the Royal Albert Hall, early in '86. Roger also played solo dates with a short tour of the east coast of America in December '85.

Monday February 8
Royal Albert Hall, Kensington, London

The Who were honoured with a Lifetime Achievement Award at the British Phonographic Industry (BPI) Awards ceremony. Appearing live, they performed ragged versions of 'My Generation', 'Substitute', and 'Who Are You' but the transmission was cut off during the latter song as it overran into the 9 pm news bulletin. Angry words were exchanged backstage, particularly from Pete who had been forced to dash from his daughter Aminta's side after she had been rushed to hospital earlier that day suffering from a serious viral infection.

This was Kenney Jones's last appearance with The Who.

John undertook a lengthy American club tour in July and August. He had previously done a short string of East Coast gigs the year before with a band called Rat Race Choir.

A quarter of a century had passed since the formation of The Who, and 20 years since the release of *Tommy*. The three original members of the group decided to observe the twofold celebration with a massive tour of the US. Joined by drummer Simon Phillips (who had played with Pete on his solo albums and shows), they were augmented by no less than 11 other musicians. As Pete commented from the stage on various dates, "We have the enormous cheek, the unmitigated gall to call this The Who." It wasn't, of course; it was a golden oldies show, songs The Who used to play performed by three blokes who used to be in The Who. Ironically, in view of their distinguished past, it was the most financially lucrative tour they ever undertook.

The 'Kids Are Alright' tour played to big crowds in big stadiums in big cities for big money. True to the celebratory nature of the tour, the band performed material from deep within their back catalogue as well as favourite covers and a few songs from Pete's solo albums. In New York and Los Angeles, the band performed *Tommy* in its entirety. The Radio City Music Hall concert on June 27 was broadcast live on the Westwood One FM radio network, the LA show taped for home video release. Both these events raised considerable sums for charity.

The Who ensemble certainly gave audiences their money's worth. Most shows ran for three hours or longer. Drummer Simon Phillips, in particular, was a shot in the arm to the overall sound. His thunderous but pinpoint style gave the group the kick it needed, something that had been lacking with Kenney Jones's more rudimentary approach.

For the 40 performances, The Who rehearsed a colossal 70 songs, playing on average 35 songs per show. A wide variety of cover versions were also included. Each show started with *Tommy*, usually 'Overture', '1921', 'Amazing Journey', 'Sparks', 'Acid Queen', 'Pinball Wizard', 'Do You Think It's Alright?', 'Fiddle About', 'I'm Free', 'Tommy's Holiday Camp', 'We're Not Gonna Take It', and 'See Me, Feel Me'.

For the special charity gala concerts of June 27, August 24, October 31 and November 2, *Tommy* also included 'Eyesight To The Blind', 'Christmas', 'Cousin Kevin', 'There's A Doctor', 'Go To The Mirror', 'Smash The Mirror', 'Tommy Can You Hear Me', 'Miracle Cure', 'Sensation' and 'Sally Simpson'.

Other basic staples of the act were 'I Can't Explain', 'Substitute', 'I Can See For Miles', 'My Generation', 'Magic Bus', 'Who Are You', 'Baba O'Riley', '5.15', 'Love Reign O'er Me', 'Sister Disco', 'Join Together', 'You Better You Bet', 'Behind Blue Eyes', 'Won't Get Fooled Again', 'Trick Of The Light', 'Boris The Spider' and 'My Wife'. Also regularly performed was the Pete Townshend solo material: 'A Friend Is A Friend', 'A Little Is Enough', 'Rough Boys' and 'Face The Face'. Less frequent performances were given of 'Pictures Of Lily', 'Mary Anne With The Shaky Hand', 'I'm A Boy', 'Tattoo', 'Naked Eye', 'Too Much Of Anything', 'I'm One', 'Eminence Front', 'The Real Me', the Townshend solo songs 'I Won't Run Anymore', 'All Shall Be Well', 'Give Blood', 'Let My Love Open The Door', 'Secondhand Love', 'Dig' and John Entwistle's solo song 'Too Late The Hero'. Cover versions played were 'Save It For Later' (The Beat), 'Hey Joe' (styled after the slow Jimi Hendrix Experience version), 'Summertime Blues' (Eddie Cochran), 'Love Hurts' (Everly Brothers), 'Born On The Bayou' (Creedence Clearwater Revival), 'Barefootin'' (Robert Parker), 'Shakin' All Over' (Johnny Kidd And The Pirates), 'I'm A Man' (Bo Diddley) and 'Night Train' (James Brown).

Wednesday June 21
Glens Falls Civic Center, Glens Falls, New York

Reunited for the 25th Anniversary tour, the augmented Who kicked off the summer long jaunt with a show in this small town in upstate New York. This was one of the very few shows they would play in venues with under 10,000 seats, and was drummer Simon Phillips first performance with The Who.

Friday June 23
CNE Stadium, Toronto, Ontario, Canada

The band attracted 92,589 fans over two nights in Toronto.

Saturday June 24
CNE Stadium, Toronto, Ontario, Canada

Gross for the two Toronto gigs came to $2,297,204.

RADIO CITY ● MUSIC HALL.
50TH STREET & AVENUE OF THE AMERICAS

The Rock and Roll Hall of Fame Presents

THE WHO

Performing $4 50

"TOMMY"

A benefit concert for the Nordoff-Robbins Music Therapy
Foundation Inc. for the treatment of autistic children and
to the Rock and Roll Hall of Fame.

TUESDAY, JUNE 27, 1989   8:00 P. M.

ORCHESTRA   Use 6th Avenue Entrance

Tuesday June 27
Radio City Music Hall, New York City, New York

Thursday June 29
The Meadowlands-Giants Stadium, East Rutherford, New Jersey
The Who were still a stronger draw here than in any other market, and all four nights were sell-outs.

Review/**Rock**

The Who, Reunited, Performs 'Tommy'

Friday June 30
The Meadowlands-Giants Stadium, East Rutherford, New Jersey
The group tallied their largest gross for any one city with the
Meadowlands gigs, receipts totalled $5 million.

.Sunday July 2
The Meadowlands-Giants Stadium, East Rutherford, New Jersey

Monday July 3
The Meadowlands-Giants Stadium, East Rutherford, New Jersey
The group played for almost a quarter of a million people in just four nights at the Meadowlands.

Thursday July 6
RFK Stadium, Washington, DC
Gate receipts were $1,952,145 from 86,762 fans.

Friday July 7
RFK Stadium, Washington, DC

Sunday July 9
Veterans Stadium, Philadelphia, Pennsylvania
The band earned $2,279,443 for their two nights work in Philadelphia.

Monday July 10
Veterans Stadium, Philadelphia, Pennsylvania
Attendance for the two dates was 102,101 spectators.

Wednesday July 12
Sullivan Stadium, Foxboro, Massachusetts
Two nights in Foxboro attracted 106,816 fans.

Friday July 14
Sullivan Stadium, Foxboro, Massachusetts
Gate receipts here came to $2,510,176.

Sunday July 16
Three Rivers Stadium, Pittsburgh, Pennsylvania
The show grossed $1,131,000 from 45,924 fans.

Tuesday July 18
Rich Stadium, Orchard Park, New York
   About 35,000 people saw this performance.

Wednesday July 19
Municipal Stadium, Cleveland, Ohio
   More than 61,000 people attended the show for a tally of $1,405,760.

Friday July 21
Alpine Valley Music Theater, East Troy, Wisconsin
   Just over 110,000 people came to see the group over three nights.

Saturday July 22
Alpine Valley Music Theater, East Troy, Wisconsin
   Many people travelled to these Alpine Valley gigs from the Chicago area as there were no dates scheduled for that city.

Sunday July 23
Alpine Valley Music Theater, East Troy, Wisconsin
   Ticket sales amounted to $3,146,704 for the three nights here.

Tuesday July 25
The Silverdome, Pontiac, Michigan
   A crowd of 46,000 fans filled the Dome for a gross of $1,058,000.

Thursday July 27
Carter-Finley Stadium, Raleigh, North Carolina
   More than 53,000 fans waited in the rain to see a three-hour-plus performance.

Saturday July 29
Tampa Stadium, Tampa, Florida
   Attendance was 55,303 with receipts totalling $1,244,318.

Monday July 31
Joe Robbie Stadium, Miami, Florida
   The show was a sell-out with 54,339 spectators in the stands for a gross of $1,222,628.

Saturday August 5
Arrowhead Stadium, Kansas City, Missouri
   A crowd of 40,000 people paid $900,000 at this gig, one of only five outdoor dates that grossed less than one million dollars.

Monday August 7
Lakewood Amphitheatre, Atlanta, Georgia
   A three-night stand in Atlanta was attended by 50,720 fans.

Tuesday August 8
Lakewood Amphitheatre, Atlanta, Georgia

Wednesday August 9
Lakewood Amphitheatre, Atlanta, Georgia

Friday August 11
Busch Stadium, St. Louis, Missouri
   Another million-dollar gate from 47,181 fans.

Sunday August 13
Folsom Field, Boulder, Colorado
   A crowd of 46,300 fans came to Folsom Field, paying out $1,088,050 at the gate.

Wednesday August 16
The Tacoma Dome, Tacoma, Washington

The LA Times reported: "Pete Townshend barely escaped serious injury Wednesday during a Who concert at the Tacoma Dome when the tremolo arm ('whammy bar') of his electric guitar pierced the webbing between the fifth and fourth fingers on his right hand. Townshend was executing his trademark windmill strum during 'Won't Get Fooled Again' – the final song before the encores – when his hand was snagged by the metal bar. The band went ahead with encores of 'Twist And Shout' and 'Hey Joe' without its leader who was rushed to a nearby hospital. It was determined that he had suffered no nerve, bone or tendon damage and no stitches were needed."

Friday August 18
B.C. Place, Vancouver, British Columbia, Canada

A crowd of 48,000 fans came to the first of two nights in Vancouver.

Saturday August 19
B.C. Place, Vancouver, British Columbia, Canada

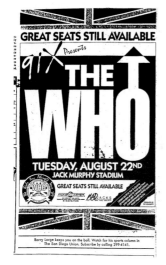

Tuesday August 22
Jack Murphy Stadium, San Diego, California

A little over 40,000 attended the show for a gross of $902,273.

Thursday August 24
Universal Amphitheatre, Los Angeles, California

The ensemble put on a charity performance, beginning at 7:30 pm, with proceeds to benefit The Gilbert W. Lindsay Children's Center, United Friends of the Children, The Westside Children's Center and the Rock and Roll Hall of Fame. An all-star guest line-up played the various roles in the *Tommy* segment of the show, one of only two complete performances of the rock opera on the tour: Elton John as the Pinball Wizard, Phil Collins as Uncle Ernie, Patti LaBelle as the Acid Queen, Billy Idol as Cousin Kevin and Steve Winwood as the Hawker.

The show easily sold out, with ticket sales totalling $2,050,782 from the crowd of 5,812. In addition, the performance was broadcast live as a pay-per-view television event and recorded for inclusion on a subsequent live album and video.

Saturday August 26
Los Angeles Memorial Coliseum, Los Angeles, California

Unlike the Farewell tour in 1982, this gig fell about 18,000 seats short of a sell-out. Still in all, more than 65,000 fans came to the show.

Tuesday August 29
Alameda County Stadium, Oakland, California

Two nights here attracted almost 102,000 fans for a gross of $2,548,325.

Wednesday August 30
Alameda County Stadium, Oakland, California

Saturday September 2
The Astrodome, Houston, Texas

The two Texas dates were the only gigs on the tour to include support acts. Consequently, audiences saw 30 minutes less of The Who but were treated to sets by two Texas bands, Stevie Ray Vaughan & Double Trouble, and his brother Jimmie Vaughan's band, The Fabulous Thunderbirds.

Sunday September 3
The Cotton Bowl, Dallas, Texas
The last gig of the 25th Anniversary "The Kids Are Alright" tour, the longest trek of The Who's career. The concert was broadcast live on the Westwood One FM radio on Labor Day. Support acts were again Stevie Ray Vaughan & Double Trouble, and The Fabulous Thunderbirds.
Total gate receipts for the tour were $34,027,052.

Friday October 6
NEC Arena, Birmingham
The Who played a mini-tour of England, starting with four nights in Birmingham.

Saturday October 7
NEC Arena, Birmingham

Monday October 9
NEC Arena, Birmingham
The first two shows in Birmingham sold out, prompting the addition of two extra dates on the 9th and 10th. This was also John's 45th birthday and an after-show party was thrown at his Gloucestershire mansion.

Tuesday October 10
NEC Arena, Birmingham

Monday October 23
Wembley Arena, Wembley, North London
All Wembley dates had sold out by October 7.

Tuesday October 24
Wembley Arena, Wembley, North London

Thursday October 26
Wembley Arena, Wembley, North London
Chris Charlesworth: "I'd lost touch with The Who after Keith died. I hadn't been to see them with Kenney Jones. All I had to remember of the glory days were the *Leeds* album, a few bootlegs and *The Kids Are Alright* video, which I'd virtually worn out. But a friend had a spare ticket for this Wembley show, and I went along more for old time's sake than anything else. I'd mellowed a bit after feeling slightly let down by what happened after Keith died. I was a bit late arriving and the band were playing 'Substitute' as I found my seat, followed by 'I Can't Explain'. Of course, it wasn't The Who up there, not The Who that I'd known and loved so much, but it brought all the old memories flooding back and in spite of it all, I enjoyed myself. Indeed, this night rekindled my interest in The Who and inspired me to get back in touch with Pete and, eventually, to get involved with producing their box set.
"I liked it when the three of them came back

Rog had the flu. Pete also made a deeply self-deprecating speech about how they were only doing it for the money which was at least honest. Most big rock bands who reform try to kid people it's for artistic reasons but The Who had never lied to their fans before and they didn't start now. He paid tribute to Keith, partly because they were in Wembley, where Keith was born. 'We've never been able to replace him,' he admitted. 'I asked Roger if he wanted to come on to do an encore and he told me to fuck off,' said Pete, adding, 'not for the first time.' Indeed not, I thought. They closed the show with John taking the vocals on 'Twist And Shout'."

alone after the interval – that was a nice touch – but Roger's voice was shot. It was clear that he was hoarse and having difficulty hitting the right notes. Mid-way through 'Behind Blue Eyes' he walked off stage in apparent disgust at himself, not to return. Pete took over on vocals and finished the song, then sang throughout 'Won't Get Fooled Again'. In a curious way this set my adrenaline flowing, because I knew it would put them on the back foot and they'd have to improvise. It was the old 'anything can happen at a Who concert' scenario all over again, and it was obvious that Pete was not best pleased at this turn of events. Great! An angry Townshend is an exciting Townshend! During 'Won't Get Fooled Again' he whacked his Schecter Stratocaster against the monitors at the front but it wouldn't break, so he just tossed it aside in that wonderfully imperious way he has with guitars that displease him, and picked up another one.

"When the band returned for an encore Pete apologised on behalf of Roger, explaining that

Friday October 27
Wembley Arena, Wembley, North London

Tuesday October 31
Royal Albert Hall, Kensington, London

Thursday November 2
Royal Albert Hall, London

The closing night of the UK tour and the last live concert Daltrey, Entwistle, and Townshend would play together until 1996.

The Nineties began on a high note for The Who when, in January 1990, Pete, Roger, John and Keith (represented by his daughter Mandy) were inducted into the Rock and Roll Hall of Fame by U2's Adam Clayton during the fifth annual induction dinner, held at New York's Waldorf Astoria Hotel. The following year Pete Townshend received a Living Legend Award at the third annual International Rock Awards at London's Docklands Arena.

The stage version of *Tommy*, for which Townshend was Musical Director, opened on Broadway in the summer 1993. A box office smash, it won three Tony Awards at the annual drama awards in New York. The show also played in California and, later, in Frankfurt and London. Also in '93, Pete toured the US behind his *Psychoderelict* solo concept album and played various charity shows. Townshend delighted in issuing the odd controversial missive and, at times, seemed almost apologetic for (and dismissive of) his work with The Who. Eternally quixotic, he was likely to change his opinions overnight and because of this, his relationship with Roger Daltrey fluctuated accordingly. Out of the spotlight, Townshend's most contented moments were (and are) spent sailing his boat around Cornwall and France.

On March 23 and 24, 1994, Roger marked his 50th birthday with a "Daltrey Sings Townshend" concert at New York's Carnegie Hall. Among those appearing were The Spin Doctors, Alice Cooper, Lou Reed, Sinead O'Connor, Eddie Vedder, The Chieftains, 4 Non-Blondes and The Juillard Orchestra, as well as John Entwistle and Pete Townshend. Apart from participating in the all-star finale, the three former Who colleagues did not perform on stage together.

Roger had planned to take the "Daltrey Sings Townshend" show on a full-scale US tour but this was curtailed after a handful of shows due to poor ticket sales, and the expense involved in taking a full orchestra on the road. Daltrey continued his work as an actor, both on film and television, as well as campaigning for charity by guesting on records and at concerts. Apparently ageless, the passing years had no effect whatsoever on his robust physique, the result of a healthy outdoor lifestyle and regular sessions in the gym. It was

Roger who did his best to keep The Who's flag flying during those times when Pete appeared to have turned his back on the past. Daltrey seemed alternately bemused and incensed by this changeable attitude. "Listen... can you ever fathom The 'Oo out? No-one can predict what's going to happen with The 'Oo. I can't and I'm the bloody singer," he said.

John also took to the road in the US with his own band, performing in clubs and demonstrating his extraordinary technique to young bass guitarists. Off the road, he kept the lowest profile, settling into rural life on his Gloucestershire estate where he established a commercial recording studio, managed by Bob Pridden, The Who's oldest and most loyal employee. Silver-haired, slightly deaf and an accomplished cartoonist, John 'Thunderfingers' Entwistle was still regarded as one of the world's greatest bass guitarists.

As the Nineties progressed, The Who became part of rock's elder aristocracy, revered by younger generations of rock performers for their influence and pioneering style, especially in America where their legendary status remained undimmed. Starting with the shortlived Grunge phenomenon, a new wave of young American musicians took their cue from The Who's untutored, visceral approach, particularly Seattle's Pearl Jam, whose songwriting leader Eddie Vedder was to become a close Who associate.

Their increasing influence was also partly due to a four-CD career retrospective box set, *Thirty Years Of Maximum R&B*, which was released to glowing reviews in 1994. The following year saw the release of a newly remixed and remastered edition of *Live At Leeds* which contained all the songs performed at the legendary Leeds University concert on February 14 1970, bar the majority of *Tommy* (which eventually followed as an extended double Deluxe Edition in 2001). This outstanding document to The Who's live power was the first step in a wholesale reissue and upgrading of The Who's back catalogue in which all of their albums were reissued in deluxe remixed or remastered compact disc editions featuring bonus tracks on each, as well as 24-page booklets containing lengthy essays, pictures, memorabilia and informative track listings.

With the advent of the Britpop phenomenon that gripped the UK in the mid-Nineties, The

Who bore a pronounced influence on bands such as Oasis, Blur, and Cast, whose best-selling debut album, *All Change*, was recorded at John Entwistle's studio, Hammerhead, and produced by Bob Pridden.

On September 16, 1995, Roger and John performed together with Simon Townshend standing in for his elder brother to climax a Who Fan Convention at The Bottom Line, Shepherd's Bush, West London. Unexpectedly, a large part of the show was occupied by the *Quadrophenia* album, which, as subsequent events attested, laid the foundation for the re-emergence of The Who the following year.

As renewed interest in The Who gathered momentum, the launch of a fanzine called *Naked Eye* and the back catalogue reissue programme, which included a new *Greatest Hits* LP that saw The Who back in the upper reaches of the album charts, the time was clearly ripe for some form of group activity. Thus, when Pete was invited by the Prince's Trust to perform at an all star gathering featuring Eric Clapton and Bob Dylan in London's Hyde Park, he chose to perform *Quadrophenia* in its entirety with a large band of guest musicians, including Roger and John with Ringo Starr's son Zak Starkey (Ringo's son) on drums. The Who bandwagon was rolling again – even though, initially, they weren't billed as The Who – and the Hyde Park show was followed by five similar *Quadrophenia* shows in New York.

In October and November, the *Quadrophenia* show hit the road in America, visiting 21 cities over a six week period, and in December Pete, Roger and John, together with the extra musicians, performed *Quadrophenia* before sell out audiences at London's Earls Court Arena and at Manchester's Belle Vue.

Saturday June 29
Hyde Park, London

The three former members of The Who took part in the 1996 Prince's Trust "Masters Of Music"

Benefit Concert staged in London's Hyde Park, sponsored by Mastercard. The ensemble performed a segment of *Quadrophenia* with special guests Gary Glitter, Phil Daniels (who played Jimmy in the 1979 film version), Trevor McDonald (British newsreader) and the comedians Stephen Fry and Adrian Edmondson. The band included Dave Gilmour and Geoff Whitehorn (guitars), Zak Starkey (drums), Rabbit Bundrick and Jon Carin (keyboards), Jody Linscott (percussion), Simon Townshend (guitar/backing vocals) as well as musical director Billy Nicholls leading three other singers on backing vocals. There was also a five-piece brass section.

During rehearsals there was an unfortunate incident when Gary Glitter swung his mikestand which accidentally connected with Roger's right eye. Ever the trouper, Daltrey played the show sporting a bullseye target eyepatch.

The order of the concert went as follows: Jools Holland and his R&B Orchestra, Alanis Morrisette, Bob Dylan (and band, featuring Ron Wood on guitar), *Quadrophenia*, and Eric Clapton and his band.

Tuesday July 16
Madison Square Garden, New York

The *Quadrophenia* show (credited to "Pete Townshend, Roger Daltrey, John Entwistle") played six nights at New York's Madison Square Garden. The Godfather was played by a hilariously high-camp Gary Glitter, unknown in America,

although his 'Rock'n'Roll Part Two' was well known to sports fans. The Ace Face was played by Billy Idol. Supporting acts were Joan Osborne (16 to 18) and Me'Shell Ndegeocello (20 to 22).

Wednesday July 17
Madison Square Garden, New York

Thursday July 18
Madison Square Garden, New York

Saturday July 20
Madison Square Garden, New York

Sunday July 21
Madison Square Garden, New York

Monday July 22
Madison Square Garden, New York

A total of 85,810 people saw the *Quadrophenia* show over six nights, proving The Who were as popular as ever in New York. They had played four shows at the Garden in June 1974 and a five-night stand in September 1979 but the attendance figures on those dates were eclipsed by the 1996 concerts.

With the success of the *Quad* show in London and New York, the band set its sights on America for a full-scale tour in the autumn. Although

many shows were not sold out, reviews were mostly favourable and it appeared that *Quadrophenia* had matured and grown even more remarkable with the passage of 23 years.

Sunday October 13
Rose Garden Arena, Portland, Oregon

The *Quadrophenia* stage show that was presented in London and New York was given ample airing on the road in America during the autumn of 1996. 25 shows were set in 20 cities starting on the west coast and ending in the New York area. It's ironic that the first date of the tour brought the show to Portland on October 13 since The Who began their 1976 autumn tour in the very same city on the exact same date.

Monday October 14
The Tacoma Dome, Tacoma, Washington

The tour played in a partitioned 'half house' Dome but still did not sell out the venue with only 7,432 in attendance. This was partly due to the fact that the tour was still being billed under the individuals' names –

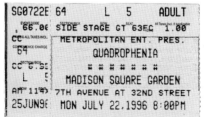

and not as "The Who".

Late in the show Pete launched his guitar about 20 feet into the air, let it fall to the floor, then smashed it. After the concert Pete called his brother Simon and asked him to take over on electric guitar. Simon flew in and spent two days rehearsing with the band in time for the Vancouver show. For the rest of the *Quadrophenia* tour Pete mostly played acoustic.

Wednesday October 16
General Motors Palace, Vancouver, B.C., Canada
Thursday October 17
General Motors Palace, Vancouver, B. C., Canada

The Who and opening act Matthew Good were seen by a total of 15,663 over two nights.

Saturday October 19
San Jose Arena, San Jose, California

On this date Pete made a surprise solo appearance at the 10th Annual Bridge Benefit concert at the Shoreline Amphitheatre, Mountain View, California. (First organised by Neil Young in 1986, the concerts raise money for handicapped children.) Pete appeared as the second act on the show, playing a short set before dashing up to San Jose to perform with The Who. (The other artists on the Bridge bill were Pearl Jam, David Bowie, Cowboy Junkies, Patti Smith and Neil Young.)

Sunday October 20
San Jose Arena, San Jose, California

The Bay Area had always been a favourite stop for The Who, and fans had always reciprocated in kind but the two San Jose dates failed to sell out. A still impressive 17,846 of the faithful turned out.

Tuesday October 22
The Great Western Forum, Los Angeles, California

Ryan Downe was the opening act. The (Great Western) Forum was one of 11 venues visited on the original US *Quadrophenia* tour in 1973. The return of the *Quad* show was well worth the wait as the band put on a tremendous performance for the 11,662 fans gathered, slightly less than a sell-out house. A smattering of California Mods were in the audience sporting parkas, desert boots, polo shirts and very un-Modlike bronzed surfer tans!

Wednesday October 23
The America West Arena, Phoenix, Arizona

Friday October 25
Arrowhead Pond, Anaheim, California

The second southern Californian date drew a crowd of 10,242.

Saturday October 26
MGM Grand Garden, Las Vegas, Nevada

Although this was the first appearance by the three original members of The Who in Las Vegas, the gig was not a sell-out in the 9,068 capacity Grand Garden with only 6,210 fans in attendance. (Roger, with John on bass, had played here on the "Daltrey Sings Townshend" tour in October 1994.)

Tuesday October 29
McNichol's Arena, Denver, Colorado

The Who played to a near sell-out crowd, ending the show with the standard encores of 'Won't Get Fooled Again', 'Behind Blue Eyes' and 'Who Are You'.

Thursday October 31
The United Center, Chicago, Illinois

Always a good "Who town", both nights in Chicago were sell-outs with 27,811 fans packing the United Center over two nights for a gross of $1,424,590.

Friday November 1
The United Center, Chicago, Illinois

The United Center replaced the old Chicago Stadium which had stood directly across the street until its demolition in 1994. The Who had played that arena in December 1975.

Sunday November 3
The Palace of Auburn Hills, Auburn Hills, Michigan

The Who had been popular in the Detroit area ever since 'I Can't Explain' had 'broken out' there when released in 1965. This concert attracted 15,681 fans to a Michigan venue the band had not played before.

Monday November 4
The Ervin J. Nutter Center, Dayton, Ohio

The Who had played Dayton only once before during the August 1971 US tour. The arena was far from sold out with 4,864 empty seats in the 12,210-capacity venue, one of the lowest turnouts of the entire *Quad* tour.

Wednesday November 6
Gund Arena, Cleveland, Ohio

The Who, supported by The Heads, performed for 10,463 spectators.

Friday November 8
Civic Arena, Pittsburgh, Pennsylvania

Saturday November 9
Marine Midland Arena, Buffalo, New York

The Who, with opening act Linda Perry (formerly with 4 Non-Blondes), were seen by 11,381 people with gate receipts tallied at $499,520.

Monday November 11
US Air Arena, Landover, Maryland

The show sold exactly 12,000 tickets for a gross of $733,952.

Tuesday November 12
The Centrum, Worcester, Massachusetts

Thursday November 14
The Centrum, Worcester, Massachusetts

Two nights at The Centrum grossed just over one million dollars with a total of 20,844 people in attendance.

Friday November 15
Nassau Coliseum, Uniondale, Long Island, New York

Despite their many visits to the New York City area, The Who had never appeared at this venue before. Surprisingly, the crowd of 10,907 was rather passive in its reaction to the performance.

Sunday November 17
Core States Center, Philadelphia, Pennsylvania

The opening act on this sold out show was Ocean Colour Scene. A second scheduled night here was cancelled.

Monday November 18
Knickerbocker Arena, Albany, New York

This city was added to the tour when the second show in Philadelphia was cancelled. The Who had played Albany only once before on November 10, 1969 during the US *Tommy* tour.

Tuesday November 19
Continental Airlines Arena, East Rutherford, New Jersey

Friday December 6
Earls Court, London

After the ensemble had performed *Quadrophenia*, Pete and Roger returned to the stage alone to perform 'Won't Get Fooled Again' together with Pete on acoustic guitar. John joined them halfway through. "It's nice to be able to perform *Quadrophenia* in front of some real old Mods," Pete told the audience. "The reason I'm playing acoustic guitar is because I like it. I'm not deaf," he added. The three then began 'Behind Blue Eyes' and were joined by the entire ensemble after the second verse. The show ended with a terrific performance of 'Who Are You', the first verse sung by Roger accompanying himself alone on one of Pete's acoustic guitars.

Saturday December 7
Earls Court, London

As on the previous night, the original members of The Who returned after *Quadrophenia* for several songs, this time adding 'Substitute' to the set. Supported by The Stereophonics.

Wednesday December 11
Nynex Arena, Manchester

1997

With the *Quadrophenia* stage show now honed to precision, the concerts continued throughout Europe during the spring and America over the summer. The 1996 *Quad* shows had been credited to Townshend, Entwistle & Daltrey, or TED, as John liked to call them. In fact, the '97 tour was going to be called 'TED In The Shed' but commercial considerations resulted in it being credited to The Who. The slightly smaller band of backing musicians included Sixties singer P. J. Proby, who replaced Gary Glitter, and unknown actor Ben Waters who took on Billy Idol's role as the Ace Face.

At selected dates, Pete played electric guitar on 'The Real Me', 'Is It In My Head?', 'I've Had Enough', '5.15', 'Sea And Sand', 'The Rock', 'Love Reign O'er Me' and on certain encore numbers, chosen from 'Won't Get Fooled Again' (sometimes performed in a medley with 'Pinball Wizard'), 'Behind Blue Eyes', 'Substitute', 'Naked Eye', 'Magic Bus', 'I Can See For Miles', 'The Kids Are Alright' and 'Who Are You'.

Wednesday April 23
Forum, Copenhagen, Denmark

Friday April 25
Globe Arena, Stockholm, Sweden

Saturday April 26
Oslo Spektrum, Oslo, Norway
This show was unusual in that it started with 'Substitute' and 'I Can't Explain', preceding *Quadrophenia*. During the encore, Roger left the stage and Pete tried to sing the opening verses of 'Magic Bus'. Roger returned and sang the correct lyrics.

Monday April 28
Ostseehalle, Kiel, Germany

Tuesday April 29
Deutschlandhalle, Berlin, Germany

Thursday May 1
Stadthalle, Vienna
During the encore, Roger forgot the words to 'Won't Get Fooled Again'. "I can't believe it!" he laughed, "I must've sung this hundreds of times!"

Sunday May 4
Olympiahalle, Munich, Germany

Monday May 5
Hans-Martin-Schleyer-Halle, Stuttgart, Germany

Tuesday May 6
Festhalle, Frankfurt, Germany

Friday May 9
Westfalenhalle, Dortmund, Germany

Saturday May 10
Forest National, Brussels, Belgium

Sunday May 11
The Ahoy, Rotterdam, The Netherlands

Tuesday May 13
The Zenith, Paris, France

Wednesday May 14
The Zenith, Paris, France

Friday May 16
Hallenstadion, Zurich, Switzerland

Sunday May 18
Wembley Arena, London, England
A packed and enthusiastic crowd welcomed Pete, Roger, John and the additional musicians back to London for the final show of the European *Quadrophenia* tour. For most of the show the audience sang along with the band. Pete

was on particularly fine form at this show, playing far more electric guitar than at the Earls Court concerts in November and '5.15', with outstanding soloing from both John and Pete, was the undoubted highlight of the *Quad* segment.

Returning for encores, as had become the norm Pete and Roger began 'Won't Get Fooled Again' as a duo, before John joined them on bass. At one point Pete raised audience expectations by strumming the main intro riff to 'Pinball Wizard', then worked his way back into 'Won't Get Fooled Again'. This was followed by 'Behind Blue Eyes', by the end of which the entire band was back on stage. 'Substitute' and 'I Can't Explain' were both given powerhouse treatments, especially the latter, and the show closed with 'Who Are You', again featuring Roger on acoustic guitar. The following day being Pete's birthday, Roger embarrassed his lifelong partner by leading a sing-along of 'Happy Birthday'. Pete looked far from amused!

Acknowledging the band at the end of the night, Pete mentioned that Keith Moon's mother was present which prevented him from saying anything rude about their late drummer. He also mentioned how much he'd enjoyed working with Roger on making the back-projection film that was shown while the band played *Quadrophenia*. "It was the first time I had ever collaborated on anything creatively with Roger," he added.

Saturday July 19
Riverport Amphitheatre, Maryland Heights, Missouri

Sunday July 20
New World Music Theatre, Tinley Park, Chicago, Illinois

Tuesday July 22
Target Center, Minneapolis, Minnesota

Wednesday July 23
Marcus Amphitheatre, Milwaukee, Wisconsin

Friday July 25
Pine Knob Music Theatre, Clarkston, Mississippi

Saturday July 26
Deer Creek Music Center, Noblesville, Indiana

The debut of John's lengthy bass solo showcase during '5.15'. At the end of 'Who Are You', Pete threw his guitar into the air, sending it crashing to the ground. He kicked at it, turned and strode off stage, not to return. As John and Roger began to leave the stage, Roger picked up the guitar, lifting it into the air as if he were going to smash it, bringing a mighty roar from the crowd. He said, "I think I'll nick it and tell Pete that it's broke!"

Monday July 28
Molson Centre, Montreal, Quebec, Canada

Tuesday July 29
Molson Amphitheatre, Toronto, Ontario, Canada

Thursday July 31
Great Woods Center, Mansfield, Massachusetts

Saturday August 2
Meadows Music Theatre, Hartford, Connecticut

Sunday August 3
P.N.C. Bank Arts Center, Holmdel, New Jersey

Tuesday August 5
Darien Lake P.A.C., Darien Center, New York

Wednesday August 6
Blockbuster - Sony Center, Camden, New Jersey

Thursday August 7
Nissan Pavilion, Bristow, Virginia

Saturday August 9
Virginia Beach Amphitheater, Virginia Beach, Virginia

Sunday August 10
Walnut Creek Amphitheatre, Raleigh, North Carolina

Tuesday August 12
Blockbuster Pavilion, Charlotte, North Carolina

Wednesday August 13
Lakewood Amphitheatre, Atlanta, Georgia

Friday August 15
Ice Palace, Tampa, Florida

Saturday August 16
Coral Sky Amphitheatre, West Palm Beach, Florida

The end of the millennium brought a welcome rush of unexpected Who activity, largely inspired by the group's charitable leanings. In October, the band (now sensibly slimmed down to the crucial three, plus Rabbit Bundrick and Zak Starkey) rehearsed for a week at Asylum Studios in West London before playing a one-off pay per view internet show in Las Vegas, followed by two charity concerts at the Chicago House of Blues, and two acoustic shows for Neil Young's Bridge School in the San Francisco Bay Area the following month.

In December, at fairly short notice and with little advertising (ticket touts were demanding up to £200 outside), The Who played two Christmas shows at the Shepherd's Bush Empire, awing 1,800 fans each night with truly dynamic sets that acknowledged their illustrious past. The two nights were marred only by the unsteadiness of Roger, John and Pete's voices, the victims of a vicious flu bug that was doing the rounds. However, all was forgiven when witnessing the welcome sight of Pete Townshend strapping on one of several red Eric Clapton signature model Stratocasters, proof positive of his tacit acknowledgment that, after all the years of tinnitus complaints, his public liked their Townshend electric and LOUD. The odd leap and windmill movement didn't go amiss either. It was a good omen that more shows might follow…

Friday October 29
MGM Grand Garden, Las Vegas, Nevada

Set: 'I Can't Explain', 'Substitute', 'Anyway Anyhow Anywhere', 'Pinball Wizard', 'See Me Feel Me', 'Baba O'Riley', 'My Wife', '5:15', 'Behind Blue Eyes', 'Who Are You', 'Magic Bus', 'Won't Get Fooled Again', 'The Kids Are Alright', 'My Generation'.

The Who's return to the stage was praised by Mike Weatherford in the *Las Vegas Review Journal* (October 31, 1999), headlined "The Who Show Muscle In Marvelous Return": "The singer's microphone did a lasso twirl and the guitarist's arm windmill-whirled, all before the end of the first song. The Who were back, all right. They've been back now and then, but Friday night they were back the way most people have wanted to see them. No horns, no background singers, no

concept albums. Just hunkering down to play the hits, loudly.

"The legendary rockers presumably accepted a big paycheck (though the live gate was donated to charity) to be the focal point for a new Internet company, Pixelon.com. The company hired them to headline its promotional iBash Friday at the MGM Grand Garden, and will post the concert on its new full-screen video site…

"Still vigorous in their 50s, Pete Townshend, Roger Daltrey and John Entwistle recaptured the macho rock side of The Who that's been missing since at least 1989. Past get-togethers have emphasized the concept albums *Tommy* and *Quadrophenia*, and thereby focused on the grand, theatrical side of the band.

"But there are many facets of Who history, and it was nice to see the power trio flex its muscles again. Friday's show was more like the *Live At Leeds* album, though longtime keyboardist John 'Rabbit' Bundrick played on every song, filling them in without getting in the way. (You wouldn't want to hear 'Baba O'Riley' without a synthesiser, would you?)

"No one bothered to explain what happened to that hearing problem that had Townshend swearing off the electric guitar and/or playing behind Plexiglass in the recent past. But he was plugged in and wailing away, reminding the sold-out crowd he's a phenomenal guitarist as well as a songwriter. He supplied both the power chords and intricate melodies on big-finish tunes such as 'Pinball Wizard' and 'Listening To You' (*sic*) without the help of a rhythm guitarist.

"The 90-minute set kick-started with 'Can't Explain' and finished with 'My Generation', sticking to the standard FM playlist and ignoring everything from its post-Keith Moon catalogue. Ringo's son Zak Starkey stuck faithfully to the Moon drum sound for honest versions of 'Who Are You?' and '5:15.' Daltrey sounded great too, though the only thing that came close to a ballad was the first half of 'Behind Blue Eyes'. Along with a little more breathing space, the set could have used some more surprises. But die-hard fans had to settle for only one dusted-off rarity – 'Anyway, Anyhow, Anywhere' - and a rhythmic reworking of 'Magic Bus' that sounded like it might have been a nod to the funk-metal wave of the mid-'90s.

"A few slip-ups, such as a hesitant version of Entwistle's raggedly-sung 'My Wife', were easy to forgive from a band that hasn't played together in a few years. They made the show seem, shall we say, more human than a Kiss set earlier in the evening that many observers suspect was lip-synched. Townshend has resisted doing a hits tour for years now, perhaps fearing The Who would come off like a washed-up oldies revue. But after a playful night onstage Friday, he hopefully will look at recent shows by The Rolling Stones - longtime rivals for the 'World's Best Rock Band' title - to see what can happen when veteran rockers get back to work on a regular schedule.

"With any luck, Friday's show will not be seen as a last hurrah preserved as a digital museum piece, but as a new beginning."

Saturday October 30
Shoreline Amphitheatre, Mountain View, California

Set: 'Substitute', 'I Can't Explain', 'Pinball Wizard', 'Behind Blue Eyes', 'Tattoo', 'Mary Anne With The Shaky Hand', 'Boris The Spider', 'Who Are You', 'I Walk The Line/Ring Of Fire', 'Won't Get Fooled Again', 'The Kids Are Alright'.

The Who appeared as part of Neil Young's annual Bridge School benefit concerts, closing the show on both nights. *The San Francisco Chronicle* critic Joel Selvin reported: "Even though the capacity crowd Saturday had already sat through eight hours of music by eight acts - including extraordinary performances by Brian Wilson, Pearl Jam, Tom Waits and Green Day - everybody stayed well past midnight for this eagerly anticipated finale.

"It was not The Who of yore, 10 years after the storied English rock band's farewell tour, more than 20 years past its prime. This most electric of rock bands played unplugged, as is the custom at the Bridge benefit. Guitarist Pete Townshend even pulled up a chair to play his clattering solo on 'Who Are You.' They may look like old bankers, but the Who's members played like juvenile delinquents. It was utterly magnificent… a towering close to an epic concert."

Friday October 31
Shoreline Amphitheatre, Mountain View, California

Set: as per October 30 (minus 'Tattoo')

Friday November 12
House Of Blues, Chicago, Illinois

Set: 'I Can't Explain', 'Substitute', 'Anyway Anyhow Anywhere', 'Pinball Wizard', 'My Wife', 'Baba O'Riley', 'Pure And Easy', 'Getting In Tune', 'You Better You Bet', 'Behind Blue Eyes', 'Tattoo', 'Mary Anne With The Shaky Hand', 'I'm A Boy', 'Boris the Spider', 'Eminence Front', 'After The Fire', '5:15', 'Who Are You', 'Magic Bus', 'Won't Get Fooled Again', 'The Kids Are Alright'/ 'A Legal Matter'/ 'Ring Of Fire', 'My Generation', 'Let's See Action'.

Support Act was C-Average, featuring Eddie Vedder (of Pearl Jam). Vedder joined The Who for the second encore, 'Let's See Action'.

Rolling Stone's Kevin McKeough filed a lukewarm report, "The Who Are Just Alright In Chicago": "Introducing the first encore of The Who's benefit concert at Chicago's House of Blues Friday night, Pete Townshend advised the packed house, 'This is not a song about being young. This is a song about our kids.' The rendition of 'The Kids Are Alright' that followed that statement matched Townshend's perspective. Full of chiming acoustic guitar, pretty keyboards and Roger Daltrey's gentle, golden singing, it was a sweetly reflective moment from a band that spent much of the evening laboring to match the ferocity of its own youth.

"Friday night's show was the first of two that Townshend, Daltrey and John Entwistle performed over the weekend, aided by drummer Zak Starkey (Ringo Starr's son) and keyboardist John 'Rabbit' Bundrick. The concerts, which came with a $300 price tag (scalpers allegedly were getting five times that much), benefited Maryville

Academy, a Chicago-area charity that provides housing and aid to abused and neglected children...

"The deep-pocketed crowd may not have minded the absurdity of a middle-aged Daltrey belting out 'hope I die before I get old' during the inevitable rendition of 'My Generation,' but The Who's years, and years apart (the show was only their third since reuniting after a three-year lay-off), were evident in the way the song petered out in the end, as if Townshend just lost interest in it. Much of the show similarly found The Who too distracted, too rusty or too (gasp!) mellowed by age to make their sound and fury convincing. Conserving his voice, Daltrey favored deliberate, restrained singing to his roaring delivery of old. He crooned rather than belted his way through the show-opening 'I Can't Explain' and forgot the words mid-way through 'Getting In Tune'.

"Townshend's obvious discomfort with the proceedings ('Pete doesn't look happy,' one observant crowd member remarked of Townshend's dour expression and fleeting bursts of intensity) may account for the rote renditions of such warhorses as 'Pinball Wizard' and 'Baba O'Riley'. For all Townshend's brittle soloing, 'Eminence Front' had a dulled edge, and Starkey's straightforward backbeat limited 'The Magic Bus' to an ill-advised funk-rock work-out more suited for the Red Hot Chili Peppers. On this night, Entwistle was clearly The Who's most dangerous member. His pummeling, rapid-fire bass lines darted through the songs like a fighter pilot on a bombing run, and he sounded dark and mean as he spat out the words of 'My Wife'. His slashing solo on '5:15' earned the wildest cheers of the evening and egged Townshend into his most abandoned solo as well.

"To be fair, a small club may not have been the right venue for a band that deals in epics. Although he struck his familiar rock god poses, Daltrey in particular seemed inhibited, unable to move around much on the small stage, and the reduced scale stripped both the music and the men performing it of their grandeur. The Who were most engaged in their music when they broke out the acoustic guitars, adapting to their location and their matured sensibilities. Legs apart, Townshend rocked on his heels as he strummed 'After The Fire' like a flamenco musician on steroids, while Daltrey's understated delivery of 'Behind Blue Eyes' quietly gave the song an intensity that even the plugged-in rendition of 'Won't Get Fooled Again' never achieved.

"Being up close and personal also allowed for some playful moments, including Daltrey's medley of Johnny Cash songs during a country rendition of 'A Legal Matter' and Townshend's teasing Entwistle about the thermos he brought onstage. 'It's fucking started already,' Entwistle responded, and the band's legendary internal tensions at times bubbled up beneath the surface, particularly when Townshend told Daltrey his harmonica playing on 'The Magic Bus' was 'shit...[and] it went on a bit.' It was hugs all around at the end though, as Townshend embraced Daltrey during the encores, then brought Eddie Vedder and Olympia, Washington band C-Average (who together had performed an opening set of garage rock, heavy on Eighties cover tunes) out for a grand finale of 'Let's See Action'.

"Daltrey and Vedder's mutual admiration was

evident as they hugged at the end like a pair of divas, but so was Townshend's awkwardness as he drew the singer and Entwistle around him for a final curtain call. Standing together, the members of The Who seemed not so much like rock titans as three men bound by a history they could repeat more easily than enhance."

Saturday November 13
House Of Blues, Chicago, Illinois

Set: 'I Can't Explain', 'Substitute', 'Anyway Anyhow Anywhere', 'Pinball Wizard', 'My Wife', 'Baba O'Riley', 'Pure And Easy', 'You Better You Bet', 'Getting In Tune', 'Behind Blue Eyes', 'Magic Bus', 'Boris The Spider', 'The Seeker', 'After The Fire', 'Who Are You', '5:15', 'Won't Get Fooled Again', 'The Kids Are Alright', 'My Generation', 'Let's See Action', 'Eminence Front'.

After 'Anyway Anyhow Anywhere', The Who presented a cheque to Father Smith from the Maryville Academy for $1,000,000. Roger sang a few lines of 'The Seeker' just before 'Boris The Spider'. Support act was again Eddie Vedder's C-Average and Vedder repeated his first night trick of joining The Who to sing 'Let's See Action'.

Wednesday December 22
Shepherd's Bush Empire, Shepherd's Bush, West London

Set: 'I Can't Explain', 'Substitute', 'Anyway Anyhow Anywhere', 'Pinball Wizard', 'My Wife', 'Baba O'Riley', 'Pure And Easy', 'Getting In Tune', 'Behind Blue Eyes', 'You Better You Bet', 'Happy Jack', 'Magic Bus', 'Boris The Spider', 'Who Are You', 'After The Fire', '5:15', 'Won't Get Fooled Again', 'The Kids Are Alright', 'Naked Eye', 'My Generation'.

Chris Charlesworth (*Record Collector*, February 2000): "Barring visits to the BBC TV Studios in Wood Lane, this was the first time since December 3, 1965, that The Who had played in Shepherd's Bush, the area of London eternally synonymous with the band. 34 years down the line, Townshend, Entwistle, and Daltrey had lost little of the passion that drove the Who onwards and upwards until, at their peak, they truly were the greatest live act on the planet…

"Nostalgic it may have been but comfortable it wasn't. 'My ears have gone,' Daltrey complained towards the end. 'You don't need to hear any-

thing these days,' Townshend quipped. 'There's nothing worth listening to these days. It was different when I was a lad!'"

The incident-packed evening climaxed with Townshend trashing a gold Stratocaster in a genuine rage. He looked rather sheepish as faithful roadies, including old retainers Alan Rogan and Bob Pridden, swept up the pieces.

Thursday December 23
Shepherd's Bush Empire, Shepherd's Bush, West London

Set: 'I Can't Explain', 'Substitute', 'Anyway Anyhow Anywhere', 'Pinball Wizard', 'My Wife', 'Baba O'Riley', 'Pure And Easy', 'You Better You Bet', 'Happy Jack', 'I'm A Boy', 'Getting In Tune', 'The Real Me', 'Behind Blue Eyes', 'Magic Bus', 'Boris The Spider', 'Who Are You', '5:15', 'Won't Get Fooled Again', 'The Kids Are Alright', 'I Walk The Line'/'Ring Of Fire', 'Mary Anne With The Shaky Hand', 'Naked Eye', 'My Generation'.

Chris Charlesworth: "The venue was packed by the time the band took the stage shortly after 8.20. The roar that greeted them sounded like Charlton, 1976.

The opening salvo - 'I Can't Explain', 'Substitute' and 'Anyway Anyhow Anywhere' - was almost perfect, the only flaw being a slight mix-up before the instrumental bars that lead to the climax of 'Substitute'. Pete windmilled his way through the solo on 'Explain' and brought 'Anyhow' to a close by drawing piercing feedback, the kind he pioneered on stage and record long before his peers.

"'Pinball Wizard', the only *Tommy* song of the night, followed, again loud, raw and flawless, before John took the mic for 'My Wife'. Unusually, Roger sang backup throughout, an indication that the world's greatest bass player can no longer sing as well as he once could, even if his fingers are still the quickest anywhere. Barely missing a beat, the familiar synthesiser loop heralded 'Baba O'Riley' and, after Roger's stirring opening verse, it became clear for the first time that Pete, too, was having problems with his vocals. Since the audience sang along at maximum volume, it didn't seem to matter too much but as the evening wore on it became clear that Pete's singing voice was shot.

"On the previous night the seldom played but potentially epic 'Pure And Easy' had gone horri

were croaky and 'The Real Me' from *Quadrophenia* served more as a showcase for John's extraordinary bass playing than anything else.

"Introduced by Pete as The Who's only ballad, 'Behind Blue Eyes' would have been a show stopper but for the nagging vocal problem. It lacked the shimmering harmonies on the second verse that were once such a highlight of live performances, but again it made up in emotion what it missed in technical expertise. The crowd of 1,800 sang along, urging the band on. 'Magic Bus', brought in by some fine blues playing by Pete, was on safer ground and came to a raucous climax, Roger throwing numerous mouth organs into the crowd, before John zipped good naturedly through 'Boris The Spider', his voice again a croak.

"'Who Are You' had been an outstanding highlight the night before, largely because Pete took an extended, jazz influenced solo that veered from delicate, astonishingly quick runs on his top two strings to plucked arpeggios and full-throttle chord work. Tonight, Pete was having none of it and, after a few seconds noodling, he crashed back into the melody and brought things to a head by windmilling furiously. '5.15' followed, much extended, featuring John's superb solo. Then it was into a full tilt 'Won't Get Fooled Again', more windmilling, a glorious scream from Roger and a fine climax to the show... or so we thought.

"In their prime The Who rarely played encores and instead of going through the laboured formality of leaving the stage, only to return a few minutes later, Roger acknowledged the tremendous ovation by strapping on an acoustic Gibson J200, paying tribute to the support the band had always received from its West London fan base and leading the millennium Who through 'The Kids Are Alright' (which featured an extended ending with Pete ad-libbing 'My kids are alright, your kids are alright', etc.) This was followed by a Johnny Cash interlude, a medley of 'I Walk The Line' and 'Ring Of Fire', as performed recently in the US, then a gloriously nostalgic 'Mary Anne With The Shaky Hand', a valiant, shattering stab at 'Naked Eye' and, as a crowd pleaser extraordinaire, 'My Generation' which descended into a blues work-out, and climaxed with a violent chord attack."

bly wrong, Pete having opened the song in a different key to Entwistle and Bundrick. Evidently he'd put in bit of practice in the meantime for the band now turned in a rousing, noble performance of a song much requested by fans which hadn't been played live since a few isolated shows in the summer of 1971. Unfortunately the vocals were again lacking, with Roger the main culprit as he strove for a top note that was neither pure nor easy.

"'You Better You Bet', the only post-Moon song in the set, suited Daltrey's voice better, and was followed by vintage performances of a sprightly 'Happy Jack' and 'I'm A Boy'. On 'Jack', Zak Starkey rumbled away through the tricky dynamics just as Moon once did and at the close there was a crowd pleasing shout of 'I saw yer'! Indeed, Zak's playing throughout frequently paid homage to Keith while maintaining an energy that was all his own. Of the three drummers that have occupied the hot seat in The Who since 1978, Zak is best suited to the onerous demands of the job. 'Getting In Tune' from *Who's Next* followed and featured a fine guitar solo from Pete though again his vocals

I f the unheralded shows of 1999 had lit the torch paper, the 2000 shows were a genuine revelation. Like contemporaries The Rolling Stones, no one in their right mind would make a case for The Who still being a genuine 'cutting edge' force. However, the "Millenium Who" were able to do justice to their considerable legacy. Without the excess baggage of horn sections and backing singers, the five-man band gelled as a unit, while it did the heart good to see Pete Townshend appear genuinely happy to be back on stage.

For those who had gradually lost interest in The Who following Keith Moon's death, it was a case of faith being reaffirmed. This was The Who stripped down, lean and back to basics. A new generation of fans came away astounded, while older fans talked of the best shows they'd seen since the band "officially" imploded in the early '80s; some even going further to say they were the best Who shows since the last Keith Moon tour of 1976. Zak stepped into the considerable shoes of Moon with daring aplomb, hammering the toms with all the force of the old master without being over-reverential. Rabbit's keyboards, at times intrusive in the past, attained the right level of enhancement. Roger's voice continued to improve throughout the tour, so much so, that by the time of the English dates in November, he sounded like a young rock singer in his prime. John stood as stoic as ever, dressed in a series of grotesque stage suits, occasionally raising an eyebrow as his lightning quick runs, particularly an extended solo in '5:15', brought gasps of amazement from both band and audience alike. To the delight of all concerned, Pete was playing electric guitar with conviction, and a solo acoustic spot proved that his rhythmic flair showed no signs of diminishing. A frenzied spate of windmilling or the odd leap, no matter how Pavlovian or undignified Townshend may have considered such behaviour for a musician in his mid-Fifties, usually brought the biggest cheers of the evening.

The basic set for the tour was as follows: 'I Can't Explain', 'Substitute', 'Anyway Anyhow Anywhere', 'Pinball Wizard', 'My Wife', 'Baba O'Riley', 'You Better You Bet', 'Behind Blue Eyes', 'Magic Bus', 'The Real Me', 'Who Are You', '5:15', 'Won't Get Fooled Again', 'The Kids Are Alright', 'My Generation'.

Additions to the list at alternate dates were: 'The Seeker' (dropped after the first four shows), 'The Relay', 'I Don't Even Know Myself', 'Getting In Tune', 'Bargain', 'Drowned', 'I'm One', 'See Me, Feel Me', 'Naked Eye', and 'Let's See Action'.

N.B: Unless otherwise stated, The Who's concerts to February 2002 featured Roger Daltrey, Pete Townshend, John Entwistle, John 'Rabbit' Bundrick, and Zak Starkey.

Tuesday June 6
Jacob K Javits Centre, New York

Set: 'I Can't Explain', 'Substitute', 'Anyway Anyhow Anywhere', 'Pinball Wizard', 'My Wife', 'Baba O'Riley', 'You Better You Bet', 'Behind Blue Eyes', 'Magic Bus', 'The Real Me', 'Who Are You', '5:15', 'Won't Get Fooled Again', 'The Kids Are Alright', 'My Generation'.

A benefit show in aid of the Robin Hood Foundation, featuring Simon Phillips sitting in for an indisposed Zak Starkey. An estimated $10 million was raised.

Sunday June 25
The World Theater, Chicago, Illinois

In a review headed "The Who Open US Run In Good Spirits", Troy Carpenter wrote: "Nobody's making any excuses for The Who these days, 18 years after their original 'farewell' tour. Drummer Keith Moon's fatal drug overdose in 1978 was considered by many to be the creative death of the band, even as the three remaining members produced two more albums and sporadically continued to tour. In the sense that The Who are still a viable band, the post-Moon era now spans a longer (though markedly less significant) period in the band's existence.

"But while the majority of the material played at Sunday night's show was at least two decades old, the pluck and tenacity of Townshend, Entwistle, and Daltrey had to be admired. Daltrey's mere presence on stage, at age 56, unbuttoning his shirt, swinging around his microphone and singing youth anthems with irony-laden lyrics like 'I'm in tune' and the classic 'I hope I die before I get old' was a sight to behold. Entwistle put the night in perspective when he took over vocal duties for 'My Wife': 'We used to make jokes about wives here,' he quipped, 'but my second ex-wife is in the audience, so we'll just play the song.'

"Entwistle's characteristically spidery bass lines were very much up to par, showing off with some impressive soloing in an exquisite rendition of '5:15,' from the 1973 rock opera *Quadrophenia*. The song ended with Townshend crooning 'Why should I care / why should I care,' and after a chorus of applause, he added a coda: 'We care because we love you so, Chicago'.

"For his part, Townshend showed plenty of flash and stellar fretwork worthy of his reputation as one of rock's greatest all-time guitarists. Supported by Starkey's manic drumming and Entwistle's thunderous bass barrage, Townshend pulled off some great riff-and-distortion workouts in songs like 'Magic Bus,' 'The Seeker,' and the *Who's Next* classic 'Won't Get Fooled Again'... Though the Who is certainly past its prime, the band is a well-oiled engine that, at this late date, can still put on an affecting stadium rock show. Sunday's performance proved that diehard Who fans planning to see the elder masters on this tour won't be disappointed."

Tuesday June 27
The Palace, Detroit, Michigan

Thursday June 29
Star Lake Amphitheater, Pittsburgh, Pennsylvania

'Bargain' and 'I'm One' were played for the first time on the tour.

Saturday July 1
PNC Bank Arts Center, Holmdel, New Jersey

Jim Farber of *The New York Daily Post* (July 3) turned in a sardonic appraisal: "Think about it: A bunch of 55-year-old geezers would be performing decades-old songs of adolescent defiance, scores of which have been sold to any Madison Avenue ad man who would have them. True, the group hadn't launched an official Who tour in 11 years, but they've put in so many one-off appearances and concept shows (like the *Quadrophenia* tour) that they now seem about as elusive a concert act as Elton John.

"To boot, The Who would be performing songs that still eat up so much time on radio, they practically rate as biohazards - material that should be buried for hundreds of years until it can once

again seem fresh. So why was The Who's reunion show at the PNC Bank Arts Center Saturday such an all-out blast? For two-and-a-half hours, remaining Who members Townshend, Roger Daltrey and John Entwistle (backed by drummer Zak Starkey and keyboardist John Bundrick) whipped through their amazing catalogue with so much edge and joy, it erased all the baggage the band and material arrived with. In this super fast night, the group sounded hard and lean, honoring the songs' original vigor. At one point, Townshend announced, 'We're being The Who tonight,' as if describing an actor assuming a role. 'If you know what that means, tell us,' he joked.

"From all evidence, 'being The Who' meant allowing the band to find the younger selves that still kick within them... A few rarities broke up the torrent of hits, including 1973's (sic) 'Relay', 'I Don't Even Know Myself' (from *Lifehouse*) and '72's (sic) 'Let's See Action'. Toward the end, Townshend did acknowledge the connection between the tragedy at Pearl Jam's Copenhagen concert Friday (in which nine people were crushed to death) and The Who's similar 1982 (sic) incident in Cincinnati. He said only that he talked to Eddie Vedder and prayed for the families. Nothing so newsworthy was needed, however, to make this show seem like the last thing one expected: an event taking place in the present tense."

Monday July 3
Tweeter Center, Mansfield, Massachusetts

Supported by UnAmerican, a four-man English band led by former World Party singer-guitarist Steve McEwan. *The Boston Herald* music critic Dean Johnson wrote: "This is what the audience saw during 'I Can't Explain', the opening song in last night's two-hour marathon Who concert: singer Roger Daltrey swinging his mike cord like a lariat and guitarist Pete Townshend wind-milling big chords from his guitar as he fell to one knee. OK, everybody, you can all go home now. You've already got your money's worth. But, of course, it was only the beginning of a striking 21-song set that put to shame the Tweeter Center's previous two shows over the holiday weekend featuring Sting and Jimmy Page with The Black Crowes.

"Blues greats like Muddy Waters were once the standard used to measure the way rock bands should age gracefully. Forget that. Maturing rockers should look at what The Who and The Rolling Stones are doing in their senior years, and based on last night's Who concert, they should be afraid. Very afraid. With Zak Starkey on drums, Rabbit Bundrick on keyboards, and John Entwistle on bass, the band just chewed up and devoured classic Who tunes like 'My Wife', 'Bargain', and 'Won't Get Fooled Again', as well as lesser-known songs such as 'Relay' and 'Naked Eye'.

"Daltrey's voice was a tad road-worn, but he still sports a washboard stomach and a riveting stage presence. Townshend was a marvel. Still one of rock's most physical guitarists, he abused his instruments all night - sometimes even repeatedly pummeling them with a fist - to get them to create great chopping riffs and torrid staccato washes. But being a gentleman rocker sometimes has its drawbacks. Several times, in the middle of scintillating breaks, Townshend had to stop in mid-stroke to gently tuck the hem of his sports coat behind his Fender… Daltrey and Townshend kiddingly bickered with each other (after 'See Me, Feel Me') and the audience for much of the night. When Entwistle blew the roaring bass lines that kick off 'Pinball Wizard', (Townshend) just made everyone start over.

"'I'm proud of the re-emergence of this band,' Townshend admitted. And rock fans everywhere should be grateful."

Wednesday July 5
Nissan Pavilion, Washington, D.C

"The Who aren't exactly lovey-dovey these days," wrote the *Washington Post*'s David Segal, "aside from the requisite pre-encore hugs, barely a flicker of genuine warmth surfaced the whole night - but their days of mutual loathing are clearly behind them. Townshend giggled a bit when Daltrey wheezed for air at the end of a song ('It's pretty fun, isn't it? If you get to see Roger Daltrey die from lack of oxygen during "Can't You See The Real Me?"'), though his needling never approached flat-out animosity. In the old days, Townshend would have considered Daltrey's breathing trouble an opportune moment to choke the guy.

"On Wednesday night, Townshend aimed his best jabs at himself. He ridiculed the ending to 'Baba O'Riley' as evidence of his 'Polish genes',

belittling it as a revved-up polka. He derided his age (55) by noting that a nasal problem, not drugs, explained his sniffles: 'I'm too old for cocaine, so there's none of that going on here.' And he made fun of his famously oversize nose, musing aloud that a plastic surgeon could tip it slightly upward and give him the Nicolas Cage look."

Friday July 7
E Center, Camden, New Jersey

Sunday July 9
Jones Beach, Wantagh, Long Island, New York

Despite the wind and rain, Pete said Jones Beach was his "favourite place to play in the whole wide world". (He last played here in 1993 on his solo *Psychoderelict* tour). "There must be something in the sea air…"

Pete performed 'Drowned' by himself on acoustic, with Roger joining in on harmonica towards the end, and smashed a guitar during 'Won't Get Fooled Again'.

Monday August 14
Hollywood Bowl, Los Angeles, California

The entire band, especially Pete, was in convivial mood, even though Roger's voice was shot and the show was generally sloppy. Roger teased John for actually breaking a sweat as he introduced 'My Wife' which John dedicated to "all his ex-wifes", one of whom, he stated, was in the audience. Before 'The Real Me' Pete told an entertaining story about the last time The Who played the Bowl (on November 19, 1967) which ended with Bobby Pridden being arrested for the use of smoke bombs. Pridden was threatened with 18 months in jail. "What did we do? I think we went back to the hotel," Townshend quipped.

Townshend stopped 'Magic Bus' after about two minutes, only to restart it complaining he "could not think at that fucking tempo". When they returned for the encore, he publicly apologised for insulting Zak over the comment and theatrically gave the drummer a bunch of flowers.

Wednesday August 16
Irvine Verizon Wireless Meadows Amphitheater, Irvine, California

Thursday August 17
Sports Arena, San Diego, California

Saturday August 19
Gorge Amphitheatre, George, Washington

A show unusually located in the middle of a natural valley with superb acoustics. Pete commented that the arena was "in the middle of nowhere", with there being no place to "land his helicopter" and the lack of "proper toilets". He did concede, however, that it was "a beautiful venue".

Monday August 21
Shoreline Amphitheatre, Mt. View, California

Tuesday August 22
Sacramento Valley Amphitheatre, Marysville, California

Thursday August 24
Pepsi Center, Denver, Colorado

Friday August 25
Mesa Del Sol Ampitheater, Alburquerque, New Mexico

Sunday August 27
Reunion Arena, Dallas, Texas

Tuesday August 29
Woodlands Pavilion, Woodlands, Texas

Sunday September 24
Mars Music Amphitheatre, West Palm Beach, Florida

Headlined "Great Generation" the *Sun Sentinel*'s Sean Piccoli review began: "Nothing gets in their way, not even old age... The Who opened the last leg of its latest rebound on amazingly strong legs. The British invaders busted out one of rock's most hallowed back catalogs on Sunday night and, before 16,284 people at Mars Music Amphitheatre near West Palm Beach, flung it around for more than two hours in what guitarist-singer Pete Townshend gleefully called "a greatest-hits show." "But we don't give a ..." he added.

Tuesday September 26
Ice Palace, Tampa, Florida

Thursday, September 28
Phillips Arena, Atlanta, Georgia

After 'Baba O' Riley', Pete told the audience about a "brilliant idea" he'd had on stage in the '70s. Being a humid night, he coaxed the entire audience to blow toward the stage, thinking they'd get a nice pleasant breeze. "It smelt of 25,000 types of mint." During the furious strumming in his solo acoustic version of 'Drowned' Townshend started slamming his hand into the guitar, exacerbating an old injury in his right hand.

Saturday, September 30
Gund Arena, Cleveland, Ohio

To rest his damaged hand, Pete played a one-off solo performance of 'Sheraton Gibson' in place of 'Drowned'.

Tuesday October 3
Madison Square Garden, New York

Supported by The Wallflowers, featuring Bob Dylan's son, Jakob. "The Kids Are Alright - But The Who Ain't" wailed Dan Aquilante's review in

The New York Post (October 4): "In the last gasps of The Who show at Madison Square Garden last night, during the encore rendition of 'My Generation', Roger Daltrey stuttered the classic line: 'I hope I die before I get old'. Too late… the band, whose principals include singer Daltrey, guitarist Pete Townshend and bassist John Entwistle, were all bluster, relying on the greatness of the music to carry the night rather than on the quality of the performance. For most at the nearly sold-out show, that was good enough, but in comparison to the performance that The Who offered concertgoers at the PNC Bank Arts Center and at Jones Beach this summer, the MSG performance was a pale reflection…

"The evening wasn't without its fun. Townshend actually whacked himself in the nose during one of the windmill maneuvers, which probably accounts for his between-song babbling, which often made little or no sense. Whenever Townshend would start to ramble, Daltrey seemed to cringe at what nonsense the man would utter next. Still, since Townshend's thick accent and clipped diction is nearly unintelligible, it hardly mattered.

"While the babbling patter was a major waste of time, what was at the bottom of most of it was that the music of The Who is often about identity crisis. Who? That's right. Still, the band hit all the notes, and the devoted fans loved the withered performance, but it all seemed so tired, as if no one except young Starkey cared. What was interesting about the show is how the band extended individual songs with jams that often did nothing to enhance the tune except make it longer. As the songs were longer, so was the show, which wound up after midnight…"

Wednesday October 4
Madison Square Garden, New York

Friday October 6
Madison Square Garden, New York

Saturday October 7
Madison Square Garden, New York

Sunday October 30
Birmingham NEC, Birmingham

Support on each of the UK dates was Joe Strummer and The Mescaleros. An acoustic 'Mary Anne With The Shaky Hand' was added to the encore on certain dates.

Thursday November 2
Nynex Arena, Manchester

Friday November 3
SECC, Glasgow, Scotland

Sunday November 5
SECC, Glasgow, Scotland

Monday November 6
Newcastle Arena, Newcastle

Wednesday November 8
Birmingham NEC, Birmingham

Friday November 10
Sheffield Arena, Sheffield

Monday November 13
Docklands Arena, East London

In a *Times* review (November 14) headed "Who You Kidding?" Paul Sexton astutely pointed out the juxtaposition of having "punk legend" Joe Strummer support "dinosaur legends", The Who. "Even Junior's *First Punk Primer* spells out that in 1976, bands such as The Clash existed to nuke old grizzlers such as The Who. Suggesting that, a quarter century later, the leader of the former might support the remains of the latter, in a series of soulless arena settings, would have been like nominating the Pistols to open for Zeppelin.

"In the intervening lifetime, the two extremes of Seventies rock have met in a middle ground of survivors whose initial spark remains connected to the mains. So no one batted an eye to see Joe Strummer guesting on the 'Oo's latest reunion tour, and those who arrived on time at London Arena on Monday witnessed one of the most storming warm-ups of the year... For all the tediously unimaginative media derision, they *didn't* die before they got old - so get over it... Townshend welcomed us to the "bumhole of London" and told us to "f#*k off" - the sort of abuse that was strangely reassuring.

"What unfolded thereafter was quite unmissable but also troublingly uneven... During the encore, Daltrey strapped on an acoustic guitar and was considerably more at ease, even mastering a falsetto detail at the end of a winning 'The Kids Are Alright'. However, the elongation effect was especially upsetting on the closing 'My Generation', which started out with fuel injection in the outside lane but ended up puttering along lamely on the hard shoulder. The Who had arrived in an MG, but left in a bubble car."

Wednesday November 15
Wembley Arena, North London

Thursday November 16
Wembley Arena, North London
'Drowned' was dropped from the set; Pete

apologizing because of his heavy cold. As a form of compensation, the band ended the closing 'My Generation' jam with a brief snatch of the 'You Are Forgiven' finale from 'A Quick One (While He's Away)'.

Monday November 27
Royal Albert Hall, London
Set: 'I Can't Explain,' 'Anyway Anyhow Anywhere', 'Pinball Wizard', 'The Relay', 'My Wife', 'The Kids Are Alright', 'Mary Anne With The Shaky Hand', 'Bargain', 'Magic Bus', 'Baba O'Riley', 'Drowned', 'Heart To Hang Onto', 'So Sad About Us', 'I'm One', 'Getting In Tune', 'Behind Blue Eyes', 'You Better You Bet', 'The Real Me', '5.15', 'Won't Get Fooled Again', 'Substitute', 'Let's See Action', 'My Generation', 'See Me Feel Me'.

A special charity show organized for the Teenage Cancer Trust. Special guests featured: Nigel Kennedy (violin on 'Baba O'Riley'), Paul Weller (guitar and vocal duet with Pete on 'So Sad About Us'), Eddie Vedder ('I'm One', 'Getting In Tune', 'Let's See Action', 'See Me, Feel Me'), Bryan Adams ('Behind Blue Eyes', 'See Me Feel Me'), Noel Gallagher ('Won't Get Fooled Again'), and Kelly Jones (from The Stereophonics) ('Substitute').

The show was filmed and released on DVD in 2001 as *The Who And Special Guests: Live At The Royal Albert Hall*, November 27, 2000. It was re-released in 2003 as part of a 3-CD set *The Who Live At The Royal Albert Hall*, included a four-track bonus disc of the bands RAH shows in 2002, John's last public performances with the band.

2001

Saturday October 20
Madison Square Garden, New York
Set: 'Who Are You', 'Baba O'Riley', 'Behind Blue Eyes', 'Won't Get Fooled Again'.

The Concert For New York - a benefit show for the victims of the September 11 tragedy. Jon Carin played keyboards in place of John 'Rabbit' Bundrick. Pete, Roger and others participating in the show joined Paul McCartney to sing 'Let It Be' and 'Freedom' during the finale of the concert. The Who's set was considered by most commentators as the highlight of the whole event.

With almost unanimous praise for their show-stealing performance at the 9/11 Fireman's Benefit the previous October, The Who were set to continue touring throughout 2002. Although the low-key warm-up shows at the start of the year featured essentially the same song selection as the 2000 tour, with the addition of some resurrected *Tommy* selections and old stage chestnuts 'Summertime Blues', 'Young Man Blues' and 'Baby Don't You Do It', every indication showed that the re-energised Who were still on fire. There was also talk of a new Who album that would hopefully expunge the memory of the generally underwhelming post-Moon albums, *Face Dances*, and *It's Hard*, now some 20 years old.

On June 10, the five members of the 21st Century Who gathered at Pete's Eel Pie Studio in Twickenham to rehearse for the upcoming American tour, as well as try out two new compositions earmarked for the album: Roger's 'Certified Rose' and Pete's 'Real Good-Looking Boy'. Among the Who tracks auditioned for the tour were 'I Can See For Miles', John's 'Trick Of The Light' and even the mini-opera. John spent the majority of the rehearsals, playing with seated, though few remarked on this at the time.

It was an omen, though, for on June 27, on the eve of the tour in Las Vegas, John Entwistle passed away in his sleep from a heart attack caused by a blocked artery exacerbated by cocaine use. The lurid headlines concentrating on cocaine use and the presence of a Vegas "showgirl" in his hotel room failed to dwell on how much of a brilliant musician The Ox had been. Ironically, the same thing occurred when Keith Moon, his closest bandmate within The Who, had passed away. A further irony was that John was one day away from where he was happiest: on the road, performing in front of an audience. Solace could be taken from the fact that John had recently been voted "Rock Bass Player Of The Millenium" in a poll among fellow musicians.

The first two dates of the tour were immediately cancelled while Roger and Pete considered their options. Eventually, after much deliberation and with the blessing of the Entwistle family, the band opted to honour the tour (the two cancelled dates being moved to the end of the itinerary),

which predictably polarised opinion among Who fans and commentators. "I simply believe we have a duty to go on, to ourselves, ticket buyers, staff, promoters, big and little people," said Townshend in a message posted on his website. Daily diaries and footage from the tour were posted by Matt Kent on the band's website.

A phone call from Pete enlisted session bassist Pino Palladino who had played with Tears For Fears, Eric Clapton and Elton John, and who happened to be in America at the time. "I made it clear we do not expect him to attempt to emulate, parody or copy John Entwistle in any way," Townshend said via his web site. "Pino is a master in his own way, but the one request I made was that - at first - he play as loud as he can bear!" After two days of intense rehearsals in Burbank, Pino's baptism of fire occurred on July 1 at the Hollywood Bowl, where the band received a standing ovation before a note was played. Palladino played the first few songs off to the side, often in shadow. The tour continued without further incident, receiving generally rave, if not sympathetic notices, ending in Toronto on September 28.

Sunday January 27
Guildhall, Portsmouth

Set: 'I Can't Explain', 'Substitute', 'Anyway Anyhow Anywhere', 'Amazing Journey', 'Sparks', 'My Wife', 'Baba O'Riley', 'Drowned', 'Behind Blue Eyes', 'I'm Free', 'Pinball Wizard', 'You Better You Bet', 'Who Are You', '5:15', 'Won't Get Fooled Again', 'The Kids Are Alright', 'Summertime Blues', 'Baby Don't You Do It', 'My Generation'.#

At the end of the show Pete destroyed a black Fender Stratocaster.

Monday January 28
Guildhall, Portsmouth

Set: 'I Can't Explain', 'Substitute', 'Anyway Anyhow Anywhere', 'Boris The Spider', 'Relay', 'Baba O'Riley', 'Overture', 'It's A Boy', 'Amazing Journey', 'Sparks', 'Pinball Wizard', 'I'm Free', 'I'm One', 'Drowned', 'Behind Blue Eyes', 'You Better You Bet', 'Who Are You', '5:15', 'Won't Get Fooled Again', 'The Kids Are Alright', 'Summertime Blues', 'Magic Bus', 'My Generation'.

Irish Jack: "This was a very poignant gig for me in more ways than one. The last time I had been in Portsmouth was at the very same venue *just* a matter of some twenty-eight years earlier when The Who played the Guildhall in a 'thank you' show for the *Tommy* extras, most of whom were local Polytechnic students. It might be worth noting that before the '74 show back then I had dinner with Roger, Chris Stamp and Wiggy (John Wolff), and later that night Keith Moon paid for my hotel room. When Chris Stamp and I arrived backstage we discovered the band had very little room to play. Chris and I stood behind a speaker cabinet scrunched up against Ann-Margaret and Oliver Reed who had come from the *Tommy* film set - who had never seen The Who before. Despite a few hitches the band were positively pulsating that night and it may have been the presence of two of the film worlds' icons that spurred the band to the dizzy heights they reached. As the four of us stood peering out from behind the speaker with our collective brandies held shoulder high, Pete slid twelve feet across the stage on his knees with a Gibson droning feedback like a low flying aeroplane - naturally he was wearing knee pads! It was a moment to behold. Ann-Margaret looked speechless, and behind me I heard an unforgettable comment of appreciation from Oliver Reed delivered like an Oxford don: 'Now that's what I call rock'n'*rule!*' Twenty-eight years *later* I found myself back at the same Guildhall. We were all there again except for dear old Keith. Mickey Double handed me a set list and I wandered into John's dressing room to say hello. Cyrano was there and he joked about my staying sober. I sat down next to John with a drink in my hand and quite unexpectedly he enquired if I had a set list on me. I looked back at him incredulously and taking it from my pocket handed it to him whereupon he began to study it

closely with punctuated 'Hmmmm's, and 'Ohhhh's I looked at Cyrano and all he did was wink. I told John he would have to memorise the set because I wanted the list as a souvenir. He broke into a big smile. And that's the Ox and that's the smile that I remember best. God bless him.

Thursday January 31
Coliseum, Watford

Set: 'I Can't Explain', 'Substitute', 'Anyway Anyhow Anywhere', 'I Don't Even Know Myself', 'Amazing Journey', 'Sparks', 'Pinball Wizard', 'I'm Free', 'My Wife', 'Who Are You', 'Getting In Tune', 'Behind Blue Eyes', 'Drowned', 'Baba O' Riley', 'The Real Me', 'You Better You Bet', '5:15', 'Won't Get Fooled Again', 'The Kids Are Alright', 'Baby Don't You Do It', 'My Generation', 'Summertime Blues', 'Young Man Blues'.

A boisterous show as far as band and crowd were concerned with a fight breaking out, at one point, near the front row. Roger and Pete admonished several hecklers, with Pete at one point "threatening to ram a marble down your throat", which had stayed on his mind after reading newspaper reports about a current murder trial. His ill-advised outburst caused a minor controversy in the UK tabloid press. Roger commented that the band hadn't played Watford since the Sixties while Pete retorted "actually it was July 1971", a reference to the low key shows the band undertook after the Young Vic Lifehouse shows.

Thursday February 7
Royal Albert Hall, London

Set: 'I Can't Explain', 'Substitute', 'Anyway Anyhow Anywhere', 'I Don't Even Know Myself', 'Amazing Journey', 'Pinball Wizard', 'I'm Free', 'My Wife', 'Who Are You', 'Getting In Tune', 'Behind Blue Eyes', 'Drowned', 'I'm One', 'Baba O'Riley', 'You Better You Bet', '5:15', 'Won't Get Fooled Again', 'The Kids Are Alright', 'Summertime Blues' (false start), 'Summertime Blues', 'Young Man Blues', 'My Generation'.

John Entwistle's last shows before an audience – two benefit shows for the Teenage Cancer Trust.

Friday February 8
Royal Albert Hall, London

Set: 'I Can't Explain', 'Substitute', 'Anyway

Anyhow Anywhere', 'I Don't Even Know Myself', 'Amazing Journey', 'Pinball Wizard', 'I'm Free', 'My Wife', 'Who Are You', 'Getting In Tune', 'Behind Blue Eyes', 'Drowned', 'I'm One', 'Baba O'Riley', 'Relay', '5.15', 'Won't Get Fooled Again', 'The Kids Are Alright', 'Summertime Blues', 'Young Man Blues', 'My Generation'.

Benefit show for the Teenage Cancer Trust. Standing on Roger's foldback monitor, Pete fell off the stage during 'Young Man Blues' and landed on fans seated in the front row. He carried on playing regardless, with the help of fan Mark Donovan, while being helped back onto the stage. Four tracks from this final show – 'I'm Free', 'I Don't Even Know Myself', 'Summertime Blues', and 'Young Man Blues' - were released on a third bonus disc with the SPV CD release *Live At The Royal Albert Hall* (2003).

Monday July 1
Hollywood Bowl, Los Angeles, California

After cancelling the first two shows of the tour – at Las Vegas (June 28; rescheduled to September 14) and Irvine, CA (June 29; rescheduled to September 15), this was the first concert to take place in the wake of John Entwistle's death, to an audience of 18,000.

The 26-show North American tour was augmented by Pete's brother, Simon Townshend on acoustic guitar and backing vocals, who rehearsed as part of the band before the tragedy occurred but now found himself taking on a bigger role than expected.

The set list ran as follows: 'I Can't Explain', 'Substitute', 'Anyway Anyhow Anywhere', 'Who Are You', 'Another Tricky Day', 'Relay', 'Bargain', 'Baba O'Riley', 'Eminence Front', 'Sea And Sand', '5:15', 'Love Reign O'er Me', 'Behind Blue Eyes', 'You Better You Bet', 'The Kids Are Alright', 'My Generation', 'Won't Get Fooled Again', 'Pinball Wizard', 'Amazing Journey', 'Sparks', 'See Me Feel Me'.

Before the show began, giant screens featured video of the group rehearsing at Pete's Eel Pie studio on June 15, filmed by tour sponsors JBL. The audience cheered and applauded each time "The Ox" appeared. The concert began on a poignant note as Daltrey and guitarist Townshend, both dressed in black, sauntered onto the stage and hugged each other. A *New York Times* report (July 2) "Who Launch Tour After Death of Bassist" said: "The Who turned their mourning into defiant energy in their first concert after the death of their longtime bassist, aged 57… 'I just wanted to say that tonight we play for John Entwistle,' Daltrey said after opening the show with the hits, 'I Can't Explain' and 'Substitute'. 'He was the true spirit of rock'n'roll and he lives on in all the music we play.' Townshend, in black sunglasses, lightened the mood a few songs later when he compared the Bowl's white shell-like stage to a 'white vagina', while the giant spheres suspended from the ceiling looked like a 'testicle factory'. While noting the absence of Entwistle's 'huge harmonic noise', he congratulated Pino's playing. 'For fans that have followed us for many years, this is gonna be very difficult,' Townshend said. 'We understand. We're not pretending that nothing's happened.'"

At the end of the show, Roger and Pete clutched bouquets of flowers, embraced and waved farewell to giant video screens that flanked the stage on which were projected images of John from his youth onwards, put together that day by Matt Kent. A male fan ran up and hugged a compliant Townshend. "Live every moment of your lives," Daltrey told the crowd before Townshend dragged him off.

Wednesday July 3
Shoreline Amphitheatre, Mountain View, California

"Raw, Ragged Tribute" was the verdict in the *SF Chronicle*: "Death is a paradox that inspires life even as it takes it" wrote Neva Chonin. "Wednesday in Mountain View, just six days after Who bassist and co-founder John Entwistle died in Las Vegas of an apparent heart attack, the

band's surviving members responded to his loss by defiantly spitting into the abyss - at high volume. And when they did, what was booked months ago as just another reunion concert by a classic cash cow became a raging testament to musical and emotional endurance.

"The second show of The Who's near-aborted US tour saw none of the spoken eulogies that marked their opening night in Los Angeles, but it was a tribute nonetheless. 'What can I say that hasn't already been said?' Roger Daltrey told the Shoreline Amphitheatre's near-capacity crowd three songs into the set. 'It's one day at a time for us. It ain't f— easy. Rock'n'roll isn't easy. Nor is life. It's just best to get on with it.'

"And they did get on with it, turning in an impassioned two-hour and 15-minute performance that was alternately ragged, painful and breathtaking. The band suffered its share of missed cues and botched lines; with only days to rehearse, replacement bassist Pino Palladino still needed sheet music for backup; there were periodic sound problems. But sleek perfection is the trait of a well-oiled music machine, and Wednesday The Who were all frayed edges and exposed nerves… By the time the Who left the stage after an encore medley from *Tommy*, questions of whether the band will continue beyond this tour, or whether it should have started this tour at all, seemed suddenly incidental. They were simply blown away in a final explosion of rock'n'roll grit that left the band drained and audience roaring.

"Again, paradoxes. Faced with death, The Who sound more alive than they have in years. Maybe it's that grief has pushed the band mercilessly out of its comfort zone and into a more daring space.

Or maybe it's just that, for the first time in decades, The Who have something to prove. Judging by Wednesday's performance, they're up to the challenge."

Tuesday July 4
Auto West Amphitheatre, Sacramento, California.

Independence Day show, supported by Counting Crows, who supported on all the first leg shows. "If those firemen in New York City had given up," explained Daltrey halfway through the show, "New York would still be a mess. We ain't givin' up, either."

"Life goes on," Pete added.

Saturday July 6
The Gorge, George, Washington

At the climax of 'Won't Get Fooled Again' Pete broke a string, before smashing his Stratocaster to bits.

Friday July 26
Tweeter Amphitheatre, Mansfield, Massachusetts

Robert Plant (and band) supported on the East Coast dates. 'I Can See For Miles' was played at this show in place of 'Bargain'. The day before the news broke that John Entwistle had traces of cocaine in his system when he died. "Some of us are still careful about what we eat and what we drink," said Townshend onstage. "We might not have as much fun as John Entwistle was having in Las Vegas; we're pretty sure he was enjoying himself - it's not to be recommended."

Despite the 11 p.m. curfew, the capacity 19,900 crowd wouldn't let The Who leave until the band had come back to perform the *Tommy* encore. They returned to play the venue on September 27.

Saturday July 27
Tweeter Amphitheatre, Camden, New Jersey

During the show, Pete remarked "John Entwistle, wherever you are, get well soon." Townshend acknowledged that Pino had "saved our bacon", and introduced Zak as the replacement for "another Who corpse".

Monday July 29
Hershey Park, Hershey, Pennsylvania

Wednesday July 31
Madison Square Garden, New York

During 'Won't Get Fooled Again' Roger's arm got hit by a Coke bottle that a fan threw from the side of the stage. Roger was incredibly angry and at the end of the song, offered the fan up onto the stage. Of course the culprit didn't show. "I should see how far I can stick this up your arse!" Roger said, when picking up the bottle. When the band reappeared for the encore, Pete joked about what should be thrown onstage, "Money, wallets, flowers, credit cards, girlfriends…" A person threw a wadded bill onstage which Pete opened and exclaimed "A five! Is that all I'm worth?" Another fan threw another bill and Pete again opened it yelling "A twenty, that's more like it!… This money will go towards Roger's hospital bill."

Thursday August 1
Madison Square Garden, New York

'I'm One' was performed by Pete solo before 'Sea And Sand'.

Saturday August 3
Madison Square Garden, New York

Sunday August 4
Madison Square Garden, New York

Friday August 23
Palace Of Auburn Hills, Auburn Hills, Michigan

The third leg of the tour, again supported by Robert Plant.

Saturday August 24
Tweeter Center, Tinley Park, Illinois

During 'Love Reign O'er Me', squealing feedback from the monitors threw Roger off, making him forget the words to the middle section of the song. After bawling out Bob Pridden (the Who's traditional fall guy), he demanded that the band start the song from scratch, which they did.

Sunday August 25
Verizon Wireless Music Center, Noblesville, Indiana

Tuesday August 27
Van Andel Arena, Grand Rapids, Michigan

Wednesday August 28
Polaris Amphitheater, Columbus, Ohio

Friday August 30
P.N.C. Bank Arts Center, Holmdel, New Jersey

"I'm One' was played at this and the next three shows.

Saturday August 31
Jones Beach Theater, Wantagh, Long Island, New York

Townshend once again spoke of the quiet man known fondly as 'The Ox'.

"'We used to share that red wine. It wasn't worth a dime. We'll have to share it some other time. See ya, John.' Someday, perhaps. But for now, Townshend, Daltrey & Co. will continue on, proving that two of the original Who are still far better than none."

Saturday September 14
The Joint, Hard Rock Hotel, Las Vegas, Nevada

The Who returned for the fourth and final leg of the American tour, commencing with this fateful re-scheduled show from June 28, with tickets priced from $155 to $355. It was an emotional and intense return to the scene of Entwistle's death. At one stage, during a searing guitar solo, Townshend ran to the front of the stage monitors and yelled "This one's for you John" (or words to that effect!). Spencer Patterson of the *Las Vegas Sun* wrote (September 16): "Saturday night at The Joint at the Hard Rock Hotel, The Who erased any doubts about whether it remains a viable live act post-John Entwistle, serving up a blistering two-hour set to an enthusiastic sold-out crowd.

"Strange as it may have seemed to see replacement bassist Pino Palladino manning Entwistle's post at stage left, the truth is the new unit may actually rock harder than The Who has in years. Palladino sounded quite comfortable working his way through the band's considerable catalog of classics. And while his bass lines may not have vibrated quite as long in your ribcage as Entwistle's once did, in the intimate, 1,600-person hall, that didn't seem like such a bad thing…

"Notably silent between songs for much of the night, Townshend and Daltrey finally paid tribute to their fallen comrade late in the show during an extended take on 'The Kids Are Alright'. While the band played softly behind them and the crowd hushed to listen, both men took a turn at the mike, telling stories about the days when they too were kids. 'I met this guy. He had a horn. It became a bass. He gave me his hand. I joined his band,' Townshend said… Then, as 'My

Sunday September 15
Verizon Wireless Amphitheatre, Irvine, California

Counting Crows supported again for the fourth leg but failed to show for this gig and a local band, taken off a local radio stage, supported instead.

Second rescheduled show from June 29. Roger forgot an entire verse of 'Won't Get Fooled Again'. As the rest of the band exited the stage, Daltrey sheepishly remained to apologise. "Well, we've done it right before," he said. He men

tioned the smell of manure had something to do with it. "I thought I was back home on my pig farm."

Tuesday September 17
Greek Theatre, Los Angeles, California
Pete delivered a long tirade against the Hard Rock where John had died.

Thursday September 19
Fiddler's Green Amphitheatre, Englewood, Colorado

Saturday September 21
American Airlines Center, Dallas, Texas

Monday September 23
House Of Blues, Chicago, Illinois
Set: 'I Can't Explain', 'Substitute', 'Anyway Anyhow Anywhere', 'Who Are You', 'I Don't Even Know Myself', 'Baba O'Riley', 'Sea And Sand', '5:15', 'Love Reign O'er Me', 'Eminence Front', 'Behind Blue Eyes', 'The Kids Are Alright', 'My Generation', 'Wont Get Fooled Again', 'Pinball Wizard', 'Amazing Journey', 'Sparks', 'See Me Feel Me'.
Benefit performance for the Maryville Academy, supported by Pearl Jam. It was the fifth benefit that The Who had performed for Maryville over the last three and a half years, thanks to Townshend's friendship with one of the academy's key fund-raisers, Marybeth Nawa. Some concertgoers purchased balcony boxes for $25,000, while less priviliged Who fans paid $400

each to attend.
"When I was a teenager, I never, ever realised that one day we would be able to use our music to help kids," said Townshend. "There has been some controversy regarding the way Maryville does business, and I can tell you, I never do anything like this without first going through the books and going through the underwear drawer. This one is kosher!" Townshend dedicated 'The Kids Are Alright' to the Rev. John P. Smyth who ran the facility.

Tuesday September 24
Xcel Energy Center, St. Paul, Minnesota

Friday September 27
Tweeter Center, Mansfield, Massachusetts
Pete opened the show by saying it was The Who's last show ever, then followed up by saying he was kidding. Typically, he went on to confuse matters by saying that he was "apparently the only one" who could determine if they'd be back in town again, and that they emphatically would!

Saturday September 28
Air Canada Centre, Toronto, Ontario, Canada

Jane Stevenson of the *Toronto Sun* (September 29) wrote: "The Who's John Entwistleless tour wrapped up last night at the Air Canada Centre with two hours and 15 minutes of passionate, loud and often exciting music that went a long way towards explaining why the seminal rock band was on the road in the first place...

"The Who, who played their 'final' concert at Maple Leaf Gardens back in 1982, have come to designate Toronto as the place to either begin or end their tours. Whether or not he and Daltrey will continue on as The Who - now that they've proven they can successfully tour as a twosome - remains to be seen."

After The Who returned to Britain, no other concerts were scheduled. To all intents and purposes, there was an air of finality. Or was there? In 2003, after the controversial arrest (and subsequent dropping of charges) of Pete Townshend on accessing child pornography via the internet, both Roger and Pete made separate statements indicating interest in continuing The Who with an album and worldwide tour in 2004..

Whether this will promise to be a new renewal or a crushing embarrassment remains to be seen. One thing's for sure, to borrow a Who line, "the doors aren't shut as tight as they might seem"...

POSTSCRIPT

As this book has attempted to emphasise, the uniquely precious quality of The Who remained untarnished by commercial compromise or musical diversion for over a decade, and continued right through to the last 'classic' Who concert in Toronto on October 21, 1976. At this show, the band thrashed out 'I Can't Explain', 'Substitute' and 'My Generation' (and, indeed, Pete smashed his guitar) with as much explosive energy, drive and adrenaline as they had done at the Marquee Club over a decade earlier. Passing years did not dampen their fire.

During the time leading up to this point, The Who made definitive the aesthetics of rock and roll performance art. Each monumental show added to the most solid and enduring reputation of any rock and roll act that chose to communicate its credo by blasting an exciting powerhouse of sound from a concert platform. The experience of attending a *real* Who concert was perhaps the only means of gaining a taste of the magic of the band as they really were. However, bits of that magic (short of the whole experience) can be glimpsed from the insights into Who performances offered here in this book, and in the body of their recordings. These documents will remain for future generations to explore and enjoy. The Who never did capture their true magic on film or tape, it just wasn't possible. However, a few CDs and videotapes give an accurate indication of something of what went on at those remarkable shows, and the following is a list of recommended releases.

Films, videotapes & DVDs containing live Who material with Keith Moon:

Monterey Pop (Virgin Home Video/Rhino DVD Box Set)
'My Generation' (Monterey Pop Festival, June 18, 1967). An interesting film in itself but meagre on Who content. Most of the Who's set has been restored on Rhino's 3-DVD box-set (2003)

The Rolling Stones' Rock'n'Roll Circus (Warners/ABKCO Home Video)
'A Quick One (While He's Away)' (*The Rolling Stones' Rock 'n' Roll Circus* TV special, December 11, 1968). The Who's grandstanding performance

on the Stones ill-fated television special finally saw the light of day in complete form in 1996. It had only taken 28 years.

Woodstock (Warner Home Video)
'See Me, Feel Me' and 'Summertime Blues' (Woodstock Festival, August 17, 1969). The Who's power cuts through some elaborate split-screen editing which now seems a little dated. A three-part 1994 TV special *Woodstock Diary* (now on Warners video/DVD), also made available 'My Generation'.

The Kids Are Alright (Polygram/MCA)
'Baba O'Riley' (Shepperton Sound Stage, May 25, 1978), 'Shout And Shimmy' (Richmond Athletic Grounds, August 6, 1965), 'Young Man Blues' (London Coliseum, December 14, 1969), 'Pinball Wizard', 'See Me, Feel Me', 'Sparks' (Woodstock Festival August 17, 1969), 'Road Runner', 'My Generation Blues' (Pontiac Silverdome, December 6, 1975), 'My Generation' (Monterey Pop Festival, June 18, 1967), 'Won't Get Fooled Again' (Shepperton Sound Stage, May 25, 1978).

A classic documentary film of timeless appeal; every home should have a copy! Re-released in definitive, pristine form as a double DVD package by Akai (in the US) in 2003.

Who's Better Who's Best (Polygram/MCA 1988):
'My Generation' (Marquee Club, March 2, 1967), 'Magic Bus' (*Popgala*, Voorburg, March 10, 1973), 'Pinball Wizard' (Woodstock Festival, August 17, 1969), 'I'm Free' (London Coliseum, December 14, 1969), 'See Me, Feel Me' (Woodstock Festival, August 17, 1969), 'Won't Get Fooled Again' (Shepperton Sound Stage, May 25, 1978).

A mixture of material from *The Kids Are Alright* and some previously unissued footage. Designed as a quick video-version of a greatest hits album, this is less essential but useful for Who completists.

Thirty Years Of Maximum R&B Live (Polygram/MCA 1994)
'Anyway Anyhow Anywhere' (*Shindig Goes To London!*, Richmond Athletic Grounds, August 6, 1965), 'So Sad About Us' (*Beat Club*, Marquee

Club, March 2, 1967), 'A Quick One, While He's Away' (Monterey Pop Festival, June 18, 1967), 'Happy Jack' (London Coliseum, December 14, 1969), 'Heaven And Hell', 'I Can't Explain', 'Water' (Tanglewood Music Shed, July 7, 1970), 'Young Man Blues', 'I Don't Even Know Myself' (Isle Of Wight Festival, August 29, 1970), 'My Generation' (*Popgala*, Voorburg, March 10, 1973), 'Substitute', 'Drowned', 'Bell Boy', 'My Generation Blues' (*2nd House*, Charlton Football Ground, May 18, 1974), 'Dreaming From The Waist' (Cleveland Coliseum, December 9, 1975), (remainder post-Moon material).

A carefully compiled and meticulously annotated live video history that unearthed much forgotten and rare material. Highly recommended as an introduction to The Who live as well as to hard-core fans: it carefully mixes performances of famous songs and hits with more obscure material.

Listening To You - Live At the Isle Of Wight Festival 1970 (Warner Music Vision 1995)
'Heaven And Hell', 'I Can't Explain', 'Young Man Blues', 'I Don't Even Know Myself', 'Water', 'Shakin' All Over/Spoonful/Twist And Shout', 'Summertime Blues', 'My Generation', 'Magic Bus', 'Overture', 'It's A Boy', 'Eyesight To The Blind', 'Christmas', 'Acid Queen', 'Pinball Wizard', 'Do You Think It's Alright?', 'Fiddle About', 'Go To The Mirror', 'Miracle Cure', 'I'm Free', 'We're Not Gonna Take It', 'See Me, Feel Me, 'Tommy Can You Hear Me?'.

A very good, albeit belated, release of a great concert. Slightly marred by the idiosyncratic editing, which was necessitated by much missing footage. This release salvaged everything that remained, and thankfully included a plethora of great musical moments and the band's timeless good humour. (This release omits the crucial 'Naked Eye', which is only available on the complete festival film *Message To Love* released by Warners in 1995.)

CDs containing live material recorded with Keith Moon:

'Live At Leeds – Deluxe Edition' (Polydor/MCA 088 112 618-2, 2002)
Disc One: 'Heaven And Hell', 'I Can't Explain', 'Fortune Teller', 'Tattoo', 'Young Man Blues', 'Substitute', 'Happy Jack', 'I'm A Boy', 'A Quick One (While He's Away)', 'Summertime Blues', 'Shakin 'All Over', 'My Generation', 'Magic Bus'

Disc Two: 'Overture', 'It's A Boy', ''1921', 'Amazing Journey' 'Sparks', 'Eyesight To The Blind', 'Christmas', 'The Acid Queen', 'Pinball Wizard', 'Do You Think It's Alright?', 'Fiddle About', 'Tommy Can You Hear Me?, 'There's A Doctor', 'Go To The Mirror', 'Smash The Mirror', 'Miracle Cure', 'Sally Simpson', 'I'm Free', 'Tommy's Holiday Camp', 'We're Not Gonna Take It', 'See Me, Feel Me' (Leeds University, February 14, 1970).

The first (and still the best) live Who album – first remixed, remastered and expanded in 1995 - was eventually released in full over two discs in 2002. A strong contender for 'best live album ever released' simply because it captured The Who's live sound with a convincing authenticity. No amount of decibels can ever do it justice!

The Kids Are Alright (Polydor/MCA
Includes 'Happy Jack' (Leeds University, February 14, 1970), 'Young Man Blues' (London Coliseum, December 14, 1969), 'My Wife' (Kilburn, December 15, 1977), 'Baba O'Riley' (Shepperton Sound Stage, May 25, 1978), 'Sparks', 'Pinball Wizard', 'See Me, Feel Me' (Woodstock, August 17, 1969), 'Join Together', 'Road Runner', 'My Generation Blues' (Pontiac Silverdome, December 6, 1975), 'Won't Get Fooled Again' (Shepperton Sound Stage, May 25, 1978).

A patchwork collection of soundtrack material of varying quality, this remains interesting rather than essential. Some CD issues omit the Pontiac material.

Rarities (Polydor): 'Baby Don't You Do It' (San Francisco Civic Auditorium, December 13, 1971). Originally the B-side of the 'Join Together' single in 1972, this is a valuable memento of a fondly-remembered cover version from the 1971 tour.

Who's Missing (Polydor/MCA): 'Bargain' (San Francisco Civic Auditorium, December 13, 1971). A brilliant live performance of 'Bargain' which it is difficult to imagine ever being surpassed.

Two's Missing (Polydor/MCA): 'My Wife' and 'Going Down' (San Francisco Civic Auditorium, December 13, 1971). Two more gems from San Francisco – a great version of 'My Wife' and the rare jam on Feddie King's 'Going Down'.

Monterey International Pop Festival (Rhino): 'Substitute', 'Summertime Blues', 'Pictures Of Lily', 'A Quick One', 'Happy Jack', 'My Generation' (Monterey Pop Festival, June 18, 1967). Of historical interest only, the Monterey material has an appealing simplicity about it but simply fails to generate real Who power.

Thirty Years Of Maximum R&B (Polydor/MCA box set)
'Substitute' (Leeds University, February 14, 1970), 'Sparks' (Woodstock, August 17, 1969), 'See Me, Feel Me' 'Young Man Blues', 'Summertime Blues', 'Shakin' All Over' (Leeds University, February 14, 1970), 'Bargain' (San Francisco Civic Auditorium, December 13, 1971), 'Bony Moronie', 'Naked Eye' (Young Vic, April 26, 1971), 'Dreaming From The Waist', 'My Wife' (Swansea Football Ground, June 12, 1976).

A random delve into the archives collected a few previously released live songs (including the great 'Bony Moronie', of which to this day Pete Townshend has a low opinion!) with some great unreleased performances, such as 'Dreaming From The Waist' and 'My Wife' from Swansea, perhaps the last great Who concert to be recorded.

Who's Next – Deluxe Edition (Polydor/MCA 088 113 056-2, 2003):
As well as an upgraded version of the original 1971 album and assorted studio out-takes, the second disc constituted virtually a whole live show from the Young Vic Theatre on April 26, 1971. Tracks: 'Love Ain't For Keeping', 'Pure And Easy', 'Young Man Blues', 'Time Is Passing', 'Behind Blue Eyes', 'I Don't Even Know Myself', 'Too Much Of Anything', 'Getting In Tune', 'Bargain', 'Water'*, 'My Generation', 'Road Runner', 'Naked Eye'*, 'Won't Get Fooled Again'

Apart from the tracks marked * this concert had lain unreleased in The Who's tape vault. Because of space constrictions, 'Baby, Don't You Do It', 'Pinball Wizard', 'See Me, Feel Me', and 'Boney Maronie' were left off. ('Boney Maronie' had first appeared as a bonus track on the re-release of 'Won't Get Fooled Again' as a single in 1988, and then again on the *30 Years Of Maximum R&B* box-set in 1994).

Live At The Isle Of Wight Festival 1970 (Castle) 'Heaven And Hell', 'I Can't Explain', 'Young Man Blues', 'I Don't Even Know Myself', 'Water', Tommy ('Overture', 'It's A Boy', '1921', 'Amazing Journey', 'Sparks', 'Eyesight To The Blind', 'Christmas', 'Acid Queen', 'Pinball Wizard', 'Do You Think It's Alright?', 'Fiddle About', 'Tommy Can You Hear Me?', 'There's A Doctor', 'Go To The Mirror', 'Smash The Mirror', 'Miracle Cure', 'I'm Free', 'Tommy's Holiday Camp', 'We're Not Gonna Take It', 'See Me, Feel Me'), 'Summertime Blues', 'Shakin' All Over/Spoonful/Twist And Shout', 'Substitute', 'My Generation', 'Naked Eye', 'Magic Bus'

A faithful and accurate representation of a whole Who concert (Isle Of Wight Festival, August 29, 1970) from their peak period. Ragged at times and certainly not as tight as the Leeds set, this nevertheless is much valued by Who fans and contains much exceptional music.

The Who By Numbers (Polydor/MCA): 'Squeeze Box', 'Behind Blue Eyes', 'Dreaming From The Waist' (Swansea Football Ground, June 12, 1976). This release added two more songs from the excellent Swansea concert.